Key Concepts in Modern Indian Studies

Key Concepts
in
Modern Indian Studies

Edited by
Gita Dharampal-Frick
Monika Kirloskar-Steinbach
Rachel Dwyer
Jahnavi Phalkey

OXFORD
UNIVERSITY PRESS

OXFORD
UNIVERSITY PRESS

Oxford University Press is a department of the University of Oxford.
It furthers the University's objective of excellence in research, scholarship,
and education by publishing worldwide. Oxford is a registered trademark of
Oxford University Press in the UK and in certain other countries

Published in India by
Oxford University Press
YMCA Library Building, 1 Jai Singh Road, New Delhi 110001, India

© Oxford University Press 2015

The moral rights of the authors have been asserted

First Edition published in 2015

ISBN-13: 978-0-19-945275-0
ISBN-10: 0-19-945275-X

Not for sale in North America

Typeset in Adobe Jenson Pro 10.5/13
by The Graphics Solution, New Delhi 110 092
Printed in India at Rakmo Press, New Delhi 110 020

Contents

Introduction

During the last couple of decades, modern Indian studies have become a site for new, creative, and thought-provoking debates extending over a broad canvas of crucial issues. Conceptually and historically grounded interrogations—with far-reaching philosophical, cultural, political, and sociological implications pertaining to developments in the subcontinent over the past two centuries—have defined the content of academic seminars and university teaching syllabi; likewise, international conferences have provided the arena for stimulating discussions on these issues. Concrete exemplification of this discursive interest in modern Indian studies is to be found in the in-depth studies that abound in this burgeoning field. Yet, surprisingly, an easy-to-access reference volume on the terminology that populates cultural studies and the social sciences relating to India remains a desideratum. Hence, in compiling this volume on key concepts in modern Indian studies, our primary aim is to contribute in some small way towards filling this unfortunate lacuna. Second, in recruiting a select number of internationally recognized experts to write individual entries on concepts central to their respective fields of specialization, our avowed intention is to introduce both students and interested general readers to scholars whose work has defined or refined the meaning of these terms. With this two-pronged agenda, *Key Concepts in Modern Indian Studies* hopes to provide some tangible entry points to modern Indian studies, in general, and to highlight some crucial issues and debates, in particular.

Given the diverse and complex range of this multidisciplinary field, our volume, needless to say, does not aspire to be more than an initial, modest attempt at bringing together ideas, issues, and debates salient to modern Indian studies. Constituting a kind of conceptual toolkit, its purpose is to serve as a handy resource guide to familiarize the reader with a whole gamut of questions defining not only academic concerns but also underscoring the social, cultural, political, and economic processes at work in the subcontinent during the last two hundred years. An underlying ambition of our pioneering venture is that it will pave the way for more extensive and intensive interest in specific debates, issues, and ideas that characterize modern India and render its study so stimulating.

This, in short, is the raison d'être of the present volume. Comprising an editorial quartet trained in four complementary academic disciplines (social and intellectual history, philosophy, cultural and media studies, and the history of science), we opted for a broad multidisciplinary approach. In deciding on a selection of over one hundred key concepts, we endeavoured to cast our net as expansively as possible to take into consideration the panoply of the subcontinent's shared vocabulary, which, in turn, exemplifies the vast array of shared experiences of its peoples. Yet, to endow this conceptually variegated landscape with distinct contours, we depended on the contributions of scholars whose expertise was called for to underscore in a lucid, concise manner—focusing on their allotted key concept—the versatility of the shared conceptual syntax. Not wanting to constrain the individual author's creative élan, only a minimal set of criteria was stipulated for structuring the respective entry (namely, to posit a concise definition of the key concept, accompanied by a critical analysis of its trajectory and a succinct discussion of its significance in the academic arena as well as in the public sphere; to provide indispensable references and list a maximum of five key texts for further reading; and, lastly, to abide by a suggested word limit). That not all authors complied with these suggestions—or only tangentially—is not *per se* problematic. Rather the non-uniformity of the individual entries is indicative of the respective authors' differing research methodologies. This explains their varying degree of emphasis either on theoretical issues or on empirical data. Whatever be the case, these essays, constituting distinctive individual contributions of the respective scholar, offer the reader glimpses of cherished research interests that make Indian studies come alive. Needless to say, exercising our prerogative as editors, we did negotiate certain textual revisions. However, we have allowed unconventional presentations to hold sway—intent as we are on displaying as wide a spectrum of academic ingenuity as possible. Indeed, the multifarious diversity of scholarly production heightens its attractiveness and accessibility, especially for a student readership.

A few more clarificatory words about our own agenda would help obviate misconceptions. Our volume is not intended to deliver a focused, neat, and tight exposition of conceptual categories. Nor did we want—through these concepts—to merely document changes brought about since the onset of modernity in India. Rather, we were concerned with underscoring the historical trajectory of a select number of key concepts themselves. More precisely, we considered it of epistemic value to show how—as a result of sociopolitical transformations, in particular at the interstices of colonialism and postcolonialism—certain concepts (such as 'Ahimsa', 'Caste', 'Darshan', and 'Race', just to name a few prominent ones) have, during the last two centuries, taken on different meanings. This being the case, seeking fixed definitions or stable meanings, therefore, seemed a pointless exercise. Furthermore, we would like to stress that in discussing or delineating the trajectory of a key concept, there is no 'wrong' or 'correct' way *per se*. Viewed from this perspective, some of our authors' seemingly idiosyncratic delineations of specific key concepts reflect just one instance of the differing ways in which the phenomena can be—and have been—perceived or interpreted during the past, and this multiperspective tendency has perhaps intensified in the contemporary period. Testifying to the constant interplay between theory and practice in the field of modern Indian studies, this heuristic device is employed quite ingeniously—albeit inadvertently—by many of the entries in this volume. While some demonstrate how concepts impinge upon practices, and develop, shape, as well as make inroads into geographical regions, thereby 'encroaching' upon their inhabitants, other entries, contrastively, discuss how practices and their agents for their part challenge and change given conceptual frameworks.

Thus, our task was to collate an assemblage of different conceptual 'narratives', representing an array of different 'readings' of sociocultural experience. In doing this, we, as editors, would like to not only sensitize the reader to the vibrancy of academic discussions but also draw attention to inherent contestations and tensions riddling scholarly interpretations. Far from diminishing the relevance of individual expositions, such discursive contentions enhance the crucial significance of academic debate, mirroring as the latter does similar contestations in the public sphere. Moreover, while taking into account the shaping and reshaping of key concepts, we have become all the more acutely aware of the many omissions in this present volume. Accordingly, we would appreciate receiving critical comments and suggestions as to crucial additional concepts for future editions; simultaneously, we wish to stress the urgent need for further concerted research in this dynamic field.

With regard to the actual selection of key concepts, the terms were chosen in accordance with themes central to modern Indian studies (pertaining to society and culture; political and economic developments, both colonial and postcolonial; the religious sphere; environment, education, and science). However, an arrangement in thematic clusters—constructing artificial compartments of multifariously interconnecting key concepts—was considered less viable than the present alphabetical listing which was chosen preferentially to facilitate easy usage.

In further elucidating the organizational rationale governing this volume, it is essential to mention some of the challenges we faced, for collating a cross-section of the shared vocabulary of modern India could only be achieved by tracking down concepts situated at ideational, linguistic, sociological, political, and cultural levels. But it was almost impossible to assemble a vocabulary representative of all the different languages of the Indian subcontinent. Even the task of selecting between terms germane to Indian languages and English terms was quite daunting. Should, for instance, an entry on 'Itihasa' be included instead of 'History', and 'Khandan' instead of 'Family'? In such cases we opted for the indigenous alternatives because they, in our view, can viably capture the cognitive implications and empirical specificities of the respective Indian conception and phenomenon. For the same reason, 'Hijra' was preferred as against 'Transgender'. Further, Hindi's role and status as a contested national language prompted our choice of terms like 'Samaj', 'Samachar', and 'Swadeshi'. We fully realize that supplementing them with regional equivalents as well as broaching the separate issue of loanwords remains a crucial desideratum for subsequent research.

Given our broad multidisciplinary approach, it was deemed necessary to have separate entries on terms which, in conventional contexts, are either clubbed together or pitted against each other. 'Darshan', 'Dharma', 'Indian Philosophy', and 'Religion' are considered separately to underscore their individual specificities. Similarly, 'Bhakti' and 'Theosophy' could have been linked up with 'Religion'. Yet, in our view, their substantive and volatile aspects can be adequately brought to the fore only when dealt with individually. The same holds true for 'Science', 'Ayurveda', and 'Unani'. To fully understand the historical processes and the ideological underpinnings with which these and other terms are intimately entangled, a short essay on 'Knowledge Formation' was considered an essential conceptual ingredient entitled to a place in our volume.

Political, economic, and religious issues taking centre stage during the struggle for Independence comprise another notable cluster of terms. Due to their salience in understanding the history of modern India, we considered it necessary to expand the scope of key concepts to integrate these crucial events and movements such as 'Indian Uprising of 1857', 'Hindu Reform Movements in British India', 'Muslim Religious Reform Movements', 'Cow Protection', 'Drain of Wealth', and 'Khalifa/Khalifat/ Khilafat'; contrastively, 'Freedom', truly a key concept, makes up for this apparent slippage. Other key concepts like 'Feminism' and 'Land Revenue/Land Reform' bridge the divide between India's past and her present. Some other entries dwell on socioeconomic constellations, geopolitical developments, and movements of resistance characterizing particular regions ('Dharavi', 'Dravidian', 'Girangaon', 'Malabar', 'Khalistan', 'Kashmiriyat', 'Maoist Movement', 'Self-Respect Movement', and 'Seven Sisters')—all are crucial to understanding the subcontinent's dynamic diversity.

Further, vernacular terms like 'Biradari', or contested ones like 'Caste' and 'Dowry', delineate social practices and, more significantly, trace, on the one hand, the shifting historical discourse and, on the other, the regional variations impinging on their multiple understandings in the contemporary period. 'Ambedkarite', 'Bhoodan/Gramdan', 'Communalism', 'Dalit', 'Development', 'Green Revolution', 'Emergency', 'Family Planning/ Population Control', 'Liberalization', 'Mandal Commssion', 'Secularism', 'Strategic Enclave', and so on, examine certain key sociopolitical and economic developments defining the public sphere since India's Independence. 'Adab', 'Atman', 'Ahimsa', 'Bhadralok/Bhadramahila', 'Bhakti', 'Dharma', 'Imam', 'Iman', 'Izzat', 'Manuvad', and 'Samvad' take on pivotal concepts characterizing social and religious practices and beliefs, as well as age-old philosophical notions that continue to rank high in the public sphere. Furthermore, a volume dedicated to modern India cannot afford to omit terms like 'Bollywood' and 'Goonda' that have impacted deeply, albeit in divergent ways, the sociocultural life in this region. 'Monsoon' and 'Indian Ocean' discuss the Asian subcontinent's climatological and geomorphological specificity, highlighting its captivating features. 'Biopiracy', 'Business Rajahs', and 'Metro' delineate recent trends that are very likely to influence India's future.

Longer entries like 'Democracy', 'Environment', 'Nationalism', 'Political Economy', and 'Religion' cross-cut many debates in post-Independence India. Others like 'Race' trace the trajectory of a controversial term that continues to be prevalent in debates, albeit in the garb of ethnicity. In comparison, some shorter articles (such as 'Sanskrit', coupled with a longer entry on 'Language') deal with terms that exemplify philological developments, whereby the authors of these entries perspicaciously show how these concepts are intimately entangled with past and contemporary cultural and sociopolitical constellations. Importantly, the length of an article is not necessarily indicative of the respective key concept's salience for modern Indian studies, but rather reflects the respective authors' proclivity, as well as testifies to our editorial quartet's liberal flexibility.

An additional feature of this volume is its multipurpose use. A reader searching for a quick elucidation of a key concept will find the term in the respective individual entry, but along with this concise overview s/he will be introduced via the bibliographical references to major published works (mentioned Chicago-style in the text, supplemented by further readings at the end of each entry, with all references being assembled and given in full in the extensive, alphabetically arranged consolidated bibliography at the end of the volume). Hence, each entry could serve as a springboard— or gateway—for subsequent detailed research. Further, individual entries, though functioning as stand-alone pieces, are, nonetheless, interconnected with a vast web of conceptually and historically related terms. This is prominently the case with entries such as 'Gandhian' and 'Nehruvian', the former being linked closely with terms like 'Ahimsa', 'Swadeshi', and 'Swaraj', and the latter with entries on 'Democracy', 'Development', and 'Secularism'. And since the individual entries have been authored by different scholars, multiperspective readings of these key concepts are made available to the attentive reader. Simultaneously, cardinal concepts (such as 'Karma' and 'Non-alignment'), which regrettably do not have separate entries, are catered for in thematically related contexts (such as

'Ahimsa', 'Atman', 'Dharma', and even 'Theosophy' for the former concept and, not surprisingly, in 'Nehruvian' for the latter term). In this way, any terminological gaps or overlaps are dealt with effectively so that the reader may reap optimal benefit from a close reading of our volume. The use of diacritics has been avoided (basically to streamline the technical process); instead, the formal international standard for Indic transliteration has been adhered to.

This project began independently in London and in Heidelberg, with very similar goals. The original SOAS, University of London, project was for longer essays (of about 3,000 words) to be published online. This was in the fairly early days of Internet publishing and although some entries appeared (http://www.soas.ac.uk/southasianstudies/keywords/), many authors did not want to contribute to an online-only publication, while others felt the open-ended nature of the project meant that deadlines could be pushed forward. As chance would have it, a parallel initiative in Heidelberg envisaged a book publication with an interdisciplinary thrust. This fortuitous coincidence provided the ideal synergy to revive a useful project and to replenish it with new life. The enthusiastic response we have received from a whole range of international specialists has also made us appreciate the enduring popularity of the printed word.

To all our contributors we would like to extend our deep appreciation for their sincere commitment, enduring patience, and generous encouragement to see this volume through to its successful conclusion. Without the empathetic support coupled with the judicious advice of the publisher this volume would not have seen the light of day.

With this innovative initiative, we hope to facilitate the reading and understanding of India's social, cultural, and political past, as well as of its present. We would not only like to draw the readers' attention to the vitality, richness, and academic rigour in the study of modern India but also, through our chosen concepts, to make them aware of their relevance to the larger corpus of scholarship in the humanities and social sciences. In enhancing the shared framework of understanding about the Indian subcontinent, we hope our volume, with its wide spectrum of key concepts, will provide the reader with insights into vital debates about the region, underscoring the compelling issues of colonialism and postcolonialism. Last, but not least, our efforts would not have been in vain if this pioneering venture opens a window for the reader (expert and non-expert alike) to engage with the intriguing intricacies of daily life on the subcontinent and its enthralling recent past.

Gita Dharampal-Frick
Monika Kirloskar-Steinbach
Rachel Dwyer
Jahnavi Phalkey

Adab

*A*dab (plural *Adaab*) relates, for many Muslims in South Asia, to ideal principles of *savoir-vivre*, or 'how to live correctly'. It is an intimate guide to personal activity, the principle behind a consciously imbibed personal and social etiquette that is simultaneously in keeping with a properly 'Islamic' demeanour or way of being. There is a long tradition of philosophical writing on *adab*, relating it to literature, art, craft, and popular religion (Metcalf 1984). This entry explores the meaning of *adab* in practice and how such practices are morally and ethically underpinned by conceptions of relatedness, the body, and social hierarchy. *Adab* is related in this regard to the cultivation of the habits of life and the development of a personal character, as exemplified by the Prophet Mohammed and elaborated in the *Sunnah* (alternative spelling: *Sunnat*). In this regard, *adab* is a form of ethical practice; it applies to thoughts, words, and actions to create an ideal code of conduct that informs all aspects of life.

Generally, in the South Asian traditions, there appear to be two methods of subdividing the practices of *adab*: between inner and outer modes of being and between the individual and social. In everyday life, there are guidelines for how to eat, partake in meals communally, sleep, speak, greet, take leave, wash, treat subordinates and superiors, travel, and act as hosts and guests. There are also guidelines on correct emotional responses to misfortune, illness, and death. *Adab* also inheres in dress and is the custodian of virtue.

On another level, *adab* lays out the principles of the relationship between an individual and God, a spiritual guide (*Sheikh*, *Saiyed*), family, and elders. Elevated among these codes are those that organize and structure relationships between spiritual guides, as putative descendants of the Prophet Mohammed, and their disciples. Upon pledging loyalty, the disciple enters a dual process of scrutinizing his faults (and attempting to remove them) and his virtues (and attempting to improve on them). He internalizes the image of perfection represented by the *pir* ('saint'); and through recitation, practice, prayer and study, the *murid* ('follower') passes through a series of reciprocal transformations between the image he has of the *pir* and the image of himself. Through the refinement of habit the self is refined. There is a transformative relationship between inner conditions and outer actions which is often conceived of as a three-stage hierarchical path: Islam ('submission', 'the embodiment of practice'), *iman* ('cultivating religious faith', 'understanding'), and *ishan* ('intentionality guided by cultivated spiritual faith').

Ideally, the profane or the everyday, and sacred relationships, are premised on the same diagram of power. As Metcalf writes: 'Whether one is learning a craft, or poetry and language, or music, or moral and spiritual qualities, the process of outer practice, the creation of habit, and finally a realization of that process in one's being is precisely the same' (1984: 11). The idea is that one's physical actions in the world transform the constituent parts of one's soul as one becomes increasingly adept and disciplined by the task: *adab*.

Adab is also about emulation of exemplary figures and striving to become similar to them. The figure of the Prophet is held in infallible esteem as a model of dignity, wisdom, temperance, and fortitude. His example forms the basis of canonical prayer, personal dignity, integrity, decorum, modesty, wisdom, and personal and social order. To follow his model is *adab*; hence *Sunnah* is popularly understood as a rough guide to *adab*. Thus, it is *Sunnah* to perform one's ritual ablutions in a certain manner, just as one is often reminded that it is *Sunnah* to round off one's meal with a morsel of something sweet.

Further reading: Alam 2004; Gabrieli 2013; Metcalf 1984.

—EDWARD SIMPSON, *Professor in Social Anthropology,*
SOAS, University of London

—FARHANA IBRAHIM, *Assistant Professor of Sociology and*
Social Anthropology, Indian Institute of Technology, Delhi

— ◦•◦ —

Adivasi

A divasi' is a collective term for a range of communities found throughout India that are considered 'indigenous' or 'aboriginal'. In 2001, there were over four hundred Adivasi communities, with a population of over 84 million, making up 8.2 per cent of the population (GOI 2001). The largest concentrations of people so classed are found in the Northeast. Elsewhere, many reside in the central-eastern region, in what is now the state of Jharkhand and areas adjoining it in Bengal, Orissa, Chhattisgarh, and Andhra Pradesh, and in a belt in western India running across the four modern Indian states of Rajasthan, Gujarat, Madhya Pradesh, and Maharashtra.

In the precolonial period, there was an awareness that the peoples who inhabited the more inaccessible hill and forest tracts were different from those who lived in the plains regions. They were generally regarded with contempt and some fear, as in the *Laws of Manu* that described the tribal *pulkasa* as being amongst 'the lowest of men'; they were held to be the reincarnation of 'priest-killers' who were said to supply dangerous herbal concoctions used in malevolent rituals (Doniger and Smith 1991: 236, 240, 283). Derogatory terms were frequently deployed in modern vernaculars, as in the Gujarati *jangli jati* ('wild people') or *kaliparaj* ('black or dirty people') (Desai 1898: 379; Belsare 1904: 264). More commonly, however, they were known by a range of disparate community names, such as Gond, Santal, Oraon, Munda, and Bhil. Where they were found alongside caste Hindus, these communities became essentially caste-like in form. The British attempted to categorize them sociologically as an all-India collective, applying a range of shifting terms and concepts. Initially, they were classed as 'aboriginals', 'early tribes', or 'jungle tribes', being characterized by their supposedly 'primitive' lifestyle. Attempts by late-nineteenth-century racist officials to categorize them as of Australoid or Negrito race floundered when anthropometric measurement found that physically they were no different from the surrounding peoples; and similar unsuccessful efforts were made to prove that their languages were of a distinct autochthonous sort (Hardiman 2008: 20–4). Additionally, an attempt was made to list and enumerate them in the censuses from

1881 to 1911 as a separate religious group known as 'animists'. This failed due to much local confusion as to whether or not they were 'really' Hindu.

In the late 1930s, these discredited attempts to define these peoples in social, racial, linguistic, religious, or other such ways, were displaced by a new political category, that of Adivasi. This was first proposed in the Chhotanagpur region by a group of politically active tribal people who formed the Adivasi Mahasabha in 1938. The term is a combination of the Hindi terms *adi* ('beginning' or 'of earliest times') and *vasi* ('resident of'). The idea was that the Adivasis were the original inhabitants of the respective lands, and that they had a prior right of control over and above later interlopers—namely, the 'landgrabbers', moneylenders, and officials of different communities—who had moved in following the 'pacification' of these tracts in the nineteenth century. The term was taken up by the Gandhian social worker A.V. Thakkar (1869–1951) in the 1940s, and Mohandas Karamchand Gandhi (1869–1948) himself adopted it in 1941 (Gandhi 1999: 369–70). It was rejected by many Hindu nationalists, who refused to accept the notion that such people had been displaced and exploited by mostly Hindu invaders. They introduced alternative terms, such as *girijan* ('mountain people'), or *vanvasi* ('forest dwellers') (Hansen 1999: 103–7). To this day, the use of such terms indicates a person's political persuasion.

The Government of India Act of 1935 also introduced a category of 'Scheduled', allowing for positive discrimination for disadvantaged peoples. Lists of tribal communities were drawn up, and different communities were placed in the category of 'Scheduled Tribe' (ST). After Independence, the STs were granted reservations in educational institutions and for official posts. Certain electoral constituencies were designated as reserved only for ST candidates. As ST is a less contentious term, it was adopted in official circles after Independence as the preferred term for these peoples, though Adivasi has in general become more widely used in recent years, providing a positive assertion of identity for a group that feels increasingly oppressed and marginalized in the development strategies of the modern Indian state.

Further reading: Hardiman 1987; Rycroft and Dasgupta 2011.

—DAVID HARDIMAN, *Emeritus Professor, Department of History,*
University of Warwick

Ahimsa

Ahimsa or 'non-violence' is a strong motif in Hindu, Jain, and Buddhist traditions, but its modern prominence has much to do with its use by Mohandas Karamchand Gandhi (1869–1948). A conceptual history of Gandhi's use of that word would have to begin by recognizing the influence of his mentor, the Jain thinker Shrimad Rajchandra (1867–1901). The latter understood ahimsa in terms of *daya* or 'compassion'—he repeatedly called for *dayadharma*, or 'religion of compassion'.

Gandhi's readings from the 1900s subtly radicalized these terms, infusing them with a more political connotation, and understanding ahimsa as involving the renunciation of any form of domination of other beings. By the 1910s and 1920s, he articulated this understanding by drawing also on Hindu and Buddhist traditions. His *daya* is premised on a distinctive *advaita* ('non-duality') interpretation which stresses not just that *satya* ('being' or 'truth') is marked by the absolute unity of 'all that lives', but also that this unity requires absolute equality. Relatedly, such equality presumes irreconcilable difference, for absolute equality does not allow for a common measure or comparison. Only by sustaining irreconcilable multiplicity is it possible thus to abide by the unity of *satya*. Perhaps to emphasize this giving and receiving of absolute equality and difference, Gandhi sometimes describes ahimsa as *abhayadana*. In some Jain traditions, *abhayadana* or the 'gift of fearlessness' (though Gandhi translates this on one occasion as 'gift of life') is the highest gift (Laidlaw 2000).

Gandhi describes ahimsa and *satya* as two sides of the same coin because ahimsa sustains this multiplicity of being. It does so by recognizing that *satya* is constitutively marked by its own 'notness', and that this notness entails the multiplicity of being. Gandhi thinks notness through the advaitic term *neti neti* ('not this, not this') or the Buddhist term *shunyata*, while he thinks multiplicity through the Jain phrase *anekantvada* ('multiplicity of truths') (Skaria forthcoming).

Drawing on these traditions, he rejects an understanding of ahimsa simply as an individual abstention from 'direct' himsa ('violence'), or as an exemplary attenuation of force. Rather, he thinks of it as a force greater than violence—as self-sacrifice rather than the sacrifice of others. He reads the Bhagavadgita's stress on nishkamakarma ('disinterested action') as action done as self-sacrifice, or non-calculable action—action outside the means/end problematic. This is why for him the Gita is already within the problematic of ahimsa. Gandhi describes this form of self-sacrifice as satyagraha—the 'insistence' (agraha) on satya. In their self-sacrifice, satyagrahis become infused by the notness of being, they become 'ciphers' or shunya.

This self-sacrifice makes ahimsa the 'extreme limit of forgiveness'. Gandhi stresses that while ahimsa involves forgiving, the institutional justice involved in law—which is based on the principle of the third party—cannot forgive. But here the concept of forgiveness must itself be rethought. Usually, absolute forgiveness is understood as a forgetting without reserve—as a forgiveness that forgets the offence against it and so forgets also that it has forgotten. When Gandhi tries to affirm forgiveness in this sense, he finds it to be impossible, for it would involve forgiving the unforgiveable—as, for instance, the immense violence of the British.

Ahimsa, therefore, is the extreme limit of forgiveness in quite another sense. Satyagrahis refuse either to punish the unforgiveable (if they did so, they would themselves assume the role of the sovereign) or to forgive the unforgiveable (if they did so, they would become complicit in the unforgiveable). Instead, satyagrahis resist the unforgiveable by offering themselves in self-sacrifice. Here, what they give as a gift is precisely the refusal to forgive, and the possibility of atonement that this refusal to forgive offers to both them and their antagonists.

Any conceptual history of ahimsa must be supplemented by recognition of its social history. Here, there is space to stress only two points. First, the masses who rallied around Gandhi as a figure often appropriated him to local agendas, and had a very different understanding of him and his politics than he did himself (Amin 1984). Second, as ideology, Gandhian ahimsa accomplished a 'most important historical task'— that of enabling the 'political appropriation of the subaltern classes by a bourgeoisie aspiring for political hegemony in the new nation-state' (Chatterjee 1983: 100).

Further reading: Amin 1984; Bilgrami 2003; Chatterjee 1983; Gandhi 1999; Laidlaw 2000; Skaria 2009, [forthcoming].

—AJAY SKARIA, *Associate Professor, Department of History,*
University of Minnesota

— •◦• —

Ambedkarite

It is difficult to specify the juncture when the term 'Ambedkarite' and its regional equivalents such as *Ambedkarvadi*—literally meaning 'speaking/advocating Ambedkar'—akin to *Marxvadi* ('Marxist'), *udaravadi* ('liberal'), or *Ambedkar vicharvadi* ('subscribing to Ambedkar's thought') came to gain currency, particularly given the uneven reach and spread of Bhimrao Ramji Ambedkar's (1891–1956) ideas and influence in the different regions of India.

In the early days, the term was used disparagingly (Jivaka 1959) by critics and opponents, or evocatively by adherents and admirers; the latter, particularly after Ambedkar's *diksha* ceremony ('initiation ceremony') to Buddhism in October 1956. The Republican Party of India (RPI) popularized the term after its inception in 1957. By the early 1960s, the term, or its equivalents in regional languages, was widely used across India to denote a distinctive mode of beliefs and values, mobilization, and organization (as in Ambedkarvadi Yuvak Sangh [Ambedkarite Youth League]), or even literary currents and religious pursuits (Kshirsagar 1994). With the Dalit Panther Movement and the popularization of the invocation Dalit from the 1970s—especially with the militant mass uprising of Dalits in Maharashtra, the term lost its force in the public domain to a certain extent, but continued to be employed either as an equivalent or additional specification (Murugkar 1994). However, émigré followers of Ambedkar have preferred to describe themselves as Ambedkarites rather than Dalits (Hardtmann 2009: 159), stressing a distinctive perspective on life, rather than a condition of being.

While there are certain core determinants attached to Ambedkarite, its substantive meanings vary widely. In a narrow sense, this perspective argues that untouchability is a distinct but despicable social practice integral to Hinduism, and a democratic polity while upholding equality of citizenship should pursue such measures as preferential considerations and affirmative action policies to uphold fair treatment. Such pursuits, however, should be carried out within the framework of a constitutional order. In a broader sense, it proposes a comprehensive critique of hierarchically organized social orders that subject sections of society to degradation and humiliation and suggest their replacement with an egalitarian ethic such as Buddhism. Violence, however, is not seen as appropriate to fight against the abominable condition of untouchability, but mass awakening and assertions for democratic inclusion are (Omvedt 1996).

Attempts to bond Ambedkarism with Marxism (or with comprehensive secularism, or with certain perspectives of liberation theology that focus on suffering, stigma, and victimhood) have not been very successful. The attempts of Dalit Panthers to invoke Ambedkar as an inclusive appeal against exploitation and conditions of oppression in general have not made much headway so far. The popularization of the term 'Dalit' has not generally helped in exploring some of the seminal ideas that Ambedkar advanced concerning knowledge and understanding, modernity, democracy and constitutionalism, representation, non-violent social action, significance of religion, nation and culture, and what it means to be human. Such tensions and deficiencies will invariably subject both the terms, 'Ambedkarite' and 'Dalit', and the perspectives underlying them, to demanding scrutiny in times to come.

Further reading: Dangle 1992; Hardtmann 2009; Jondhale and Beltz 2004; Kshirsagar 1994; Murugkar 1994; Omvedt 1996; Rodrigues 2002; Thorat and Thorat 2007; Zelliot 1992.

—VALERIAN RODRIGUES, *Professor, Centre for Political Studies, Jawaharlal Nehru University, New Delhi*

— ·•· —

Anglo-Indians

Anglo-Indians are a mixed-race Indo-European group who are defined and protected as an Indian minority community in the Constitution of India with special safeguards and nominated seats in the Lok Sabha ('House of the People' or lower house of the Indian Parliament) and state legislatures.

From the 1940s onwards, many Anglo-Indians migrated to Britain, Australia, and other Anglosphere countries, creating a global diaspora. Originating from India's European mercantile and imperial presence, Anglo-Indians' ancestry can include British, Portuguese, Dutch, French, Irish, and other European progenitors. Prior to the 1911 Census of India, they were referred to as Eurasians, East Indians, Indo-Britons or, more pejoratively, half-castes, while the term 'Anglo-Indian' was associated with Britons living in India (a usage that occasionally persists in contemporary scholarship). During the twentieth century they largely subsumed Luso-Indians. As a result of their upbringing and the major avenues to social and material advancement available to them during the colonial era, Anglo-Indians tended to strongly identify with the European side of their ancestry: speaking English as their first language; practising Christianity; and embracing what they perceived to be European dress, culture, and cuisine. However, like Anglo-Indians themselves, their distinctive cuisine embodies an Indo-European hybridity.

The British East India Company initially encouraged racial intermarriage, but banned mixed-race offspring from its service in 1791. The Raj's evolving socioracial hierarchy extended to excluding Europeans of Indian domicile from 'whiteness'. Due to their overlapping social and economic existence with Anglo-Indians, both were conjoined as 'the domiciled community'. Depicted as 'poor whites', Domiciled Europeans actually included many Anglo-Indians engaging in racial passing (which refers to the passing off by a person possessing some characteristics of a particular socioracial category as belonging entirely to another). The British perceived the presence and poverty of the domiciled as a threat to their racial prestige and responded by endowing schools and orphanages for them. However, neither group was uniformly poor, and both came to enjoy an intermediary position within the Raj's socioracial employment hierarchy, with rank and remuneration above those of Indian subordinates and below those of transient Britons. Employed in the railways, telegraph offices, and customs departments, and made (as a condition of employment) to serve in auxiliary military forces, the domiciled community was relied upon by the Raj to secure its transportation and communication infrastructure, which was necessary for the rapid redeployment of troops during civil unrest.

The 1935 Government of India Act definition of an Anglo-Indian (which survived into the Indian Constitution) was carefully crafted, specifying European ancestry in the male line, but omitting direct reference to Indian ancestry. This excluded the offspring of Indian men and Anglo-Indian or European women, but allowed for the inclusion of whites domiciled in India as well as those of mixed-race who denied their Indian ancestry (whether they self-identified as Anglo-Indian or domiciled European). The Anglo-Indian leader Henry Gidney attempted to shift Anglo-Indian attachment to Britain towards a dualistic embrace of Britain as fatherland and India as motherland. His successor Frank Anthony went further by embracing Indian nationalism and thereby secured Anglo-Indians' status as a constitutionally recognized minority. Since Independence, Anglo-Indians have continued to make prominent contributions to Indian public life in the armed forces, education, nursing, sports, and entertainment.

Further reading: Blunt 2005; Caplan 2003; Ghosh 2008; Hawes 1996; Mizutani 2011.

—UTHER CHARLTON-STEVENS, *Associate Professor, Institute of World Economy & Finance, Volgograd State University, Volgograd*

— ·◆· —

Aryan

The discussion of the terms *arya* and *anarya* is normally dominated, on the one hand, by linguistics and archaeology, and, on the other, increasingly in the context of the politics of knowledge as reflected in colonial and postcolonial histories of South Asia. Even in the ancient and classical period in India, these terms played an equally significant role expressing conceptions of linguistic, ethnic, moral, and spiritual identity, purity, and superiority. In the Hindu religious–legal tradition (*dharmashastra*), the term *arya* came to refer to the three higher social groups—the Brahmins, Kshatriyas, and Vaishyas—but the ancient law-giver Manu also speaks of *arya* languages and modes of behaviour (Bronkhorst and Deshpande 1999).

The term 'Aryan' was later used in Indo-European linguistics in two ways that emphasised both the affinity of Sanskrit with Greek and Latin, as well as their derivation from a common linguistic source. This branch of linguistics was initiated with the address of Sir William Jones (1746–1794) to the Asiatic Society in Calcutta in 1786. A detailed elaboration of the Indo-European family was worked out later, mostly by German philologists like Franz Bopp (1791–1867), August Schleicher (1821–1868), Karl Brugmann (1849–1919), and Berthold Delbrück (1842–1922), and was further consolidated in the work of Friedrich Max Müller (1823–1900), and the French scholar Antoine Meillet (1866–1936). Gradually, the notion of a common linguistic origin was extended to the common origin of races or peoples and of religious and mythological ideas. These theories were developed by scholars like Max Müller and Georges Dumézil (1898–1986). For a general history of Indo-European studies, see Mallory (1989).

The term 'Aryan' is now used to refer to the speakers of Indo-Iranian languages, Indo-Iranian itself being a branch of the larger Indo-European language family. The term *arya* as a self-referring term, meaning 'civilized' or 'noble', is found only in ancient linguistic materials in Iran (Avestan and Old Persian) and India (Vedic Sanskrit), both regions claiming to be the home of the Aryas.

However, in less careful and yet extensive usage, the term 'Aryan' is sometimes used to refer to the entire Indo-European language family. With the uncritical equation of language and race in the nineteenth century, the term 'Aryan' came to assume a racial significance, and it was extensively employed in that manner by western colonial administrators, historians, and politicians, particularly by the Nazis, and still continues to be used that way by white supremacist groups in many parts of the world. The term 'Aryan race' also appears in many Indian writings of the nineteenth and twentieth centuries, where it also referred to a revivalist purist Hindu identity by groups like the Arya Samaj, and it continues to resonate until today with Hindu nationalist groups vocal in their rejection of the 'Aryan Invasion Theory', which holds that the indigenous population of India became dominated by culturally superior Aryan invaders, and argue for the 'Out of India Theory', claiming that it was the superior Indian Aryans who migrated outward, and civilized the rest of the world (Bronkhorst and Deshpande 1999; Bryant and Patton 2005).

What is often not realized is that people speaking the same language can belong to different 'racial' backgrounds, and people of the same 'racial' background may speak different languages. The speakers of Indo-Aryan Marathi and the neighbouring, but linguistically unrelated Dravidian language, Kannada, can hardly be distinguished from each other on biological grounds, and yet these two languages belong to different linguistic families. When the Rigvedic poets invoked their gods to help the Arya community and destroy the Dasa/Dasyus, they were dealing with culturally perceived differences, rather than 'race' as understood in the twentieth century. Even during the Rigvedic period, there appears to have been a gradual move away from the earlier violent conflicts between the Arya and the Dasa communities towards some sort of a cooperative and collaborative relationship between them. There is a good deal of research showing how a slow intercultural and linguistic convergence may have come about in ancient India (Bronkhorst and Deshpande 1999), leading to linguistic and cultural Aryanization of the originally non-Aryan communities, and a localization of the original Aryan communities by incorporation of the others' linguistic and cultural traits. This process eventually resulted in what Murray B. Emeneau (1904–2005) called 'India as a linguistic area'. In this process, languages originally belonging to the Indo-Aryan and Dravidian language families came to share a common set of linguistic features.

In more recent research, the search for Aryan/Indo-European origins has been extended to the domains of archaeology and genetics. Exciting as this research is in opening new avenues (Mallory 1989; Anthony 2007; Kuz'mina 2007), it still remains contested due to difficulties involved in the mapping of linguistic, cultural, and biological identities, since these are essentially independent variables.

Further reading: Anthony 2007; Bronkhorst and Deshpande 1999; Bryant and Patton 2005; Kuz'mina 2007; Mallory 1989.

—MADHAV M. DESHPANDE, *Professor of South Asian Literature and Linguistics, University of Michigan*

— •• —

Atman

'As to this [Atman] even the ancient gods had doubts, for it is hard to understand, it is a subtle doctrine'. This is how the dialogue on the nature of *atman* begins in one of the famous *Upanishads* (*Katha* 1.21, ca. 450 BCE, see *Dashopanishadah* 1937), the ancient Indian texts on philosophy.

Like many other Indian terms, *atman* has been used in various ways in different contexts, but, commonly, in many philosophical, political, and social contexts, it refers to 'self', 'soul', 'individual', 'person', 'I', 'being', and so on. The Vedic belief is that *atman* is 'life' or 'being', which is unborn (*aja*), hence imperishable, undying (*amartya*); the non-physical entity of a human being remaining after the body's destruction (*Bhagavadgita* 2.20). For ancient philosophers, *atman* became a subject of deep intro-spection to understand that 'I-ness', and to ruminate on it to realize freedom from the vicissitudes of life. However, the ancient seers, phi-losophers of the *Upanishads*, advocated that a proper understanding of *atman* alone would lead to wisdom and, eventually, to freedom from the cycle of death and birth; it is also suggested there that understanding the subtle and true nature of *atman* requires the intervention of a teacher or a guide (*Brhadaranyaka Upanishad* 5.15.1, see *Dashopanishadah* 1937). Therefore, in the Upanishadic dialogues on the nature of *atman*, one witnesses a hint of helplessness on the part of the preacher. Besides, the term is frequently used by people to address 'oneself', the first-person pronoun, 'I'. It is suggested in Indian philosophical debates on the *atman* (particularly between the Nyaya and Buddhists schools) that to justify one's intuitions, knowledge, and the things belonging to a person, *atman* is necessary; without *atman* it would not be possible to distinguish between different bodies, different shapes, and colours. However, Vedanta philosophy (espoused by the Upanishadic texts of ca. 500 BCE) distinguishes this type of *atman* from the larger, indivisible self of which the *Upanishads* also spoke as 'smaller than small, larger than large', all-pervading Brahman (*Brahmasutrabhasya* 1.1.31, see Acharya 1948). In the Nyaya ('realist') and Vedanta ('monist') philosophies of India, *atman* has been explained as consciousness and reflexive awareness (*svasamvedana* or 'self-cognition'). This becomes linked to another major epistemological concept, 'memory', which requires, in the process of perception and cognition, recollection of previous awareness.

The Nyaya school of Indian philosophy (comprising logic or the systematic exposition of the means to knowledge) defends the existence of *atman*; it propounds that without an entity, effects of human activities will remain unexperienced. Moreover, such an experience would need a subject, a substratum. In the absence of *atman*, all this would vanish with the perishing of the body; the endeavour to seek freedom and liberation, therefore, would prove futile (*Nyayasutras* 1.1.1–25; 3.1.1 and their commentaries by Vatsyayana, ca. fourth–sixth century CE, see Jha 1939). Elsewhere in the *Upanishads*, this *atman* is also interpreted as the one consisting of 'vital breath', 'mind', 'body', 'perception', and 'bliss' (*Taittiriya* 2.3.2–25, see *Dashopanishadah* 1937). This analysis of the *Upanishads* has been more or less endorsed by Vaishesika philosophy (or the realist school of Indian philosophy), where the perception of *atman* is linked to the body (*Vaishesikasutra* 3.2.1, see Jambuvijayaji 1961). Jaina philosophers concurred that *atman* cannot be envisaged in the absence of the senses, which are the main constituents of the body. Advaita Vedanta describes the plurality of *atman* as an illusion; for it, the ultimate *atman* is the only reality: 'the difference between the self and the highest self is unreal; it appears real due to ignorance' (*Brahmsutrabhasya* 1.4.22, see Acharya 1948). However, *Vishistadvaita* ('monism with a difference') believes in the multitudes of *atman*, under the supervision of one, ultimate *atman*, called *ishvara*, the 'supreme lord'.

The *purusha* of Samkhya (a dualist school of Indian philosophy) is not very different from *atman* except that it is inactive, aloof, and disinterested, yet affected by the effects of the body (the epistemology of Samkhya, ca. 500 BCE, deals with the notion of self, *purusha*, and matter, *prakriti*, cf. *Samkhyakarika*, ca. 400 CE, see Pandeya 1967). Buddhists do not accept *atman* as an entity as understood by orthodox schools of Indian philosophy, that is, those schools that recognize Vedic texts as the authoritative source of knowledge, namely, Mimamsa, Vedanta, Nyaya, Vaishesika, Samkhya, and Yoga. The Buddhist 'no self' (*anatma, anatta*, in Pali) theory was supported by the fourth-century philosopher Vasubandhu who belonged to the Madhyamika school; the Madhyamika believes that what is 'real' has no *atman*; in other words, what appears to be the nature of *atman* is in fact nothing but an ever-changing combination of the five constituents (*skandha*; in Pali, *khandha*): body (*rupa*), sensation (*vedana*), perception (*samjna, sanna*), impression (*samskara*), and consciousness (*vijnana, vinnana*). These five 'building blocks' are explained by employing the metaphor of a chariot, which appears as an entity only until its parts are pulled apart. Thus the reality, *atman*, by its nature is impermanent (*Milindapanha* 2.1.1, see Trenckner 1962). The Buddha himself is believed to have said that one's fear of 'non-being' can be overcome only when one realizes that 'I' is itself a fiction. This level of scepticism also raised the moral question of human action, but not of the kind that Carvaka, the materialist, would like us to believe—that each action is justified as long as it brings about physical pleasure, *sukha*.

The scepticism of Vedanta, similar to that in the Bhagavadgita (or the *Mahabharata* in general, see van Buitenen 1981), seems to entail the theory of karma which suggests that each result is qualitatively proportionate to its action: good actions will accrue meritorious fruits and bad actions will bring about evil effects. The sage of the *Brhadaranyaka Upanishad*, Yajnavalkya, says: 'A man becomes good by good action and evil by bad action' (*punyo punyena karmani bhavati papah papeneti*: 3.3.2). The Bhagavadgita explains *atman* in ethical terms as immortal, unassailable, and never-changing. Both in the Bhagavadgita as well in the *Ramayana*, *atman* has also been explained as one's essential nature, pure spirit, immutable, permanent and, above all, pure consciousness of good people where the truth or dharma resides. Mohandas Karamchand Gandhi (1869–1948) was no doubt inspired by the Upanishadic notion of truth when he exhorted his countrymen to insist on exorcizing the veil (of foreign, unethical rule) from the truth (of self-rule) through *satyagraha*. In the modern Indian, or even in a global, context leaders from all professions promote the fashionable slogan, 'discover your self', which signifies enhancing one's self-confidence, boldness, and courage. In this sense, the concept of *atman*, self, is wide, even opaque, both in India and the West. What cannot be denied, however, is that certain common, human experiences, like pain, pleasure and desire, and ontological cognitions would be difficult to sustain without pointing to an entity called *atman*.

Further reading: Buitenen 1981; Dasgupta 1922 [1932]; Hiriyanna 1949; Jambuvijayaji 1961; Jha 1939; Olivelle 1998; Vasubandhu 1973.

—HEERAMAN TIWARI, *Assistant Professor, Centre for Historical Studies, Jawaharlal Nehru University, New Delhi; Senior Fellow at the Israel Institute for Advanced Studies, The Hebrew University of Jerusalem, Israel*

— ·•· —

Ayurveda

Ayurveda is the oldest extant medical system in the South Asian subcontinent. Scholars date Ayurveda's beginning to medical concepts discussed in the *Atharvaveda* (the last of the Vedic scriptures). Its origins are more commonly dated to the compilations of the *Shusruta* and *Charaka Samhitas*, composed after a series of symposia on medicine between the second and sixth centuries, in which medical traditions are first formally expanded and codified. Ayurveda is framed as a biomoral tradition based on the linking of ritual, embodiment, philosophy, and cosmology in Hindu thought. Its entrenchment within the social worlds of Hindus meant that it was generally at arm's length from the formal politics of the state, giving *vaids* ('ayurvedic physicians') autonomy over the tradition, even during periods of Mughal state sponsorship (Wujastyk 2003). The major shift during the modern era is thus evidenced by Ayurveda's incorporation into the logic of medical planning, witnessed by the nineteenth-century attempts to limit its influence, and levelled by interwar medical planning in which the indigenous medical systems were relied upon to implement new health measures.

The relationship between medicine and the state shifted starkly with the introduction of British colonial medical culture. Early imperial traders and travellers held Ayurveda and other indigenous medical traditions in some regard and often partook of these cures. However, the formalization of a British colonial biopolitic in the nineteenth century resulted in a singular biomedical focus, and Ayurveda was condemned as overly ritualized and unscientific. What persisted, however, was the authority of the *vaid* as a figure of medical authority, and by the turn of the twentieth century, *vaids* and other indigenous medical practitioners were relied upon for their trusted place amongst Indians sceptical of allopathic medical treatment, including vaccination and sanitation campaigns (Attewell 2007).

Ayurveda came to fruition as a medical system deemed capable of addressing the ills of modernity in the interwar period. The advent of a dyarchic devolution of power resulted in the transfer of responsibility for local medical services from the central to the provincial governments of British India. The provinces were now responsible for organizing and funding the expansion of medical services, bringing the state of the public's health within the purview of local government for the first time. Biomedical techniques and therapies were too expensive to use universally, and so provincial governments turned to pre-extant medical infrastructures. Between 1923 and 1939, the provinces released reports streamlining Ayurvedic and other indigenous medical systems along the lines of techno-scientific practice, which resulted in: attempts to standardize medical texts; the formalization of measures by which practitioners were trained, registered, and certified; seizing government control over the distribution of Ayurvedic and other therapeutic and pharmaceutical products; and the development of new educational and dispensary institutions (Berger 2013).

Ayurveda also had a role in determining the cultural politics of the national body during the nationalist period. The increase in publications dealing with indigenous medicine—while also drawing on eugenic and other ideas about the propagation of the nation—came to constitute a discourse about the measure of the 'ideal' Indian body. In this context, Ayurveda's association with a Hindu Indian past was resurrected to suit a communal politic, in which Ayurveda came to be associated solely with the 'Hindu' body, legitimate as the 'true' Indian body.

The success of Ayurveda's incorporation into medical planning in the interwar period, coupled with its cost-effectiveness, ensured its entry into postcolonial medical planning. Through the early 1950s and until India's second Five Year Plan, Ayurveda was a cornerstone of provincial planning. The Bhore Report (GOI 1946) and the Chopra Report (1948) spelt out possibilities for its incorporation into serious state planning at the central and, eventually, federal level, but the shift to Nehruvian technoscience, and the incursion of foreign medical aid in the 1950s, resulted in this pos-sibility falling by the wayside. Ayurveda was brought under the jurisdic-tion of the federal government in the early 1970s, along with Unani, Yoga, and Siddha, all of which were cast as primarily complementary and also historically indigenous health practices.

Further reading: Alavi 2010; Attewell 2007; Berger 2013; Mukharji 2009; Sivaramakrishnan 2006; Smith and Wujastyk 2008; Wujastyk 2003.

—RACHEL BERGER, *Associate Professor, Department of History, Concordia University, Montreal*

— ••• —

Bazaar

The dictionary definition of a bazaar refers to an Oriental market held all year long, consisting of shops and stalls with an assortment of goods for sale. The *Oxford English Dictionary* (OED) notes the presence of such markets in Oriental camps of yore, and also in more recent times, 'a fancy fair in imitation of the Eastern Bazaar'. The bazaar has slipped into the English language with a remarkable degree of fluidity and breadth of meaning.

It is hard to say when or where exactly this Arabic term, also adopted by Persian, made its way into the common vocabulary of Indian languages, but its widespread usage can be noted in courtly accounts dating back at least to the early period of the Delhi Sultanate (1206–1526). Thus the Persian words *bazargan*, *bazari*, and *bazariyan* ('marketers' and 'market-goers') describe a visibly identifiable community.

Any city worth its name was known by its bazaars. The Mughals built covered marketplaces that functioned much like whole cities in keeping with its peripatetic court-and-camp mode of rule (Mohammed 1989). Akbar constructed the Fatehpur Sikri Bazaar according to the classic four-sided (*chahar suq*) style, where the market stalls were arranged around a spacious square to accommodate royal processions. The open market square (*chauk*, *chabutara*) became an established feature of urban architecture in northern India (Rizvi 1972: 16).

Patronized by royalty, aristocracy, and *zamindar*s in their country seats, often attached to mosques, temples, and Sufi hospices, bazaars were indispensable to everyday trade and commerce across the Indian subcontinent (Sen 1998: 14–5, 52–3). More than that, however, the bazaar came to represent the world at large, including the common, vulgar, and the profane. This is nowhere more evident than in literature, especially poetry, where the bazaar denotes both fair and unfair exchange, serving as a metaphor for things both exotic and mundane. The literary and allegorical use of the word 'bazaar' can be seen readily in Urdu verse, but such usage can be traced much further back in time to the common man's parlance adopted by heterodox mystic poets of the *bhakti* movement in northern India, dating back at least to the fifteenth century CE.

In crowded bazaars, distinctions of caste, wealth, and social standing were difficult to maintain. Yet, the medieval Indian market was not necessarily an anonymous or independent public domain. Heads of temples, guardians of mosques and tombs, and hosts of major pilgrimages all derived power and sustenance from the bazaar through levies and tolls. Market exchange was thus subject to legitimate authority as well as the caprice of arbitrary power.

By the beginning of the eighteenth century, markets and trade routes were in disarray in the Mughal heartland. As the effective authority of Delhi declined, fortunes of many prominent cities and their bazaars were visibly affected. There was a period of uncertainty as northern India came under the sway of the East India Company's authority, and conflict over marketplaces with local rulers became frequent during the later eighteenth century. Consolidation of British rule during the nineteenth century saw a resurgence of market towns and military bazaars, with a rising class of traders and intermediaries replacing some of the traditional political elite (Bayly 1983: 15–16, 213–15).

The bazaar thus stands for much more than just a place of economic exchange; it remains infused with cultural and social connotations of much greater antiquity. The prevalence and significance of bazaars articulate the vitality of material life that has long been a part of Indian culture, well before the advent of colonial or even global capital. It also suggests that like any complex social category forged over such a long duration, the bazaar is an imaginary that both inhabits and transcends in equal measure the mundane periodicity of everyday culture.

Further reading: Bayly 1983; Mohammed 1989; Rizvi 1972; Sen 1998.

—SUDIPTA SEN, *Professor of History, Department of Social Sciences and Humanities, University of California, Davis*

— ·◆· —

Bhadralok/Bhadramahila

Our understanding of the history and the sociology of nine-teenth-century Bengal has been dominated by the category of the *bhadralok*, and the related figure of the *bhadramahila*. Members of the *bhadralok* ('respectable men', 'gentlemen', almost always upper- or intermediate-caste Hindu) were distinguished from *chhotolok*, or the 'lower orders'. The former were broadly divided into two categories. The first consisted of the *abhijat bhadralok*, who had acquired their fortunes in the late eighteenth and nineteenth centuries as business agents of the British, and who sustained their fortunes from mid-century onwards through rural rentiership. The second comprised the *grihasta* or *madhyabitta bhadralok*, a middle-income group characterized by English education, professional occupations, and salaried status. It is the latter group that has come to be associated most powerfully with the term *bhadralok* (Mukherjee 1987; Sarkar 1997: 168–9).

Deindustrialization, a feudalized agrarian system, and discriminatory colonial policies that disadvantaged indigenous enterprise kept the *bhadralok* from many of the spheres of bourgeois activity and social transformation that characterized Europe. By mid-century most had turned to bureaucratic, intellectual, and professional occupations rather than to capitalist enterprise. While a fair number enjoyed some rentier income through intermediate tenure holdings, these incomes were usually insufficient to sustain respectable living standards (Sinha 1978: 16–17). English education thus became necessary to the practice of *bhadra* ('respectable') professions such as law, teaching, medicine, journalism, and bureaucratic and clerical work in government and mercantile offices. The number of *bhadralok*, however, with such an education soon outstripped the racially restricted employment opportunities available. Besides, for most *bhadralok* men office work, a defining feature of *bhadralok* masculinity in Calcutta and other urban centres, was humiliating and poorly paid; Sumit Sarkar notes that the *kerani* ('clerk') became a symbolically freighted figure of classed uncertainty and colonial abasement even for well-established *bhadralok* (Sarkar 1997: 282–357). These anxieties were aided by some of the most caustic 'anti-babu' satires of the century, produced by the cheap presses of Bat-tala in north Calcutta, by Anglo-Indian commentators, and by *bhadralok* writers such as Bhabanicharan Bandyopadhyay (1787–1848), Pearychand Mitra (1814–1883), Kaliprasanna Sinha (1841–1870), and, most importantly, Bankimchandra Chattopadhyay (1838–1894).

Nevertheless, the *bhadralok* produced a remarkable efflorescence of new cultural forms, especially the novel, the theatre, and vernacular journalism. In addition, *bhadralok* males, who prided themselves on being members of an enlightened and reforming intellectual class, applied themselves to a number of projects of social reform; many focused on the amelioration of the lives of their female kin, the *bhadramahila*. Spurred by the criticisms of Utilitarian, Evangelical, and missionary commentators, who saw the degraded condition of *bhadra* women as symptomatic of Indian civiliza-tional backwardness, many of the *bhadralok* dedicated themselves to the abolition of *sati* ('ritual immolation of widows'), child marriage, purdah, and *kulin* ('high-ranking') Brahmin male polygamy and to the promotion of widow remarriage, female education, sartorial reforms for women, and new norms of conjugality. These efforts were combined with a commit-ment to redefining the role of the *bhadramahila*, and to making them into the suitably refined and enlightened helpmates of *bhadralok* males and the informed, efficient mothers of *bhadralok* children. The *bhadramahila* had a variety of responses to these changes. Some resented what they saw as forced induction into new forms of servitude, such as compulsory literacy, new-found puritanical norms of speech, association, and entertainment, and the very institution of companionate marriage (Walsh 2004: 51–86). Others, especially members of the reformist Brahmo Samaj, took the initiative in pressing for reforms and seized whatever educational oppor-tunities were available (Borthwick 1984).

Not all *bhadralok* were reformist in their orientation; by the end of the century, the impetus to reform had come to be trumped by a variety of nationalist and Hindu revivalist movements. Besides, the reform move-ments had clear intellectual and ethical limits. Caste remained obdurately entrenched among reformers, as did anti-Muslim sentiment; the lower orders were frequently associated with indecency and waywardness; and, in the arena of gendered reform, new forms of patriarchy sometimes replaced older ones (Banerjee 1989; Walsh 2004).

It was not until the early twentieth century that the term *bhadralok* came to be applied to an educated Muslim middle class; in the preceding century, Muslim elites were denominated as *ashraf*. Like their Brahmo and Hindu counterparts, Muslim *bhadralok*, at the turn of the century, were the recipients of English education and were drawn from the ranks of administrative, educational, and judicial service personnel as well as the intermediate ranks of landholders (Amin 1996: 27–9). The reformist development known as the 'Muslim awakening' was influenced both by Brahmo developments and by the language of a rationalist and liberal Islam that emanated from the Aligarh movement of the late nineteenth century; the latter was dedicated to educational uplift and modernization among the subcontinent's Muslims (Amin 1996: 24–35). The reformist impulses of the 'awakening' were deployed against polygamy, child marriage, and extreme forms of purdah, and in favour of women's education (Amin 1996).

The movement from *ashraf* to *bhadralok/bhadramahila* status of an educated, salaried, and professional Muslim community in Bengal can be said to be a signal moment in the standardization of what was at least as much an ethos or a world view as it was a class/status position. *Bhadralok* values permeate middle-class Bengali society today, the *bhadralok* (and the *bhadramahila*) no longer being regarded as contentious agents of ongoing social transformation. As objects of continuing critical fascination and critique, they belong not to the domain of public culture but to the sizeable scholarship on colonial Bengal.

Further reading: Amin 1996; Banerjee 1989; Bhattacharya 2005; Borthwick 1984; Mukherjee 1987; Sarkar 1997; Sarkar 2001; Sinha 1978; Walsh 2004.

—PARAMA ROY, *Professor, Department of English, University of California, Davis*

— •◆• —

Bhakti

The Sanskrit noun *bhakti*, derived from the verb *bhaj*—to share or to possess—occupies a semantic field that encapsulates notions of belonging, loyalty, loving, or even simply liking. It depicts an aspect of Indian religion in which the devotee's personal engagement with a divinity constitutes the core of religious life, and it has often been felt to be naturally constitutive of a community of sharing that draws people together in ways far deeper than the ordinary.

Bhakti of the strongly emotional type is usually said to have had its origins in early Tamil culture (ca. sixth to tenth century). Genuine continuities, such as the singing of devotional songs composed in vernacular language by 'poet-saints', the consideration of both sexes and all social strata as potential devotees, and the cultivation of personal experience in the face of any external pressures can be found in all geographical and historical stages of what has often been called the '*bhakti* movement'. Together, these characteristics form a considerable contrast to Vedic ritual traditions and the differential social distinctions that are often considered to lie at the core of Hindu religion.

Even if the ancient roots of *bhakti*, in contrast to those of Vedic practice, are difficult to establish, it would be a mistake to conclude that *bhakti* is necessarily a more recent phenomenon. Evidence gathered in early Buddhist and Jain texts suggests that many elements of *bhakti* existed in non-Vedic religions, and it is clearly to be found in the Bhagavadgita (ca. first century), which had its own quarrels with *Veda*. In the *Gita*, Krishna, speaking as Arjuna's mortal charioteer, states that he would accept the simplest offerings if they were presented to him in the spirit of *bhakti*. Interpreters disagree as to whether this statement implies the emotionalism of later *bhakti* or refers to a form of mental concentration of the sort we meet elsewhere in the *Gita*'s teaching. In the text overall, however, it is clear that *bhakti* is considered to constitute one of the three disciplines (*yoga*) constitutive of the seriously considered, well-lived life.

The *bhakti* of the Bhagavadgita stands at some distance from that of the early Tamil singer-saints. For the latter, *bhakti* is basic, even alimentary, and never simply cerebral. The new tone that *bhakti* attains when devotion verges on possession leads to the creation of communities of those possessed—possessed through a musical, poetic idiom. In South India, the development of institutions to capture this sensibility is clearly traceable. One begins with the Alvars and Nayanars, Vaishnava and Shaiva poet-musicians respectively whose appeal to faith is direct. Later, their utterances became ritualized as features of temple worship. In time, the Sri Vaishnava community, dominated by Brahmans and Vellalas, comes to view the Alvars as its forebears, while the Shaiva Siddhanta community, led more exclusively by Vellalas, roots itself in the Nayanars. Anthological and hagiographical corpuses develop in both cases, and a body of theological reflection to match.

Although these Tamil Vaishnavite and Shaivite *bhakti* institutions were managed and administered by powerful Brahman and Vellala elites, the poets to whom these elites looked for inspiration were neither exclusively upper caste nor male. Accounts of the lives of the 'humbler' of these saints sometimes underline the point that their *bhakti* had the power to propel them ahead of members of the 'purer' castes. The fundamental institutions that developed in the aftermath of around the twelfth-century Virashaiva ('extreme' Shaiva) saints of Karnataka were even more strongly defined in these counterstructural terms. Hence, classically, the emblem (*linga*) of Shiva was to be recognized in one's own body rather than in any institutionally acceptable temple or shrine.

The poet-saints of Maharashtra in western India come from a variety of social backgrounds, but again the inner freedom to serve God questions the validity of caste exclusivity. To read this as pure egalitarianism would usually not be right, but a Brahmin *bhakta* like Eknath (sixteenth century) is widely remembered and celebrated for his insistence on eating with 'Untouchables'. Even so, those same Untouchables, as in the case of Chokhamela (date uncertain), are often remembered for having been denied entrance into the great temple of Vitthal (Vishnu), who is the common point of reference for the paradigmatic *bhakta*s of Maharashtra.

From the sixteenth century onwards, a certain number of references on the part of the *bhakti* poet-saints of North India to their predecessors elsewhere—notably the Bengali Jayadev (twelfth century) and the Maharashtrian Namdev (fourteenth century?)—testify to an interregional network of *bhakti* transmission. Yet, whether we can really think of this as giving evidence of a pan-Indian '*bhakti* movement', said to begin in the south in the Tamil region in the sixth century and to move beyond that region until it arrives in northern India in the fifteenth or sixteenth, remains a question. We must keep in mind that in its mature form, this *bhakti* movement' idea was a product of nationally motivated thinking in North India in the decades just preceding Independence. It may, therefore, be better to think of a *bhakti* network than a *bhakti* movement as a way to describe the thematic and stylistic similarities that characterize the mutually echoing *bhakti* poetry and hagiographical anthologies that emerge in many parts of India. If one prefers to retain the concept of 'movement', it may, similarly, be best to envision several parallel or interdependent *bhakti* streams rather than a single, common current. *Bhakti* anthologies, usually delimited by language, rarely display the strong transregional links and narrative coherence that go with our modern conception of a unified *bhakti* movement'.

Strictly speaking, the notion of a *bhakti* movement' first developed in English in the 1920s—in the works of J.N. Farquhar (1861–1929), Ishwari Prasad, and Tara Chand. Yet an argument can be made that it was Hazariprasad Dvivedi (1907–1979), writing across the linguistic divide in Hindi (in 1936, 1940, and 1942), who had the most enduring impact on the crystallization of the concept. For it was in the study and teaching of Hindi literature that the *bhakti* movement—in Hindi, *bhakti andolan*—received its widest, most devoted readership. All this was connected to the search for pan-Indian origins that would justify Hindi as a national language. If the south served as the foundation for a unifying *bhakti* history, then it was in the north that such a history first emerged.

Further reading: Grierson 1909; Hawley [forthcoming]; Lorenzen 2004; Novetzke 2008; Shukla 1940.

—JOHN STRATTON HAWLEY, *Professor, Department of Religion, Barnard College, Columbia University*

— ·•· —

Bhoodan/Gramdan

hu (bhoo) means land, and *dana* can be translated as donation or gift. *Bhoodan* thus means the gift or donation of land by landowners to those who are landless. In *gramdan*, *grama* means a revenue village and *dana* means gift, as defined above. *Gramdan* does not mean the gift of the village, but rather the gift or sacrifice to or for the village. *Gramdan* involves the solemn resolve or vow undertaken by villagers entirely by their own volition to give their land and other wealth to the village. Therefore, a gift of village(s) in the past by the kings to someone in appreciation of his service to the king can, according to this definition, not be called *gramdan*. In *bhoodan*, giving may not be a one-time affair, it may be a continuous act; likewise for *gramdan*. Hence, there can be continuous *bhagadana* ('gift of a part') or *danadhara*, a continuous flow of *dana*.

It should be noted here that although the term *dana* is mostly used to refer to a donation or a gift, Shankaracharya (ca. 788–820) defined it as *danam sanvibhagaha* ('equitable distribution'). Vinoba Bhave (1895–1982), the 'propagator' of *bhoodan*, repeatedly urged people to remember this meaning of *dana*. Similarly, the idea of a continuous *dana* is reflected in the term *bhoodan ganga* (Ganges), which has been widely used in this context.

When India became independent in 1947, there was the choice between the Gandhian and the Nehruvian paths of socioeconomic reconstruction. Officially, the latter path, which involved Central Planning, was chosen and the first Five-Year Plan was launched in 1951–1952. Although the state and some other sections of Indian society rejected the Gandhian approach, certain thinkers and social workers in India were contemplating how to guide the nation towards the Gandhian path. Hence, when Central Planning was introduced, the Gandhian path was initiated in the form of *bhoodan/gramdan*, unaided by the State.

The first *bhoodan* took place on 18 April 1951 at Pochampalli in Andhra Pradesh with the donation of 100 acres to the landless by a landlord named Ramachandra Reddy. Similarly, on 24 May 1952 at village Mangroth in Uttar Pradesh, when all the landlords attending Vinoba Bhave's meeting unanimously decided to donate their entire land as *bhoodan*, these *gramadanavas* ('donators of villages') heralded the voluntary abolition of ownership of private property, and vested it in the community as a whole.

Subsequently, the concept of *bhoodan* extended to related ideas such as *sampattidana* ('gift of wealth'), *sammatidana* ('gift of consent'), *shramadana* ('gift of labour'), *buddhidana* ('gift of intellect'), *prakhanddana* ('gift of block division'), *zilladana* ('gift of district'), and so on. Although the *bhoodan* approach has not been practised extensively, it was perceived by its adherents as an ideal instrument of socioeconomic reconstruction for independent India.

Further reading: Bhave 1965, 1996; Nargolkar 1963; Ostergaard 1985.

—LAXMAN MADHAO BHOLE
Department of Humanities and Social Sciences
Indian Institute of Technology, Mumbai

— ·•· —

Biopiracy

Conjoining 'bio' with 'piracy' to constitute biopiracy, a term entering the *Oxford English Dictionary* (*OED*) in 1993, aims at tracing a range of colonial practices that persist in contemporary times in new and evolving forms. It is attributed to Pat Roy Mooney (b. 1947), a Canadian activist who leads the Rural Advancement Fund International (RAFI, now called Action Group on Erosion, Technology and Concentration, ETC). A probable first use was with reference to US plant patents on naturally coloured cotton granted to Sally Fox (b. 1955) who merely developed a variety from seed samples held by the US Department of Agriculture that were collected in the Andes (Shand 1993).

Shiva (2001: 49) defines biopiracy as 'the use of intellectual property systems to legitimize the exclusive ownership and control over biological resources and biological products and processes that have been used over centuries in non-industrial countries'. In the mid-1990s, biopiracy was estimated at US$ 5.4 billion annually. With changing practices the ideas co-constituting biopiracy have also been transformed. Partly as counter-discourse, the term critiques a neoliberal reframing of these exploitative transactions as 'development' (Hayden 2003), thus interrogating their inherent legitimacy of such activities and illuminating the systemic inequity (Mgbeoji 2005; Robinson 2010). As a postcolonial moment, the rhetoric of biopiracy channels debates concerning ownership in and dispositional rights to genetic resources. The term also aligns with a property turn in identity politics where arguments of cultural survival and human rights get entangled to constitute the normative basis for authorial recognition (Sunder 2006). Illustratively, not only is a trademark like 'Texmati' deceptive and a misappropriation, but 'Basmati' itself merits intellectual property protection.

Mapping shared elements across the different instances of biopiracy, Mgbeoji (2005) identifies three reinforcing elements. First, in a sociocultural sense, the contributions of farmers, artisans, and traditional communities are denigrated and not recognized. Symptomatic is the classification of plant genetic resources that indigenous and farming communities curate as 'wild relatives' and 'landraces'. Second, are the institutional processes that have enabled the historic collection, transfer, and documentation of genetic resources from the South. Implicated here are colonial-era botanical gardens and contemporary proliferation of agricultural research centres in the tropics. The third factor, the intellectual property system, bridges these two through the juridical construction of intellectual property standards that are biased against traditional knowledge. This cognitive injustice is witnessed in the case of *Neem*: in granting the patents, the system fails to acknowledge oral traditions as prior art, and then in revoking some of the patents, it fails to consider evidence from farmers, but required documentation of industrial production in India.

These struggles against biopiracy have contributed noteworthy norms and principles to the existing legal codex whilst also pioneering counter-practices. Notable here is the Traditional Knowledge Digital Library: a Government of India initiative that seeks to document traditional knowledge, such as Ayurveda, Siddha, Unani, and Yoga, among others, and grants access to patent examiners in the North, in the hope that fraudulent novelty claims will be defeated. Resistance to biopiracy has also generated juridical principles, such as access and benefit-sharing, prior informed consent, and disclosure of origin that—if globally instituted into practice—would hopefully check some misappropriation. While the global inequity of biopiracy-like transactions make a compelling case for these norms and principles as matters of justice, their transformative potential may only be partial (Schroeder and Pogge 2009). For that matter, often unacknowledged is the challenge of respecting customary practices of traditional communities themselves, as well as of adhering to their norms of sacred and secret knowledge.

Further reading: Hayden 2003; Mgbeoji 2005; Robinson 2010; Schroeder and Pogge 2009; Shand 1993; Shiva 2001.

—DWIJEN RANGNEKAR, *Associate Professor of Law, School of Law, University of Warwick*

— •◦• —

Biradari

B *iradari*, alternative spelling *biraderi* (lit. 'brotherhood'), is a widely misunderstood concept. As a folk term, *biradari* is said to refer to a patrilineage of equal 'brothers' but, in reality, *biradaris* for both North Indian Hindus and Muslims are endogamous categories *within* their caste, and also the primary vehicle of strategic marriage alliances and caste mobility.

Parry defines *biradari* minimally as 'a group of clans of the same caste which are reckoned to be roughly of equal status and which exchange women on a symmetrical basis' (1979: 318). Given, however, that *biradari* is an elastic concept with a 'sliding semantic structure' (Alavi 1972), internally differentiated (Alvi 2007), it may refer, situationally, to a hierarchy of ranked segments or, alternatively, to an unbounded, maximal lineage—

or family-focused affinal network (Parry 1979; Alvi 2001). Whereas castes or *zats* (following Dumont [1972], named, endogamous groups hierarchically ranked according to principles of purity/pollution and/or power) are in reality ranked social categories whose members are widely scattered, *biradaris* are more local, and frequently refer to the effective units of 'recognition' and 'participation' (Mayer 1960); though, as Parry (1979) argues, *biradaris* are not bounded corporate units: not all their members cooperate or even know each other. Rajput *biradaris* are said to have a distinctive lifestyle, and express ranking through commensality and avoidance practices. Among more egalitarian Punjabi Muslims, the term is often used as a euphemism for caste, *zat* or *qaum*, probably due to Muslims' reluctance to admit to exclusive, hierarchical divisions among themselves (Werbner 1990, 2002; Alvi 2001).

Since marriage is hypergamous for North Indians (on Muslims, see Werth 2001), *biradaris* are ranked according to the direction in which women move, meaning that hierarchy pervades relations within as well as among *biradaris*. This is especially so when smaller units within the *biradari* begin to negotiate new marriage alliances with more highly ranked groups and refuse to give their daughters to erstwhile marriage partners. Against the tendency towards hierarchy, however, Parry (1979) records periodic attempts made among Kangra Rajputs to limit hypergamous marriages outside the *biradari*, in order to establish equality among its constituent clans. This entailed compelling the highest-placed *biradaris*, whose women were often doomed to spinsterhood and who tended as a result to practise female infanticide, to exchange women among themselves. But such movements towards *biradari* endogamy mostly failed in the long run. Thus for both Hindus and Muslims, *biradari* encapsulates the contradictory ideas of equality and inequality. For Muslims, in particular, it disguises the immanence of caste behind a facade of fraternal kinship.

The key difference between Hindu and Muslim *biradaris* relates to the much wider rules of exogamy among Hindus who practise patrilateral and matrilateral clan as well as lineage exogamy up to the third generation (in some cases also *gotra* ['clan'] exogamy). Muslims, by contrast, permit marriage to a wide range of close kin including first parallel and cross cousins. This has radical implications for the size of *biradaris* and for their capacity to allow for upward caste mobility. As Werbner shows for overseas Muslim Punjabis, while changing their caste affiliation members of an extended family can intermarry among themselves with an extremely close range of kin. Endogamy among close kin also means that Muslim *biradari*s beyond the village resemble loosely defined affinal networks more than their Hindu counterparts do. Hence, *biradari* is only seen as denoting homogeneous status when viewed from the outside (Parry 1979: 278) or when leaders make claims for political influence.

Further reading: Alavi 1972; Alvi 2001, 2007; Parry 1979; Mayer 1960; Sahai 2005; Werbner 1990, 2002; Werth 2001.

—PNINA WERBNER, *Professor Emerita, School of Sociology and Criminology, Keele University*

— .•. —

Bollywood

Bollywood is currently the internationally recognized term for popular or mainstream Hindi cinema made in Bombay/Mumbai. Although the term is much disliked by many in the film industry, it has spread from its origins in the 1970s or 1980s, becoming used mostly by the diaspora to being the standard term in journalism and beyond.

Most people limit the term to the popular Hindi cinema but its historical reach is more nebulous. In academic circles, Bollywood is usually restricted to the last twenty years, when cinema becomes part of the wider entertainment industry (Rajadhyaksha 2003). Vasudevan further limits the term to the extended commodity function of the 'high-profile, export-oriented Bombay film' (Vasudevan 2011). According to him, this is about a branding of India rather than a presentation of India as an aesthetic form, locating its beginning with *Dilwale Dulhania Le Jayenge* (directed by Aditya Chopra, 1995), a foundational film for the diasporic romance.

Indian cinema has an acknowledged unique form, distinctive styles and genres which arose from a combination of western technologies, and modes such as melodrama, with indigenous visual and performative traditions. With the coming of sound in the 1930s, Indian cinema soon devolved into many cinemas, mostly divided by language, including major cinemas in Bengali, Tamil, Marathi, and Telugu. However, cinema also united the incipient nation as it spread the use of the lingua franca, 'Hindustani', a language which can be loosely identified as the colloquial form both of Hindi, which became the official language of the Union of India after Independence, and also of Urdu, later the national language of Pakistan. After Independence and Partition in 1947, other popular national cinemas evolved, notably in Pakistan, including that based in Lahore ('Lollywood'), and important 'regional' cinemas, notably in South India, continued to develop. Hindi cinema, which aspires to be India's national cinema, finds major audiences across the entire region, even where there have been attempts to restrict it, such as in Pakistan.

India has other cinemas that have different production and distribution circuits from the Hindi cinema, notably a realist cinema encompassing the films of Satyajit Ray (1921–1992), one of world cinema's most acclaimed directors, the 'middle cinema' (also known as 'new cinema', 'parallel cinema'), typified by the work of Shyam Benegal (b. 1932), and the multiplex and *hatke* ('different', 'independent') cinema of the present (Dwyer 2011). This realist cinema is aimed at an audience familiar with world cinema, and even though their films are not usually released beyond the festival circuit, they can be seen via other media.

Indian cinema is also a global phenomenon, though different in scale from that of Hollywood. It is hugely popular outside western Europe and the USA, where it is often preferred to local and Hollywood cinemas. Some Hindi films have proved to be massive international hits such as *Awaara/The Vagabond* (directed by Raj Kapoor, 1951). One of the reasons for the wide appeal of Hindi cinema is that it was cheaper to screen than Hollywood, but it is also celebrated as a non-western form, upholding other traditions and values, in particular its depiction of love within the larger family in a changing, often westernizing, society.

Hindi cinema received little recognition in Europe and North America until the 1990s. Hindi films were screened here only for the diasporic Asian markets, but since the 1990s they have begun to find a niche interest, and are now viewed in multiplex theatres, although they have only a limited penetration of mainstream audiences. It is still early to assess the lasting impact on cinema of the massive changes that occurred in the India of the 1990s, including the media explosion, the shifts that took place within the films and the film industry, and a reorientation of government policy towards its relations with the global Indian diaspora.

Further reading: Dwyer 2005, 2011; Ganti 2004; Rajadhyaksha 2003; Vasudevan 2011.

—RACHEL DWYER, *Professor of Indian Cultures and Cinema,*
SOAS, University of London

— .•. —

Business Rajahs

Apopular term that emerged in circulation in the 1990s shortly after the official launch of economic liberalization, 'business rajahs' refers to the heads of the business dynasties that constitute the elite of Indian industry and finance (Piramal 1997; Kripilani 1997). Like the Rockefellers and Carnegies, some of the most influential business groups in India today have long histories dating back to at least the middle of the nineteenth century (for example, the Tata, Birla, Bajaj, and Godrej groups) while other currently powerful global players have emerged more recently (Ambani and Mahindra). The current term, 'business rajah', evokes the distinct history of corporate capitalism in India.

Many of India's top business conglomerates first operated as extended family businesses buttressed by the networks of their traditional commercial castes or ethnic groups. These included Hindu and Muslim traders (*banias*) from Gujarat and North India, Marwaris from Rajasthan, Parsis, Punjabi Khatris, Sindhis, and Tamil-speaking Chettiars (Tripathi 1984). Highlighting the disparity between the super wealthy and the rest, the term may also evoke the grandiose consumption associated with newer magnates.

The business rajahs emerged from the trading world of the bazaar (Ray 1992; Bayly 1983; Siddiqi 1995; Subrahmanyam 1990). Mughal emperors, rulers of Indian kingdoms, empires, and sultanates as diverse as Vijayanagara, Hyderabad, and Jaipur, and later, the British colonial regime, relied on merchants to finance the salaries of government officials, military campaigns, and agricultural production. Indian traders operated through sophisticated networks of trust: clan members would be identified going back at least seven generations; patriarchal family networks secured extensive capital flows across geographic regions within and outside the subcontinent. The prominent Indian family firms generally held diverse portfolios, engaging in banking, the financing of primary production, as well as wholesale and retail trade (Bayly and Subrahmanyam 1988).

The kinship-based organization of Indian capitalism fell under critical scrutiny by modernizers in the late nineteenth century. They argued that Indian merchants' market organization reflected anachronistic worldviews that would hold them back from economic innovation (Birla 2009). Historians of entrepreneurship have emphasized in contrast that cultural forms of business organization have not been a deterrent to capitalist development, detailing the adaptability and benefits of family-based organization in unstable economic environments (Ray 1992; Bayly 1983). Postcolonial approaches have highlighted that the very parameters of the culture versus economy debate had been set by the imperial context: the colonial legal modernization of market practices coded the family firm as a cultural *rather than* as an economic formation, at once delegitimizing it as a model for business organization, while simultaneously enabling its reproduction, and its patriarchies, under personal law (Birla 2009). These colonial debates echo in contemporary questions about the nature of legitimate business practice in India and in the term 'business rajah' itself.

A genealogy of contemporary business rajahs would certainly date back to World War I, when commodity speculation fuelled by global instability enabled extensive capital accumulation, and import substitution buttressed already nascent Indian industry (Bagchi 1972). Cotton-spinning mills had emerged in western India when Indian cotton took over the global market during the American Civil War. The period from 1870 to 1900 saw expansion in Indian-owned textile mills and the early nationalist Swadeshi Movement that fuelled the demand for locally made textiles (Tripathi 1990). The global demand for gunny sacks and hessian during World War I benefited the British-dominated jute industry in eastern India and its predominantly Marwari exporters, who then set up their own factories. These early industries exercised full control over labour, and strikes throughout the 1920s and the worldwide depression of the 1930s reflected the politicization of the labouring classes (Chandavarkar 1994). The macroeconomics of World War II enabled another period of consistent growth for Indian industry, its diversification, and the consolidation of wealth among prosperous business houses. Indian capitalists joined the nationalist cause, most supporting the Indian National Congress (INC) and the Gandhian call, beginning in the 1920s. As such, a preferential relationship between the state and influential business families emerged during the nationalist period. Shortly after Independence, a small number of companies were given contracts in major sectors of industry such as steel and motor vehicles (Tripathi 2004; Markovits 1983; Chandavarkar 1994). The operations of a few family conglomerates grew to account for 15 per cent of the Indian economy (Kripilani 1997).

Despite the dynastic quality of the large business houses, the picture for Indian industry since Independence has evinced new actors at different stages of India's economic development. In the two decades after Independence, British firms that had conducted activities in India (such as Martin Burn and Andrew Yule) were taken over by Indian firms, allowing for the consolidation of indigenous business houses that had been expanding their corporate organization (Misra 2000; Tomlinson 1981). Several new business houses such as Thapar, Mafatlal, and Nagarmull emerged in this period and joined the ranks of the older business houses. In the 1970s and 1980s, the Ambani group, which runs Reliance Industries, one of India's first global multinationals, established its foothold (Piramal 1997). In the 1990s, economic liberalization, which criticized 'licence raj' and its monopolies, challenged old guard dynasties to remain competitive while at the same time opening space for important newer ones such as Mahindra & Mahindra in vehicles and automotive technology (Tripathi and Jumani 2007).

Since the 1990s, the boom in information technology has pushed older established business houses to diversify into arenas like telecommunications, and has brought new social and ethnic groups not traditionally associated with trade to the ranks of the business elite. Companies such as Infosys and Wipro are changing the character of the business rajahs. Infosys Technologies, the first Indian company to be listed on the American stock exchange in 1999, was founded by N.R. Narayana Murthy (b. 1946), a South Indian Brahmin with a background in electrical engineering. Azim Premji (b. 1945), scion of a Gujarati Ismaili Muslim mercantile group, and founder and chairman of Wipro, the giant in outsourcing for the global IT industry, has distinguished himself as a leader in innovative strategies for business as well as philanthropy (Tripathi and Jumani 2007: 209–11).

Further reading: Chandavarkar 1994; Markovits 1983; Ray 1992; Tripathi 1984; Tripathi and Jumani 2007.

—RITU BIRLA, *Associate Professor of History and Director, Centre for South Asian Studies, University of Toronto*

— ••• —

Caste

A cademic writing on caste is in a contradictory state, marked, on the one hand, by its essentialization, fulfilling thereby the compelling need for a defining feature of Indian society, and, on the other, by its marginalization, testifying to an attempt to efface caste from an assumed centrality. By reviewing briefly the historical genealogy of caste discourse, some insights may be gained into the many shifts in perspective, significant as they are for mirroring caste's epistemological and phenomenological multidimensionality.

The term 'caste' (*casta*) was first applied to the Indian context by the Portuguese in the early decades of the sixteenth century and embraced several meanings such as 'family', 'stock', 'kind', 'strain', 'clan', 'tribe', or 'race', and interestingly also designated religious communities, besides Hindu ones, such as the 'caste of Moors' and the 'caste of Christians' (Yule and

Burnell 1989; Dharampal-Frick 1994: 182ff.). Hereby not only was the plurivalency of Indian social formations highlighted, but also the later ascribed 'racist' notion of 'purity of blood' deduced from the etymological derivation from the Latin *castus*, meaning 'chaste' or 'pure', was by no means predominant. Moreover, though the term 'caste' had been coined in the initial stages of European contact with India, given that in most early reports other more familiar terms (such as guild, family, estate) were preferred, it appears that the distinctive traits perceived in Indian society were being brought in line with apparently similar European social divisions (Dharampal-Frick 1995). This implicit acknowledgement of a coeval relationship between India and Europe in the pre- and early colonial epoch constitutes a striking contrast to later nineteenth and early twentieth century western attitudes when India had become conquered territory (Inden 1990). Furthermore, this use of equivalent European sociological terminology underscores that the religious connotations of caste, defined along the axis of purity/impurity *à la* Dumont, which were to become so prominent in the later discourse, were not crucial in the early emphasis on communitarian organizational features of Indian societal order (Dharampal-Frick 1994: 228).

Yet, despite this initial recognition of empirical heterogeneity in the late eighteenth century, caste came to conceptually circumscribe a scaled ordering of four *varnas*—Brahmin, Kshatriya, Vaishya, and Shudra—with the so-called Untouchables occupying an ambivalent place below, or outside, the *varna* scheme. *Varna*, which is primarily a conceptual category, was interpreted as constituting actual social strata (namely the priestly class, the kings or warriors, the merchants and craftsmen, and the peasants and labourers, respectively) with the empirical entities, or *jatis*, representing subgroups of the fourfold varna divisions (Dharampal-Frick and Götzen 2011). This codification of multivalent social relations into a single hierarchical register was facilitated by early Orientalist appropriations of selected Sanskrit scriptural traditions (such as the *Manusmriti*, or *The Code of Manu*, Jones 1794), entailing a certain measure of collaboration with indigenous Brahmin scholars who laid emphasis on ritualistic hierarchical status which underscored their pre-eminence (Pollock 2003). Consequently, the canonization of brahmanical scriptural lore, amenable as it was to colonial policies, validated the thesis that *varna* hierarchy, as *the* defining feature of the caste system, was based on the ritualistic and prescriptive *varnashramadharma* ('socioreligious ranked order'), and constituted an all-pervasive feature, determining social life, polity, and religion in India. Serving as a blueprint for establishing control over early nineteenth century Indian society, and despite empirical data gained through regional surveys (carried out by Colin Mackenzie [1754–1821], Thomas Munro [1761–1827], and so on, cf. Cohn 1987a) about the latter's hermeneutical multidimensionality (with regard to occupation, rules governing property, inheritance, endogamy, and commensality, and so on), caste organization became projected not only as hierarchical, but increasingly also as discriminatory and stultifyingly ritualized. This view was reinforced by evangelical missionaries and utilitarian-minded administrator-scholars alike. The former, exasperated by the stubborn resistance to Christian conversion offered by cohesive *jati* communities, castigated caste as 'a prison which immures many innocent beings' (William Carey [1761–1834], cited by Forrester 1980: 26), and polemically declared it to be the 'most cursed invention of the Devil that ever existed' (cited by Dirks 2001: 27), which demanded a Christian crusade against the system (Grant 1793). Subsequently, by equating caste with slavery, William Wilberforce (1759–1833) in a parliamentary speech in 1813 induced the British government to endorse full-scale missionary activity on the subcontinent (Wilberforce 1813). Conclusively, for the utilitarian James Mill (1773–1836), freeing India from the slavery of caste necessitated Britain's civilizing mission (Mill 1858 [1817]: vol. I, 131).

In the aftermath of 1857, the Brahmanical *varna* scheme, besides serving as a necessary controlling adjunct to colonial authority, metamorphozed into a racialized avatar, with communities from northwestern India, designated as 'martial races', were enlisted to revamp the army, whereas oppositional forces were branded as criminal tribes and castes (Bates 1995: 25–6). More significantly, through philological expertise, misconstrued translation of the crucial term *varna* (that in Sanskrit signifies 'category' or 'quality', and 'colour' only in a symbolic ritual context) gave rise to an influential rendering (which still holds sway), interpreting it as denoting 'skin colour' or 'pigmentation', so that the fourfold conceptual hierarchy could be explained in line with racial categories (Trautmann 1997: 209–11). Similarly, other Sanskrit terms concerned with descent groups and kinship relations, such as *vamsa*, *kula*, *jati*, and *gotra*, were also given racial connotations (Monier-Williams 1976: 652; Thapar 1980: 96). Further, endogamous *jatis* were perceived as ideal specimens to verify the anthropometrical and criminological theories of French anthropologists, such as Broca

(1824–1880) and Topinard (1830–1911), as well as the criminologist Bertillon (1853–1914) about categorizing different bodily features as race markers; this new scientific methodology was zealously applied by scholar/ administrators of the decennial census, and foremost by Herbert Risley (1851–1911; Risley 1915) and Edgar Thurston (1855–1935; Thurston 1909), with the aim of fixing the social ranking of communities in line with their nasal index. Compounding this notorious attempt at social engineering, the Aryan invasion theory was instrumentalized by Risley (1915: 275) to explain the genesis of the caste system as engendered out of an inherent racial antagonism, whereby the upper castes were deduced to be the descendants of the aquiline-nosed fair-skinned Aryans or *arya-varna*, supposedly constituted by the Brahmins, Kshatriyas, and Vaishyas, while the lower castes or Shudras were categorized as the conquered snub-nosed dark-pigmented indigenous inhabitants comprising the *dasa-varna*. This racial taxonomic scheme simultaneously explained the Aryan/Dravidian divide, with the European dichotomy between Aryan and Semitic serving as a conceptual fulcrum.

Moreover, caste, reified as a rigid Brahmanical system, was held responsible, by Risley (1915: 272–3) and others, for rendering Indians politically impotent, making them the pliable subjects of conquerors. Due to its fragmentary tendencies resulting from racial animosities, caste was considered antithetical to the development of a strong nation state and inimical to national unity. On the one hand, this latter fissiparous characteristic was to a certain extent borne out by nineteenth and early twentieth century movements of self-assertive resistance, entangled as they were in the net of colonialist rhetoric; led by low-caste or non-Brahmin spokesmen in various regions of India, such movements proactively applied the racist theories, in inverse order, to resist systems of economic exploitation and political domination (for instance, Jyotiba Phule [1827–1890] in Maharashtra and E.V. Ramaswamy Naicker [alias Periyar, 1879–1973] in the Tamil region laid claims to racial indigeneity or Dravidian origins in reassertion against Brahmanical or Aryan subjugation, cf. Dirks 2001: chs 7 and 12). On the other hand, nationalist politicians such as Mohandas Karamchand Gandhi (1869–1948), in an attempt to disprove the colonialist verdict, attempted to reform caste society, also by providing more integrative understandings of Indian social ordering (Stein 1998). Interestingly, Bhimrao Ambedkar (1891–1956), leader of the 'Untouchables' and one of India's most vehement opponents of the caste system, castigated in no uncertain terms the racist interpretation of its origins; in his meticulous exegesis of the Vedic scriptures, he convincingly shows that the implied hostility between different social groups was due to differing cultic practices and did not stem from racial animosity (Ambedkar 1970). Yet, the racist constructions of caste had long-lasting repercussions leading to seismic societal schisms, the resonances of which continue to be felt in India today, both discursively and empirically.

By the early twentieth century, less ideologically slanted anthropological studies defined caste primarily as a non-monetary, non-market, interdependent and self-sufficient exchange system among traditional landholding and occupational castes of village communities (Wiser 1936). This communitarian interpretation was soon superseded by influential works, projecting caste as a religious mode of social organization (Dumont 1970). In counterposing western society as egalitarian and individualistic against Indian society as hierarchical and holistic, Dumont understood caste as *the* defining institution, with the ritual purity of the pre-eminent Brahmin constituting the key ideological principle. In this scenario, with the ritual-religious authority of the Brahmin 'encompassing' the political power of the king, not only were economic and political relations given marginal importance, but due to its ideological and structural uniformity, diversity was neglected (Fuller 1997). Subsequent approaches going beyond Dumont's simple binary opposition of the pure/impure (Heesterman 1985) explored divergent patterns and conceptual categories as reference points, both in scripture and everyday ethnographic reality. Arguing that the *varna* model produced a wrong and distorted image of caste, M.N. Srinivas (1916–1999) made a plea to foreground a 'field view' as against the hitherto hegemonic 'book view' of Indian society (1962). Yet, his theory of 'Sanskritisation' (designating a process of upward social mobility) did implicitly underscore the exemplary pre-eminence of the Brahmin in caste society. Other scholars (Cohn 1987a; Inden 1990; Dharampal-Frick 1995; Dirks 2001) demonstrated the far-reaching effects of the colonial reconfiguration of caste in an attempt to historicize and contextualize it as a discursive phenomenon.

In post-Independence India, though caste as a stratification system was considered to have lost its moral–social legitimacy, it surprisingly attained a new lease of life, donning a 'secular' identity in democratic politics (Srinivas 1962; Béteille 1992; Gupta 2004), rather than dying out under the threefold onslaught of urbanization/secularization/modernization.

The tenacity of caste in adapting to conditions of modernity (Rudolph 1968; Kothari 1970) would seem to belie the modernist–universalist desire to transcend narrow sectional identities (Nigam 2006), as also to underscore the political acumen of lower castes who have used their franchise as a tool of empowerment to wrest state legislatures from the hands of the upper castes (Jaffrelot 2003). Inter-caste competition for higher socioeconomic status has received state support through the recommendation of the Mandal Commission (1980) which provided for mandatory job reservations of 27 per cent for so-called backward castes in central and state legislatures as well as in state educational institutions, thus attempting to attenuate inequality and reduce exploitation. Recent studies on this increased political and social assertiveness attribute thereby an epistemic privilege to the experiences of being Shudra or Dalit (Ilaiah 1996; Guru and Geetha 2000; Pandian 2007).

Needless to say, more viable measures are required to empower (politically, socially, and economically) the many disadvantaged groups so that the subcontinent's social, cultural, and ethnic diversity may finally shed the classifying trammels bequeathed by colonialism. In view of India's societal complexity and historical dynamism, mapping the trajectory of caste studies, taking note of their reorientation and the recasting of their mediated realities, remains necessarily an incomplete task. Yet, in this ongoing process, the primacy of caste with its variegated possibilities will continue to stimulate further research.

Further reading: Bayly 1999; Cohn 1987a; Dharampal-Frick and Götzen 2010; Dirks 2001; Dumont 1970; Ilaiah 1996; Inden 1990; Kothari 1970; Risley 1915; Srinivas 1962; Stein 1998.

—GITA DHARAMPAL-FRICK, *Professor of History, South Asia Institute, University of Heidelberg*
—SUDHA SITHARAMAN, *Department of Sociology, Pondicherry University*

— .•. —

Colonial (and Postcolonial) Education and Language Policies

On 2 February 1835 Lord Thomas B. Macaulay (1800–1859), then a member of the Executive Council for the East India Company (EIC), declared: 'We must at present do our best to form a class who may be interpreters between us and the millions whom we govern—a class of persons Indian in blood and colour, but English in tastes, in opinions, in morals and in intellect' (Sharp 1920). The commonplace of Macaulay's minute has dominated many discussions of educational matters in nineteenth century India. In India and Britain, constant reference to this minute has slanted an understanding of British colonial policy, suggesting that all knowledge to be imparted to Indian subjects was western and should be taught in English. This, however, does little justice to the complexities of the colonial education debate which lasted well over sixty years, pitting those favouring the study of 'Indian classics' (the Orientalists) against the partisans of English education (the Anglicists) in a controversy culminating in the 1830s.

Far from espousing Macaulay's depreciatory judgement on Indian civilization and ancient languages, Orientalist British scholars exerted their efforts towards their preservation and transmission. Orientalists played a prominent role prior to Macaulay's minute with Horace Hayman Wilson (1786–1860) heading the General Committee of Public Instruction established in 1823. They were later superseded by Anglicists as a more utilitarian and reformist perspective progressively imposed itself from the late 1830s and early 1840s onwards (Zastoupil and Moir 1999).

Rather than being a mere tool in the hands of British Orientalists and/ or administrators, Indians, too, played a significant part in building the educational systems of the various presidencies. Siding with Orientalists— as did *munshis* ('secretaries or language teachers') employed in oriental institutions such as the Hindu College at Calcutta—or with Anglicists, for instance by petitioning governing bodies for the opening of English-medium schools, the indigenous elite actively shaped colonial policies. Furthermore, in advocating the teaching of English, western knowledge and science, or, conversely, voicing their concerns over the introduction of English education in place of Sanskrit, Arabic, or the 'vernaculars', members of various local elites pursued their own interests with regard to social mobility, social reform, knowledge, conservatism, and so on.

Thus the Language Policies designed by the British were the result of much-negotiated interaction, locally. Therein, although often absent from the quarrels between Orientalists and Anglicists, the place of vernaculars as a medium of instruction was a recurrent concern for utilitarian administrators and religious missionaries. These were united by their common backgrounds, including a shared belief in their 'British mission to Christianise South Asia'.

Undergirding such Christianization was a sanitary and moral enterprise primarily reflected in the teaching of languages, which also motivated translating European works, composing original vernacular ones, and reforming and codifying vernacular languages from within. Hence the extraordinary amount of work produced from the middle to late nineteenth century on grammar, lexicality, syntax, and so on. The model predicating this codificatory enterprise was clearly British, with English constituting the reference language. Such configuration, however, was not specific to the British Raj. Comparable endeavours occurred on the European continent at that time. In India, this reformist and codificatory project was jointly conducted by *pandits* and British educationalists. Importantly, the rhetoric of morality traversed British and Indian pedagogues writing on vernaculars, as well as indigenous teachers in government and missionary schools. Possibly the success of such a moral dimension lay in the convergence of European and Indian ideals and notions of morality during that period (Benei 2002).

Arguably, a similar notion of morality operated in the formation of linguistic nationalist movements, congruently with the awakening of anticolonialist claims from the late nineteenth century onwards. Thus the well-known Hindi language ideology was integral to redefining an exacerbated nationalism in northern India, where language increasingly became a politically divisive issue among nationalists of various backgrounds and religious origins. Hindustani, the hitherto popular language used across the northern peninsula by Hindus and Muslims alike, underwent a process of Sanskritization whereby Urdu words were extirpated. Such crystallization of popular Hindi/Hindu communalist trends is encapsulated by the motto of 'Hindi! Hindu! Hindustan!' in the belief that language, faith, and country together should guide the future of a new, independent Indian nation.

Although this proposition failed to rally the builders of the new nation, constituted as secular, linguistic issues have, nonetheless, been crucial in the postcolonial context. Resonating with the ideological trinitarian association of 'one language, one faith, one country/region', regional states were carved out of the new national territory on vernacular linguistic bases. Numerous debates and controversies ensued over topics ranging from language delimitation to preferred medium of instruction in each state (vernacular over English, vernacular over another vernacular). Lending poignancy to these controversies is the visceral attachment many citizens/speakers developed towards their 'mother tongue', itself a modern notion fashioned alongside nationalist and regionalist ideologies (Ramaswamy 1997). This explains, for instance, the strong antagonism between 'Dravidian' languages (for example, Tamil) and the now 'official' northern Hindi language that lasted for several decades in southern states where English was favoured as a lingua franca. (Interestingly, Hindi today has secured its dominant position for interstate administrative and political communication across the country through Hindi Bollywood cinema.) The Marathi language offers yet another example, uniting its speakers through an emotional and embodied bond mediated by a regional/national mother-goddess figure (Benei 2008, 2009).

These developments have occurred simultaneously with the nation-wide spread of the pedagogic 'three-language formula'. Education is provided in a given state's official linguistic medium (for example, Kannada in Karnataka, Marathi in Maharashtra, and so on) or a child's native tongue for the first ten years of primary and secondary schooling. Additionally, Hindi plus a third language are taught from Class V onwards. The third language may be English. This three-, even four-tier linguistic scheme has been crucial to the creation of an integrated Indian nation. Yet, this model also refracts tensions between local/regional identities, national identities, and opportunities brought about by economic liberalization and 'globalization'. Especially in states where regional vernaculars gradually replaced English for administrative purposes in the late 1990s, renewed interest in this language is fraught with difficulties—ideological, moral, and economic. This time, members of the Indian upper and upper-middle classes are those opposing alleged widespread embrace of English on the part of the expanding middle and lower-middle classes. Some of the debates about education and language policies thus generated, however, bear an uncanny resemblance to their earlier, colonial counterparts.

Further reading: Benei 2002, 2008, 2009; Crook 1996; Ghosh 1995; Kumar 1991; Ramaswamy 1997; Sharp 1920; Zastoupil and Moir 1999.

—VERONIQUE BENEI, *Senior Research Fellow (Research Director)*
in Anthropology, Centre National de la recherche scientifique, Institut
Interdisciplinaire de l'Anthropologie du contemporain/Laboratoire
d'Anthropologie des Institutions et des Organisations Sociales, Paris

— ••• —

Communalism

During the last two hundred years, intercommunity relationships in South Asia have increasingly come under the influence of communalism. Communalism is primarily a relationship between communities governed by mutual distrust, enmity, and antagonism which, in due course of time, engulfs all areas of human existence, particularly social relations and political life. Although violence has been integral to communalism, expressed through physical confrontation between the members of different communities, the more overarching manifestation has been its political ideology.

Early historians of communalism have identified communal riots as an end product of communal politics (Smith 1946; Chandra 1984) and have traced their origin and development to the colonial era; more specifically, as a by-product of the 'divide and rule' policy of the British. Recent research suggests that community tensions and conflicts occurred even previously, but during colonial rule they became qualitatively different: the conflicts no more remained localized as before, but became widespread and simultaneous, and there was substantial increase in their frequency.

More importantly, during the last decade or so the brutality of communal violence has steadily increased, as is evident from the events of Gujarat in 2002 and Orissa in 2004. Physical conflicts are the most visible and, therefore, more perceivable dimension of communalism. But communalism is not confined to violence alone; it is a multifaceted phenomenon of which humanism is the first casualty. It assumes different shapes in order to suit different social conditions (Panikkar 1991).

The articulation of communalism in the second half of the nineteenth century draws upon the social consciousness engendered by primordial identities of caste and religion. Such primordial identities, which were non-antagonistic in the traditional order, underwent fundamental changes in the colonial and postcolonial periods. Among the factors which contributed to this transformation, two are particularly important: first, community-oriented administrative policies of the colonial government, and second, the internal consolidation of religious and caste communities during the course of the nineteenth century. Colonial rule treated Indian society as a conglomeration of warring religious communities and tried to play upon their differences in order to maintain control. Such a social balancing was resorted to because colonial rule had no social base of its own and therefore had to seek the support of different communities. In this process, it extended patronage to sections of society most amenable to its influence at a given point of time, according to its own shifting interest. For example, in the beginning the colonial administrators had treated the Muslims as a hostile community, having been the 'rulers' from whom the British captured power. Once the Empire found firm political and territorial footing they tried to win over the Muslims. After the Revolt of 1857, believed to be the result of a Muslim conspiracy by a section of British administrators, Muslims were treated as enemies and patronage was shifted to the Hindu feudal classes. In the wake of the national movement, which was seen as a Hindu movement, the policy was reversed to befriend Muslim communities. Such a periodical change in British attitude generated mutual suspicion among different religious communities, straining their relations in the process (Prasad 2001).

Simultaneously, community formation and consolidation were also occurring both among Hindus and Muslims. Such a process was aided by social and religious reform movements as they engendered a community-oriented perspective which eventually led to the internal consolidation of communities. Most of the reforms among Hindus were caste specific, yet they functioned within the general rubric of religion. In organization, social practices, and ideological perspectives, these movements not only drew upon religious traditions but also sought their sanction; even the movements among the lower castes were not exceptions to this case. During colonial rule, therefore, communities increasingly functioned within caste and religious boundaries, thereby restricting their consciousness within these limits. As a result, the identity of belonging to a given religion was publicly articulated. A very suggestive example is the self-description of nineteenth-century newspaper correspondents who expressed their identity in religious terms. Needless to say, though religious identity was not the sole factor leading to communalism, the role of religion in the making of communal identity cannot be overlooked either. Nineteenth-century India witnessed the formation of communitarian consciousness, which eventually transformed into communal identity (Panikkar 1999).

This transformation was primarily due to the mediation of politics. The emergence of the national movement in the last quarter of the nineteenth century generated a fear of majoritarianism among Muslims. They were advised by Sayyid Ahmad Khan (1817–1898), reformer and founder of the Aligarh movement, to keep away from the anti-colonial movement which he characterized as a Hindu project. Influential Muslims soon came to the conclusion that the progress of their community was best achieved through the instrumentality of the British. With British support, this led to the formation of the Muslim League in 1906. Almost simultaneously, the Hindu Mahasabha was formed in 1914. Such a development was based on a two-nation theory, enunciated first by the Hindu ideologue Vinayak Damodar Savarkar (1883–1966) and later by Muhammad Ali Jinnah (1876–1948).

The implications of the two-nation theory shaped the political and cultural agenda of communalism. The political project of communalism was essentially to establish the assumed Hindu origins of the Indian nation, the recorded lineage of which has been traced to the period of the Indus Valley civilization. Hindu ideologues identified artefacts of this civilization with Hindu religious symbols; more importantly, evidence was interpreted, and even manufactured, to prove an ancient Vedic Aryan presence in the Indus Valley. One of the crude attempts in this direction was the transformation of a unicorn into a horse through computer manipulation (Rajaram and Frawley 1994; Jha and Rajaram 2000). This was meant to discredit the theory of Aryan migration to India and to replace it by that of indigenous origin. The political importance of this historical 'interpretation' was to ascribe to the Hindus the status of original inhabitants of the land. It also had another objective: once the Aryan 'original invader' was indigenized, all non-Hindus could be labelled as outsiders to the nation. The argument for establishing a Hindu nation could, thus, gain historical validity. It was within this rubric that the Hindi–Urdu controversy in Uttar Pradesh and the cow protection movement in the late nineteenth century, as well as the politics of temple reconstruction in the twentieth, assumed a communal character (Thapar 2011).

Muslim communalism, on the other hand, exploited the minority syndrome and anchored its politics on separatism, which was encouraged by colonial rulers. Constitutional arrangements since the Minto–Morley Reforms in 1909 progressively conceded the principle of separation, culminating in the Partition of India. Partition was the outcome of the communalization of both Hindu and Muslim communities. However, it did not eliminate communalism from the politics of India; instead it served as an instigation for further communalization of the subcontinent (Hasan 1979).

Further reading: Chandra 1984; Hasan 1979; Pandey 1990; Panikkar 1991, 1999; Prasad 2001; Thapar 2011.

—K.N. PANIKKAR, *Chairman, Kerala State Council for Historical Research*

—— •◦• ——

Cow Protection

The origin of an organized political movement of cow protection, demanding an end to cow-slaughter in British India (inspired mainly due to the Hindu belief in the sanctity of the cow) can be traced back to the 1860s and to the Namdhari sect among the Sikhs in Punjab (Jones 1989; O'Toole 2003; Dharampal and Mukundan 2002).

The movement for cow protection began to assume a more organized form in the 1890s with eminent *sanyasis* like Gopalanand Swami (1781–1852), Swami Bhaskarananda (1833–99), government employees, politicians, and local merchants, *sadhus*, and fakirs. Cow protection rose to prominence when organizations, in particular the Arya Samaj, called for mass participation. Its founder, Dayananda Saraswati (1824–83), besides branding cow-slaughter as an immoral act in his 1881 treatise *Gaukarunanidhi* ('Ocean of Mercy to the Cow'), provided cow protection with a highly functional rationale, underscoring the cow's practical utility for agricultural productivity, though basically eschewing any communal sentiment. Further, cow protection was integrated into a reformist discourse, along with issues like opposition to child marriage, widow burning and the bar on widow remarriage, caste discrimination, idol worship, and so on. Hence, cow protection assumed a crucial role in revitalizing the Hindu community in the service of the nation with the aim of protecting it from colonial aggression (O'Toole 2003: 86–7). From 1882, Gaurakshani Sabhas ('societies for the protection of the cow') were founded in large parts of northern, western, and eastern India, with the cow emerging as an enormously potent symbol of mobilization, uniting Hindus of all sects (Tejani 2007). Campaigning in villages, the Gaurakshani Sabhas called upon people to donate funds to establish *gaushalas* ('cattle sanctuaries'), where hundreds of old and unproductive cows were kept, bought from fairs and markets and saved from slaughterhouses; extensive signature and pamphleteering campaigns were also initiated to ban cow-slaughter. Interestingly, some prominent Muslims supported these mass agitations which, as recent archival research into the extensive colonial reports has underscored (Dharampal and Mukundan 2002), were initially directed against the British who (with their large armies and personnel) were the main consumers of beef. Some officials perceptively underscored the strong political (anti-colonial) motives behind the movement (Letter from Commissioner Gibbon, Bettiah, 1.9.1893, cited in Dharampal and Mukundan 2002: 408ff.).

Yet, given the non-compliance of the British government with the plea for banning cow-slaughter, and the concomitant intensification of the cow protection movement (with attempts to physically prohibit the slaughter and sacrifice of cows), administrative endeavours to legislate (emphasizing the Muslim 'right' to slaughter and that of Hindus to protect cows) led to a deepening of religious communal animosities and ensuing conflict, exemplified by riots in Azamgarh district in 1893 (Pandey 1993: 123; Freitag 1990; Tejani 2007). Coupled with a legislative 'divide and rule' policy (as perceived by some sections of the indigenous press), stringent controlling mechanisms (restriction of movement and participation of government employees and notables, press censorship) ensured that the movement subsided by 1894, albeit leaving a legacy of communal strife in its wake.

Recent academic debates on the increasing 'communalization' of society underscore that issues such as cow protection are again being used as a tool for political mobilization (Jaffrelot 1996: 206). Yet the question why people feel so passionate about protecting the cow needs to be addressed outside the politics of Hindu right-wing nationalism.

Further reading: Ambedkar 1990; Dharampal and Mukundan 2002; Freitag 1990; Gupta 2001; Jaffrelot 1996; Jha 2004; Jones 1989; O'Toole 2003; Pandey 1993; Tejani 2007; Veer 1994.

—SUDHA SITHARAMAN, *Department of Sociology,*
Pondicherry University
—GITA DHARAMPAL-FRICK, *Professor of History,*
South Asia Institute, University of Heidelberg

— •◆• —

Dalit

T he word 'Dalit' is one of the terms used to designate a social category that, for quite some time, had no fixed name. The caste system described in the *Rig Veda*, the oldest text of the Hindu tradition, acknowledges only four *varnas* (lit. 'colours', 'groups'): the Brahmins ('priests'), the Kshatriyas ('warriors'), the Vaishyas ('traders'/'artisans') and the Shudras ('servants of the three previous groups'—mostly tillers of the land). However, in the oldest texts of Hinduism, an even lower caste is alluded to: Camanna in the *Rig Veda* or Panchana in the *Manusmriti* (200 BCE–200 CE) (Smith 1994).

Yet the most common label that the first ethnographers encountered while doing fieldwork in North India was 'Untouchables' (*achhut*) because they were supposed to be the most 'impure' of the Hindus (Smith 1994). Even if they are sometimes called 'Outcastes', the 'Untouchables' are definitely part of the caste system: they represent one of its structuring poles, Brahmin being the opposing one.

During social reforms under the British Raj (1858–1947), new terms were introduced to avoid the derogatory connotations of these earlier terms to give, at least theoretically, recognition of human dignity. Three new competing terms were used. The state coined bureaucratic euphemisms like Depressed Classes; from the 1930s, Scheduled Castes became an official label that the Indian republic retained after 1947. Mohandas Karamchand Gandhi (1869–1948) propagated a name that was used in a few Gujarati circles, Harijan ('People of God'), in order to elevate the status of this social group. However, some educated 'Untouchables' who did not want to seek equality with other Hindus in spiritual terms, before God, but rather in social terms, in the everyday, rejected a name they found condescending. They opted instead for the term 'Dalit' (Smith 1994).

Etymologically, Dalit comes from Sanskrit, meaning 'broken', 'crushed', and so on. It was first used to designate the 'Untouchables' by Jyotirao Phule (1827–90), a 'low-caste', anti-Brahmin reformer from modern Maharashtra who denounced upper caste oppression, arguing that the latter were Aryan invaders (a description that was widespread in South India where lower castes claimed to be indigenous peoples), and played a pioneering part in promoting the cause and education of Dalits (including of girls and women). The first pan-Indian Dalit leader, Bhimrao Ambedkar (1891–1956), also from Maharashtra, propagated this term in defence of his caste fellows. He even endowed the Dalits with an alternative cultural identity. First, he claimed that they were the descendants of the first Buddhist converts who had been punished by the upper castes for their conversion.

Second, in 1956, he offered them an escape from their former Hindu identity via conversion to Buddhism (Smith 1994). For Ambedkar, the word 'Dalit' offered the advantages of a generic term bracketing together all 'untouchable' *jati*s which were locked in traditional rivalries, the hierarchical rationale of the caste system applying to the 'untouchable' subgroups too. However, Ambedkar did not use the word 'Dalit' in a systematic way, as is evident from the names of his parties (cf. the Scheduled Castes Federation, for instance) or the title of his books where he uses the expression 'Untouchables' (cf. Ambedkar 1990a, 1990b).

The word 'Dalit' gained wider acceptance after the emergence of a body of writings which came to be known as 'Dalit literature'. This literary genre crystallized in the 1950s in Maharashtra. It mostly comprised poems and autobiographies, usually in Marathi, of educated Dalits who evoked their (and their community's) condition. Writers in Hindi, Tamil, Kannada, and so on, subsequently developed variants of this genre.

In the 1970s, Dalit writers from Maharashtra emulated the Black Panthers of the United States of America to develop a new movement, the Dalit Panthers. Like their American role models, they intended to fight like the Panthers for their rights. Socially revolutionary, they contested elections, but had very little success (Smith 1994).

The notion of Dalit assumed an important dimension in India's public life through politics after the foundation of the Dalit Samaj Soshit Sangharsh Samiti (Committee to Fight for the Community of the Exploited and the Oppressed) by Kanshiram (1934–2006) on 6 December 1981—Ambedkar's death anniversary. Though this party was replaced by another one in 1984, the Bahujan Samaj Party (Party of the Masses), from whose name the word 'Dalit' was discarded, the BSP popularized this notion and promoted it as a concomitant social category. Known as a 'Dalit party', the BSP won the election in India's largest state, Uttar Pradesh, in 2007.

Further reading: Ambedkar 1990a, 1990b; Jaffrelot 2005; Smith 1994.

—CHRISTOPHE JAFFRELOT, *Senior Research Fellow at CERI-Sciences Po/CNRS, Paris and Visiting Professor, King's India Institute, London*

— ·•· —

Darshan

The concept of *darshan* has come to occupy a central place in the studies of India's visual culture. As a Sanskrit word, usually translated as 'vision' or 'gaze', it is most commonly used nowadays in three different contexts: in everyday religious discourses; in mass media and popular culture studies, explaining cultural differences in the popular usage of visual culture; and as a paradigm considered specific to an Indian or Hindu manner of seeing.

The everyday use of the word *darshan* mostly refers to the act of seeing and being seen by the image of a deity, a major reason for Hindus to visit a temple. This act is at the core of religious pilgrimages to cities, rivers, or mountains that play a central role in the sacred geography of Hinduism. In these cases, *darshan* is not only associated with seeing the image of a divinity, but also encapsulates a more diffuse interaction with the sacred place as a whole. *Darshan* is used as well with reference to holy people, embodying an important dimension of the relationship between a guru and his disciple. The term also occurs in the context of people who exercise secular power, such as politicians (most famously Gandhi and Nehru) or film stars; this underscores the way in which different forms of social and religious power in India may interact and overlap.

A significant feature of *darshan* is its conception of vision that intimately connects seeing and being seen with the senses of sight and touch. In some cases, eye contact is ostensibly associated with tactile contact; Babb has described the *darshan* of a god or a guru as a metaphorical way of 'drinking' his power (Babb 1981). But the corollary of this intimacy established between beings of different statuses, such as a devotee and a god, involves the risk of polluting the superior being and hurting or destroying the inferior.

The term *darshan* also connotes an important philosophical category, approximately equivalent to a specific school of thought, thus linking seeing with knowing. According to Yogic tradition, knowledge is acquired both through the medium of texts and also by practising meditation.

Unlike many other South Asian concepts used by social scientists, *darshan* has attracted only relatively recently the attention of foreign scholars, following the seminal works of Diana Eck (1981) and Lawrence Babb (1981) which deal mostly with religious contexts of Indian culture and society where *darshan* is the term used by the people themselves. As a non-western concept of vision, *darshan* also appeals to scholars who explore non-ethnocentric theories, in particular through the study of mass media and popular culture. *Darshan* is often used to explain cultural differences in the way people look at photographs or popular prints or watch cinema in India (Pinney 1997, among other scholars of visual culture), giving the term new currency as a specific Indian or a Hindu manner of seeing. *Darshan* is now used for the study of non-Indian culture (notably by Gell 1998) as well as a way of contrasting Indian ways of seeing with other western or non-western ones (Nelson 2002).

Although *darshan* may constitute in some aspects 'a Hindu manner of seeing', many characteristics which define the concept may be found in other cultures. This is seen clearly with some aspects of the notion of extra-mission which played a central role in the conceptions of vision in the Arab and western worlds. Similarly, there are many other cultures where the visual interaction between people of different statuses has been considered potentially dangerous. More fundamentally, however, the idea of *darshan* as a unique Hindu manner of seeing is problematic because conceptions of vision vary not only historically but also synchronically, for example in different social groups. Given the cultural diversity of India, and its interactions with western and Islamic thought, the idea of a seemingly unchanging, purely Hindu manner of seeing is problematic.

Further reading: Babb 1981; Eck 1981; Gell 1998; Nelson 2000; Pinney 1997.

—DENIS VIDAL, *Directeur de recherche, IRD-Université deParis, Diderot, Paris and Research Associate, Centre d'études de l'Inde et de l'Asie du Sud, École des Hautes Études en Sciences Sociales, Paris*

— ••• —

Democracy

D
emocracy, Robert Dahl notes, 'is the national ideology of India. There is no other' (2000: 162). Two assessments of Indian democracy are widely accepted. First, India is regarded as a significant exception to comparative theories of democracy. Democratic institutions such as free and fair elections, and freedom of expression and association are not supposed to survive in contexts characterized by high levels of poverty, illiteracy, and cultural diversity. Yet, despite their many failings in India, democratic institutions have proved resilient. With low levels of economic development and cultural homogeneity, India meets the criterion of institutional consolidation, namely that democracy is recognized as 'the only game in town' by all actors seeking political power (for example, Stepan, Linz, and Yadav 2011). Second, it is asserted that democracy in India is highly flawed, limited at best. Large-scale poverty and economic inequality undermine the equality of political rights. The rule of law is weak, with political institutions offering little protection to the vulnerable, and few restraints on the powerful. Corruption is widespread and accountability is minimal. Violence and discrimination against religious and caste minorities are common, often aided by state institutions such as the army and police. India is thus seen as an electoral democracy, an 'ethno-democracy' according to some (Jaffrelot 2011), where the basic rights of the poor and of minorities are not respected.

Approaches to democracy in India can be broadly divided into those that define democracy in largely institutional terms, and those that emphasize socioeconomic criteria (Jayal 1999). On many institutional criteria of democracy such as political competition and electoral participation, India appears to be a success case. Elections have been largely frequent, free, fair, and competitive (Yadav 1999), with relatively high levels of voter turnout, averaging around 60 per cent since Independence. Furthermore, democracy in India has deepened over time: Indian elections have become more competitive since Independence, with a greater number of contenders for power, closer electoral contests, and a higher turnover of incumbents (Yadav 1999; Varshney 2000). Political participation has increased, particularly among under-privileged groups, with the incidence of voting higher among the less educated, lower castes, rural groups, and women, in contrast to many Western democracies (Yadav 1999). The social profile of the political elite has also changed significantly since Independence, with many more political representatives drawn from 'backward' castes (Jaffrelot and Kumar 2009). In international terms, support for democracy in India is high, including among marginalized groups, with the very poor and Dalits reporting high levels of commitment to democracy (Stepan, Linz, and Yadav 2011: 65–6).

Yet, institutional approaches do identify deficiencies in Indian democracy. Political participation is usually limited to voting, with citizens unable to use the vote to shape the content of public policies (Yadav and Palshikar 2009). Policies have largely focused on symbolic improvements in the social status of previously denigrated groups (Varshney 2000), and selective benefits for electorally significant groups as part of a politics of patronage (Chandra 2004). Democratic institutions in India have shown little will or capacity to improve the material conditions of the disadvantaged or to deliver health, education, and basic amenities as universal goods. Nevertheless, from an international comparative perspective, democratic consolidation and deepening in India appear in a favourable light.

Approaches that define democracy in social or economic terms have on the whole been less optimistic in their assessments of Indian democracy. Some have questioned whether India can be regarded as a democracy at all, holding that it offers an example of democratic authoritarianism, where 'the meticulous observance of the ritual of elections enabled a partnership between the political leadership and the non-elected institutions of the state', masking the widespread use of force (Jalal 1995: 249). Elections and democratic institutions, more generally, are seen here to have little efficacy in relation to enduring structures of socioeconomic equality. Importantly, these are not necessarily viewed as a democratizing force, often strengthening forms of centralization and authoritarianism. Others have developed Alexis de Tocqueville's (1805–59) analysis of the consequences of democracy as a social tendency to argue that in India democratic institutions such as elections have helped erode social inequalities but done little to tackle economic inequalities that capitalist development has exacerbated (Kaviraj 2000). Elections have also produced majoritarianisms based on religion and caste: Hindu nationalism is one face of democratization in India, and the extension of quotas to electorally powerful 'backward' castes is another. As such, it is argued that democratic institutions have had illiberal consequences, strengthening the power of groups rather than individuals, and weakening restraints on political power.

Another important socioeconomic perspective suggests that democracy, like the state itself, is unevenly spread across India. Democratic institutions were the product of 'an elite dominated pact' (Heller 2000: 504) in India and have been largely ineffective in creating relations of equality between citizens. Kerala, however, represents a different case—of the successful establishment of democratic relations of equal citizenship through universal social policies. This has been achieved through a process in which class-based mobilization of subordinate groups for the expansion of basic services has played a crucial role (Heller 2000: 511). Oppositional mass-based movements, thus, *contra* influential theories of democracy (for example, Huntington), can play a crucial role in democratic advance. Perhaps the most significant contribution of social approaches to democracy has been to highlight that democratic institutions are not a panacea necessarily producing desirable consequences such as respect for rule of law, reduction in poverty, and accommodation of pluralism. Rather the historical trajectory of democracy in India serves as a useful reminder that it 'also very often gives birth to forces, desires, and imaginings of an authoritarian and anti-democratic nature' (Hansen 1999: 6), such as those found within Hindu nationalism in India, and xenophobia in Europe and beyond.

Three emerging research areas on democracy in India are of note. First, it has been suggested that democratic institutions, with all their flaws, have played a significant role in the management of diversity in India, and thereby advanced important goals such as state stability. Institutions of federal democracy encourage 'identification with the state' among citizens with different social identities (Stepan, Linz, and Yadav 2011: 62), contributing to state survival, although this remains to be established through systematic empirical research. In a similar vein, it has been suggested that elections in India, while encouraging a politics of patronage and corruption, have also offered opportunities for the reconfiguration of social identities through the building of new inter-group alliances, and thereby prevented social polarization (Chandra 2004). Conflict management and state stability are the unintended, macro-level outcomes of self-interested actions of politicians seeking political power in a context in which no social group has a stable electoral majority. A second strand of scholarship employs ethnographic approaches to illuminate the practices of elections and mass movements in India. What is the meaning of voting in the everyday life of a poor, rural Indian (Banerjee 2007)? Why do ordinary people bother to vote, given the poor performance of democratic governments, and the high levels of distrust in politicians? The spectacle and drama of elections, and the staging of popular protests against the state are not incidental but rather integral to the democratic political imaginary in India and elsewhere (Hansen 1999). Ethnographic approaches promise to illuminate not just the unique colour and texture of Indian democracy but also the expressive and performative dimensions of democracy in general. A third approach identifies democracy with the everyday practices of the poor in India and elsewhere that breach or circumvent state laws—the activities of squatters, hawkers, vagrants, and local strongmen, for instance (Chatterjee 2011). Illegal transgressions and claims for exceptions to universal laws pressed by subaltern classes, it is argued, embody a distinct non-western approach to democracy, more inclusive than dominant western approaches which privilege the modern state and universal laws. While providing a useful critique of some institutionalist approaches, the political society perspective has not yet elaborated an alternative set of criteria for democracy that establishes how deviations or exceptions from norms are democratic.

Why and how democratic institutions, with their many failings, survive in India continues to puzzle theorists of democratization. Important explanations include colonial legacies such as British-style parliamentary institutions and the subordination of the military to elected civilian leaders; the democratic dispositions of the Indian nationalist leadership combined with a long and relatively inclusive national movement (for overviews, see Varshney 1998; Kohli 2001); and the nature of India's cultural diversity, in particular, the absence of a single, stable group that is large enough to rule over all others (Dahl 2000). Recent research suggests that democratic institutions in India are supported by a broadly inclusive and flexible vocabulary of public reasoning that has endured, even as the meanings of its key normative terms have changed over time (Bajpai 2011). While the contribution of India's rich traditions of public argument (Sen 2005: 13–14) to the maintenance of its democratic institutions has been noted, India's founding ideals are usually attributed to the thought of key leaders, such as Gandhi (1869–1948), Nehru (1889–1964), and Ambedkar (1891–1956). However, more studies of everyday public reasoning are needed in sites such as legislatures, courts, and newspapers, in order to discern the role of processes of debate in the sustenance of democratic institutions (Bajpai 2011). India remains diagnostically significant for the career of democracy; its complex resolutions, often imperfect and messy, continue to challenge the prescriptive certitudes of influential theories.

Further reading: Chatterjee 2011; Dahl 2000; Guha 2007; Hansen 1999; Jayal 2001; Khilnani 2007; Kohli 2001; Stepan, Linz, and Yadav 2011; Varshney 1998.

—ROCHANA BAJPAI, *Senior Lecturer in the Politics of Asia/Africa,*
SOAS, University of London

— ••• —

Development

In a broader sense, the term 'development' is often used to refer to the gradually unfolding process as societies go from a simple to a more complex form of organization. However, development is more commonly used to denote material or economic advancement; in this sense it is often referred to as economic development. In this common usage, development would mean an increase in the standard of living of a nation which, in turn, invariably has a comparative connotation. It is not surprising, therefore, to find that the constitutive features of development are still hotly debated. Seers (1979) argued that the purpose of development is to reduce poverty, inequality, and unemployment, while Sen (1999) argues that development involves increasing freedom and broadening choices.

However, these debates must be situated within the broader historical and political context of the subcontinent. Indian economic and political history has shaped its unique perspective on development. Given India's unique features—fertile lands of the Indo-Gangetic plains and climatic conditions—the Indian peninsula was historically perhaps one of the most developed and affluent regions (Spear 1985; Thapar 2003). Drastic transformations in the state of knowledge and technology in the eighteenth and nineteenth centuries were to change this situation. These developments favoured regions that adopted technological innovations in the nineteenth and twentieth centuries. One of the consequences of such a technological advancement has been the emergence of a set of developed nations that became a benchmark for comparison. Their standard of living became the unit of measure in contemporary development debates.

From the archaeological evidences that locate one of the earliest human settlements in the world to the Indus Valley (dating back to over four to five thousand years) to the arrival of British East India Company, Indians, in general, lived in comparative prosperity (Spear 1985; Nehru 1989). The accounts of the economic condition in India at the eve of the British conquest show that average Indians had a better standard of living compared to the average British, and one of the accounts suggests that even a small town like Murshidabad in Bengal was as prosperous as eighteenth-century London (Nehru 1989: 285). As the state of knowledge and technology drastically altered, the mode of production and concept of wealth, as well as the relative standard of living in India steadily declined. The technology-driven development also produced a kind of interregional dependence between those who had access to technology, and attained a higher living standard, and those who did not adopt, or had no access to technology.

Consequently, the emerging world order in the nineteenth century led to deprivation in countries like India which had a better living standard in the pre-industrial era. In fact, the observation that a large proportion of Indians became underfed and undernourished was one of the driving forces behind the formation of the Indian National Congress (INC) in 1885 (Naoroji 1901). The issue of economic development became central to the deliberations of the INC in its struggle for self-rule. Initial debates about the diversity of development strategies culminated in the formation of the National Planning Committee (NPC) in 1934, which argued that a minimum standard of living could be ensured by an increase in national income along with a more equitable distribution of wealth.

Despite the emphasis on the reduction of mass poverty by the NPC and the adaptation of its prescriptions in economic development models (for example, Harrod–Domar and neoclassical models of growth), the rise in national income since Independence in 1947 has not necessarily led to a general rise in the standard of living. High rates of poverty, inequality, unemployment, and underemployment underline this disparity.

This paradox of continued poverty amidst rising prosperity is an outgrowth of the fundamental philosophy underlying development planning. One of the major theoretical flaws seems to be the neoclassical assumption of homogeneity of the participants or the beneficiaries of development. Despite a substantial increase in the national wealth of post-Independence India, the process of Indian development turns out to be skewed. Only certain sections of the population have benefited, while a large proportion continues to suffer from multiple deprivations. Due to the unique Indian institutional set-up that manifests itself in the form of the multicultural, multilingual, and multireligious structure of the population, the rise in the standard of living has not been inclusive. Admittedly, the recent spurt in economic growth has done much to raise confidence in the ability to achieve high levels of national productivity, and levels of poverty have declined from over 50 per cent of the population to about 27 per cent (GOI 2007). Yet, as the disparities across different social strata and regions continue to flourish, this growth has also intensified the tension between ensuring productivity growth, on the one hand, and on providing an equitable distribution of that growth, on the other.

While growth and equity are not automatically mutually exclusive, a post-socialist world order and India's increased participation in the global economy have tended to highlight their disjunction. Consequently, 'inclusive growth' has emerged as a key imperative of Indian development discourse. In this context, Sen's (1999) argument, that individual freedom is not only the principal goal of, but also a key to development, has taken on a new meaning. In different ways, civil society initiatives that demand right to education, right to food, and right to information, and stress the need to curb corruption, attempt to ensure inclusive growth.

Further reading: GOI 2007; Naoroji 1901; Nehru 1989; Seers 1969; Sen 1999; Spear 1985; Thapar 2003.

—AMARESH DUBEY, *Professor of Economics, Centre for the Study of Regional Development, Jawaharlal Nehru University, New Delhi*
—SONALDE DESAI, *Professor of Sociology, University of Maryland*

— .•. —

Dharavi

Dharavi is a collection of neighbourhoods, each layered with its own diversity: of language, economic activities, festivals, rituals, and aspirations. Historically, the Koli fishing community comprised the oldest residents of the fishing village of Dharavi-Koliwada, situated on the western side of present-day Dharavi between the localities of Sion and Mahim. Colonial records like the *Gazetteer of Bombay–Thane* consider the Kolis to be an indigenous community dating back to the sixteenth century, at least in this region. In the first half of the twentieth century, *khumbars* ('potters') from Gujarat and leather tanners from Tamil Nadu and Maharashtra made this swampy, mosquito-infested land their home. Embroidery, food-processing, recycling, and many of the industrial activities that characterize this locality emerged from the community/caste-based artisanal occupations of its populations that migrated from all over the subcontinent and adapted to the needs of a modernizing urban economy.

Today, it is a tapestry of communities, marked by religious and ethnic shrines, mostly from economically and culturally marginal communities. This peripheral part of the city grew on its own steam, with no or very little civic support. It was widely, but not accurately, designated as the largest slum in Asia just a few decades after India's Independence, attracting national and global media attention.

In reality, Dharavi is just one among many of the city's neighbourhoods and destinations populated by poor migrant groups, though certainly one of the oldest. Many, even larger habitats, grew around the city's airport and its numerous industries located in the suburbs, but without receiving similar attention. The reason could be that Dharavi is unique in many ways. With little capital and resources, its migrant families, individuals, and communities harnessed whatever they could in terms of land, artisanal skills, and labour, to plug into the city's economic activities and make their neighbourhood a hub of its own.

Dharavi continues to be hugely productive. Many residents treat their house as a tool of production as much as a living space for themselves or for their workers. These dwellings are typically built by local contractors according to individual means, needs, and requirements, with no help from architects, engineers, or other formally qualified construction professionals. This makes its landscape uneven and unpredictable.

Most homes double up as a productive space of some sort. A 'tool-house' emerges when every wall, nook, and corner becomes an extension of the tools of the trade of its inhabitants; when the furnace and the cooking hearth exchange roles and when sleeping competes with warehouse space. Consequently, the density of the neighbourhood becomes a resource in itself. If there are enough people passing by (and there always are), one is inevitably able to sell something to someone. It can be seen as the libertarian version of totalitarian Chinese sweatshops, producing just as much, but with a frugal and decentralized web of producers.

Today, an increasing number of students, researchers, activists, and writers are feeding off Dharavi to produce new concepts, participatory methodologies, and architectural systems. Their intention is not to combat Dharavi's poverty but to learn from it, as a model of self-reliant urban growth. The Net Generation in particular recognizes itself in the story of this self-developing city, which is powered by the collective intelligence and individual aspirations of hundreds of thousands of people.

Yet, for municipal authorities, Dharavi is merely a slum. Their own civic failure to provide good sewage, water connections, and roads is blamed on the neighbourhood. This is then translated into a story of victimization of the residents. Under the official aegis of the Slum Rehabilitation Scheme (SRS) (instituted in 1995 and still fundamentally influential in spite of subsequent modifications), municipal authorities are intent on providing residents tiny bits of dwelling, in high-rises that will break the fragile enmeshing of economic and residential functions that the present fabric facilitates. In reality, developers and the civic authorities have simply realized the economic value of the land on which Dharavi is located and seek to exploit this for real-estate development alone.

The state government and its Dharavi Redevelopment Project, presented to the residents by the Slum Rehabilitation Authority, the prime executive body of the SRS, in any of its several expressions floated since the mid-2000s, have been accused by local activists such as Ramchandra ('Bhau') Y. Korde as putting 'land development' before 'human development', the latter represented by the hard-working and urbane inhabitants of this misrepresented place.

Further reading: Bhide 2008; Burgman 2009; Echanove and Srivastava 2008, 2010, 2011; Edwardes 1909–10; Sharma 2000.

—MATIAS ECHANOVE *and* RAHUL SRIVASTAVA,
Co-directors of the Institute of Urbanology, Mumbai

—— •••• ——

Dharma in the Hindu Epics

The Hindu epic poems, the *Ramayana* and the *Mahabharata*, serve to this day as significant ethical models influencing Indian theories of rights, justice, and social and individual morality. The *Mahabharata* is a prominent example of ethical controversy as a product of human nature, whereas the *Ramayana* represents a paradigm for human behaviour as conveyed by the gods in reincarnated forms on earth. In this regard, the *Mahabharata* plays a bigger role in defining the themes that shape premodern Indian ethical thinking, namely dharma.

The ethical implications of the *Mahabharata* are based on philosophical principles that give meaning to life. The underlying natural order in the Hindu belief system that connects individuals, society, and the universe as a whole is known as *rita* ('universal order'). This constitutes the overarching social, moral, and natural order that must be maintained and relies on human compliance by renouncing selfish desires and accepting individual responsibility. *Rita* conveys the struggle for balance in the world and for the welfare of all beings, including humans, gods, and animals. The interconnectedness of humanity and nature is a recurring idea in the epics and is the foundation of the traditional ethical system (Matilal 1989).

The all-encompassing cosmic order must be upheld by dharma, defined as the embodiment of rights, duties, laws, justice, virtue, and truth. Dharma has no direct English translation—it is a broad concept that establishes individual duties, obligations, and place within society and on earth. Alterity is a key idea here; it implies that the obligations to be fulfilled are not just restricted to the individual or even to one's peers—they extend to all beings, both human and nonhuman. Thus the oneness of all living beings is emphasized, tying morality to responsibility. Dharma revolves around disinterested action; any agent must fulfil his duty without regard to the consequences that may arise (Bhagavadgita, II.39). When dharma is not followed, for example when avarice and selfishness overcome righteousness, *adharma*, the negation of dharma, prevails. Adherence to dharma, that is, the fulfilling of one's predetermined obligations, minimizes the burden of karma (Bilimoria 2007).

Karma puts forth the idea that every action creates impacts that go beyond the immediate effect of that action. It is manifested in the transmigration of the soul, which continues on through a cycle of rebirth. Karma is an action–retribution system in which the fulfilment of one's dharma in one life may improve his or her dharma for the next. This is because dharma is regulated by *varnashramadharma*, the premodern Hindu social order. The first group comprised the Brahmins, or religious leaders and teachers; these were followed by the Kshatriyas, who were the warriors and military leaders of society, whose duty it was to fight and to govern—the Kshatriyas play a key role in the *Mahabharata*. The third group was called the Vaishya, and included merchants and landowners, and were those who kept the economy alive. Finally, at the bottom of the caste system was the Shudra group, which consisted of the manual labour force. An individual's dharma was thus dependent on his or her *varna*: duties and position in society went hand in hand (Chapple 2007). Dharma was also influenced by *ashrama*, or 'stage of life'. The first stage of life was characterized by the attainment of knowledge, then the working and householder stage, thirdly the gradual withdrawal from societal demands, and lastly transcendence through 'asceticism'. Social stratification and life-stage played important roles in determining an individual's specific role, and determined what actions he was to take in order to live an ethically appropriate life.

As mentioned before, the *Ramayana* is a more dogmatic, paradigmatic text that idealizes human behaviour by glorifying the gods. The *Mahabharata*, on the other hand, is a text that explores the conflicts of dharma faced by warriors, kings, and gods in the struggle to allow righteousness to prevail. The epic depicts a story of a deeply divided family fighting for kingship; on one side the Kauravas, blinded by greed and jealousy, and, on the other, the Pandavas, struggling with moral conflict. The height of the struggle is reached during a section of the text called the Bhagavadgita, when the commander-in-chief of the Pandava Kshatriya army, Arjuna, is preparing to fight for his brother's rightful kingship. He realizes that on the other side of the battlefield are his uncles and cousins who have wronged him and his brothers. However, he cannot bear the thought of being the one to kill his kin in the battle that is about to ensue. The *Gita* depicts the conversation between the conflicted Arjuna and his mentor, Krishna, who is a reincarnation of the supreme lord, Vishnu, and is the orchestrator of the gods' efforts to restore righteousness on earth. In this dialogue, Krishna aims to convince Arjuna to fight in the war by preaching the idea of disinterested action, asserting that Arjuna must selflessly fulfil his dharma as a Kshatriya without regard to the consequences (Mohanty 2007). Krishna also stresses the importance of devotion to God (a practice known as *bhaktiyoga*), and the existence of an imperishable, universal soul that connects all beings—thus death is not absolute. Arjuna's ethical dilemma is an example of the conflicts imposed by dharma; Krishna's solution emphasizes the duty- and action-oriented stance individuals must take when faced by moral conflicts. Here dharma is given authority to strictly define one's course of action. Action taken in accordance with dharma is seen as morally sound and only in this way can an individual achieve ultimate liberation.

The Hindu epics put forth an ethical perspective imbued with religious presuppositions which has been used in the context of politics, war, family life, and love. It is important to note that while the idea of dharma forms the basis of Hindu philosophy it has also been applied in secular ethos, for example in law and legal jurisprudence (Bilimoria 2011). Many analytical texts have placed dharma in contexts that have little to do with pious action. Disinterested action, duty and obligation, and individual liberation all rely on dharma as a presence in various aspects of society and life.

Further reading: Bilimoria et al. 2007; Bilimoria 2011; Creel 1977; Mohanty 2007; Olivelle 2009.

—PURUSHOTTAMA BILIMORIA, *University of California, Berkeley*
—LYKA SETHI, *University of Melbourne*

— •••• —

Dowry

Dowry transactions in India can probably be traced to ancient times. The bridal chest or trousseau (*kosha*) in the *Rigveda* 10.85.7 may be the oldest indication, together with the *vahatu* ('bridal procession') of the *Rigveda* 10.85.13. Innumerable local dowry practices exist among Indians today and dowry prestations appear under many names. *Jahej, daaj,* or *dahez,* also *burri,* are terms in North India used to describe gifts the bride receives from her natal family and friends to take to her new family. Different types of *shagan* or *salami,* 'wedding presents' for the bride (and groom, or both), on various occasions could be part of dowry, which concerns more than simply gifts or property.

Fieldwork-based research now presents 'the dowry problem' largely as an ideologically constructed gender issue linked to matrimonial conflicts, especially over loyalty between families and intimate relationships (Wyatt and Masood 2011), while much academic literature still confuses dowry with the Muslim 'dower' (*mahr*). Dowry is often viewed as a Hindu cultural illness which has infected Muslims and tribal communities. Many Muslims use both dower and dowry arrangements, creating 'a strange situation' (Ali and Naz 1998: 132).

Dowry may be given with the wife to the husband and/or his family. While it is often unclear what falls under dowry and what not (Menski 1998), marriage becomes a highly ritualized occasion to transfer property to daughters, often as premortem inheritance, allegedly rarely a fair share. What she brings into marriage certainly affects a woman's position, but the property seldom belongs to her exclusively. Dowry may be defined as 'women's property' (*stridhanam*), but where women themselves are treated as property, as in North India/the Punjab (Oldenburg 2002), this becomes problematic. 'Good' dowry, perceived as *sadacara,* which can be translated as 'good custom', often coexists with 'bad' dowry, property demanded by the husband's family and claimed as family property.

Manifestations of dowry are widely portrayed as dowry 'murder', bride-burning, and dowry-related domestic violence, linked to female infanticide and selective foeticide (Menski 1998). While European cultures treat dowry prestations as useful socioeconomic transfers, it appears problematic to stigmatize dowry among Indians as a spectacle of 'the Orient' (Oldenburg 2002: viii); that traditional (and modern) dowry expectations may cause multiple stresses and violence is another matter. Saavala (2010: 30) notes that middle-class families feel the pinch as 'dowry payments for daughters are [...] more and more demanding'. Such families suffer paradoxes of control when allowing female employment to ease the financial burden of providing dowries. Love marriages cause additional tensions because of the absence of dowry (Saavala 2010: 52).

Even when extremely large dowries are expected and given, there need not be a dowry 'problem'; millions of Indian marriages involving dowry do not end in violent disaster. However, dowry is constructed as problematic in terms of gendered violence and inequality, since daughters were not treated as entitled to inheritance in their own right (Basu 2005). The Hindu Succession (Amendment) Act (2005) now treats Hindu daughters as equal to sons in inheritance, but such strategies only work where there is property to distribute. Traditionally, 'it is basically the parents' duty to provide for their daughters and to give them as "the gift of a virgin", accompanied by a dowry, to the affinal family' (Saavala 2010: 43–4), but such idealizing concepts overlook the socioeconomic realities of widespread poverty among Indians, as fieldwork identifies poor people's creative strategies of managing 'reasonable' dowry adjusted according to families' financial capabilities.

Many poorer Indian women thus get a better deal out of traditional family obligations to provide decent weddings than formal entitlements to property shares could secure them. In such families, dowry becomes a carefully planned investment and mainly brothers/cousins help secure safe passage into matrimony. However, where dowry has become a tool for extortion, it legitimizes violence against women and even killing. Many families thus terminate marriage negotiations when unreasonable demands appear. While 'good' dowry and 'bad' dowry coexist, legal intervention through the Dowry Prohibition Act (1961) has been ineffective. Presently, dowry has ceased to be a prime concern for feminist activists, while many women are allegedly still killed in dowry 'murders'. Court cases now deal mainly with criminal evidence and the boundary between suicide and murder.

Politicized scholarly perceptions about the desirability of securing independent female property rights and individual autonomy clash with social contexts that expect a symbiotic relationship between spouses.

Viewing dowry merely as a patriarchal tool to repress women overlooks various practices to secure women's economic safety (Basu 2001: 225), and fails to note that many families value daughters, and also belittles women's self-interest in claiming dowries. Becoming an 'Enlightenment problem', then, South Asian dowry debates implicate culture-specific forms of violence against women as a consequence of patriarchal, patrilocal societies. Highlighting Indian dowry 'problems' becomes a convenient tool to denigrate Indian culture. While there is no necessary direct correlation between dowry and gendered violence, apprehensions about divorce remain closely implicated in dowry 'murders'.

Further reading: Ali and Naz 1998; Basu 2001, 2005; Menski 1998; Oldenburg 2002; Saavala 2010; Wyatt and Masood 2011.

—WERNER MENSKI, *Emeritus Professor of South Asian Laws, SOAS, University of London*

—— •◆• ——

Drain of Wealth

The concept of drain of wealth or 'drain theory' was coined in the 1860s in the context of British rule over India. The 'high priest' of the theory was an early nationalist in India, Dadabhai Naoroji (1825–1917) (Chandra 1966). The drain of wealth was best explicated in two seminal works, namely Naoroji's *Poverty and Un-British Rule in India* (1901) and Romesh Chandra Dutt's *The Economic History of India* (1901, 1903), presenting the Indian nationalists' economic critique of colonialism.

Basically, the drain of wealth referred to the 'tribute' or the unrequited transfer of resources from the colony to the colonial metropolis. The drain of wealth began when the British East India Company—having established political power over Bengal in the mid-eighteenth century—stopped paying with bullion (worth about 3.1 million Rupees in 1757–8) for the huge amount of Indian textiles it imported from India. Instead, the Company's imports were henceforth paid for with revenues (mainly land revenue) extracted from India itself (Habib 1995; Mukherjee 2010). India thus paid for its own exports, and to the extent it did so, this constituted the drain of wealth.

The drain of wealth was to continue throughout British rule (1757–1947). Thus, for nearly two centuries 5 to 10 per cent of the GDP produced in India was annually drained out to Britain. The drain of wealth in 1801 was calculated to be 9 per cent of the GDP of the British territories in India (Habib 1995). The form that the drain of wealth took kept changing, as the composition, pattern, and direction of India's foreign trade and the composition of revenues raised through taxes changed over time. The basic process, however, was that Indian Rupee revenues were converted into remittance in Sterling by appropriating India's export surplus (Mukherjee 2010). A British government document maintained in 1930 that fiscal and monetary measures had to be imposed on India which would enable the remittance of 60 per cent of the total annual revenues of about 100 million pounds, raised in India through taxes, to cover the military and civil expenditures and other Sterling 'commitments' that Britain charged to India (India Office Records 1930). It was these charges which Indian nationalists called the 'Home Charges' and which formed a controversial constituent of the drain of wealth.

The drain of wealth was argued to be the central cause of India's poverty (Naoroji 1901). The 'capital famine' it created by draining away virtually the entire potential investible surplus of the country meant that the Indian economy did not grow in per capita terms, but experienced an actual shrinkage during colonial rule. The concept of the drain of wealth, the most popular and powerful argument against British rule, was also politically the most subversive for colonialism and hence has been rejected by colonial ideologues persistently until today (Roy 2006).

Further reading: Chandra 1966; Dutt 1901, 1903; Habib 1995; Mukherjee 2010; Naoroji 1901; Roy 2006.

—ADITYA MUKHERJEE, *Professor of Contemporary Indian History,*
Centre for Historical Studies, Jawaharlal Nehru University, New Delhi

Dravidian

In late-nineteenth- and twentieth-century South India, the term 'Dravidian' was employed to denote a politicized Tamil identity and to wage a pitched struggle for political power and supremacy over a contested Tamil ethnicity. Creating a Dravidian identity aimed at recreating idioms, terms, and images from its Tamil cultural past and superimposing it on the political present. Much of this terrain of identity formation was situated in the imaginative and rhetorical prose of political propaganda, beginning with the Justice Party in the late nineteenth century, flourishing in the early twentieth century under the leadership of E.V. Ramaswamy Naicker (1879–1973), known as Periyar. The entry of the Dravida Kazhagam (Dravidian Organization) in the 1930s and 1940s, led by C.N. Annadurai (Aringnar Anna, 1909–69), followed by Muthuvel Karunanidhi (alias Kalaignar b. 1924) and, since the 1950s, the Dravida Munnetra Kazhagam (DMK) (Dravidian Progress Federation) made singular attempts to twin the project of etching out a 'Dravidian-scape' to the creation of a collective political identity for Tamils.

Three interlinked and overlapping conceptual categories that shaped the contours of being and becoming Dravidian merit special attention since they simultaneously created a Dravidian nation, culture, and statesmen: the 'country', the 'colony', and the 'citizen'. Inherent in such discourses, as Veena Das's (1995) study of the Sikh militant discourse reveals, is the creation of a political language to forge and activate a political unity among its citizens. Here, discourses function 'more to produce a particular reality than to represent it' (1995: 125). Dravidian discourses were narratives, 'the telling of a nation and telling a particular version of it' (Kaviraj 1992: 2).

The first concept, the 'country', shows a historical obsession with recurrent themes of reclaiming a 'golden past'. The process of building a Tamil identity was essentially constructing a unified nation, language, and history. 'Dravidian' gave rise to different constructions contingent on the type of rhetoric invoked for a purpose. It could mean a genetically determined race or a linguistic community hinged upon the historical process of evolving and sharing culture, art, language, and social habits.

Linked to the concept of country is the concept of 'colony', a representation of the Dravidian country as a subjugated colony by the Aryan invasion. A powerful voice redefining the political project of reclaiming the colonized Dravidian country and the 'ethnicization' (Ramaswamy 1993) of Tamil was Annadurai, founder of the DMK (formally founded in 1949). Anna addressed all Tamils as his brothers and mothers, and used the podium for generating and shaping a 'Tamil family'. Tracing the various stages in the conquest of culture by alien forces, Anna states: 'When a culture wishes to forcibly conquer another [culturally distinct entity], it does so either by force, through unfair trade and finally by an imperial war [...]' (Annadurai 1948: 39–40). The imposition of Hindi was perceived as one such sociopolitical act of a cultural takeover by means unjust and foul. In his speeches and writings, Tamil became a concrete signifier of an ethnic and political community, tied by kinship and blood.

The third concept deals with 'being and becoming a Dravidian in thought and deed' (Rangaswamy 2004). A Dravidian was portrayed as someone who would act by subjugating his body and laying down his life in the creation of a Dravidian country, freed from the clutches of colonization. Political rhetoric clearly identified signifying practices to provide a normative account of what a Tamil citizen must embody. A Dravidian by birth, blood, or kinship had to further prove his citizenship by an unequivocal allegiance to the Tamil country. Anna's call to all his Tamil brothers was an impassioned invocation for moral action against his country's colonizers: 'If a Tamilian is equipped to safeguard his honour, if thousands who went to jail were true to their ideals, if the renaissance currently sweeping the Tamil country is true, come my Tamil men to war against the enemy' (Rangaswamy 2004: 44–5).

The discourse feeding into the creation of Dravidian identity is multilayered, inasmuch as it attempts to weave together multiple ideological positions in the project of successfully 'massifying' a political identity. Much of its supple and creative prose was drawn from the cultural mythographies of the Tamil landscape, endowing its people with legendary accomplishments and natural qualities, and conferring immortal purity and antiquity on its culture. Such a discourse needed to touch all aspects of 'being a Dravidian' and bring together the variegated Tamil people into a 'Dravidian community'. It was intended to create a Tamil popular culture transforming the perception and embodiment of a Dravidian identity. The current scenario in Tamil Nadu is remarkable for the emergence of a number of new political parties rhetorically feeding on the discourses of Tamil cultural nationalism articulated by the Dravidian movement. Contemporary Dravidian politics is now structured by the realpolitik of democratic electoral mass politics of the state. In contravention of the radical tenets of its early political rhetoric, it now feeds on Hindu nationalism, caste-based politics, and struggles between numerically dominant lower castes and Dalits (Harriss 2002).

Further reading: Barnett 1976; Hardgrave 1964–5; Harriss 2002; Pandian 2007; Sivathamby 1995; Washbrook 1989.

—NIMMI RANGASWAMY, *Senior Research Scientist at Xerox Research Centre India and Adjunct Professor, Indian Institute of Technology, Hyderabad*

— •• —

Emergency

On 25 June 1975, the President of India, Fakhruddin Ali Ahmed (1905–77), declared a state of Emergency under Article 352 of the Indian Constitution. The Prime Minister, Indira Gandhi (1917–84), had asked the President to do so, giving her unlimited powers for an unspecified period. The 'crisis' provoking the Emergency was the short-term compulsion of a government under threat. The Allahabad High Court (on 12 June 1975) served Mrs Gandhi with an unfavourable verdict for electoral corruption. Threatened by the clamour of Opposition voices, and by the political upsurge in the countryside and cities on a host of other issues, Mrs Gandhi and her Congress faction decided to stifle those voices by characterizing them as 'anti-national'. On 20 June 1975, Mrs Gandhi told a rally, 'My opponents are not only after my chair, they want to murder me and my family' (Prashad 1996: 48). The slogan 'Indira is India' only helped to clarify the centrality of Mrs Gandhi's well-being to the nation's well-being.

The serious consequences of the inflationary years (1965–7 and 1973–4) provided the objective conditions for many anti-government political projects, including the Railway Strike of 1974, the Maoist Naxalite movement, the communist agitation in West Bengal and elsewhere, the Bihar student-led agitations (which began on 18 March 1974), the United Women's Anti-Price Rise Front in Maharashtra, and the Nav Nirman movement in Gujarat (Gandhi 1996; Sheth 1977; Chandra 2003). These radical political projects demonstrated to the dominant classes that the hegemony of the various branches of the Congress was slowly losing its hold over the population. At this stage, the economic elite welcomed 'the strong hand of the leader', accepting that in such times the elite would need to agree to the removal of its notional political power to maintain its broader social power.

Indeed, Mrs Gandhi's populist authoritarianism oscillated between rhetorical concern for the masses and real collaboration with the Chambers of Commerce. The Emergency period was not the continuation of the trajectory of socialism opened up by bank nationalization (1969) and the Indo-Soviet Peace Treaty of 1971; in fact, it was its negation (Guha 2007: ch. 19; Nayar 2012: ch. 8). On 1 July 1975, Mrs Gandhi announced a 20-point programme whose basis was to draw in industrialists through cutting back on licences through the 'liberalization of investment procedures' (14th point, Prashad 1996: 49). Exports seemed to be the drive of this industrial policy, far removed from the Indian state's attempt in the 1940s to produce an economy sustained by its own requirements rather than by the whims of foreign trade. One of Mrs Gandhi's ministers told the defanged Lok Sabha in 1976 that the State would take 'further steps to encourage investment by non-resident Indians' (Gandhi 1976: 338). Industrial and finance capital, along with large landholders, were the principle beneficiaries of the Emergency policies, though supposedly this was done to benefit the poor. In the name of the poor, as well, Mrs Gandhi's son, Sanjay (1946–80), pushed an urban agenda: population control, slum clearance, tree planting, and other objectives that appealed to the urban middle class. The middle class and the elite were, myopically, more interested in the impact of poverty on themselves rather than on the lives of the poor. They were the favoured constituency of the Emergency (Tarlo 2003; Mehta 1977; Prashad 1996).

The heavy-handedness of the Emergency provoked a powerful democratic response from the people that led to the ouster of the regime by the ballot box in 1977 (Guha 2007: ch. 23). That election signalled the failure of the strategy of dictatorship from above in India. Deep-rooted liberal sentiments and brave struggle from a range of political positions prevented this form of authoritarian rule to continue. Unable to control the crisis, the dominant classes pledged themselves to a new strategy: an elitist populism that sought to reinvent the spirit of nationalism, obscure the differential class interests, and drive Indian modernity into a more *friendly* form of 'Emergency rule'.

Further reading: Chandra 2003; Ghosh 2010; Kaviraj 1986; Prashad 1996; Tandon 2006; Tarlo 2003.

—VIJAY PRASHAD, *Professor of International Studies, George and Martha Keller Chair of South Asian History, Trinity College, Hartford*

— ••• —

Environment

The natural environment has always been an important topic in South Asian thought and discourse. It was integral to classical Hindu cosmology (Bilimoria 1998): the idea of human personhood encompassed a humoral integration with the environment in Ayurveda; and many classical texts regarded the arts of clearing the land and draining the body as two aspects of the same enterprise—of managing the interactions between various fluids and humors (Zimmermann 1988). By the Mauryan era (322 to 185 BCE), the environment had become an important facet of the vocabulary of governance and statecraft; and with waves of influences, from the Greeks to Turks, Arabs, and Mongols, a rich tapestry of ideas about the environment and the habitable world emerged (Richards 2003).

In the early nineteenth century, the environment morphed from a philosophical concept to a more immediate and practical concern as large swathes of the Indian subcontinent witnessed rapid deforestation due to a growing demand for timber, the rise of corrupt contractors, an economic ideology based on laissez-faire, and a utilitarian outlook that valued revenue yielding arable land over those that were forested (Ribbentrop 1990, Tucker 1982, 1983). There were, however, some in the colonial administration—amateur naturalists in the medical, civil, and military services exposed to the international literature on the deleterious effects of deforestation—who saw deforestation as wasteful, and attempted to change resource-use policies (Grove 1996, Rajan 2006). During the middle of the nineteenth century, they built a powerful case for a new paradigm for efficient forest management. They particularly argued for the adoption of the Continental European forestry system in British India, and were eventually successful in their campaign. During the last quarter of the century, such a system was put in place by Prussian directors-general and a cadre of British officers trained initially in France and Germany (Rajan 2006). In the ensuing decades, revenue yields from timber products increased, but at a social cost: in order to sequester timber and other valuable forest products for the state—a process that benefited a new local elite comprised of developers and contractors—local communities that had enjoyed traditional usufruct rights were denied access to forests, just as their counterparts had been in Europe less than a century ago (Guha 1989; Prasad 2004).

Independence in 1947 did not change this dynamic; it only served to exacerbate the social tensions built during the colonial era—with the result that protests against forest policies intensified in the postcolonial period (Guha 2001). Crucially, in the 1970s and 1980s, these protests were joined by urban social and intellectual movements that among other things reinvented forestry; new nature–society hybrids, such as Joint Forest Management, emerged (Khare 2000). This period also saw intensification of policies to promote wildlife conservation, building on late colonial responses to near-extinction consequent to rampant hunting by expatriate and local elites. Old conservation schemes were expanded and new initiatives such as Project Tiger launched (Rangarajan 2001). However, these programmess have consistently faced many threats, such as illegal poaching, expanding populations, poor planning and execution, and the emergence, since the 1990s, of the economic governance ideology of liberalism that has accepted reckless habitat destruction as a price for development.

Another environmental legacy of British colonialism was agricultural intensification and an emphasis on cash crops and a mandate to increase yield from croplands, which, in turn, resulted in investments in water infrastructures. Existing irrigation systems were bolstered and expanded, and in some areas, such as Punjab, new networks were built (Whitcombe 1972). These canals meant that Punjab enjoyed a surplus when other provinces experienced an agricultural crisis. According to some estimates, per-capita output of crops increased by nearly 45 per cent between 1891 and 1921 (Charlesworth 1982: 26). The system, however, brought with it a wide range of social problems. It exacerbated economic inequities by privileging those who could afford the service payments—water rates for the use of canals—and engendered widespread corruption. The canal system also engendered a number of ecological problems. Foremost amongst these is the issue of salinity—a consequence of waterlogging. Many areas of Punjab, known for their well-watered soils, are today saline deserts, with alkaline and unproductive lands (Whitcombe 1972; Gilmartin 1994). The revenue success of the Punjab canal system, however, encouraged colonial planners and public works departments to attempt similar initiatives in peninsular India. While the economic benefits of these initiatives have been debated, given the challenges posed by the seasonal and rain-fed nature of peninsular rivers, the packages that accompanied irrigation schemes in the peninsula resulted in the rise of new agrarian classes that have dominated the political landscape for more than a century, while impoverishing others (Mosse 2003). More recently, the irrigation landscape has been transformed by the emergence of tube wells which have devastated water tables and disrupted agrarian political economies (Dubash 2002).

The political–ecological consequences of cash crop oriented agricultural policies continued to plague the postcolonial era. The dynamic consisted of: (a) diversion of water to cash crops; (b) cycles of consolidation of political power amongst some communities with the concomitant impoverishment of others; (c) persistent water scarcity; and (d) ecological damage due to water logging and salinity. To these, a fifth issue—dams—emerged after Independence, and has since dogged Indian environmental politics. Heeding prime minister Nehru's (1889–1964) slogan that dams were the temples of modern India, successive governments embarked upon a dam-building spree. While dams did enable irrigation and power generation in a nation that was both water and energy deficient, the political economies that dictated the control of water meant that the colonial dynamic described above continued, and often exacerbated economic inequalities. The dams of the postcolonial era also resulted in a great degree of ecological loss, and contributed staggeringly to the rise in the numbers of internally displaced persons (D'Souza 2006; Khagram 2004). The World Bank, for example, estimates that although large dams constitute only 26.6 per cent of the total Bank-funded projects causing displacement, the resulting displacement makes up 63.8 per cent of the total number of people displaced. It is also noteworthy that, according to Government of India figures, less than a quarter of the estimated 40 million people displaced by large dams during the past 60 years have been resettled (Cernea 1999).

Environmental politics in postcolonial India were largely about natural resources until 1984, when another important, but relatively dormant set of issues, dramatically burst onto the scene. On the night of 2–3 December 1984, an explosion of gas tanks storing methyl isocyanate at the Union Carbide India Limited (UCIL) pesticide plant in Bhopal instantly killed between 2,259 and 3,787 people, and maimed about half a million others and their progeny. The Bhopal Gas Disaster, as it is known, resulted in a soul-searching review of the costs and benefits of the Green Revolution and, in particular, to the threats to ecosystems and human health posed by pesticides and insecticides. The wider debate about Bhopal also raised the problem of what has been called the 'treadmill effect', wherein Green Revolution crops demand the application of progressively more chemical inputs, causing not only pollution, but also rural indebtedness (Weir 1987). Yet another issue raised by Bhopal was the adequacy of governance structures to cope with complex, multifaceted problems such as technological disasters. The Indian state, at both the central and state levels, failed first to put into place a regulatory regime that might have prevented the accident. In the aftermath of the disaster, it also failed to respond adequately. The immediate response, when thousands of people had to be evacuated, was poor, as was the longer-term approach to rehabilitation. The state bureaucracy was also unable to troubleshoot and adapt, so that what began as an acute disaster cascaded in a continuing catastrophe (Rajan 2002).

Bhopal also raised another fundamental question—about accountability. This issue is especially relevant today when national economic policies emphasize growth. At Union Carbide's factory in Bhopal, chronic lax maintenance and poor employee training resulted in a plant that was constantly plagued by accidents and mishaps, and at the time of the accident in December 1984, less than half of the original operators and supervisory staff remained in service on site, in part due to low staff morale (Chouhan 1994). The catastrophic disaster did not, however, result in any change in corporate culture. The company hired top public relations firms, lobbied governments, and embarked upon strong divestment tactics culminating in the sale to Dow Chemicals, while failing to adequately address the issue of rehabilitation (Rajan 1999). From the perspective of the survivors in Bhopal, the company simply got off scot-free. Significantly, the issue of the accountability for the management of companies was the crucial element in a landmark case in the Indian Supreme Court a year after the Bhopal incident, and the court, in its ruling, deemed the top management of a corporation criminally liable in the case of toxic industrial accidents (Bhagwati 1986). However, the track record of accountability since then has not been particularly impressive.

The environmental problem in India is, without doubt, more than forestry, irrigation, and Bhopal. The list of issues is long, and includes, among other things: population; chronic air and water pollution; the prospect of nuclear meltdown; genetically modified organisms (GMO)–related risks to ecosystems and human health; climate change; energy; and mining. However, the three issues discussed illustrate a very basic theme that defines the locus of environmental politics in India. Unlike Europe, North America, or Australia, where the topic of 'the environment' has fundamentally been about protecting nature from the ravages of humanity, in India the environment represents a crucial vector that addresses the very survival of peoples and communities. For that reason, the Indian environmental debate, ultimately, is about justice, fairness, and the viability of human life.

Further reading: Charlesworth 1982; Eckerman 2005; Groove 1996; Prasad 2004; Rajan 1999, 2002.

—RAVI RAJAN, *Department of Environmental Studies,*
University of California, Santa Cruz

— ••• —

Family Planning/Population Control

F amily Planning refers to the notion that people decide when and how many children they wish to have, while Population Control refers to planning the size of a population, usually undertaken by governments and other institutions, although the boundaries are often blurred. Guiding these notions are ideas about poverty, race, gender, and so on. Today, they are central to discussions about the environment, global warming, and immigration.

The idea that Indian poverty was due to overpopulation is an old one, first expressed by Abbé Dubois (1765–1848) around 1799 when working as a missionary in southern India. Surveying the destruction of the Indian weaving industry due to goods from Lancashire, he noted 'of these causes of misery, the chief one is the rapid increase of population' (Dubois 1906: 93). This became 'common sense' for colonial administrators taught by Thomas Robert Malthus (1766–1834) at Haileybury College, before they set sail to India. Although Malthus does not use the word 'overpopulation', the idea is named after his famous 1798 publication, *An Essay on the Principle of Population*. By 1891 in England 'overpopulation' was commonplace enough to enter into Robert Louis Stevenson's (1850–94) novel *In the South Seas*.

A product of Haileybury College, Sir Richard Strachey (1817–1908), heading the Famine Commission, noting the devastation of the famines of 1877, observed 'the statistical returns made certain what has long been suspected, that starvation and distress greatly check the fecundity of the population' (GOI 1880: 28). In 1877, at her trial in London for publishing Charles Knowlton's book on birth control in London, Annie Besant (1847–1933), then a British socialist, gave a call for population control arguing that famines 'were caused entirely by overpopulation' (Connelly 2008: 19). The Census of India (1911) argued that famines could indeed do good: '[...] the high mortality of the two extremes of life and among the weaker members of society left a population purged of its weaker elements and with constitution improved both physically and morally by the trials it has gone through' (GOI 1911: 28). The first Census to provide data on population growth, namely that of 1931, noted 'grave increase in the population of this country [...] a cause for alarm' (GOI 1933: 29).

Late in the nineteenth century, echoing what was taking place in England, Neo-Malthusian Leagues had been founded in Madras, Bombay, and Pune to enhance the use of contraception (Hodges 2008). In 1916, Wattal published *The Population Problem in India: A Census Study*, arguing that the only remedy for 'poverty and other evil effects of the principle of population' was controlling births and marriages (Wattal, cited in Ahluwalia 2008: 33). Eugenic ideas were influential for instance in the 'Sub-Committee on Population' of the *National Planning Committee* which observed, 'Man, who has come to the stage of development where he is anxious to breed carefully such species of the lower animals as dogs or horses to obtain very specific qualities [...] has not realized the possibilities of careful scientific breeding of the human race' (NPC 1948a: 7). The 'Sub-Committee on Women's Role in Planned Economy' argued that 'the state should follow a eugenic programme to make the race physically and mentally healthy', suggesting sterilization of the unfit and diseased (NPC 1948b:114). In the 'Sub-Committee on Health', a strong case was made, on the grounds of women's health, to include birth control in maternity and child health services to be provided by the state (NPC 1948c). The 'Bhore Committee' (GOI 1946), which set the blueprint for the evolution of health services in India, made the argument for family planning on three grounds: for the well-being of the national economy, eugenics, and women's health. The adoption of family planning was, therefore, seen as being in the interests of the nation, linking the family and the nation in a teleology of progress.

By the end of the Second World War eugenics had become discredited, associated as it was with the Holocaust. But population control arrived as a new global project in this period, driven by international non-governmental organizations (NGOs) such as the Ford and Rockefeller Foundations. It was in the Cold War conditions of the early sixties, with the consolidation of the global population control movement, that population control took wing, moving, in India, from the clinic approach, to the extension education approach, to the IUCD (intra-uterine contraceptive device) approach, to male sterilization and then to female sterilization (Rao 2004). Population control reached its apotheosis in the 'Emergency' period of 1975–7 when thousands of (mostly) men and women were forcibly sterilized, leading to the official deaths of 1,776 men. This proved to be politically damaging and attention now turned to the sterilization of women. The Indian family planning programme was now called the Family Welfare Programme (Rao 2004).

By the late nineteen eighties, international agencies like the World Bank were admitting that population control as a solution to the problem of poverty had been a failure. There are indeed profound problems with the underlying arguments. By focusing on numbers, what population control did not do was to investigate who was consuming resources. It was increasingly being realized that there was a need to move away from a demographic approach to the issue of poverty and that the new paradigm had to respect reproductive rights (International Conference on Population and Development [ICPD] 1995).

Further reading: Ahluwalia 2008; Connelly 2008; Hodges 2008; Rao 2004.

—MOHAN RAO, *Professor, Centre of Social Medicine and Community Health, Jawaharlal Nehru University, New Delhi*

— .•. —

Feminism

F eminism in India emerged and developed as an inextricable part of India's colonially mediated modernity. This is not to argue that India was innocent of ideas concerning women's subjugation prior to the advent of the British. Research on early Indian history (Tharu and Lalitha 1993) shows that Indian women did experience 'feminist' urges, and importantly also articulated both their sense of exclusion and denial as well as their desire for freedom and fulfilment. However, the specificity of feminism, as a vision that rests on the idea of universal and equal citizen rights (irrespective of gender and creed, to be ensured by the state), is certainly located in a modern context. Likewise, the British nineteenth-century idea of the need to educate women for national progress, which left a deep imprint on Indian feminism, also presents a historically specific, modern formulation.

Yet modernity ushered in by colonial rule was premised on—and operated within—structures that were deeply unequal and unjust, while the discourse of modernity spoke a language of freedom and equality, of progress and the inalienable right of people to self-rule. It is within this inherent contradictoriness and ambiguity of colonial modernity that feminism emerged and took shape in modern India (Chaudhuri 2011).

Indians, though aspiring to a western modernity, simultaneously wanted to mark themselves off as distinct, different from, and even superior to the West. Indian women desired to rid themselves of the oppressive structures of tradition but, at the same time, wished to reaffirm the ancientness and wisdom of that same tradition. Some have, thus, argued that the woman question, such as exemplified by *sati* in nineteenth century India, was simply an incidental site to debate questions of tradition and culture, nation, and modernity (Mani 1989). Moreover, attaining India's freedom from colonialism was seen as a necessary prelude to the freedom of women. Hence, given the close interface between feminism and western colonialism, many Indian women in both the women's and national movements disavowed being feminist (Chaudhuri 2011).

This disavowal may be read as a denial of feminist visions or as bowing to patriarchal and orthodox critiques. But it is perhaps more productive to read it as a search for a different language in which the cultural specificities of Indian feminist desires could be articulated at a time when the discourse of 'difference' was both absent and illegitimate in the dominant public sphere. This disowning can be understood as a quest for 'authentic indigenous' cultural grounds for feminism, a desire which persists in a twenty-first century still marked by global inequalities and western aggression. Contending power struggles between the 'western' and 'non-western' hemispheres have too often been fought over questions of the rights of women and the rights of culture. The 'western perspective' of women as 'nature' and men as 'culture' provides a different counterpoint to Indian women as emblems of culture (Chaudhuri 1995).

The above narrative is an important albeit a partial story of feminism in India. For western colonialism was not the only unequal structure that marked Indian society. Indian society itself was deeply unequal, defined by caste and class. The rise of Dalit feminism in the last decades of the twentieth century has drawn attention to the fact that Dalit women speak 'differently' and that an 'upper-caste' women's movement has erased their struggles from the story of the nation (Rege 2006).

It is argued that the nationalist framework—and the cultural making of the nation—shaped by the dominant upper castes and Hindu middle classes, has subsumed the woman question (Geetha 2004). In other words, questions of community and women's rights, of nationalism, secularism, and the state, did not crop up as a posterior add-on to the woman question; they were a bone of contention from the nineteenth century. For instance, it was debated whether *purdah* (lit. 'curtain', veil worn by women, also 'female segregation', for further discussion, cf. Chaudhuri 2011) was a Hindu or Muslim practice. Significantly, members of both communities blamed its origins on the other community, thereby claiming the right of 'their' women to be free from *purdah*. Even in the Constituent Assembly, which first met in 1946, it was debated whether religious rights would clash with women's rights (Chaudhuri 2011). This past history of Indian feminism is symptomatically illustrative of the perspective of a twenty-first century West itself, often caught between contending claims of multiculturalism, the concept of the state bound to secular visions, and notions of the individual rights of citizens (Asad 2006; Chaudhuri 2012).

This past remains part of Indian feminism's present. A bill proposing to reserve 33 per cent of the seats in the Indian parliament for women failed to be ratified in 2010 because leaders of a new and assertive middle class constituted by middle-caste communities saw this as a ploy of upper castes to retain hegemony over the state and Indian public life (Teltumbde 2010). Although women's organizations firmly backed the proposed measure, its realization seems to be a retreating possibility. Feminism is thus caught in the crossfire of hegemonic struggles even as they are fought in a language of social justice.

Feminism in twenty-first century India is therefore challenged by two forces: first, from a patriarchy that defends honour killing on grounds of cultural rights; second, from a neoliberal vision, which deifies the economy and demonizes collective and emancipative politics. Often both sets of views emerge from the same factions. In cases such as honour killings, the state is asked to follow the writ of patriarchally controlled communities (Chowdhry 2007). At other times, it is asked to shun social welfare measures for poor women and instead to facilitate financial institutions to deal directly with women as creditors (John 2004). The language of rights of women as citizens and workers to which the state must respond is replaced by the language of the market which is accountable to none other than the imperatives of profit maximization. Thus, the ongoing fight of 'indigenous' women to protect their livelihoods—against global mining appropriations—can be viewed as an impediment to development. If politics earlier sought to tame markets, proponents of this new form of global capitalism now use markets to tame politics. Images of individuated women, for whom an unbridled market provides endless opportunities, feed a dominant public discourse that celebrates the idea of an unfettered self—unfettered by the nation or family, community or state, or by the ideology of feminism itself (Chaudhuri 2010). Female foeticide in such climes can be defended on the grounds of individual choice. In contrast, dominant real politics witness patriarchal assertions, be they overtly defending honour killing, concertedly opposing the Women's Reservation Bill, or favouring lenient handling for those accused of rape. Feminist opposition persists even as challenges mount and become more complex and insidious.

Further reading: Chaudhuri 2004, 2010, 2011; Rege 2006; Sangari and Vaid 1989; Teltumbde 2010; Tharu and Lalita 1991, 1993.

—MAITRAYEE CHAUDHURI, *Professor, Centre for the Study of Social Systems, School of Social Sciences, Jawaharlal Nehru University, New Delhi*

— ·•· —

Freedom

India achieved freedom at midnight on 14–15 August 1947. As Jawaharlal Nehru (1889–1964) famously put it, when the world was asleep, India woke up to life and freedom. This meant the end of nearly two hundred years of British rule, for which the Indian National Congress and various other political groups had been fighting for about half a century. So naturally there was euphoria on the streets of the capital, New Delhi, as well as in the provinces. The celebrations started at 11 p.m. on 14 August when the Constituent Assembly met under the chairmanship of Rajendra Prasad (1884–1963), and Nehru delivered his emotionally charged 'Tryst with Destiny' speech, followed by the presentation of the emblems of the new nation—the flag and the anthem. The Constituent Assembly had accepted the new flag, which had been the Congress flag since 1930, with a minor change—the *charkha* ('spinning wheel') being replaced by the *chakra* ('wheel of life'). The nation, as Nehru argued, could now stand under the same flag with which they had fought against foreign rule. As for the anthem, the Constituent Assembly preferred Rabindranath Tagore's (1861–1941) *Jana-gana-mana* over the familiar *Bande mataram*, which offended the Muslims. Thus, at the moment of arrival the founding fathers carefully chose the emblems of the new nation which they expected to be secular and democratic, as well as closely associated with the legacy of the Congress (Bandyopadhyay 2009; Tan and Kudaisya 2000).

On the streets people were ecstatic that night and the following day. More than a million came to watch the evening parade at Kingsway, where the national flag was hoisted and the government buildings were illuminated. A million marched on the streets of Bombay that morning and some of them even took possession of the Secretariat Building. In Calcutta, about 200,000 people broke the police cordon and rushed into the Governor House and later the Assembly House, in a bid to reclaim what was once the most sacred space of the Raj. Numerous functions were held all over the country, where the national flag was unfurled, the national anthem sung, and patriotic speeches delivered (Bandyopadhyay 2009; Tan and Kudaisya 2000).

But not everyone was in a mood to rejoice, as freedom also arrived with the pain of Partition. Mohandas Karamchand Gandhi (1869–1948), then in Calcutta trying to stop communal riots, spent the day in prayer as an act of penance. The Hindu Mahasabha (a Hindu nationalist organization founded in 1915) did not participate in the celebrations as a protest against Partition. The Muslim League (founded in 1906) decided to join, but Muslims being a minority—like their Hindu counterparts in Pakistan—lived in a state of anxiety about an uncertain future.

Freedom at the moment of arrival thus evoked mixed emotions, and Partition was not the only cause for concern. The idea of freedom in

India had developed as a result of a productive encounter with colonial modernity that transformed the older idea of *mukti* ('an abstract spiritual notion of emancipation in the other world') into more worldly concerns for individual freedom of choice, on the one hand, and collective freedom, on the other. However, as the freedom struggle progressed, the issue of individual freedom came to be subordinated by the concept of collective freedom; and of all collective identities, the nation took precedence over others, like class, caste, or gender (Kaviraj 2002).

However, there was also tension in the ways national freedom was being conceptualized by the myriad groups of people who constituted the grand nationalist coalition and wanted to see the end of British rule. While some saw in the attainment of political sovereignty for the nation state the immediate fulfilment of the freedom struggle's goal, others preferred to expand the meaning of freedom to incorporate also the notions of economic and social freedom for the people. As Nehru reminded his countrymen in his opening speech, in 1947 the immediate goal of political freedom had been achieved, but the greater challenge was to ensure for every citizen the freedom from poverty, ignorance, disease, and inequality. And it was this challenge that caused anxiety as there was no agreement yet on how to overcome it.

Hence, freedom in 1947 did not mean a clean break with the colonial past. In the initial years, continuities could be seen in the institutional structure, in the rituals and pageantry of the state, and even in the modes of governance. Gandhi had warned in *Hind Swaraj* (1909) that India might end up with English rule without the Englishmen. The process of decolonization did not involve any complete reversal of the colonial past. Freedom was not a moment of rupture, but symbolized a process of transference and adaptation—a process of hybridization through which the meanings of freedom would be expanded exponentially.

Further reading: Bandyopadhyay 2009; Chakrabarty 2007; Kaviraj 2002; Masselos 1990; Tan and Kudaisya 2000.

—SEKHAR BANDYOPADHYAY, *Professor of Asian History,*
Victoria University of Wellington

— ••• —

Gandhian

G andhian is used either as an adjective, meaning a set of actions or life choices that conform to the teaching of Mohandas Karamchand Gandhi (1869–1948), or as a noun to describe a person who lives and/or acts in conformity to such an agenda. The terms 'Gandhism'/'Gandhist' are also used, with similar connotations. The term began to be used widely from around 1920, when Gandhi had just asserted his leadership of the Indian nationalist movement, when he exhorted the people of India to follow his methods and way of life (*Daily Telegraph*, 07.03.1921, cited in art. 'Gandhian', *Oxford English Dictionary* [*OED*] 2000). Those who responded to this plea in a wholehearted manner were thenceforth known as Gandhians. The term continued to be widely applied after Gandhi's death, both in and outside India, and is still in use to this day. It may be used in a pejorative sense by those of different ideological persuasion, such as modernizers, Marxists, Ambedkarites, or Hindu nationalists associated with the Rashtriya Swyamsevak Sangh (RSS) (National Patriotic Association).

Some of the key precepts adhered to by Gandhians are those of *satyagraha*, ahimsa, *swadeshi*, *swaraj*, and *sarvodaya*. 'Satyagraha' is a word coined by Gandhi in 1906, denoting a form of non-violent resistance that incorporates a dialogic reaching out to an opponent in a non-hating manner (Hardiman 2003: 51–4). It is an amalgamation of two Sanskrit words, *satya* ('truth') and *agraha* ('taking, seizing, holding'), the implication being that one seizes hold of the truth and impresses it on one's opponent through the sheer strength of one's convictions. Ahimsa, or non-violence, is core to *satyagraha*. In ancient texts such as the *Kapisthala Katha Samhita* of 1000–800 BCE, ahimsa meant desisting from animal sacrifices and, by extension—as seen in later texts such as the *Chandogya Upanishad* of 800–700 BCE—the harming of animals in general. Gandhi gave the term a new political dimension—meaning a refusal to cause any physical harm to political opponents. By translating ahimsa into English as 'nonviolence', Gandhi in 1920 created a new word in the English language (*OED* 2000, art. 'ahimsa', cited in Nehru's autobiography [1936, xii, 83]).

Swadeshi and *swaraj* were not terms coined by Gandhi, being key concepts in the Swadeshi Movement in Bengal of 1905–8, and dating back some years before this (Sarkar 1973). *Swaraj* basically meant 'self-rule', being what Indian nationalists demanded for the Indian people and *swadeshi* formerly meant 'self-production', and involved the revival of manufactures destroyed through colonial rule and the industrial revolution, as well as the start of new modern industries controlled and run by Indians, along with a boycott of foreign goods. Gandhi created his own original understanding of these concepts in his seminal work *Hind Swaraj* ('Indian Self-Rule'), published in 1909. Therein, he rejected attempts to implement *swaraj* and *swadeshi*, while still holding on to institutions and concepts inimical and out of harmony with the values and culture of the Indian people. He envisaged an India that was almost entirely self-sufficient, with production being carried out as much as possible at the village level through handicraft manufacture. In the early 1920s, he popularized hand-spinning on the *charka* to further this agenda, and—for his followers—this, along with the wearing of the hand-woven cloth called *khadi*, became one of the core ways in which they could demonstrate a Gandhian identity (Tarlo 1996). Sarvodaya was a word that summed up Gandhi's overall social programme. He coined the word in 1908 as a title for his Gujarati translation of John Ruskin's *Unto This Last*. It was a compound of the Sanskrit *sarva* ('all') and *udaya* ('uplift'), and meant 'the uplift of all'. In his autobiography, Gandhi defined it as 'the welfare of all' (Gandhi 1969).

Although Gandhians were involved typically in the nationalist movement against British rule in the pre-Independence period, they were also active in what was known as the 'constructive programme' (Hardiman 2003: 77–81). This involved developing alternative institutions that were believed to be more in harmony with the culture and needs of the Indian people, and which would form a model for post-Independence institutions and ways of being. Gandhian education based on the principle of *nai talim* ('basic education' which exemplified a lack of separation between intellectual knowledge and manual work) was one very important form of this, with teaching in vernacular languages and with a strong emphasis on practical manual work alongside academic learning. Nationalist schools and universities with a strong Gandhian identity were established from 1921 onwards to further this agenda. The constructive programme also involved social work, with Gandhians going to live in villages and starting *ashrams* that focused on education, sanitation, wholesome vegetarian diet, abstinence from alcohol, promotion of handicrafts and local self-reliance with appropriate technology, and the provision of help during emergencies such as natural disasters. They conducted social surveys to reveal the causes of poverty in particular areas, and provided leadership in localized campaigns of protest on issues such as excessive taxation and oppression by local officials. They fought discriminatory practices, particularly against Harijans (lit. 'God's people', 'untouchables'), and sought to promote harmony between religious groups. Gandhians of this sort were expected to live according to the ethos of *aparigraha* ('non-possessiveness'). Gandhi also promoted new forms of industrial relations, in which workers would organize themselves in unions (*majoor mahajan*) led by dedicated Gandhians to demand decent wages and living conditions, and in which businessmen would run their industries in a spirit of 'trusteeship' and *apigraha*. In all this, the emphasis was on mediation between capitalists and workers, with Gandhians trusted by both parties acting as mediators, in place of the class confrontation favoured by communists (Hardiman 2003: 81–5).

After Indian Independence in 1947 and Gandhi's assassination in 1948, some prominent Gandhians served as ministers in the central and state governments. Morarji Desai (1896–1995), who served as prime minister from 1977 to 1979, was a notable example. Gandhian policies were implemented, with varying degrees of success and longevity. Nonetheless, as the ruling Congress Party, led initially by Jawaharlal Nehru (1889–1964), favoured large-scale industrial development over and above Gandhian-style small-scale projects, the general economic policy thrust was away from Gandhian models (yet Ramachandra Guha [2003:2–4] does refer to Gandhian influence on Nehruvian politics, for example, inclusive patriotism, commitment to dialogue and democracy, decency and transparency in public life). This has continued to be the case to this day. Many Gandhians preferred to work outside formal politics, seeking to influence policy through what has been described as a 'saintly' political idiom (Morris-Jones 1962). Foremost in this respect in the immediate post-Independence period was Vinoba Bhave (1895–1982). He had worked largely within the constructive programme before 1947, and after Gandhi's death in 1948 he founded the Sarvodaya Samaj (Association for the Welfare of All) (Ostergaard and Currell 1971). Bhave sought to counter the communists, who had been gaining considerable support in many rural areas, by providing an alternative and more peaceful Gandhian model for land reform. This involved persuading landlords to transfer ownership of parts of their land to the poor and landless on a voluntary basis. This was known as *bhoodan*, from *bhu* ('earth') and *dan* ('gift'), and thus 'the gift of land'. Bhave launched his Bhoodan Movement in 1951, touring central and northern India on foot, holding meetings to persuade landlords to donate land. He was joined in this in 1953 by Jayaprakash Narayan (1902–79), a leading radical socialist and nationalist hero who, after an earlier scepticism, had embraced Gandhian philosophy after witnessing the horrors of Partition in 1947. He focused on his home state of Bihar. Bhave and Narayan then extended the movement into what they termed *gramdan* ('gift of a village'), in which ownership was held by the village community as a whole, which then governed itself. Although the Bhoodan and Gramdan Movements achieved considerable success on paper in the 1950s, they flagged thereafter, and much of the pledged land was not in practice handed over. Bhave refused to apply pressure through *satyagraha* on those who broke their pledges, arguing that there was no need for it in independent India. This quietist approach led to a growing divide between the conservatives, led by Bhave, and the radicals, led by Narayan and other Gandhian socialists such as Rammanohar Lohia (1910–67) (Ostergaard 1985).

In 1957, Bhave founded another Gandhian institution called the Shanti Sena ('peace army') that sought to oppose religious divides and communal hatred (Weber 2009: 60–3). Gandhi had first proposed such a body just before his assassination, as a reaction to the events surrounding Partition. People enrolled themselves as Shanti Sainiks ('peace workers') who tried to nip communal situations in the bud before they could escalate. When riots broke out, they sought to dampen emotions, counter rumours, and act as mediators between the two sides. The very active secretary of this organization was Narayan Desai (b. 1924), the son of Gandhi's secretary, Mahadev Desai (1892–1943). It proved extremely effective in a number of cases in the 1960s and early 1970s, but declined thereafter, even though the need for such an organization if anything increased during the period of militant aggression by the Hindu Right against Muslims in the 1990s and early 2000s. With the honourable exception of Desai, most Gandhians proved remarkably quiescent at that time.

A notable offshoot of the Sarvodaya Movement was the Chipko Movement that started in 1972 in what was then the Uttaranchal division of Uttar Pradesh. This was directed against the rampant cutting of trees in the Himalayan foothills by timber contractors. It involved people 'hanging on to' (*chipko*) or hugging trees to prevent them being felled. Although the leaders, such as Sunderlal Bahuguna (b. 1927), were *sarvodaya* workers, local people, and especially village women, took the initiative in the actual protests. The movement achieved many of its objectives by 1980, becoming an iconic event for the rapidly growing environmental movement of that time at a global level (Weber 1988).

Further reading: Gandhi 1909, 1969; Hardiman 2003; Morris-Jones 1962; Sarkar 1973, Weber 2006.

—DAVID HARDIMAN, *Emeritus Professor, Department of History, University of Warwick*

— •◦• —

Girangaon

Gaon is a common word for 'village' in most of India and *giran* or *girni* is the Marathi word for a mill—not just for textiles, but also for flour, jute, and so on. Taken together, Girangaon, or village of mills refers to the 600-odd acres of land at the centre of Mumbai's island city, that is, the southern peninsula. Consisting mainly of cotton textile mills, and mill tenements, Girangaon was once the heart of Mumbai's social and cultural ethos. In 1980, there were still 165,000 workers on the payrolls of the textile mills in Mumbai (Bakshi 1986: 36).

Cotton textile mills started up in the middle of the nineteenth century in Mumbai. Workers lived in tenements called *chawls*, which are still largely the prevalent form of housing, not just for the poor but even a part of the middle class in the island city. Mumbai's mill workers played a vanguard role in the history of the Indian working class. In 1908, Mumbai's textile workers went on a spontaneous six-day strike against the British government's sentencing of freedom fighter Bal Gangadhar Tilak (1856–1920) to six years in prison (Karnik 1967). The first trade union in India was called Bombay Millhands Association, started by a liberal social reformer N.M. Lokhande (1848–97) in the 1880s (Kadam 1995). It is ironical that the first Indian trade union was started by an anti-caste social reformer, since trade unions and the Left have traditionally emphasized class more than caste. Lokhande was a follower of the revolutionary social reformer Jyotiba Phule (1827–90), whose Satyashodak anti-caste movement included the class and gender dimension of social discrimination. In 1928, the Communist Party of India (CPI) established the Girni Kamgar Union (GKU) and dominated Girangaon, for 41 years, not only as a trade union in the mills but also as a formidable electoral force in the neighbourhoods. This was demolished by the Marathi chauvinist Shiv Sena in the 1960s. The Shiv Sena used a combination of tactics: a mass upsurge for employment of locals, violence, and chauvinist anti-communist propaganda in the neighbourhoods to uproot the communists and establish a base in Girangaon (Menon 2004).

The Shiv Sena did not enjoy the support of the workers inside the mills for long, although in the neighbourhoods they continued to have a significant base. In 1982, the maverick trade union leader Datta Samant was approached by the textile workers themselves to lead them in what became the longest workers' strike in world history, which started on 18 January 1982 and continued for a year, until it was broken by a determined Congress government led by Indira Gandhi (1917–84) (Wersch 1992).

The textile strike ended in a humiliating defeat for the workers and spelt the beginning of the end for the textile industry, the workers, and for the 'village' called Girangaon. The Indian textile sector was going through a crisis of its own, and mills were closing all over the country due to textile 'sickness'. It was only in 1990 that workers belonging to closed mills lit another spark in Girangaon with a fight for their jobs. Although the mills did not stay open, they did get an assurance of alternative employment and workers' rights to a part of mill land. The Maharashtra state government agreed to build houses for mill workers on a percentage of the mill lands, and to find other land outside as well, in order to provide houses for all the workers (Menon 2012). A small portion was also reserved for the city, as open spaces.

In land-starved Mumbai, Girangaon has turned into attractive real estate. Despite the attempts of urban planners and activists in the city, the development of mill lands was not subjected to regulations and planning that could have provided the city with much-needed public spaces or social housing (D'Monte 2002). Girangaon today is a medley of high-rise apartments, office blocks, high-end designer stores and malls, and hotels, in the midst of which the mill chimneys now look incongruous and forlorn.

Further reading: Kadam 1995; Menon 2004; Wersch 1992.

—MEENA R. MENON, *Consultant, Actionaid India, Delhi*

— ••• —

Goonda

The word *goonda* ('ruffian') surfacing from the turn of the early twentieth century in Kolkata and elsewhere was inflected with anxieties about the transformations overtaking Indian cities, in particular about the reconstitution of the urban poor as a constituency for legal and illegal forms of political and economic entrepreneurship. The *goonda* was cast as the figure through whose agency the rural migrant, instead of finding his proper place in the city as a docile coolie, might be positioned as a muscleman for a gambling den, a cocaine dealer, a factory owner, or a merchant, or make up the aggressive fringe of a picket line or a procession. The *goonda* of popular conception belonged to the world of the urban plebeian but he was not crushed by its necessities and he never seemed to be safely immobilized within it (Singha 2014). In turbulent post-war India, municipal councillors and legislators sought to capture control of localities with the help of those who had influence with the urban poor, while circumscribing simultaneously that conceptual and institutional space which would allow these figures to emerge as competitors in the field of legitimate politics.

The paperwork and protocols of colonial and postcolonial 'preventive' policing, always perched at the border of legality, lent a seeming concreteness to *goondas* and others suspected of habitual criminality by bringing them onto surveillance lists and criminal 'history-sheets'. This was a process which added to the menace of such figures, for it seemed to position them as players in another arena of 'dangerousness', that of police and executive illegality (Singha 2014). The word *goonda* entered the legal realm with the Bengal Act 1 of 1923 which set out a semi-judicial procedure for externing *goondas* from the city or province to disrupt their networks. Such provincial statutes deployed clusters of synonyms for the *goonda* rather than clear legal definitions so they could be brought into operation when any crisis of order seemed to overtake a city; the Bengal Goonda Act stated that: 'Goonda includes hooligan or other rough'; the United Provinces Goondas Act (Act 1 of 1932) added: 'hooligan, bully, rogue or badmaash'.

The insertion of 'hooligan' is an index of the transnational circulation of images about unruly plebeian behaviour in cities, surfacing in England in the 1890s, then in St Petersburg in the early twentieth century. Its juxtaposition with *badmaash*, a Hindustani word for 'rascal', shows that Goonda Acts had a lineage in the so-called *badmaashi* or 'bad-livelihood' sections of the Criminal Procedure Code which permitted bad livelihood to be deduced from general repute. However, the Goonda Act went a step further in shedding the formalities of judicial process.

The word *goonda* also evokes images of transgressive masculinity, of the presumptuous plebeian or debauched youth exercising, by lechery and violence, control over the women of a locality. The entertainment industry in India has enthusiastically mined this narrative lode. Ironically, it has also been active in getting film and video piracy added to the transgressions for which someone can be hauled up as a *goonda* (see Tamil Nadu Amending Act 32 of 2004). Public criticism of *goonda* enactments focuses largely on laxity in applying them, or police misuse of them for political favour or vendetta, not on the arbitrariness of 'preventive' policing.

Further reading: Bhattacharya 2004; Dhareshwar and Srivatsan 1996; Kidambi 2007; Nandi 2010; Singha 2014.

—RADHIKA SINGHA, *Professor, Centre for Historical Studies, Jawaharlal Nehru University, New Delhi*

— .•. —

Green Revolution

The term 'Green Revolution' was originally coined by William S. Gaud (1907–77), USAID (United States Agency for International Development), at a lecture delivered to the Society for International Development in 1968 titled 'The Green Revolution: Accomplishments and Apprehensions'. This term popularly signifies the transformation of agriculture, specifically in the Third World, through substantial increases in yields of wheat, rice, and maize. This increase was brought about by a comprehensive package for agricultural modernization which comprised agricultural science–based technologies and large-scale economic planning.

In India, Dr M.S. Swaminathan (b. 1925) and his team were instrumental in launching the Green Revolution in the 1960s. This was a combination of high-yielding varieties (HYV), chemical fertilizers and pesticides, extensive irrigation, and complementary infrastructure like minimum support prices, food procurement, distribution, credit, marketing, and rural electrification. The implementation was done on a large scale due to a combination of high levels of public investment by the Indian government and technical support, primarily from the Rockefeller and Ford Foundations (Pearse 1980). However, the seeds of the Green Revolution were sown not in India, but in Mexico.

Dr Norman Borlaug (1914–2009), agronomist and Nobel laureate, is popularly referred to as the 'Father of the Green Revolution'. In 1943, Borlaug was stationed in Mexico and is credited with developing the disease-resistant, high-yielding, semi-dwarf wheat variety. This strain of research had its lineage in the works of an Italian plant breeder, Nazareno Strampelli (1866–1942), who had started the research as early as 1900 in Camerino (Salvi, Porfiri, and Ceccarelli 2013). Strampelli's work helped Italy achieve self-sufficiency in bread wheat in the early decades of the twentieth century. Borlaug's wheat variety and subsequent mechanization helped Mexico achieve high yields in the 1940s. The Rockefeller Foundation had started funding research as early as the 1940s in the Mexican Agricultural Program, and this became a pioneering example of technical assistance and scientific agriculture which was to become the bedrock of the Green Revolution in decades to come (Brinkmann 2009).

India was grappling with food insufficiency in the decade after Independence (1947). This situation continued until the early 1960s and, therefore, India had to rely largely on the United States' PL-480 Program for importing nearly ten million tonnes of wheat in the mid-1960s. Domestic production in India stood at about seven million tonnes at the time. Reliance on US foreign aid for crucial commodities had its own share of implications for the Government of India. It was a plethora of factors which lay behind the Indian government's hurry to attempt self-reliance in food production; foreign aid implications also had a role to play. The Intensive Agriculture District Programme was launched by the Government in collaboration with the Ford Foundation in 1961, but this programme did not yield the targeted results. Since the programme lacked wheat varieties that would respond favourably this lacuna was sought to be plugged through the High Yielding Varieties Programme launched in 1966 (Cleaver 1972). In 1962, Dr Swaminathan requested the Indian Agriculture Ministry to arrange for Dr Borlaug's visit to India in view of obtaining wheat materials possessing dwarfing genes. The request was conveyed to the Rockefeller Foundation which funded Dr Borlaug's work to arrange for the visit (Swaminathan 1993).

In 1966, the Indian team left for Mexico to purchase 18,000 tonnes of seeds. Dwarf wheat was introduced in 1966–7 and, in just one year, two million hectares were added for cultivation; productivity increased from between 7 and 8 to 11 quintals per hectare and there were spectacular increases in production from 5 million to 16 million tonnes (Swaminathan 1993). The then prime minister, Indira Gandhi (1917–84) released a 'Wheat Revolution' stamp in July 1968 hailing the success of the endeavour. India declared itself self-sufficient in cereal production by the early 1980s (Swaminathan 1993). The early successes of the Green Revolution led to the spread of this model to large parts of Asia, Latin America, and Africa.

However, the persistence of hunger in these very nations amidst claims of self-sufficiency do not augur well for the credentials of any revolution. The deliberate replacement of ecologically aligned traditional farming practices with intensive irrigation-centric and chemicalized ones have led to the depletion of water tables, loss of soil fertility, and a host of health problems in the long run. There has been a concurrent rise in the cost of cultivation resulting in the crippling pressure of indebtedness amongst farmers practising these techniques across developing countries.

Further reading: Cleaver 1972; Pearse 1980; Swaminathan 1993, Brinkmann 2009.

—KAUSTAV BANERJEE, *Assistant Professor, Centre for the Study of Discrimination and Exclusion, School of Social Sciences, Jawaharlal Nehru University, New Delhi*

— ·•· —

Hijra

Although frequently described as the 'third sex' of India, as 'neither man nor woman' (Nanda 1990), recent scholarship (Cohen 1995; Reddy 2005) has argued that *hijras* cannot be understood with reference to sex and gender alone, but construct themselves in terms of a multiplicity of differences including religion, region, kinship, and class. *Hijras* are typically phenotypic men (although a minority is born intersexed) who wear female clothing, grow their hair, and enact an exaggeratedly feminine performance. *Hijra* lifeworlds encompass a range of corporeal possibilities but tend to be characterized by hierarchies of authenticity, at the apex of which stand those who undergo complete excision of the penis and testicles. This operation—referred to as *nirvan*—is believed to liberate *hijras* from sexual desire, transforming them into vehicles of the goddess Bedhraj Mata, through whom they acquire the power to bless newborn children and newly wed couples with fertility (Reddy 2005: 57).

This apparently paradoxical belief accords with the trope of the erotic ascetic in Hindu mythology, symbolized most prominently in the figure of Shiva, whose *tapasya* ('asceticism') simultaneously endows him with creative potential (Nanda 1990: 29). The abundance of gender-ambiguous figures in Hindu mythology—Arjuna (as Brhannala) and Sikhandi in the *Mahabharata*, Vishnu incarnated as Mohini, Krishna in his adoption of female guise to slay the demon Araka, and the Ardhanarishvara ('the Lord who is half woman') form of Shiva, to give just a few examples—provides an important legitimating discourse for *hijra* ontology. Yet even as they draw on Hindu mythology, many *hijras* simultaneously identify as Muslims and observe a number of Muslim religious, sartorial, and dietary customs (Reddy 2005: 98–120).

One explanation reads this as the historical consequence of patronage by Muslim rulers, particularly in princely states like Hyderabad (Jaffrey 1996). Although third sex terms such as *kliba* (itself possessing a range of meanings including eunuch, sterile, impotent, castrated, transvestite), *pandaka* ('eunuch'), *tritiyaprakriti* ('third sex'), and *napumsaka* ('neuter gender') can be found in Sanskrit (Hindu) and Pali (Buddhist) texts dating back nearly 3,000 years, the wide range of meanings encompassed by these terms makes it difficult to interpret them as the historical forerunners of contemporary *hijras*. Explicit references to eunuchs in South Asia increase with the advent of Muslim rule in the eleventh and twelfth centuries, with eunuchs occupying important positions in royal courts. Under the British Raj (1857–1947), intimacy between men was coded in the idiom of sexuality and criminalized by section 377 of the Indian Penal Code; *hijras* were classified as a 'criminal caste' under the Criminal Tribes Act (1871), a situation that persisted till 'denotification' in 1952 (Narrain and Gupta 2011: xvi–xviii). In recent years, *hijras* have been at the forefront of sexual minority activism, as a result of which they have won significant concessions in so far as state recognition of their identity is concerned. The Aravani Welfare Board in Tamil Nadu represents one of the most complex instances of government intervention in the community's affairs, with the state offering ration cards, passports, and reserved seats in government-run educational institutions, with ambivalent consequences for *hijra* organization and self-assertion (Govindan and Vasudevan 2011).

Hijras earn their living principally in three ways: through traditional ritual roles of conferring fertility blessings (*badhai hijras*), through sex work (*kandra hijras*), and by begging. They can often be seen in groups, performing their trademark handclap, and threatening—when confronted with tight-fisted interlocutors—to lift their saris to reveal their postoperative genitals, the sight of which is believed to make the viewer impotent (Cohen 1995: 283).

Hijras typically live together in households that function as residential, economic, and kinship units. Households are organized into 'houses' (symbolic descent groups), of which there are seven in India. Each household is headed by a *nayak* ('leader'), who has a number of *chelas* ('disciples') who may, in turn, serve as gurus to their own *chelas*. The *guru–chela* relationship is seen as a hierarchical but mutually beneficial one, combining elements of master–disciple and parent–child relationships. *Hijra* kinship also involves more affective 'mother–daughter' and 'sister' relationships within the household. In addition to serving as heads of their households, *nayaks* collectively constitute a *jamat* ('council') that arbitrates disputes between households and represents their houses in interregional *hijra* events. Membership in *hijra* houses is conferred through, and symbolized by, 'putting a *rit*', a ritual involving the elders of the house, the aspiring *hijra* and the guru sponsoring her entry into the community (Reddy 2005: 58).

Further reading: Cohen 1995; Nanda 1990; Reddy 2005.

—RAHUL RAO, *Department of Politics and International Studies, SOAS, University of London*

— .•. —

Hindi/Hindustani

Hindi (lit. 'Indian' in Persian)—a Neo-Indo-Aryan (NIA) language that is related to other North Indian languages (Punjabi, Gujarati, Bengali, Nepali, Marathi, and Urdu)—is a textbook example of the modern emergence of language identity and nationalism (Brass 1974), perhaps now coming towards the end of its historical trajectory.

In the multilingual world of precolonial North India, before language became a symbol of community identity that fused language and script with religious, historical, and cultural histories (captured in the slogan 'Hindi, Hindu, Hindustan'), the vernacular was used for songs and tales, in the local administration, and for popular religion since the fifteenth century (Orsini 2012). But the script in which it was written (Persian, Devanagari, or Kaithi) depended on the profession and education of the scribe, not on some intrinsic quality of the language. Unlike the 'high languages' (Sanskrit, Persian, and Arabic), the vernacular was not codified and was simply called 'language' (bhakha/bhasha), or 'Indian' (hindi, hindui, hindavi) in Persian sources (Bangha 2010; Orsini 2012).

But in the nineteenth century, with the waning of the Mughal order that had fostered a Persian-script vernacular literary culture (which we now call Urdu) under British colonial rule, and with new ideas about language and identity, groups of Hindu intellectuals began campaigning for the recognition of the Devanagari script in education and the administration because it was the 'language of the people' and the carrier of Indian ('Hindu') culture, while they stigmatized Urdu as the alien 'language of the Muslims'. 'Pure' (shuddh) Hindi became part and parcel of nationalist ideology; while its aim to replace English as the national language of India was ultimately unsuccessful, 'pure Hindi' became the dominant official language of North India (King 1994; Orsini 2002). By contrast, Hindustani (initially a colonial term for Urdu) came to denote a demotic mixed variety (in Gandhi's view, to be written in either script) (Lelyveld 1993). In Hindi cinema, which always drew upon the whole range of expressive registers, 'pure' Hindi remained decidedly marginal, too.

Now that both English and Hindi are spreading thanks to the proliferation of non-state media, the politicization of the lower castes and increase in mass education, and the street-wise glamour of a mixed urban lingo ('Hinglish'), Hindi has once again become a vibrant and more mixed language.

Further reading: Bangha 2010; Brass 1974; Dalmia 1997; King 1994; Lelyveld 1993; Orsini 2002, 2012.

—FRANCESCA ORSINI, *Professor in the Literatures of North India,
South Asia Department, SOAS, University of London*

— ·•· —

Hindu Reform Movements in British India

As with other religious communities in modern India, the quest for Hindu reform reflects a pressing concern for reformulating one's social and cultural identity. This enterprise postulated a homogeneous Hindu community and though historically untenable, Hindu reformism ably orchestrated this view, synthetically creating a unity among a people that had remained widely differentiated. Hindu reformers began by delineating certain common beliefs and practices which they took to be the defining elements of their community. Every such attempt revolved around the questions: 'Who is a Hindu?' and 'What does it mean to be a Hindu?'

But just what posed such problems of definition? For now, suffice it to say that an acute sense of self-reflexivity was induced (especially among Hindus) by the very intense and creative 'dialogue' that followed India's exposure to the material and intellectual changes occurring in contemporary Europe in the late eighteenth and nineteenth centuries. Reform, in this sense, was both a creative and reactive response to challenges posed by European modernity: creative because there was a conscious refashioning of older beliefs and practices; reactive because of the new cultural pride which sought to accept changes on its own terms. Thus, modern European knowledge was widely welcomed by the English-educated, middle-class Hindus, but without the trappings of an accompanying 'alien', Christian influence (see Sen 2003: 5–15).

Especially in the context of British India, reform implied a self-conscious attempt at changing social and religious beliefs or practices for the 'better'. Western-educated Indians readily accepted certain points of criticism appearing in European writings on India. For example, they accepted the argument, typically put forth by James Mill, that the state of a civilization may be judged by the way it treated its women. Thus, dehumanizing and unnatural practices like inequalities inherent in the caste system, the depressed social status of Hindu women, and gross irrationalities or superstition were matters that constituted reformist agendas. However, there was a lack of agreement about factors that could bring about social 'betterment'. Not everything that prima facie called for reform entered the reformist agenda. Educated Indians, for example, were only too aware of the problems of female infanticide in certain parts of India, yet very few took this up with any seriousness. Besides, reformers could be selective about issues that were otherwise interrelated. The idea of female education was generally supported, but few were willing to acknowledge that this also produced a sense of freedom and independent judgement in women. Further reformers were reluctant to significantly raise the marriageable age or allow for the girl's consent in marriage. In general, as K.T. Telang (1850–92) put it, the 'line of least resistance' was followed. In effect, this meant piecemeal reform or slowing down the pace of reform so as not to antagonize influential sections of society (Sen 2003: 94–7).

The character of reform movements varied regionally. In Bengal and the Punjab, for instance, where inter-caste conflicts had been less volatile, 'reform' tended to percolate from above; it was largely determined by upper castes and classes, with a mandate for others to follow. In Bengal, all influential reformers came from the three most advanced *jatis*—the Brahmins, Baidyas, and Kayasthas, representing the sacerdotal, physician, and the scribal castes respectively—that also made up the new Hindu intelligentsia in the nineteenth century. However, in Maharashtra and parts of South India with their long histories of caste contestation, upper-caste directives were often thrown overboard by radical movements from below. In the 1870s, this was true of the movement led by Jotiba Phule

(1827–90), who belonged to a 'ritually defiled' caste and, still later, of E.V. Ramaswamy Naicker, alias Periyar (1879–1973). Such movements demanded structural changes, not muted blows or minor social adjustments. Periyar demanded 'revolution' in place of reform; the latter he associated with the deviousness of upper castes.

By the early nineteenth century, a mental revolution had gripped the Hindu intelligentsia. India's most meaningful contact with Europe occurred at a time when that continent was itself undergoing momentous changes. England, with which India was historically tied, witnessed unprecedented material changes and the flowering of thought which produced new perspectives on human society and history. It now came to be widely believed that history chronicled universal human progress and that it was morally imperative for man to contribute to this through active intervention in worldly life. Hence, 'utility' came to be an important consideration with modern thinkers. Social and cultural institutions were now judged in terms of their practical 'usefulness' to human life. Utilitarianism, an influential philosophy in nineteenth-century Britain, was strongly oriented towards reform and harshly critical of tradition. Further, influences from Evangelism inculcated a deep sense of moral responsibility, compassion, and piety. Although not always impartial in their assessment of India, European thinkers and missionaries did make educated Indians more critically aware of their past.

The impact of the West on the mind of the educated Hindu, and the response thereto, was a complex process. Much thought and deliberation went behind the way educated Indians re-examined their tradition and prepared a blueprint for the future. However, attacks on contemporary society and religion predate the impact of modern European ideas. Rammohun Roy's (1774–1833) strong critique of contemporary religious beliefs, the *Tuhfut ul Muwahidin* (1804), was written at a time when he had little or no knowledge of the English language or of European thought (Sen 2012: 60–2). Nevertheless, as Rammohan and many others after him were to admit, European modernity was somewhat unique inasmuch as it posed some unprecedented mental and moral challenges. This, in turn, called for setting new agendas and strategies.

In hindsight, a general inclination to reform must be distinguished from institutionalized reform work. Not every Hindu thinker or reformer worked through a reformist organization. The Bengali reformer and philanthropist Iswar Chandra Vidyasagar (1820–91), who advocated Hindu widow remarriage, was never a formal member of a reformist body like the Brahmo Samaj (Community of Believers in Brahman) (see below). Rammohun's campaign against the practice of *sati* ('immolation of a widow on her husband's funeral pyre') was carried out as an individual campaigner. And yet, the virtues of organized activity soon became apparent. For one, this gave reformers a greater voice and leverage in relation to the government which alone could enact social legislation. Organized reform activity reached a high point with the founding of the Social Conference in 1887 (see Kolasker 1902 for addresses delivered at the Social Conference by its founder, M.G. Ranade).

By the late nineteenth century, reformist bodies and organizations sprang up in most of British India. Understandably enough, they were most active in the three Presidency towns of Calcutta, Bombay, and Madras in which the educated middle classes were largely concentrated. Initially trained in Hindu and Islamic scholastics, Rammohun Roy keenly followed European developments and believed that India's progress depended on breaking her intellectual isolation and constructively accepting moral and material values associated with European modernity (Sen 2012: 118–49). For this purpose, he founded the Atmiya Sabha (Society of Kindred Souls) in 1815 and the Brahmo Sabha (Community of Believers in Brahman) in 1828. Finding conventional social relations and ways of worship detrimental to such progress, Roy tried to replace them with more 'rational' and 'useful' forms. Strongly opposed to 'priestcraft', 'polytheism', and 'idol worship', he believed that none of these was integral to 'pure' or 'authentic' Hinduism. In this sense, his reformism had shades of a cultural revival.

The Brahmo Sabha (renamed Brahmo Samaj by his spiritual successors) carried out important work in the areas of adult education, temperance, widow remarriage, and movements aimed at weakening caste. It was the first Hindu reform movement with some claims to being pan-Indian but suffered two successive schisms—in 1866 and 1878—partly due to differences over social reform issues (Sastri 1974). The more conservative Brahmos spoke against radical, woman-related changes which others believed to be of utmost importance in keeping the spirit of reform alive.

Another major reform movement to have survived from this period is the Arya Samaj (Society of Aryas). It was founded by the Hindu monastic Swami Dayanand Saraswati (1824–83) who, unlike Rammohun or his followers, had no knowledge of the English language (Jordens 1998). Although founded in Bombay in 1875, the Arya Samaj was most successful in the Punjab where it was patronized by the Hindu-Punjabi trading and professional castes, particularly the Khatris, the mercantile caste. Compared to the Brahmo Samaj, the Arya Samaj reveals a more reactionary sentiment. In the 1840s, having found the *Vedas* internally inconsistent and anachronistic, Brahmo leaders renounced their faith in them as an infallible source; the Aryas, on the other hand, claimed to locate in them elements of modern science and technology. Given the history of Hindu–Muslim hostility in the Punjab, the Arya Samaj gradually adopted a more belligerent anti-Muslim attitude. In the late nineteenth century, militant Aryas started *shuddhi* ('purification') and *sangathan* ('organization') movements that aimed at reclaiming Hindu converts to Islam (Jordens 1998; Jones 1994). In his major work *Satyarth Prakash* ('The Light of Truth') (1875), Dayanand, too, is intolerant of both Islam and Christianity. However, the Aryas more actively promoted widow-marriages, discouraged caste divisions, and established a chain of secondary and higher educational institutions for both the sexes.

The Brahmo Samaj and the Arya Samaj are only two of the numerous movements that sprang up in nineteenth-century India. Their main issues and the agitational methods adopted were quite typical of reform movements of this period. Soon, an inverse relationship developed between the movement for social and political reform. As nationalistic sentiment grew and was dispersed throughout British India, a good number of Indians began showing a greater reluctance to effect changes in their social and religious institutions (Sen 2003: 24–6). First, both a reactionary conservatism and a perceived loss of power led them to argue against official British policy interventions in Hindu social and religious customs (Sen 2003: 26–30). Although not opposed to the idea of social legislation itself, many also felt that Indians alone had the right to set their house in order. Implicitly, this was a demand for greater Indian representation in law-making bodies and a measure of political power. Not surprisingly, political bodies like the Congress avoided taking up social issues. These issues, often regional in character, were felt to be divisive whereas an anti-colonial sentiment glossed over social differences. Under these circumstances, defending the social status quo became an expression of political self-determination; as India advanced into the twentieth century, the movement for social and religious reform perceptibly weakened. By this time, Indians were sharply divided over whether or not social changes should precede political ones. Interestingly, many Indian states like Mysore and Baroda, in which nationalistic sentiments were not as strong as in British India, were able to carry out meaningful social legislation more consistently.

In hindsight, Hindu social and religious reform movements appear to have achieved modest success. Female education met considerable opposition; only a few Hindu widows could be remarried despite an enabling legislation to this effect in 1856. The caste system, another favoured area of reform, was far from dismantled. On the contrary, caste identities became sharper for a variety of reasons. Nevertheless, it cannot be denied that the attempt to bring about a social reordering within the Hindu community constitutes an important aspect of Indian modernity. It sensitized a good number of Indians to the fact that political unity rests but uncomfortably on gross social inequities.

Further reading: Jones 1994; Sen 1979; Sen 2003, 2007.

—AMIYA PROSAD SEN, *Professor of Modern Indian History,*
Jamia Millia Islamia, New Delhi; Heinrich-Zimmer-Chair,
South Asia Institute, University of Heidelberg

— ·•· —

Hindutva

The word 'Hindutva' was popularized by Vinayak Damodar Savarkar (1883–1966), who used it in the title of his pioneering book, *Hindutva: Who Is a Hindu?* (1928). In 1923, this book was first published anonymously in English in Nagpur. It is the first charter of Hindu nationalism, an ideology which, precisely, has become equated with the word 'Hindutva'. (In his *Hindutva* [Calcutta 1892] Chandranath Basu employed the word 'Hindutva' in a similar fashion to Savarkar. The term itself was apparently in use in Bengal since Bankim Chandra Chatterjee's days.)

Savarkar wrote this book in prison after having been arrested in London for taking part in the plot to assassinate William Hutt Curzon Wyllie (1848–1909), a political assistant to the Secretary of State. During his 27 years in jail (between 1910 and 1937) he had come in contact with the Khilafatists whose attitude convinced him that the real enemies to the Indian nation were not the British, but the Muslims (Keer 1988: 161). His book rests on the assumption that the Hindus were vulnerable to the Muslims, whose sense of solidarity and pan-Islamic sympathies posed a threat to a Hindu majority divided into many castes and sects.

Drawing some of his inspiration from Dayananda Saraswati (1824–83), the founder of the Arya Samaj, and Bal Gangadhar Tilak (1856–1920), a fellow Chitpavan Brahmin, who helped him to study in England, Savarkar defines the nation primarily according to ethnic categories. For him, the Hindus descend from the 'Vedic fathers' who inhabited India since the dawn of history. However, ethnic bonds are not the only criteria of Hindutva; this identity also rests on other pillars which, interestingly, are not primarily religious.

Savarkar did not follow traditional rituals and did not oppose the Muslims because of their faith. In fact, those who converted to Islam from Hinduism were welcomed back, since they came from the right 'stock'. Savarkar suggested that they could be reintegrated into Hindu society, provided they paid allegiance to the Hindu culture. Thus, an important criterion of Savarkar's Hindutva is a 'common culture', a notion that reflects the crucial importance of rituals, social rules, and language. Sanskrit is cited by him as the common reference-point for all Indian languages and as 'language par excellence' (Savarkar 1989: 95).

Territory is the last major criterion of Hindutva. For Savarkar, a Hindu is primarily someone who lives in the area between the Indus River, the Himalayas, and the Indian Ocean, in a space 'so strongly entrenched that no other country in the world is so perfectly designed by the fingers of nature as a geographical unit' (Savarkar 1989: 82). This is why in the Vedic era, their forefathers 'developed a sense of nationality' (Savarkar 1989: 5). This land of the Hindus that he calls 'Hindustan' is described as a decisive factor in the unity of the population because its enclave nature favoured intermarriages: 'All Hindus claim to have in their veins the blood of the mighty race incorporated with and descended from the Vedic fathers' (Savarkar 1989: 85).

The profound originality of the notion of Hindutva 'invented' by Savarkar comes from its mixed character. At face value, it is a clear-cut illustration of a well-known type of nationalism that one may call 'ethnic' or 'cultural', in contrast to the 'universalist' or 'political' brand of nationalism. But Savarkar's nationalism is more inclusive than the former. Firstly, it incorporates a territorial dimension that is consistent with the Hindus' definition of their 'sacred land' (*matribhoomi*) and an element of openness generally associated with 'political nationalism'. Accordingly, all the citizens living within the state's borders are entitled to be part of the nation in this political variant of nationalism. Secondly, the racial dimension of Savarkar's Hindutva, paradoxically, enables him to accommodate converts from other religions.

These factors of openness have not survived for long. The Hindu nationalist movement, which has been associated with the Rashtriya Swayamsevak Sangh (RSS) (National Volunteer Organization) after 1925, has stigmatized Muslims in toto; gradually, Hindus of the diaspora have been considered as part of the Hindu nation. But most of the other mainstays of Savarkar's Hindutva have remained key features of Hindu nationalism. Until the 1960s, its proponents demanded recognition of Sanskrit or Hindi—the vernacular language closest to it—as the national idiom. More generally speaking, Hindu nationalists perpetuated a defini-tion of the nation where the majority community embodied the identity of India: Muslims (and Christians) were allowed to practise their religion and retain their culture in the private sphere, but in the public space, they were supposed to pay allegiance to Hindu culture, including 'national heroes' like Lord Ram. While this Hindutva-based discourse remained at the fringe of Indian political life until the 1980s, it asserted itself paradig-matically during the Ramjanmabhoomi movement which culminated in the demolition of the Babri Masjid in 1992.

Further reading: Jaffrelot 1996; Savarkar 1989.

—CHRISTOPHE JAFFRELOT, *Senior Research Fellow at CERI-Sciences Po/CNRS, Paris and Visiting Professor, King's India Institute, London*

— .•. —

Imam

Imam (lit.'one who leads the way', pl. *a'imma*), verbal noun of the first form of the Arabic verbal root ['-m-m], has acquired various meanings in different contexts, all of which, however, relate to religious and political guidance of the Muslim community (*umma*, or *jama'a*). Other than *khilafa*, which technically denotes only a succession, *imama* has an intrinsic eschatological dimension: The central task of an *imam* is to correctly guide the community of believers towards salvation in the Hereafter. This is physically expressed by the *imam* leading the congregational prayer, herein following the historical example of the Prophet Muhammad (Muslim 1987: 77–101).

In Sunni Islam, the *imam* was historically synonymous with the caliphs in the succession to Muhammad—a perception that, albeit only partially, was maintained until the official abolition of the Caliphate in 1924. After the enforcement of the dynastic principle in establishing leadership, however, the term *imam* became first and foremost used for the prayer leader (Crone 2004). Theoretically, the *imam* is only the first among equals; his appointment is temporal and informal and depends on the actual prayer congregation. Historically, however, the *imama*, especially for the royal mosques, had been made a permanent office, the appointment being usually the privilege of the monarch. In Mughal Delhi (1638–1857), for example, the *imama* of the Imperial Friday Mosque (*Jami' masjid*, or *Masjid-i jahan-numa*) had been made hereditary to the Bukhari family in 1656; the office is held today by the thirteenth descendant of the first *Shahi Imam*, Sayyid Ahmad Bukhari (b. 1952).

In Shia Islam, the concept of *imama* constitutes the crucial doctrine and has, therefore, been theologically thoroughly elaborated. It developed from the idea that infallible guidance of the community is vital; infallibility, in turn, had been conferred by God upon the Prophet Muhammad (Momen 1985) and is maintained through his bloodline that emerged from the marriage of his daughter Fatima and 'Ali ibn Abi Talib. The initial rather diffuse political movement, in opposition to dynastic claims by various Arab clans, gave way to various denominations that acknowledged different numbers of *a'imma* before the line of succession eventually came to an end (Halm 2004). One of the two major denominations present in South Asia are the Twelver Shi'is (Rizvi 1986) who have developed the concept of occultation of the twelfth *imam*, based on the sound tradition that 'God will never leave this earth without an *imam* and a divine proof for his servants' (al-Kulayni 1978: 452). Since the current *imam* remains hidden until the end of time, his infallible guidance has fallen to the jurists (*fuqaha*), representing the least fallible members of the community. The second common major denomination of Shi'is in the subcontinent comprises the two branches of the Isma'ilis, or Seveners (Daftary 1990). While the Nizaris, mainly to be found in Indian Gujarat and the Pakistani Northern Areas, kept the line of succession alive and possess the Aga Khan, a living *imam*, the sub-branch of Musta'lis, concentrated mainly in and around Mumbai, acknowledges only a succession of representatives (*du'at*) of the last *imam* that its adherents recognize.

Further reading: Brentjes 1964; Calder 1984; Madelung 1964.

—JAN-PETER HARTUNG, *Reader in the Study of Islam,*
SOAS, University of London

— ·•· —

Iman

*I**man** (lit. 'believe', 'faith'), verbal noun of the fourth form of the Arabic verbal root ['-m-n], is a core Islamic concept and denotes first and foremost man's unconditional belief in and loyalty to God, coupled with a notion of 'being protected' or 'feeling secure' from deviation (*bi-aman*). In a broader sense, it includes a similar belief and trust in God's successive divine revelations to man, the last of which had been the Quran, the finality of God's direct verbal communication to humankind with Muhammad, the temporality of the world, bodily resurrection, and divine judgment at the end of time. The Quranic verses 2:2–4 are commonly considered the minimal definition of a 'believer': '[...] those who fear God, who believe in the Unseen, are steadfast in prayer, and spend out of what We have provided for them, and who believe in the Revelation sent to thee, and sent before thy time, and (in their hearts) have the assurance of the Hereafter'. Classical Islamic speculative theology (*kalam*) has considered the expression of *iman* to be generally tripartite: inner certitude (*tasdiq bi'l-qalb*), verbal expression (*iqrar bi'l-lisan*), and the execution of prescribed acts (*'amal*) (Wensinck 1932).

The antonym of *iman* is *kufr*, 'unbelief', literally 'to hide, or conceal the truth', but with regard to *iman*, it denotes failure to acknowledge (for example, Q 30:13) or to reject everything that constitutes *iman*, and to be ungrateful to God (for example, Q 2:152). Close to *kufr* is the term *shirk*, 'deification of beings other than God', usually denoting the religious constitution of pre-Islamic Arabia. *Shirk* had widely been applied to the South Asian context because its legal consequences are much less harsh than those of *kufr*, and allowed, therefore, for a more peaceful coexistence between adherents of monotheistic and polytheistic religions: Muslims were thus not compelled by the regulations of the religious law to persecute non-Muslims, but to treat them rather as charges, as in the case of the so-called 'People of the Book', that is, Jews and Christians (Khalfaoui 2008). In the course of intensified religious and political reconceptualization by Indian Muslims from the late eighteenth century onwards, *kufr* became a central term for framing non-Muslims, but even more so those Muslims whose religious practices were considered deviant, hence lacking *iman* (Hartung 2004). A vivid expression of this tendency is the *Taqviyat al-iman* ('The Strengthening of Belief') by Shah Ismail Dihlavi and Sayyid Ahmad Barelvi (both killed in 1831) (Hartung 2004). Among the practices they have considered *shirk*-cum-*kufr* were various common Sufi observances that constituted first and foremost the request for intercession (*tawassul*) at the graves of saints.

Further reading: Bari 1965; Hartung 2004; Izutsu 1965; Khalfaoui 2008; Wensinck 1932.

—JAN-PETER HARTUNG, *Reader in the Study of Islam, SOAS, University of London*

— ◆ —

Indian Ocean

Historians have done much to contribute to the solidification of the Indian Ocean as a respectable postcolonial idea (Gupta, Hofmeyer, and Pearson 2010). Their panacea has been to theorize the ocean as a unified space or 'world', where the cultural confinements of the land as an opposing category can be rendered invalid. To upset this picture somewhat I first turn to fiction and then to ethnography.

The historic city of Surat in western India is the setting for a short story written by Leo Tolstoy in 1885 (*The Coffee House of Surat*). His cast includes a Persian and his African slave, a Brahmin, a Jew, a Protestant minister, a Catholic missionary, a Turk, Abyssinian Christians, Lamas from Tibet, Ismailis, Parsis, and a Chinese Confucian. A debate in a coffee shop focuses on the correct relation between man and god and the divisiveness of sectarian and nationalistic pride. Each praises his own religion and sees god in those terms alone. The Confucian, however, tells them: 'It is pride that causes error and discord among men. As with the sun, so it is with god. Each man wants to have a special god of his own, or at least a special god for his native land. Each nation wishes to confine in its own temples Him, whom the world cannot contain' (Tolstoy 2008 [1885]: 50).

Scholars have often claimed a unity for the cultural and geographical region of water between continents, defined by the movements, associations, and allegiances of people rather than by the lands around its periphery (Chaudhuri 1985; McPherson 1995; Pearson 2000). As a parable, Tolstoy's story suggests that god and truth are ubiquitous like the sun and therefore those who see the whole picture should refrain from blaming or despising those who see in their own idol a single ray of that same light. As a metaphor, the story offers a compelling glimpse into the politics of travel, difference, and debate. The story animates uncomfortable distinctions of community, religion, and nationality in what might appear at first glance to be a cosmopolitan Indian Ocean world setting.

The nation state thus sits awkwardly within the idea of the Indian Ocean as a unified world: voyages transcend national boundaries which also obscure previous empires and past voyages, while ships and sailors are known, audited, taxed, and hierarchically ordered by their national origins, rather than by the commonality of their voyages; some decry the voyages of others as anti-national, while others decry the piracy of some as terrorism; the nation state reproduces colonial myths of ancient seafaring as evidence of a lost prowess. In this final sense, nationalist sentiment also finds a way into the historiography of seafaring (see Sakarai 1980 for an example). Indian historiography notably lays emphasis on the glorious past of Indian seafaring and the conquest of East Africa by Indian merchants. Perhaps, in part, such a history compensates for the humiliation of British colonialism; the presentation of the Indian Ocean, as with occurrences afloat, cannot be detached from events on land.

The Indian Ocean became an arena of rebellion against the supposed tyranny of regional studies, providing opportunity for scholars to take their vocabulary offshore and to cast their eyes across the water. James de Vere Allen (1980) thus saw the Indian Ocean as containing three overlapping strands of unity: race, culture, and Islam. For Kirti Chaudhuri (1985), people and places were united through systems of exchange but divided by distance, changing environmental conditions, and cultural differences.

From a broader perspective, however, it is peculiar that debates on indigenous perceptions of history, social hierarchy, nationalism, learning, and religious movements have been sidelined in oceanic studies when such debates are flourishing in the social science of South Asia and East Africa. It is almost as if by taking a comparative or connected approach to interactions between the two landfalls, the activities, preoccupations and political engagements of those on the shore have been eclipsed.

Following Tolstoy, however, my thesis is that travel is more socially divisive (in terms of imaginative frameworks and status) than congealing. The ethnographic evidence from my own research in Gujarat suggests that littoral society has been formed and reformed by the movement of people (Simpson 2006). Such movement fragments space and divides people. However, the values accorded to such spaces, goods, and movements are not equal in their value and prestige or in their capacity to be absorbed into local society. Therefore, the differential values accorded to places and histories can be actively used as people attempt to change the social order. Travel in the Indian Ocean does not dissolve pride, special gods, or native lands, and so it is that travel creates hierarchical and divided societies rather than unified worlds of equals.

Further reading: Allen 1980; Chaudhuri 1985; Gupta, Hofmeyer, and Pearson 2010; McPherson 1995; Pearson 2000; Simpson 2006.

—EDWARD SIMPSON, *Professor in Social Anthropology,*
SOAS, University of London

— ·•· —

Indian Philosophy

Each of the disciplines (*shastra*) that collectively make up the intellectual culture of India has at least this in common with the others: it takes truth to be a regulative goal.

Fidelity to tradition is, to be sure, highly prized, but the value accorded to that fidelity is in the first instance instrumental: respect for the accumulated wisdom of one's tradition is seen to be a sensible policy in one's quest for truth. Thus, philosophers in India occupy a position of special importance. Certainly, they too have truths of their own of which they are in pursuit—the truths of metaphysics, ethics, and the various branches of philosophical knowledge. The greater part of their intellectual endeavour, however, the part which is called *pramana shastra* ('theory of the sources of knowledge'), is an inquiry rather into the general form of truth-oriented intellectual practices as such (Matilal 1986; Ganeri 2001, 2011).

How is a practice which is self-consciously governed by the regulative goal of truth to proceed? What are the intellectual virtues its participants must possess? Accuracy in the accumulation of information, caution in the interpolation and extrapolation of conclusions, due care with the application of terms of art and theory, and trustworthiness in the transmission and spread of information within the intellectual community—the four *pramana*s of perception, inference, analogy, and testimony—stand out as the cardinal virtues. The philosophers produce in theory an account of what others exemplify in practice, a theory of intellectual practice itself.

The contemporary intellectual who attempts an engagement with the work of premodern Indian philosophy must perforce address several issues about method. I will classify them as questions of motivation, questions of objectivity, and questions of critical engagement.

Motivation refers to the intended significance and purpose of the proposed examination: Here the sharpest distinction is between the investigator who has no expectation of being substantively informed about the subject matter of the intellectual discipline under investigation, and the investigator who does indeed anticipate that the investigation will result in substantive education. The intellectual historian of Indian astronomical sciences may expect little that would constitute an enrichment of contemporary astronomical theory; this will not form part of a conception of the purpose of the investigation. On the other hand, the investigator into Indian philosophy typically will expect the Indian discussion to be of substantive philosophical reward. In particular, there is no antecedent reason to rule out the possibility that Indian inquiry into the nature of truth-governed intellectual practice will inform the contemporary investigators' conception of the structure of intellectual practices, including the practice in which they themselves participate.

What does the demand for objectivity require of the modern intellectual engaging with Indian rational tradition? Little remains now of the nineteenth-century conception of the requirements of objectivity which call for a complete elimination of interest or perspective. Even an investigation that conceives of itself as the mere chronicling of facts presumes a deliberate selection of facts deemed to be worth chronicling, and there are many difficulties with the supposed distinction between matters of fact and matters of theory, well attested in work on empiricist philosophy of science. It is a good question, and one indeed which the contemporary intellectual profitably addresses, to ask after the Indians' own conception of the requirements and burdens of objectivity, both in theory and in practice. An important resource for the contemporary intellectual is Amartya Sen's recent elaboration of the idea of 'positional objectivity' (Sen 1993). Sen argues that an objective assessment of India's past does not require that the interpreter seek (vainly) to assume a 'view from nowhere'. There is, he claims, a clear sense in which situated interpretations—views from somewhere—achieve objectivity. Sen cites as an example the interpretation of India's intellectual past advanced by the

Indian nationalist movement, which was, as is well known, selective in its choice of materials and single-minded in the use to which it put them. In particular, he argues, it was reasonable for the Indian nationalists to give weight to themes of synthesis and convergence in Indian intellectual history, given the colonial use of supposed communal and ideological discord as a justification for the superimposition of colonial rule. Sen's idea, I take it, is that the description of the 'facts to be explained' by a theory depends on the spatial, social, or cultural position of the theorist, in ways that are not accountable for simply in terms of a notion of subjective bias. The practical reasonableness of such an interpretation, the fact that it is, as we might say, what anyone would think in those circumstances and presented with that data, commends the interpretation as an objective one, albeit positionally objective. A contemporary intellectual profitably seeks to establish the Indian philosophical self-conception of the requirements of objectivity in a pluralistic intellectual milieu, when all interpretation is situated interpretation; and the motivation for such an inquiry would consist in part in the fact that we ourselves are situated interpreters.

There are resonances with the Indian description of truth-oriented practices, their emphasis on the place of established background principles (*siddhanta*) and paradigmatic examples (*drishtanta*), as well as their use of suppositional reasoning (*tarka*) from hypothetical premises (Ganeri 2001). These all seem to be an acknowledgement that truth-seeking practices are situated, that such practices achieve objectivity though, or through, having cultural and historical location.

Michel Foucault (1969) advanced as a meta-methodological principle that the specific methods of investigation into some aspect of a system of thought must be constructed anew each time, tailored to the particular object of study (Aristotle similarly used the image of a flexible ruler, used to measure the varying shapes of fluted columns). There is no overarching single correct methodology in the human sciences. The application of this idea to philosophy is complicated by the fact that the object of study is itself a methodology of inquiry. To what extent should the inquirer into the *pramana shastra* permit their investigations into that methodology to affect the methods being employed to study it? At the very least, the great sophistication of the Indian theory implies that it would be incautious not to be willing to learn from their methodological investigations, when so much attention had been paid to the problem of intellectual practice in a pluralistic intellectual environment. More strongly, one might argue that the methods of investigation into the intellectual world of a culture must draw upon the conception of reasoned inquiry articulated by that culture itself, that the critical apparatus and standards of evaluation should be immersed rather than external. This is a central question for any reflection on a contemporary appeal to Indian philosophy. Part of the answer seems to me to rest in the notion of participation. To the extent that the interpreter of Indian philosophy is a participant in an extended intellectual community, it is appropriate to draw upon the critical resources of the tradition itself.

In considering the contemporary, postcolonial, appeal to India's premodern philosophical traditions, John Newman's analysis of the problem of development within a tradition provides a flexible account of the distinction between development and corruption within a tradition. Newman observes that 'one cause of corruption in religion is the refusal to follow the course of doctrine as it moves on, and an obstinacy in the notions of the past' (1890: 177). This amounts to an important criticism of fundamentalist readings of tradition—the ossification of an idea is the sign of unhealth and decay. Fidelity to a religious belief implies an acknowledgement of its underlying idea, but this is in no way antithetical to a respect for ways in which the articulation of the idea can change. It is, in particular, the very essence of a healthy tradition that it has the ability to absorb new ideas from outside itself:

> Doctrines and views which relate to man are not placed in a void, but in the crowded world, and make way for themselves by interpenetration, and develop by absorption. Facts and opinions, which have hitherto been regarded in other relations and grouped round other centres, henceforth are gradually attracted to new influences and subjected to a new sovereign. They are modified, laid down afresh, thrust aside, as the case may be. A new element of order and composition has come among them; and its life is proved by this capacity of expansion, without disarrangement or dissolution. An eclectic, conservative, assimilating, healing, moulding process, a unitive power, is of the essence [...] of a faithful development (1890: 186).

'Healthy traditions' are not insular; rather, they are able to absorb and assimilate external influences. The reason is surety in their inner principles, which are then brought into relationship with ideas from outside the tradition. Outside influences do not corrupt a 'healthy tradition' but rather assist it in its development. A development, then, in Newman's account, is a change in the body of the tradition that can be seen as following logically from the fundamental principles of the tradition, even if it is brought about by causes external to the tradition; it is a change consistent with those principles, and a fuller expression and articulation of them.

Let me apply these ideas to the studies of Indian intellectual culture produced by a modern interpreter, Bimal Krishna Matilal (1935–91). The context of Matilal's work (1986) is clearly the contemporary community of analytical philosophy: the study is written in English, it uses contemporary philosophical jargon; it makes references to leading participants. Matilal's willingness to participate in illocutionary acts of this kind reveals his deep immersion within the Indian intellectual traditions. Matilal was responding to an obvious historical fact, the brute fact of colonialism. The immense rupture which colonialism represents left Indian intellectuals inhabiting an anglophone intellectual culture, being taught in English-style university systems, writing in English. How is a contemporary Indian intellectual like Matilal to engage with precolonial Indian intellectual culture? This, however, presents no great new problem: Kumarila (seventh century CE) struggled to make sense of a ritual worldview that had lost social vitality, while Uddyotakara (seventh century CE) has to find a way to reappropriate the ancient texts of *Nyaya* in a new intellectual culture inaugurated by the emergence of Buddhism in Sanskrit. Jumping back across a rupture, while continuing to be indelibly marked by it, reconceptualizing the pre-rupture past in the categories of a post-rupture present, is a characteristic hallmark of Indian intellectual practice. For this reason, Matilal's work expresses far more profound continuities with the underlying principles of the Indian tradition than the visible discontinuities would suggest. His is a deeply Indian hermeneutical stance, the stance of a situated interpreter.

My proposals have been, first, that the requirement of objectivity in interpretation is that the situated interpreter achieves positional objectivity in her interpretations, and second, that immersed interpretation is positionally objective to the extent that the interpreter's situation is one of participation rather than observation. I have suggested further that the contemporary intellectual engaging with India's philosophical traditions is situated within a tradition of inquiry into the form of truth-governed intellectual practices, but outside of a tradition of metaphysical and ethical speculation, and so is both participant and witness to Indian intellectual traditions.

Further reading: Ganeri 2001, 2009, 2011; Matilal 1986; Sen 1993.

—JONARDON GANERI, *Professor, New York University, Abu Dhabi, UAE*

— ·•· —

Indian Uprising of 1857

The Indian uprising of 1857 had both material and emotional causes. It began as a mutiny within the ranks of the native *sipahi* or 'sepoy' army of the Bengal Presidency in North India. The immediate provocation for this mutiny lay in rumours that claimed, amongst other things, that the soldiers were to be issued with a new rifle, the Enfield, the cartridges for which were greased with the fat of pigs and cows. This was supposed to be a deliberate attempt to undermine the religions of both Hindu and Muslim soldiers in the army. Behind these rumours lay more general anxieties, concerning Christian missionary activities encouraged by the East India Company (EIC) and the perceived and real injustices perpetuated under Company rule. However, a more immediate cause of discontent amongst the sepoys was the General Service Enlistment Act of 1856, which threatened to remove the substantial special payments made to troops serving beyond the boundaries of British India and which proposed to diversify recruitment, thereby removing the priority accorded to sons of sepoys. This attack on the livelihoods of sepoy families was considered an act of injustice (Stokes 1986: 51).

The 19th Regiment of Bengal Native Infantry, stationed at Barrackpore just west of Calcutta, was the first regiment to take up arms against its officers (Malleson 1857: 20–3). Those involved in this mutiny were arrested and the regiment disbanded. On the day following the initial outbreak—29 March 1857—Mangal Pande of the 34th Regiment, which had been barracked alongside the 19th, fired at his commanding officer, but was overpowered. He and another sepoy were tried and executed (Mukherjee 2005). After the 34th was also disbanded, rumours about the greased cartridges and the summary disbanding of regiments spread rapidly. Six weeks later, a thousand miles away, a native regiment at Meerut was publicly humiliated for refusing even to train in the use of the (yet to be issued) cartridges, being marched in shackles to jail. The next evening (10 May), the remaining sepoys rallied around the guns of their regiments, forced open the armoury, released their colleagues from jail, and attacked and killed their British officers along with a number of civilians. The following day they marched to Delhi (Wagner 2010).

By demanding that the aged Mughal emperor in Delhi, Bahadur Shah II (1775–1862), should support their revolt, and by calling for the expulsion from India of the British *feringhi* (a pejorative term for Europeans dating back to the Crusades and etymologically derived from 'Franks'), the Meerut regiments indicated their desire for a restoration of past authority (Dalrymple 2006; Ray 2002). Simultaneously, although they had no desire for a revival of Mughal rule, many North Indian elites rose to arms to defend their respective territories following the collapse of British power. Other regiments joined the so-called mutiny eventually totalling more than 100,000 soldiers, but in the absence of effective leadership the Indian uprising degenerated into uncoordinated sieges of the surviving British garrisons in North India (Stokes 1986: 57; Bates 2007: 65–76).

The military 'mutiny' was accompanied by a widespread civil insurrection which affected most of the Indo-Gangetic plain. The fiercest fighting was in the territory of the former princely state of Awadh in eastern Uttar Pradesh, from which many sepoys had been recruited (Mukherjee 1984). The British annexation of this once-loyal kingdom, the deposition of the Nawab (formally regent of the Mughal empire), the raising of land taxes, and the displacement of aristocratic landlords (*talukdars*) were all important factors furthering the revolt. British reprisals were ruthless, and recaptured towns and cities were laid waste as well as villages that had supported the insurgents.

The British faced continual uprisings in India, but that of 1857–9 was by far the largest and bloodiest (Mukherjee 2001; Bates 2007: 78). The Indian uprising was also the most politically significant. Since British families were caught up in the fighting there was widespread public support for the sending of Government troops to India to put down the rebellion. The capture, deposition, and exile of the last Timurid Emperor in September 1857 marked the end of Mughal rule and vast new territories came under the direct control of the British, including the former Mughal imperial capital of Delhi. However, the campaign bankrupted the EIC and from 1858 onwards its Indian territories were brought under the formal rule of the British crown. The Indian uprising was of global significance, since after this date the activities of British trading corporations across the globe were replaced by the establishment of formal imperial control. Thus 1857 marked the beginning of what has been termed 'the second British Empire'. Additionally, it provided an important inspiration to later Indian nationalists.

Further reading: Bates 2007, 2013; Bhattacharya 2007; Dalrymple 2006; Malleson 1858; Mukherjee 1984; Mukherjee 2001; Ray 2002; Roy 1994; Stokes 1986; Wagner 2010.

—CRISPIN BATES, *Professor, School of History, Classics and Archaeology, University of Edinburgh*

— ·•· —

Integration

The term 'integration' is used, in the context of modern Indian studies, to describe the process whereby around 560 erstwhile Indian princely states—the Indian kingdoms which survived the British imperial conquest and remained more or less autonomous in internal affairs under the supervision, or 'paramountcy', of the colonial Political Department (and after 1935 of the office of the Crown Representative, that is, the Viceroy)—were merged with and assimilated into the postcolonial Indian and Pakistan states, roughly between 1947 and 1950.

British impatience with the failure of many states to move with the times, and pressure on the princes from the left wing of the Indian National Congress (INC), led to piecemeal reforms in the 1940s, such as the sharing of high courts and other elite institutions. On the eve of the transfer of power some of the more savvy princes entered into talks with a view to establishing federations of states covering entire regions (such as Saurashtra, roughly equivalent to the western half of modern-day Gujarat). But these plans were scotched by the States Department set up, with British consent, in June 1947, headed by Congressman Sardar Vallabhbhai Patel (1875–1950) and driven by V.P. Menon (1894–1966) as Secretary (Copland 1997: 214; Hodson 1969: 364).

Under the Cabinet Mission formula, paramountcy was slated to 'lapse' with the transfer of power; this ambiguous wording encouraged some princes to seek a postcolonial future for their states as accredited Dominions. The Viceroy, Lord Mountbatten (1900–79), and the Labour government led by Clement Attlee (1883–1967), already uneasy about Pakistan, were both opposed to a further fragmentation, or 'Balkanization' of the subcontinent, as was the Congress. Meanwhile, Mountbatten had the uphill task of reconciling Congress to Partition. To this end he put it to Patel that an accession of the states would more than compensate India for any resulting loss of territory (Copland 1995: 395). On 25 July 1947, he told the King that 'I have not yet got Patel to agree to [...] these terms' (Mansergh 1983: 338); but according to H.V. Hodson (1906–99), Mountbatten's Constitutional Advisor, the next time they met, the Sardar agreed to 'buy a basket with 565 apples [that is states]' (1969: 368). For a month, the Viceroy pressured and cajoled the princes to come on board; by 14 August all but a handful of states had signed an Instrument of Accession (IOA) signifying their willingness to join India or (in five cases) Pakistan.

However, the states were required to accede only for three central subjects: foreign policy; defence; and communications. It remains a matter of conjecture how much Mountbatten knew, or guessed, that the incoming Dominion governments would not long be satisfied with this minimal arrangement; afterwards many princes claimed to have been purposely misled; but accusations of bad faith aside, it was inevitable that further inroads would be made. In the event, the Indian government waited only four months before overseeing a merger of the Orissa and Kathiawar states, and in April 1948 Indore and Gwalior (among others) were incorporated in a new Union of Madhya Bharat (Copland 1998: 155–6). Further enforced mergers, of the Rajputana and East Punjab states, followed. Effectively, these reorganizations spelt the end of princely rule, but left the merged entities and the few states that still retained their old boundaries with a residue of local autonomy. This anomaly was extinguished in May 1948 when the Rajpramukhs ('governors') of the new unions, and the rulers of the remaining stand-alone states, were induced to sign new 'Instruments' ceding to New Delhi the power to legislate for their territories on federal and concurrent subjects. Around the same time, the unions agreed to stop collecting customs on goods transiting their borders, and under the Constitutional settlement of 1950 the Part B states (as they became known) were made liable to federal taxation (Copland 1998: 157). A similar process was pursued, though more slowly, in Pakistan.

In a speech to the Constituent Assembly, Patel described the integration of the states as a great 'bloodless revolution', an assessment that has been echoed by some historians such as William Richter (1971: 538). The hyperbole is not wholly out of place; the integration of the states totally revamped the political map of South Asia. Yet it was far from bloodless; hundreds died in popular movements on behalf of or in opposition to the change. In the case of Jammu and Kashmir, a Muslim-majority kingdom which abutted both India and Pakistan and was technically eligible, under the terms of the deal Mountbatten spelt out to the princes, to join either, opposition to its Hindu Maharaja's belated accession to India in October 1947 led to an undeclared war; to this day, its legal status remains contested and unresolved.

Further reading: Copland 1993, 1997, 1998; Hodson 1969; Menon 1956; Richter 1971; Sherman 2007.

—IAN COPLAND, *Adjunct Professor, School of Philosophical, Historical and International Studies, Monash University, Melbourne*

— •• —

Itihasa

The literal meaning of the Sanskrit term *itihasa* (*iti-hi-asa*) is 'thus indeed it was' and it refers to legend, traditional narratives, events from the past and particularly those connected with past heroes. By itself, *iti* is often used to indicate preceding words or to suggest indirect speech or refer to what is known. It refers to that which has gone before, and in this sense *itihasa* since the nineteenth century has been used for the discipline of history.

Associated with *itihasa* are a number of other words. The *aitihasika* is the one who knows about the past and is familiar with traditional and historical legends. The most frequent association of *itihasa* is with *purana* which literally means 'belonging to times past' and to that extent is thought to encapsulate traditional history. The difference between the two terms is difficult to gauge and they are often linked as a compound term. The *Purana*s took the form of texts originally recited by the *suta* ('bard'), and later by the Brahmin priests. As a narrative recounting of the past, *itihasa* is also sometimes linked to *anushasana* ('governance'), and to *dandaniti* ('administration of justice') (*Arthashastra* 1.5.14).

References to *itihasa* first occur in the Vedic corpus and more often in the *Brahmana*s (exegeses on the *Veda*s), *Upanishad*s (secret teachings and philosophical texts) and the *Shrauta-sutra*s (texts describing ritual and their meanings), largely composed between 900–600 BCE. The context was initially that of educating the householder, including the *raja* ('clan chief'). Gradually, the function of *itihasa* focused more on educating the king. The reason for using it as a compound term, *itihasa-purana*, is not clear. Possibly *purana* was a general reference to narratives about the past, whereas *itihasa* may have been more specific and implied some historicity. The *Shatapatha Brahmana* states that studying the *Veda*s and the *Itihasa-purana* is a way of satisfying the gods and is equivalent to an offering of milk and flesh (11.5.7.4–9). A daily study of these brings affluence, security, a long life, progeny, and blessings (11.5.6.8). One *Upanishad* describes it as the fifth *Veda*, a term also used for the *Mahabharata*, one of the two major Sanskrit epics. This is difficult to define, but presumably applies to those compositions that may not actually be a *Veda* but have a similar importance (*Chandogya Upanishad* 7.1.2.). The *Shrauta-sutras* recommend the recitation of the *Itihasaveda* and the *Puranaveda* as part of the *ashvamedha* sacrifice (a horse sacrifice conducted to establish control over territory, to assert authority, and to ensure fertility, *Ashvalayana* 10.7). *Itihasa* is here embedded in the performance of ritual.

By the early centuries CE, references to *itihasa* are found in treatises on educating the king about governance and the need for him to know these texts, as kings of ancient times who failed to do so came to grief, but those who did so succeeded. This in a sense demonstrates the significance of knowing about the past (*Manu* 7.40–43; *Arthashastra* 1.5.12; 1.2.6). The same advice is repeated in the *Mahabharata* and the *Puranas*, both initially recited by a *suta* and subsequently by *brahmanas*. The *Mahabharata* is described as an *itihasa*. The *Puranas* indicate the occasions when it is to be recited. But some *Puranas* contain a specifically historical segment, the *Vamshanucharita* (*Vishnu Purana* IV). This records what is believed to be the descent of the ancient heroes of the *suryavamsha* ('solar') and *chandra-vamsha* ('lunar') lineages, and then gives the dynastic lists for the ruling families from the Shishunaga (413 BCE) up to the Guptas (320–550 CE). These genealogies, culled from various sources, became the core of the *itihasa* tradition.

Buddhists and Jainas maintained histories of their *sanghas* (organizations for the sects in both religions) and of the evolution of dissident sects. The sects and monasteries were holders of property through royal grants and other forms of patronage whose records had also to be maintained; correlating important monks with contemporary rulers gave a sharper historical edge to their records, as in the *Mahavamsha* in Sri Lanka. From the post-Gupta period the genealogies were central to the legitimation of new ruling families who had to be provided with an ancestry linked to ancient lineages. There was an interdependence of political power and legitimation provided by those Brahmins who had taken over the *Puranas*. *Itihasa* was taken out of its ritual context and was now seen as central to governance. It took the form of *charitas* ('royal biographies'), *prashastis* ('eulogies') or histories of dynasties recorded in inscriptions, and *vamshavalis* ('chronicles'). These texts, recognized as *itihasa*, were akin to a more secular historical tradition and constitute the major sources for reconstructing the history of this period. History, as we know it today, is a post-Enlightenment concept where the narrative of the past is based on factual evidence. *Itihasa*, as used in premodern texts, has a wider meaning to include historical consciousness and perceptions.

Further reading: Bhattacharya 2010; Singh 2003; Thapar 1986.

—ROMILA THAPAR, *Professor Emerita of History, Jawaharlal Nehru University, New Delhi*

— .•. —

Izzat

Izzat ('honour') is a vital concept across South Asia, used by Hindu, Sikh, and Muslim communities, but most often associated with northern India and Pakistan. It suggests the upholding and protection of the honour of the community or kin (often *biradari*), tribe, *jati* (caste or immediate family), or that of the individual. *Izzat* has connotations of respectability and dignity and is sometimes twinned, conversely, with *sharam* ('shame'). It has its roots in notions of reciprocity and equality, in both hospitality and enmity, and is cited as the motivation for action in numerous situations: in warfare, in politics, in the law courts, in family disputes, and in instances of violent retribution. It also has a more quotidian meaning, used by South Asians to describe their own self-respect.

Before Independence, seeking to maintain *izzat* could motivate anticolonial resistance and shape responses to imperial rule (Metcalf 1985). Princes might perceive colonial intervention in their states as an assault on their *izzat*. Muslim Leaguers campaigning for the new state of Pakistan in 1947 often phrased their struggle in the language of upholding the community *izzat* (Gilmartin 1988: 189–224). Today, Dalit leaders in contemporary India might express an election victory as upholding the *izzat* of their followers. More mundanely, an educated unemployed youth who seeks to maintain his self-worth among his peers, despite difficulties finding work, might use the term (Jeffrey, Jeffrey, and Jeffrey 2004: 179). In 2009, the West Bengal politician Mamata Banerjee launched a new rail travel subsidy and called it the 'Izzat Scheme', suggesting that it would bring dignity to the poor.

A living concept that has shaped many South Asian daily lives, *izzat* was also accentuated by the intervention of colonial officials who regarded it as a crucial organizing principle of South Asian society. It was particularly regarded as a characteristic feature of the 'martial races'. Appeals were made to community *izzat* when recruiting for soldiers for the Indian Army and the word was often incorporated into regimental mottos. *The Martial Races of India* of 1933 describes an encounter between an Indian *subedar* ('officer') and a British officer, 'his chief remarks were to his sense of gratitude for the supreme honour that the Sahib had done him, and how his *izzat* was exalted for ever, which could easily be imagined in a country where honour and consideration are so prized' (MacMunn 1933: 313). The behaviour of Pashtun tribesmen and their recourse to customary laws in the Afghan borderlands was attributed to the notion of *izzat* by colonial officials and associated with *badal*, the taking of revenge. This perception continues to inform simplified understandings of *izzat* in the region today.

Izzat has also become an increasingly gendered term, reductively understood as relating to the protection of women, and the community's right to seek retribution in response to any infringement of a woman's chastity. Honour killings or revenge attacks are often described as stemming from a desire to protect *izzat*. In studies of the South Asian diaspora, the term has increasingly been linked to patriarchal values, domestic violence, forced marriages, and to the seclusion of women (Ballard 1994). However, this thinning of the meaning of *izzat* overlooks the complexities of the concept and the richer uses to which it has historically been applied.

Further reading: Ballard 1994; Gilmartin 1988; Jeffrey, Jeffrey and Jeffrey 2004; MacMunn 1933; Metcalf 2006.

—YASMIN KHAN, *Associate Professor, Department for Contnuing Education, University of Oxford*

— •••• —

Kaliyuga

The fourth era (*yuga*) of the quaternary time cycle of Hinduism, Kaliyuga represents our own time, one that signifies decline, corruption, and moral crisis. The concept of the four declining ages first appeared in the *Mahabharata* and some of the *Puranas* and was developed between the fourth century BCE and the fourth century CE. The specific chronological parameters of the *yuga* system, with the Kaliyuga spanning 432,000 years, were adopted by astronomers about the second century CE (Pingree 1990: 276). The *yuga* system continues to be a central conceptual and calendrical feature of present-day Hinduism.

The virtue or dharma of the early *yugas* disintegrates through the ages. The bull of dharma, who stood square on all four legs in the virtuous Kritayuga, wobbles on a single leg in the fourth age. In the age of the demon Kali, dharma will continue to degenerate until the point of complete annihilation and the inauguration of another cycle of eras. Dharma is opposed by the forces of *adharma*, comprising untruth, violence, discontent, and enmity. Brahmins fail in their duty, Shudras become kings, heretics and barbarians rule, castes mingle, and crime prevails. The earth is ravaged and peasants are overtaxed. People fail to heed dharma and devote themselves to food and sex. It is an era when standards are reversed and misery reigns (Kane 1946: 891–5).

While the idea of decadence is common to many world religions, the specific features of decline in the Kaliyuga—such as invasions (by groups such as the Yavanas, Shakas, and Hunas between ca. 300 BCE and 300 CE) from the northwest and the emergence of a new ruling class—may reflect historical crisis and theological adaptation. The degenerate Kaliyuga is also the age in which *bhakti* or personal devotion offers the greatest potential for salvation. While liberation took ten years to achieve in the Kritayuga, it can be achieved by anyone in a day in the Kaliyuga with simple devotional practices of singing and recitation (Stietencron 2005: 35, 45).

The open-ended imagery of Kaliyuga became popular in medieval religious texts; it appears in Kabir, Nanak, Tulsidas, and countless other poets' writings since. For some, the degeneracy of the Kaliyuga provides the rationale for the entry of the destroyer or redeemer who will punish wrongdoers and restore the primal age of truth. This could be Kalki, the awaited tenth avatara of Vishnu, or the avatara of the age (*yugavatara*), an open-ended concept assumed by scores of religious figures, from the early-sixteenth-century figure Krishna Chaitanya, the originator of Gaudiya Vaishnavism, to the semi-mythical half-Hindu, half-Muslim holy man Satya Pir/Satyanarayana in Bengal (Stewart 2000: 24, 30). This vocabulary continues to resonate: the late Sathya Sai Baba (1926–2011) is represented as both *yugavatara* and as a manifestation of Kalki.

Kalyug, a 1981 film by Shyam Benegal, reworks the definitive Kaliyuga epic, the *Mahabharata*, in its depiction of the family drama of an embattled business house. The popularity of pornography is lamented in another film with the same title by Mohit Suri and Mahesh Bhatt in 2005. Social critics, devotees, and artists continue to find fertile ground in the vocabulary of Kaliyuga.

Further reading: Kane 1946; Pingree 1990; Stewart 2000; Stietencron 2005.

—**SAMIRA SHEIKH**, *Associate Professor of History and Asian Studies, Vanderbilt University, Nashville*

— ••• —

Kashmiriyat

K ashmiriyat' (Urdu: 'Kashmiri-ness'; also spelled *kashmiriat*) is a word that plays a key role within discourse on the territorial dispute over the region of Jammu and Kashmir, but one whose meaning is blurred by multiple significations and contrasting deployments by differently positioned political groups. At its simplest, 'Kashmiriyat' indicates the common cultural ground between Hindus and Muslims of the Kashmir Valley, who share the Kashmiri language as mother tongue as well as votive, culinary, and sartorial practices.

The word has also been claimed by Pahari speakers (Aggarwal 2008: 228), who hail from parts of the erstwhile Dogra-ruled Princely State of Jammu and Kashmir that are under Pakistani state control since 1948 and which topographically fell outside the Kashmir Valley; to these groups, Kashmiriyat signifies a *communitas* originating from membership of the original Dogra kingdom that came largely under Indian jurisdiction in 1947 (Kabir 2009).

Most crucially, Indian left-liberal discourse has staked a claim to Kashmiriyat. Although the precise moment of its coinage is unclear, it certainly gained ascendancy amongst media and cultural pundits during the 1990s, exactly when an armed insurgency against the Indian State, spearheaded by the JKLF (Jammu and Kashmir Liberation Front) and its ideological associates, became the conflict's visible front. Indeed, the associations and uses of Kashmiriyat condense the emotional entanglement between the discourses of Indian and indigenous Kashmiri nationalisms (Zutshi 2004: 1–5).

An Indian perspective sees Kashmiriyat as the agreeable blend of Islamic and Hindu mystic strands in Kashmiri culture (Zutshi 2004; Kabir 2009). It thereby signals the overlap between Kashmiri Sufi practices and Indian secularism, with the latter also aligned with South Asian Sufism as a set of practices that pull Islam away from a threatening orthodoxy towards a benevolently fuzzy syncretism. Because such alignments support Kashmir's ideological and historical nestling within the idea of a secular India, the word 'Kashmiriyat' is often rejected by different parties from Kashmir, who consider its appropriation by the Indian establishment as undermining Kashmiri claims to independence or, at the very least, autonomy and self-determination (Aggarwal 2008). At the same time, other Kashmiris, particularly from the Valley, invoke Kashmiriyat as a set of shared but eroded values. The psychosocial repercussions of political conflict are attributed to the suspension of Kashmiriyat, and *azadi* ('freedom', 'self-rule') relied upon to ensure its restoration: when the Kashmiris will have obtained *azadi*, Kashmiriyat will have returned to them. In these contexts, which are often poetic and creative (Kabir 2009), Kashmiriyat works as strategic essentialism, nourished by a political spiritualism deeply connected to the Valley's geography, to embodied craft and folk practices, and to the (Kashmiri) body's return to the over-celebrated

Kashmiri landscape (Ali 1998). This 'reclaiming' is different from that of Kashmiriyat's Indian votaries (for example, Rushdie 2005), for whom Kashmiriyat needs to be protected because it is a cipher for the health of Indian secularism, read as religious and cultural syncretism. The continuing struggles over the meaning of Kashmiriyat are intrinsic to the struggle over territory, desire, and representation that mark the Kashmir conflict; its overloaded semantics offer an alternative map of the conflict's complex emotional and discursive terrain.

Further reading: Aggarwal 2008; Ali 1998; Kabir 2009; Rushdie 2005; Zutshi 2004.

—ANANYA JAHANARA KABIR, *Professor of English Literature, King's College, London*

— ∙•∙ —

Khadi

K*hadi* or *khaddar* refers to coarse cotton cloth, hand woven using hand-spun yarn. It was commonly worn by peasant and artisan groups in pre-industrial India and became a key visual symbol of India's nationalist struggle in the early 1920s. Central to its revival was Mohandas Karamchand Gandhi (1869–1948) who dramatically shed his western dress in favour of simple Indian styles, promoted *khadi* as a national fabric, and tried to reorganize the textile industry around hand-spinning and weaving (Tarlo 1996: ch. 3).

To Gandhi, *khadi* was more than simply cloth; it was the material embodiment of an ideal, representing freedom from the yoke of colonialism, and standing for economic self-sufficiency, political independence, spiritual humility, moral purity, national integrity, communal unity, social equality, a challenge to untouchability, and the embrace of non-violence.

By choosing a simple, non-elitist textile as national dress, he sought to encourage people of different castes, classes, ages, regions, and genders into the nationalist struggle, creating a powerful visual language with which to confront colonialism. Whilst the wearing of *khadi* became a national duty, hand-spinning was encouraged as an act of prayer and the spinning wheel (*charka*) promoted as a weapon of non-violent resistance and the foundation of a future craft-based society (Gandhi 1999: vol. 73, 241).

Khadi and the *charka* played an important role in creating an imagined national community which, for the first time, incorporated the non-literate majority. The Congress Party recognized their significance by placing them at the centre of the Non-Cooperation campaign of 1920–1 and the Civil Disobedience movement of 1930 which included boycotts of the import and sale of foreign cloth, and the staging of public bonfires in which foreign cloth was burnt and replaced by simple white *khadi* garments. Eventually the Congress Party adopted *khadi* as its official fabric, placed the spinning wheel at the centre of the national flag, and introduced daily spinning for its members. Meanwhile, the All-India Spinners Association organized *khadi* tours throughout the country, replete with exhibitions, sales of cloth, and demonstrations of spinning in rural areas (Trivedi 2003). In effect, Gandhi transformed the visual culture of Indian politics. By designing a small white *khadi* cap (later known as the Gandhi cap) which people of any background could wear, he not only challenged European sartorial hierarchies, but also Indian ones, creating a powerful image of national unity (Tarlo 1996: 82–6).

Gandhi's promotion of *khadi* was met with opposition from several quarters, including prominent figures such as Rabindranath Tagore (1861–1941) and Bhimrao Ambedkar (1891–1956), both of whom perceived hand-spinning as retrogressive (Tarlo 1996: 92). There were also economic problems that haunted the *khadi* campaign such as the cost of raw cotton and the comparative cheapness of imported, machine-spun yarn. Gandhi's decision to adopt a short *dhoti* or loincloth in 1921 was partly a response to this situation. He wished to evoke the poverty to which India had been reduced through colonial policies and convey the necessity of re-establishing economic self-sufficiency. Many, however, wrongly interpreted his loincloth as the natural dress of a religious ascetic—something Winston Churchill (1874–1965) picked up on in his famous description of Gandhi as a seditious lawyer 'posing as a half-naked fakir' (Tarlo 1996: 78–9).

Gandhi's dream that *khadi* would become the everyday textile of Indians after Independence was never realized. Ironically, the white *khadi* worn by politicians is associated more with hypocrisy and corruption than purity. Yet *khadi* continues to represent an alternative, distinctly Indian, modernity at a time when globalist capitalist values have majority appeal. When artists, academics, and social activists wear coloured *khadi* they recognize its continued capacity to represent alternative lifestyles, aesthetics, and values.

The ambiguous status of *khadi* in politics is echoed by its problematic economic position. In 1956, the Khadi and Village Industries Commission (KVIC) was established with a view to stimulating *khadi* and other village industries in rural areas. Yet, despite high levels of government subsidy, the *khadi* industry has always struggled to sustain itself and has been further marginalized since the liberalization of the Indian economy in the 1990s (Reddy and Bhaskar 2005). Today, there are numerous attempts to update the industry through aggressive marketing at home, abroad, and over the Internet, as well as through the promotion of different varieties, from 'polyester khadi' to 'bio-khadi'. What past and present revivals of *khadi* reveal are ongoing tensions between capitalist development and alternative economic and moral principles. At a symbolic level, *khadi* retains its place in national memory as the cloth of India's freedom struggle.

Further reading: Bayly 1986; Chakrabarty 2001; Gandhi 1999; Reddy and Bhaskar 2005; Tarlo 1996; Trivedi 2003.

—EMMA TARLO, *Professor of Anthropology, Goldsmiths,*
University of London

— ·•· —

Khalifa/Khalifat/Khilafat

The terms *khalifa* and *khilafat* have specific translations in English as caliph and caliphate. They embrace, however, an idea of great power in Islamic civilization, the idea of succession (Gibb 1962: 54–8). Thus, in the early twentieth century, South Asian Muslims might have regarded the Ottoman caliph as the successor to the Prophet Muhammad as the leader of the Muslim community. More generally, they regarded themselves as the successors in their generation to great traditions, passed down from the time of the Prophet and the subsequent classical Islamic period. This was symbolized, for instance, in the *ijaza* ('licence') to teach a book that would be given to a student when he completed one of the books of the *madrasa* (lit. 'school', 'college', esp. a college for Islamic instruction) curriculum and which would state how the book had been transmitted from the original author down the centuries to him. It was symbolized, too, in the *shijra* ('family tree'), which the Sufi master would give his disciples, amongst whom the most favoured would be designated *khalifa*. The *shijra* would state the record of the handing down of spiritual knowledge from the Prophet's nephew and son-in-law, Ali, through the founding saint of the Sufi order down to his master. This sense of civilizational succession was felt through many aspects of Indo-Islamic life (Robinson 1996).

In the nineteenth century, the onset of British power in South Asia undermined the idea of civilizational succession and the authority of the past that came with it. To confront the challenges of British rule in religious matters, some Muslims abandoned the authority of transmission through time and sought new forms of authority ranging from a direct return to the Quran and *hadith* (lit. 'tradition', a collection of traditions containing sayings of the Prophet Muhammad which, with accounts of his daily practice, constitute the major source of guidance for Muslims apart from the Quran) and to western science (Troll 1978). In material matters, others looked increasingly beyond their civilization to find inspiration across a broad front—from western technology and philosophy to western poetry. These breaks with the past were traumatic, a feeling expounded in Hali's popular elegy of 1879 on the rise and fall of Islam (Shackle and Majeed 1997).

Muslim protest against the rupture with many of the central traditions of Islamic civilization was symbolized by the Khilafat Movement from 1919 to 1924 (Minault 1982). From the mid-nineteenth century, *ulama* came to recognize Ottoman claims to the caliphate (which had been revived in the treaty of Kucuk Kainarji with the Russians in 1774), and which came to be promoted vigorously after the accession of Abdul Hamid II in 1876 (Ahmad 1967: 124–31). From 1911, the overwhelming of the Ottoman dominions by Europe sparked acute concern. The years from the formation of the Indian Khilafat Organisation (1919) to Ataturk's abolition of the Ottoman Khalifat (1924) witnessed the greatest mass movement India had ever seen (Minault 1982). Amongst the reasons for the vigour of the movement were: the economic disruption caused by World War I, the hardline stupidity of the Government of India's Rowlatt Acts (1919 legislation which turned the emergency laws of World War I, enabling trial without jury and internment without trial, into permanent law), the political fluidity and uncertainty created by the Montagu–Chelmsford reforms (1919 legislative council reforms which devolved substantial new powers on Indians), the vitality of the response of the Muslim press to developments in the wider Muslim world, and the mobilizing skills of both the *ulama* and Mohandas Karamchand Gandhi (1869–1948). But to all of these must be added the iconic power of the decline of the *khalifat*. Consciously, and for many subconsciously, the threat to the *khalifat*, and its final demise, symbolized the fractures, and the loss of contact with the past that Indian Muslims were experiencing.

The dissolution of the *khalifat* did not bring to an end the salience of the word *khilafat* in twentieth-century India. At the very time that one meaning of the word was losing contemporary relevance, another was emerging—the caliphate of man. The new meaning reached back to the Quran but gained force as a result of the religious changes brought about by the Muslim revival from the nineteenth century. In the context of Muslim loss of power, reformers placed a new emphasis on direct contact with revelation, on the realities of the Day of Judgment, and on the undesirability of seeking intercession with God for man on earth. The aim was to fashion the individual human conscience as the basis of Muslim society. Men knew that they had to act on earth to be saved. This 'activist Muslim', as Muhammad Iqbal (1877–1938) explained so well in his *Reconstruction of Religious Thought in Islam* (1930), was God's *khalifa*, God's successor on earth. It was an idea of great power which was taken up by Maulana Maududi (1903–79) and by Muslim reformers in the Middle East from Sayyid Qutb (1906–66) to Ayatollah Khomeini (1902–89) (Robinson 2004).

Further reading: Ahmad 1964; Minault 1982; Robinson 2004; Shackle and Majeed 1997.

—FRANCIS ROBINSON, *Professor of South Asian History,*
Royal Holloway College, University of London; Sultan of Oman Fellow,
Oxford Centre for Islamic Studies, University of Oxford

— .◆. —

Khalistan

The concept of a sovereign Sikh State, Khalistan, was first formulated by a medical practitioner from Ludhiana, V.S. Bhatti, in 1940. Strategically as well as semantically, this concept was a mimetic, and simultaneous, response to the demand for Pakistan by the Muslim League. Pakistan and Khalistan both refer to a 'land of the pure'; the latter term also refers to the Khalsa, founded by the last Sikh Guru, Gobind Singh (1666–1708), in 1699 (Singh 2004).

Sikh leaders like Master Tara Singh (1885–1967) and Giani Kartar Singh (1902–74) did toy with the idea of an independent Sikh state during the negotiations around the transfer of power from British to Indian hands, in 1946–7, but to no avail (Grewal and Banga 2000). This separatist project resurfaced in the early 1970s around another medical practitioner, Jagjit Singh Chauhan (1929–2007). In 1971, he placed an advertisement in the *New York Times* advocating the creation of an independent Sikh state in Punjab. His call for Khalistan was echoed by other diasporic Sikhs in later years (Tatla 1999), such as the Washington-based

Ganga Singh Dhillon (b. 1931), who became the first advocate for this cause on Capitol Hill.

Until 1984, this separatist project evoked indifference, if not worse, from the Sikhs of India (sixteen million individuals) and the diaspora (two million, mostly in the UK, Canada, and the US). Indeed, in Hindi and Punjabi, the term *Khali-stan* can also mean 'the empty country', and the 'Khalistanis' were primarily an object of derision. But this situation changed brutally after the Indian army, under Indira Gandhi's (1917–84) command, launched a full-fledged assault against a group of Sikh extremists entrenched in the holiest Sikh shrine, the Golden Temple of Amritsar. Sant Jarnail Singh Bhindranwale (1947–84) and hundreds of his companions—as well as an equivalent number of pilgrims—were 'martyred' during this military intervention, code-named 'Operation Bluestar' (Tully and Jacob 1985). These deaths, and the profanation of the Golden Temple, infuriated Sikhs of all persuasion, in India as well as in the diaspora, and gave a new resonance to separatist demands.

Following this attack, hundreds of young Sikhs (including a small number of women) crossed over to Pakistan in search of armed support for the 'liberation' of Khalistan. Initially reluctant to oblige, the Pakistanis regrouped most of these potential recruits in special quarters of the Faisalabad Jail; only after 1986 did Pakistani intelligence agencies start to train and provide military support to Sikh insurgents, who gradually organized politically and militarily (Gayer 2009).

From the beginning, this insurgent movement has suffered from fissiparous tendencies, which have greatly weakened it. The Khalistan Commando Force (KCF), founded in 1986, was gradually sidelined by other armed groups such as the Babbar Khalsa and the Khalistan Liberation Force (KLF), whose political agenda focused less on the liberation of Punjab from the Indian yoke than on the moralization of the Sikhs (Keppley-Mahmood 1996).

From 1992 onwards, this armed struggle started receding in Punjab, in a context of gradual political normalization. In 1995, the Khalistanis perpetrated their first—and last—suicide attack, which cost the life of Punjab's chief minister, Beant Singh (1922–95). Far from signalling a revival of militancy in Punjab, this act of sacrificial violence turned out to be the swan song of a waning insurgency. Even if the demand for Khalistan were to retain some support in the diaspora, most insurgents have been either killed, have defected, or joined the political mainstream (Grewal 2004).

Further reading: Gayer 2009; Grewal 2004; Grewal and Banga 2000; Keppley-Mahmood 1996; Singh 2004; Tatla 1999.

—LAURENT GAYER, *Research Fellow, CERI-Sciences Po, Paris*

— .•. —

Khandaan

For those conversant with the recent history of North Indian popular culture, be it cinema or television serials, this Hindustani term conjures up a multigenerational, co-residential unit, comprised mostly of patri-kin—fathers, sons, and grandsons, their wives, daughters-in-law, and other female relatives. This apparently cohesive kinship unit in such representations would also have a few faithful family retainers thrown in, who would have lived with the family for generations, and hence be considered its 'members'. Periodically, this fact, of the structuring of affect via residence and sharing of food, would be reiterated, thereby underscoring the enduring nature of the *khandaan* as a kinship unit within Indian society (for representative discussions see Shah 1998; Uberoi 1994).

Despite these rather baroque representations of households as sites of sharing, mutuality, and affect, bulging at their seams with happiness, these repeated popular cultural iterations become an interesting entry point to unpack the meaning of the term. Needless to say, linguistic variations in India, with their attendant etymologies, themselves point to differences in what is loosely translated as 'the household' in English. However, that notwithstanding, what is significant is whether, despite variations, there are any generalizable elements constituting the *khandaan*, understood as a loose approximation of household, and how one might arrive at isolating these for analytical purposes. Predictably, these issues become vexatious when in recent times households are qualified in any number of ways, including terms such as 'female-headed' and 'single-person', amongst others. Yet, it is precisely these differences that point to at least one feature that is singularly important in an attempt to understand the meaning of the term 'households'—that it is not a static, unchanging entity that lends itself to easy definition. Households are not merely a sum of different characteristics; these change in shape, size, and constitution depending on the histories of their formation, political and economic conditions, and even the sites from which information is culled to 'define' them. Be it the law or the state (the census is an excellent source for tracking changes in the definition of the term), the 'household' is often seen as the basic unit of society—for purposes of governance, economic analysis, or simply for organizing systems of enumeration.

In disciplinary terms, the predominant amount of writing on the household is sociological (or anthropological) and historical (for India see Arunima 2003; Patel 2005; Shah 1998; for the non-Indian context, see Netting et al. 1984). Despite differences in thrust or emphasis, by the 1980s scholars like Robert Netting and Richard Wilk, amongst others, working on understanding the evolution of this kinship form and its changing meanings over time, agreed on the fact that it defied easy categorization. Equally, they warned against a tendency of going by what were termed as 'classificatory catchwords' (for instance, defining a household as matrilocal or patrilocal) as 'residence rules might be followed, ignored, or temporarily observed' (Netting et al. 1984: 14). The more substantive point, of course, was the mismatch between theoretical 'rules'—often formulated by external observers—and the complex, and changing, histories of social practice that informed marriage, family, household, and kinship itself. This is linked to a second issue that is germane to what one might term as a 'definitional crisis'. This is the distinction, often maintained, especially in early anthropological literature, between the 'family' and the 'household'. In essence, this devolved on the assumption that while the former was constituted by kindred, the latter could have non-kin members who were long-term associates of the household (for instance, housemaids, feudal retainers, and so on) (Netting et al. 1984: 14). While there is some merit in maintaining this distinction, in that it alerts us to the differences in relationships, including questions of rights and authority within the domestic group, for the most part it simply obscures the messy, and overlapping, nature of these units. Besides, if the presence of non-kin members alone were to be a criterion for distinguishing families from households, then one may find that the latter was the preserve of the upper classes, and the landed elite (Netting et al. 1984: 14; for an example from the Indian context, see Arunima 1992).

Indeed, particular types of households were certainly restricted to the wealthy and the well-endowed. For instance, a nineteenth-century Malayalam proverb decreed that 'you may be a Nayar, but to count as one you must be born in a *taravad*' (Arunima 2003). The *taravad*, or matrilineal 'household' of the Nayars of Kerala, signified power, prestige, and landed wealth. Though over a period of time the term itself was used more loosely to refer to any household—here referring to both a shared right in resources and a multigenerational interest group for the most part—it is significant that in this early usage it emphasized property ownership, and its attendant privileges, as a key criterion for defining a household (Arunima 2003).

Equally, the substantial body of work of feminist scholars, both anthropologists and historians, has alerted us to the messy nature of this term, the difficulty in making easing distinctions between household and the family, and, most significantly, to caution against working with ideas of the household as strictly bounded or performing merely specific functions. Like elsewhere, scholarship in India too has moved to exploring the 'household' as a changing, and dynamic, form—integrated into social, economic, and political processes, but also structured by ideological imperatives that influence both its internal structure, as indeed its integration within wider society (for representative examples, see the essays in Chatterjee 2004; Chowdhry 2009; Ghosh 2006.)

More recently, particularly within historical scholarship focusing on issues of gender and women's rights that has framed an understanding of the household, one can see at least three broad analytical trends. The first, evident in the work of scholars like Carroll (1983) or Arunima (1992, 2003), focuses on the dynamic and changing nature of the household, and attempts to locate this within an intersection of the law and state. Through the nineteenth century, the colonial state attempted to create standardized laws governing different types of kinship relations. These legal changes attempted to modify both household 'structure'—for instance, rights pertaining to property, authority, or residence—while redefining 'personal' issues like marriage, divorce, inheritance, and maintenance (Carroll 1983). Predictably, changes in any one of these would have an effect on all else;

however, if one were to examine an overall trend in the transformation of the wealthier households by the mid-twentieth century, it appears that most of these became, at least legally, co-residential, kin-based units, where age and gender were principal factors in determining property rights and structures of authority, as indeed questions of mobility and of labour (see for instance Sen 1999). The second body of research that sheds light on another dimension of the household is the literature on the nineteenth-century 'woman question'. The debates generated by the work of Tanika Sarkar (2001), Uma Chakravarti (1998), Kumkum Sangari, and Sudesh Vaid, amongst others (1989), particularly on 'marriage' ('child', 'widows', and 'age of consent'), direct our attention to the household as an ideological site whose form and function cannot be understood without accounting for structures of power, legitimation, and desire that constantly mould and shape both the relationships of the people within it, as indeed of it to wider society.

However, how accurate would it be to see the colonial period merely as relentless patriarchal governmentality, wherein ideas and institutions of marriage, family, and the household, alongside those of gender and sexuality, are streamlined and easily regulated? Often diversity in household forms that reflect differences in class, caste, community, region, and economic activity also attests to the need to critically situate the state's regulatory interventions. Equally, histories of migration, labour, and urbanization are also influential in determining changes in household structures, size, membership, as also relationships of 'interest and emotion' (Medick and Sabean 1984). This constitutes the third, quite differentiated, 'trend', in the literature on households. For instance, compulsory ascetic widowhood for the Bengali *bhadralok* (literally, respectable people, a term used for the middle class) women implied that many upper-caste households would have had ageing older, dependant women living a life of 'social death' within them (Chakravarti and Gill 2007). This was a pattern commonly found in other upper-caste households too, particularly in parts of southern India, including Karnataka and Tamilnadu. On the contrary, the prevalence of *karewa* marriage, or levirate, amongst the Jat peasantry meant that household structure would adapt to this social history of practice (Chowdhry 1994). Interestingly, while it might be argued that both these (ascetic widowhood and levirate) were instances of forms of patriarchy, the outcomes, in social and material terms, and the shape of the household, varied greatly.

This takes us back to the problem of an analysis driven by rules and definitions in understanding household formation, both historically, and as a dynamic contemporary social process. For every multigenerational patrilineal, 'patriarchal' household, following strict caste rules, there have been households based on interracial marriages, or on slavery and concubinage (Chatterjee 2004). Even contemporary assumptions that female-headed households are a recent phenomenon are belied in the face of extraordinary histories such as those of Begum Samru (ca. 1753–1836), who had no known biological or affinal relations. She was sold into slavery in her youth, lived sequentially as a Muslim courtesan, domestic slave/purchased mistress of a Catholic European mercenary, converting herself to Catholicism, and ended her life as a virtually independent ruler of a princely state. She also was an 'adoptive mother' of several generations of the relatives of her master-turned-consort (see Fisher 2004b). Households such as hers bear testimony to the fact that the 'exception' needs far greater attention than it is normally accorded. Moreover, such examples point to the fact that not simply the household, but other analytical criteria like caste or class, otherwise assumed to be stable, are likewise messy categories. Not only does the recent body of literature on the household by Ghosh, Chatterjee, and Fisher, amongst others, complicate questions about its origin, structure, and function, but it also fronts issues like cross-class sexual intimacy and power (as in the case of slaves as concubines) as constitutive of household formation in certain historical and cultural contexts.

Finally, then, what are the implications of 'diversity' for an analysis of the 'household'? Historical and cultural variations found in property rights, residence patterns, authority structures, or rules relating to marriage, divorce, maintenance, and inheritance are simultaneously accompanied by legal and statist attempts to circumscribe, regulate, and thereby thematize them. In post-Independence India, 'personal law' reforms of all communities have affected changes in laws pertaining to marriage, adoption, maintenance, and succession (Agnes 2005). Ironically, these are accompanied by new social phenomena like cross-regional marriages (men from Haryana marrying Malayali women)—often a by-product of low sex ratios in bride-seeking regions (Kaur 2006). While it is too soon to predict the implications of these practices for understanding contemporary changes in the household, it certainly highlights the difficulty in merely adopting state policy, legislative histories, or notions of unilineal change as ways of understanding a complex, and mutating, domestic group like the household.

Further reading: Agnes 2005; Arunima 2003; Chakravarti and Gill 2007; Chatterjee 2004; Chowdhry 1994; Medick and Sabean 1984; Shah 1998; Sangari and Vaid 1989; Saradamoni 1992.

—G. ARUNIMA, *Associate Professor, Centre for Women's Studies, School of Social Sciences, Jawaharlal Nehru University, New Delhi*

— .•. —

Knowledge Formation

The question of knowledge formation has been one of the most contentious issues in recent studies of South Asia and lies at the heart of the problematic understanding of the relationship between knowledge and power, especially in the context of colonial rule in India. One school of interpretation, drawing intellectual authority from the writings of Antonio Gramsci (1891–1937) and Michel Foucault (1926–84), and more especially from Edward Said's *Orientalism* (1978), has identified a radical disjuncture in the dominant knowledge system in India with the advent of British rule in the late eighteenth and early nineteenth centuries. As Bernard Cohn observed in an essay first published in 1985: 'The conquest of India was a conquest of knowledge' (Cohn 1996: 16).

While some scholars have argued that Orientalist epistemology facilitated colonial conquest in the first place, or made possible its initial consolidation, the prevalent view has been that it was only once foreign rule had been established that the need arose for an epistemological space within which Orientalism could flourish. As rulers, the British quest for knowledge about India was driven by largely utilitarian motives—to achieve their political and economic objectives, uphold a (highly racialized) sense of difference from the colonized, and seek legitimation for alien rule by extolling the virtues of their own civilization and denigrating that of their subjects (Chatterjee 1995; Dirks 2001). For Cohn, the process of knowledge acquisition, begun by obtaining an effective command of India's languages, grew rapidly to encompass Indian law, religion, revenue systems, and ethnography. Knowledge formation entailed the use of indigenous texts and local informants, but it was a pursuit of knowledge shaped by the West's Enlightenment, informed by a specifically western understanding of India, and was a task to which the British brought 'their own forms of knowing and thinking' (Cohn 1996: 53). One of its earliest and most influential manifestations was the Orientalist scholarship (notably in Sanskrit and Persian) associated with the founding of the Asiatic Society of Bengal by Sir William Jones (1746–94) in 1784 and pursued by subsequent generations of East India Company (EIC) scholar-officials. This brand of Orientalism, Gyan Prakash observed, following Said, 'was a European enterprise from the very beginning. The scholars were European; the audience was European'. Indians figured only as 'inert objects of knowledge'. In this semi-official scholarship, the western Orientalist invariably 'spoke for the Indian' (Prakash 1990: 384). But other scholars have suggested a more constrained and interactive process, with Lata Mani remarking that 'the colonial state's will to knowledge, unlike that of the metropolitan, required negotiating a radically different cognitive universe, one which it grasped only imperfectly and which it was never to wholly comprehend or subdue' (Mani 1988: 12–13). As colonial rule evolved, its knowledge systems became more systematically institutionalized and integrated into the apparatus of state power. Cohn regarded the gathering, ordering, and classifying of 'objective' knowledge about India as requiring several different techniques or 'investigative modalities' (Cohn 1996: 5–10)—ranging from the historiographic and observational to the museological and surveillance modalities. Particularly influential in his view were the government surveys as well as settlement and census reports. Subsequent scholarship has broadened the remit of colonial knowledge to include such fields as medicine, science, cartography, ethnology, philosophy, law, and education, and has demonstrated the importance of such strategic sites for the garnering of colonial knowledge—and hence for the exercise of colonial power—as the army, the police, the mental asylum, and the prison (Viswanathan 1990 on education; Arnold 1993 on medicine). By the late nineteenth century, this 'useful' knowledge had been refined and consolidated into census reports, district gazetteers, and such functional texts as the manuals of 'criminal tribes' and 'martial races'. It informed a set of stereotypical, essentializing understandings of India, typically constructed around ideas of regional difference, religious bigotry, innate criminality, immutable caste hierarchies, gender oppression, and a pervasive sense of poverty, fatalism, timelessness, and tradition (Inden 1990; Metcalf 1994).

Knowledge formation is understood as a colonially constructed discursive project, one which aspired (despite its many internal contradictions) to create a coherent and systematic western understanding of India and thereby assist in creating and maintaining India's dual subordination to colonialism and capitalism. Colonial knowledge formation implied, firstly, a radical disjuncture from what had gone before—an 'epistemic violence' that marked off the colonial regime from all its Indian predecessors. Secondly, it was associated with the formation of new (or at the least substantially reconstituted) institutions and agencies, novel sites of observation and practice, by which and through which colonial knowledge of India was acquired, refined, and disseminated. But, thirdly, knowledge formation was understood as an ongoing historical process, by which an initial phase of acquisition and formulation, spearheaded by Orientalist scholarship and missionary propaganda, was largely superseded by an array of state institutions (such as the army and the jails, the surveys and censuses). This colonial activity in turn made possible an Indian appropriation, internalization, and hybridization of ideas that had their origin within the domain of colonial knowledge or through interaction with it and so became part of an emergent 'national knowledge' (Guha-Thakurta 1995; Ludden 1993: 271–4).

This broadly Foucauldian and Saidian understanding of knowledge formation, as an essentializing and yet utilitarian Orientalist-colonialist project, has been contested by a number of South Asia scholars. Some have doubted the very validity of the power/knowledge nexus, preferring to speak instead of 'information' and 'communication' (Bayly 1996; Dirks 2001: 307–13), and have reasserted the primacy of a historical and sociological understanding of India grounded in class (rather than knowledge) formation and in capitalist materialism rather than the real (or imagined) effects of alien epistemologies (Chandavarkar 1994). A substantial body of criticism has returned to a pre-existing notion of the relative fragility and superficiality of the colonial presence in India, and, in something of a reiteration of a once-spurned concept of 'collaboration', has resurrected the idea of British rule on the subcontinent as being a mutually interdependent Anglo-Indian enterprise rather than a function of alien imposition and externally driven innovation (Frykenberg 1999). Critics of Said further point to the long-established and multiple knowledge systems that existed in India well before the advent of British rule—embodied in ancient Vedic texts, in philosophical, religious, and legal treatises, in medical and scientific works dating back to Buddhist times, in Islamic scholarship on history, religion, and literature from the late medieval era onwards, to say nothing of the complex interweaving and regional variations of and between these different knowledge systems or the varieties of subaltern knowledge with which they intersected and at times came into conflict. In particular, from the sixteenth century onwards, the Mughals and Marathas are seen as having pioneered many of the knowledge-gathering tools and the means of collecting, systematizing, and classifying knowledge later identified with the British (O'Hanlon and Washbrook 1991; Washbrook 1999).

Rather than knowledge formation being a one-sided enterprise, it can be argued that the British derived much of their understanding of India from Indians themselves, especially at a time when the British remained acutely aware of the insecurity of their political and military ascendancy over India and when, before the 1830s, the lines of social exchange and cultural communication were more open and more reciprocal than they became in the post-1857 period. Indian informants, such as Brahmin pandits or members of the Muslim elite, deliberately or unconsciously imbued the British with their own understanding of Indian society, law, religion, and culture, and these partisan 'native' epistemologies, or hybrid versions of them, were then given new (arguably unprecedented) authority through colonial legal codes, census categories, bureaucratic procedures, and military recruitment practices (O'Hanlon and Washbrook 1991; Dirks 1993). Much that was already entrenched in India thus remained relatively intact beneath the carapace of colonial rule, or was sufficiently viable, versatile, and robust to engage in dialogue with the local representatives of Company rule. Hence, as Eugene Irschick has claimed, social meanings and institutions as they emerged in early colonial South India were more the product of 'negotiation' than 'imposition,' or gave rise, through local processes of mediation and innovation, to new forms of knowledge (Irschick 1994: ix, 6, 8). This line of argument eschews the kind of oversimplified binary between East and West, 'indigenous' and 'colonial', attributed to Said and his followers: it also seeks to give Indians (at least Indians of a privileged social position or intermediary authority) effective agency in the process of knowledge formation, and hence in the making of an Indian modernity that was more than simply a passive replication of western modernity. Such a line of argument suggests, too, that the frailty and superficiality of the colonial knowledge system rendered British power—far from being all-knowing—weak and vulnerable to unforeseen eruptions like the Indian uprising of 1857–8, since it lacked reliable intelligence about the attitudes and grievances of the mass of the population and hence the means to anticipate and counter them (Bayly 1996: ch. 9).

The debate over colonial knowledge raged most fiercely in the 1990s as the arguments of Cohn and Said were absorbed and responded to. More recent scholarship has tended to seek a more nuanced and less dichotomous understanding of knowledge formation. One move has been to step back from the colonial era and to see it as merely a phase in a far longer history of knowledge creation and transformation, of syncretism between 'systems', of processes through which new or once-external ideas, institutions, and practices were articulated, amended, and absorbed, thereby downplaying the special epistemological status assigned to colonialism and its peculiar forms of knowledge. Knowledge is seen as circulating over a long period of time between Indians and Europeans (Grove 1996), as being the product of their mutual engagement and 'co-production' rather than extracted by imperial agency or imposed by imperial fiat (Raj 2003), or it is seen as arising from or through non-state agencies, such as foreign missionaries (Sharma 2011). Significantly, some of the most formative influences are seen as emanating from continental Europe or from America and so less likely to be representative of a specifically British colonial system of power/knowledge. There has, besides, been a growing tendency to see knowledge formation in more fluid and migratory terms, with essentializing ideas, emblematic objects, and technical practices moving with relative freedom (but also shifting shades of meaning and adaptive usages) between precolonial cultures and British India or as fragments of 'cosmopolitan knowledge' that circulated between the subcontinent and other disseminating sites of information and power (Sivasundaram 2005; Kumar 2012). And yet, despite this move to interaction and circularity, something of the former pro- and anti-Saidian polarity remains, especially among those scholars across a range of disciplines—history, anthropology, geography, and postcolonial studies—who continue to believe in the historical exceptionality of colonialism and in its unparalleled processes of coercion, exploitation, and knowledge formation.

Further reading: Cohn 1996; Irschick 1994; O'Hanlon and Washbrook 1991; Prakash 1990; Sivasundaram 2005.

—DAVID ARNOLD, *Emeritus Professor, Department of History,*
University of Warwick

— .•. —

Kumbh Mela

The Kumbh Mela is a Hindu festival occurring at regular intervals over a twelve-year cycle at four places in India: Allahabad, Haridwar, Nashik, and Ujjain. Allahabad and Haridwar also hold 'half' Kumbh Melas six years after their 'full' melas. A full Kumbh Mela took place at Allahabad in 2001. In 2003 there was a Kumbh Mela at Nashik and in 2004 there was a full Kumbh Mela at Ujjain and a half Kumb Mela at Haridwar. In 2007, there was a half Kumbh Mela at Allahabad. In 2010 and 2013, there were full Kumbh Melas at Haridwar and Allahabad, respectively, and then the cycle started again.

The most important dates at each Kumbh Mela are those of the three *shahi snans* ('royal baths'), whose exact times are fixed by astrologers. On these days it is deemed particularly auspicious to bathe in the sacred rivers at each of the sites (the 'confluence' or *sangam* of the Ganga and Yamuna at Allahabad, the Ganga at Haridwar, the Godavari at Nashik, and the Shipra at Ujjain).

Kumbh Melas last for up to three months. Many pilgrims stay for the duration of the festival in a tented city (those who do so are called *kalpavasis*), but their numbers increase greatly for a few days around the time of each royal bath. Estimates of the number of pilgrims that attend are notoriously inaccurate but at the most recent Kumbh Mela, that at Allahabad in 2013, officials reported that over 30 million people bathed on the day of the main royal bath (Rashid 2013).

The Kumbh Mela is said to be the biggest gathering of people in the world. It is claimed by many of its participants to be an ancient institution. There is evidence that large gatherings of pilgrims have happened at Allahabad since at least the middle of the first millennium CE, and at the other sites since the medieval period (Clark 2006: 294–7), but their systematization into four linked Kumbh Melas dates to the late nineteenth century and was a strategy employed by the priests of Allahabad to ensure that the British recognized the festival and their rights over it (Maclean 2008: 83–110).

At the heart of the festival are the camps of the sadhus. Kumbh Melas are where the sadhu orders make all important organizational decisions and appointments, as well as initiate new recruits. The right to bathe at the most auspicious times was, along with more mundane concerns, the cause of frequent bloody battles between the different *akhara*s ('militant sadhu regiments') at Haridwar during the eighteenth century, at which time the sadhus controlled the festival. In the nineteenth century, the East India Company (EIC), seeking both to suppress the unruly sadhus as well as to control the lucrative tax and trade revenues associated with the Haridwar *mela*, intervened, and the layout of the camps and order of bathing has remained the same since (Maclean 2008: 23–4). After the 1857 rebellion, the British administration was in charge of the *mela*s at all four sites and fixed the order of bathing. After Independence, the Government of India took over the administrative duties and they now provide the infrastructure necessary for the festival.

Further reading: Clark 2006; Lochtefeld 2004; Maclean 2008, Rashid 2013.

—JAMES MALLINSON, *Lecturer in Sanskrit and Classical Indian Studies, SOAS, University of London*

— ·•· —

Land Revenue/Land Reform

W hy tax land? From the early modern period, Indian territorial states, dominating lands and inhabitants, often found it easier to tax agricultural produce than immoveable property, trade, or invisibles such as interest and profit, let alone hunting and gathering. Forced or slave labour was expensive to manage, as was exacting tribute by agreement or invasion. Taxes on persons or dwellings were hard to collect, and anyway, in a largely agrarian society, were indirect levies on farming. Commerce and industry, also difficult to tap, were often less rewarding fiscally for the central government than might be thought from the many dues on artisans and markets, and the local tolls on roads and at landing places. Agricultural output was relatively predictable, cyclical, tangible, and exchangeable. Producers or land controllers were identifiable, and less mobile than most wealth creators. To encourage payment, lords offered protection and investment alongside their depredations, as did some states. Agriculture required investment—to break in new lands, develop artificial irrigation, and recuperate from climatic or demographic reverses; and, of course, credit was needed in the natural gap between input (ploughing, sowing) and return (harvest, marketing).

Setting the land tax was fundamental to landownership and the nature of states and societies. In precolonial India, even the Delhi sultans (1206–1526) but particularly the Mughals from about 1580 (cf. the statistical survey of Todar Mal, ca. 1515–89, minister to the emperor Akbar, 1542–1605) tried to scrutinize, regulate, and increase the taxation of rural surplus, not only on state or dynastic lands (*khalsa*) but across their domains (see Richards 1995). British rule (1772–1947) brought major changes, mainly by distinguishing between land rights, gradually protected even against the sovereign or the state, and more contingent insecure possession where a despotic sovereign was ultimate landlord. David Landes' (1998: 31) orthodox account of Europe's early economic advantages notes:'linked to the opposition between Greek democracy and oriental despotism was that between private property and ruler-owns-all'. Both possession and transfer existed in precolonial India, but arbitrary and potentially unlimited taxation made landholding insecure, even where holders were unlikely to be ousted by force. British colonial administrators, sometimes pretending they inherited ultimate proprietorship from the Mughals, could not escape their own history: they limited state power in order to protect private property.

The British sought raised income, economic development and trade benefiting rulers and people, and groups to control society and support the state. Sometimes captivated by theories of unearned surplus, calling it rent, after David Ricardo (1772–1823), they were consistently concerned with the economic potential of secure, industrious producers. Though referring to theory, they were pragmatic and political when setting the land tax. They also sought to recognize, not create, rights and relationships on the land. Later, their attitude resembled corrections made in political economy by Richard Jones (1790–1855) and others, emphasizing the variety of landholding and its particular, national significance (Barber 1975). However, British rule also standardized the meanings of rent (payment for possession of land) and real property (bounded territory held by legal right). Anomalies always existed, but the trend was towards norms and regulation. Formalizing and recording types of land right, under the rule of law, the British transformed the nature of property and the concepts of rights in India.

First, the permanent settlement of Bengal (1793) placed its faith in superior landlords, fashioned out of the varieties of *zamindars* ('Mughal land controllers and revenue payers'), replacing temporary revenue farmers discredited by theory and practice. Little or no reassessment was undertaken; many existing rates were confirmed. The land tax was fixed, reducing real income over time. (It had to be augmented by other taxes, dues, user fees, and strenuous efforts to check titles, define estates and boundaries, resume revenue-free holdings on to the revenue roll, and monitor the partition and inheritance of larger estates.) The state relinquished what hold it had over local records of landholding and land use, though state officials did measure and record estates that were partitioned, sold for revenue arrears, brought under protection of the Court of Wards, or subject to action at law. During the nineteenth century, new rules defined landlords, tenure holders, and tenants. Landlord rights were never absolute, but first strengthened and then qualified. Rents were fixed for a few tenure holders. Permanent heritable occupancy rights were recorded for large proportions of the superior tenants, redefined in the Acts of 1859 and 1885. By the end of the century, districtwide surveys and records of rights were beginning. Property markets developed slowly, but rents (always related to physical, economic, and sociopolitical conditions) became more economic than sociopolitical in character, set on a competitive basis—despite indigenous notions of fairness, a largely fruitless British search for *pargana* ('district') rates, and laws controlling rent increases on occupancy holdings. Actual cultivators, subtenants, sharecroppers, and labourers were little protected, despite meliorative measures in the twentieth century (Robb 1996).

In southern India, *raiyats* ('landholding cultivators') and village officers were the key, after the survey and settlement of Baramahal (1792–9) by Alexander Read (1751–1804). The system was popularized by Thomas Munro (1761–1827) as settlement officer and Presidency Governor, with endorsement from the British parliament's Fifth Report on the East India Company (EIC) (1812). Initially hampered for want of 'sufficiently minute investigation' (Munro's words), it implied closer local administration, less subject to rules and courts. Raiyatwari settlements were temporary: in both southern and western India, land revenue payments related to actual production, year-on-year, for individual holdings, at rates determined periodically by elaborate survey and settlement. The baseline assessments initially attempted to set the demand 'scientifically', at half the estimated 'unearned' profit, considering soils and ignoring variations relating to crops or caste. But, no advocate for a large interventionist state, Munro sought the minimum needed by government rather than the maximum the *raiyat* could pay (Beaglehole 1966: 19–20). Most rates were soon adjusted to match what seemed affordable and likely to increase production—pragmatic calculations of general economic conditions and capacity. As in the permanently settled areas, privileging and entrenching certain roles and powerful groups changed the legal and political character of landed property. Landownership was strengthened, encroaching upon common rights, especially to 'waste' lands, to harvest shares, and to rent-free provision or other exemptions for religious foundations, artisans, and village officers. Local revenue officials and village headmen benefited.

Another change in British understanding was marked by the famous image of village communities, in the account of Thomas Metcalfe (1795–1853), and by an ideology of caste and tribe, especially prevalent in the Punjab cadre of the Indian Civil Service (ICS). In the 1820s, the revenue minutes of Holt Mackenzie (1787–1876) and William Bentinck (1774–1839) translated some of these ideas into land policy, supposedly to reflect the building blocks of Indian society. Thereafter, most settlements, notably in North India, envisaged co-parcenary 'brotherhoods' or village communities with several and collective rights over land. The landholders comprised rent receivers, cultivators, village servants, and artisans (the last two recorded for their rent-free holdings). These settlements too were temporary, or rather periodic (several decades at a time). Once again, repeated revenue surveys investigated, mediated, and recorded a range of land rights, establishing landownership, the size and boundaries of estates and holdings, and their revenue payment and rents (Stokes 1959; Metcalf 1979). For all the talk of not disturbing pre-existing rights, the British assumed all land must be owned, and that use ought to be productive. These settlements too changed the basis and nature of rights. Different revenue systems produced societies and governments of different character, as did residual features including landlord or caste rights and obligations (social authority, bonded labour, credit, water management), and the interdependence provided by the village community, co-parcenary unit, or (still persisting) joint family. Some *zamindars*, such as in Burdwan or Darbhanga, with vast tracts of land, became important for wealth, patronage, and political influence. More generally in colonial India, ownership and rights became the language of legal and political discourse. Individual forms of ownership were preferred, even when land was held jointly. Increasing definition, fixity, and opportunity in the countryside led to more commercialized and sometimes more mechanized production, the generation of social and political capital for rural elites, and greater poverty and debt. Social differentiation widened, seen in absentee landlords, rich peasants, 'sub-infeudation', sharecropping, and landlessness. Women were discriminated against (Agrawal 1994).

From the later nineteenth century, economic nationalists believed an exorbitant land tax caused Indian poverty and famine. In practice, the colonial state's overall taxation was high enough to underwrite Britain's trade and development, but too low to galvanize the Indian economy through large productive investment (science, education, infrastructure) or redistribution (reducing vulnerability, increasing consumption). A greater problem was probably that modern law, bureaucracy, records, and coercion were imposed from outside rather than developed from within. Indian society reacted in ways peculiar to itself. Landed interests became organized: for example, the *zamindari* associations, Awadhi *taluqdars* ('superior landowners'), *kisan sabhas* ('peasant societies'), and, more locally, Gujarati *patidars* ('members of a rich peasant caste', formerly called *kanbis*), Bengali and Bihari indigo cultivators, and Punjab canal colonists.

Struggles against revenue or rent were significant in India's Independence movement (Sarkar 1983). Disorder persistently involved disputes over land rights, from the Faraizi movement in nineteenth-century Bengal to the Naxalites in central and eastern India today.

In the 1940s, amendment to India's constitutional property rights permitted states to abolish *zamindari*. Some undertook serious, long-term reviews of landholding and agrarian policy. The United Provinces, for example, concluded that intermediaries between cultivator and state were an 'exotic growth not suited to the genius of the people' (Report of the United Provinces Zamindari Abolition Committee, vol. 1, 1948: 519), whereas rights of cultivators were permanent and heritable. Their polemical ideas derived from nineteenth-century colonial debates and nationalist rhetoric, with added influence from Soviet-style planning. The inquiry proposed social engineering that was expected to produce a more efficient, equitable agrarian economy, and to eradicate poverty. It calculated that more progressive taxation, continuing the shift from land tax to income tax that started in the nineteenth century, would raise state revenues while allowing superior owners' land to be confiscated with compensation (based on average rents).

Numbers of rent receivers increased during the first few decades of the twentieth century, substantially in areas such as Sindh and Punjab. India's abolition laws brought no wholesale confiscations (anyway a threat to economic prosperity). Landlord rights persist in Pakistan, though *zamindari* was formally abolished in what became Bangladesh, by the East Bengal State Acquisition and Tenancy Act of 1950. In India, most property and other rights remain entrenched, in laws built on the past. The intelligentsia as well as business and industrial interests have gained influence, especially in burgeoning cities, but the politics of the still-large rural sector are often shaped by powerful landed interests. These adapted to adult franchise from positions of legal and economic strength traceable to the agrarian policies and administration of the British Raj.

Further reading: Guha 1963; Kumar 1998; McLane 1993; Robb 1996; Saumarez Smith 1996; Stein 1992; Stokes 1959.

—**PETER ROBB**, *Research Professor of the History of India,*
SOAS, University of London

— .•. —

Language

A glance at a rupee note gives an intimation of the significance of language in South Asia: the currency of the Republic of India records its denomination in fifteen separate languages. Since prehistory, South Asia has been home to a remarkably complex linguistic ecosystem, with representatives of three language families widely attested: Indo-Aryan, Dravidian, and Munda.

The first of these, itself a subgroup of the wider Indo-European family, possesses the widest distribution—the New Indo-Aryan languages can be found throughout much of the subcontinent and beyond (Sinhala, spoken in Sri Lanka, is also a member of the family)—and the family's linguistic history has received by far the most scholarly attention. From its origins in the Old Indo-Aryan forms of Vedic and classical Sanskrit, the family proliferated into a number of attested Middle Indo-Aryan literary languages, including Pali and the wide variety of dialects and registers classed as Prakrits and forms of Apabhramsha. The Dravidian family is concentrated in the far southern peninsula; however, one member of the family, Brahui, is spoken in Pakistan and Afghanistan. Several of the family's languages possess an ancient written record: Tamil, Kannada, Telugu, and Malayalam, in descending order of antiquity. All of these languages demonstrate a productive and mutual relationship with Indo-Aryan at the level of lexicon and syntax. Alongside these literary languages, the Dravidian group includes many other representatives, many of which were only documented in the last century (Steever 1981: 1–40). This also holds true for the far-flung Munda family scattered throughout the subcontinent's Northeast, which—like the smaller members of the Dravidian family—are spoken by so-called tribal peoples. While no Munda language possesses a premodern literature, the family's antiquity can be seen in very early lexical borrowings into the historical languages of the other two groups (Southworth 2005: 39–97). The presence of these genetic families must be set alongside the remarkable assimilation of the extra-areal languages of Persian and Arabic over the past millennium and the languages of Europe, especially English, over the last several centuries.

Besides this luxuriant linguistic diversity, India has been home to some of humanity's greatest innovators in the reflection upon language. An outstanding figure here is the Sanskrit grammarian Panini (fourth century BCE), whose algebraic *Ashtadhyayi*, which, with its complex form of aphoristic *sutras*, supplied a model for much subsequent systematic thought of whatever genre. In this, the influence of Panini's grammar has been compared to Euclid's *Axioms* in the western and Islamic worlds (Staal 1965). Panini was concerned almost exclusively with morphological analysis; later authors such as Patanjali (second century BCE) and Bhartrhari (fifth century CE?) supplemented this with reflections on syntax, semantics, and the metaphysics of language, while further innovations in discourse analysis and sentential pragmatics were argued for by the ritualist Kumarila Bhatta (ca. seventh century CE) (Houben 1995; Matilal 1990). Rival systems of grammar and the philosophy of language, for instance the one associated with Buddhist authors following the innovations of the fifth century CE theorist Dignaga, interacted with the post-Paninian traditions in complex ways (Hayes 1988; McCrea and Patil 2010). Working largely independently of these Sanskritic systems, the Tamil *Tolkappiyam* (early centuries CE?) adopted a more capacious intellectual object, including rules of poetic composition within the domain of language analysis (Zvelebil 1973: 131–54; Trautmann 2006: 42–72).

The second millennium CE witnessed the widespread grammaticalization of languages throughout South Asia (Pollock 2006). In many cases, the prestige of the Paninian system led to the codification of languages as different as Kannada and Kashmiri into grammars composed in Sanskrit. From the early modern period, South Asia also became the home to thoroughgoing linguistic and philological scholarship on Persian (Alam 1998, 2004). Among the many extraordinary Indian Persian intellectuals, Siraj al-Din 'Ali Khan Arzu (1687–1756) deserves to be singled out (Kinra 2011). In a career that ranged from literary criticism and lexicography to bitter polemics with his Iranian contemporaries, Arzu was probably the first scholar to notice the structural affinities between Persian and Sanskrit, preceding Sir William Jones' proposal of the common Indo-European heritage of Sanskrit, Latin, and Greek by more than a generation.

India furnishes many examples of language's central place in political contestation and in the making and unmaking of collective selves. The speciation of two separate and religiously identified script-languages,

Hindi and Urdu, was largely the product of the colonial state's effort to regiment the social identities of its subject population, tying language and religious confession together in a way without strong historical precedent in South Asia (King 1994). Independence witnessed the vituperative resistance to the adoption of Hindi as a single national language, especially in the Tamil-speaking South, where language devotion has provided one of the major driving forces in political and intellectual life (Irschick 1969; Ramaswamy 1997; Venkatachalapathy 2006). Independent India's reorganization of states along linguistic lines in 1956 is a further testament to the complex and problematic linkages between language and belonging, as is the recent rush to declare the supposed 'classical' status of many of South Asia's historical languages (Pollock 2011). Ironically, this process of classical canonization is underway at a time when the linguistic diversity of India is under unprecedented pressure. The markedly declining competence in India's historical languages at the moment of their state-decreed classicization is a problem yet to be systematically formulated, much less addressed. As elsewhere in the world, minority languages are rapidly declining in the face of the ascendant registers of media and of global capitalism. There are countervailing tendencies: for instance, the cinema of such subregional languages as Bhojpuri continues to thrive in India and in the diaspora, and the Internet has created new avenues and forums of expression. The trend nevertheless has been towards increasing homogenization. This is a sobering thought, although the remarkable linguistic capacities that the region has evinced over the millennia suggest that the death of South Asia's linguistic diversity should not be diagnosed prematurely.

Further reading: Emeneau 1956; Grierson 1903–22; Pollock 2003.

—**WHITNEY COX**, *Associate Professor, University of Chicago*

— .•. —

Liberalization

After Independence, Nehru and his political heirs opted for a planned economy, and invested in heavy industries and the agricultural sector, whilst trade and business remained severely restricted. The 'idea of India' (Khilnani 1997) linked economic policies to modernist ideologies of development that were intended to benefit the poor through state-led programmes. But the reality of democratic processes forced consecutive governments to bow to local and national elites, and increased debts and deficits, whilst the poor, at whom the state-run programmes were directed, did not reap the fruits of the state-subsidized 'licence raj', the rule of tenders for materials and services supplied for state projects.

The political crisis of the 1980s brought about by the rise of upwardly mobile castes, and an increasingly dissatisfied middle class brought the encompassing Hindu nationalist organizations to power, who then initiated economic reforms (Corbridge and Harriss 2000).

In 1991, India's government was forced to take out a foreign loan, which required acceptance of adjustment policies and the gradual opening of the Indian economy to export markets, foreign investment, and imported consumer goods, as well as reform of taxation and the privatization of the state-owned public sector undertakings (PSUs). Though the unevenness of economic growth since then has been well documented, the reforms led to an expansion of particular sectors, for instance in trade and services, whilst others were scaled back, especially PSUs. The main beneficiaries belong to the so-called new middle classes, a heterogeneous group of citizen-consumers. In post-liberalization India, middle-class lifestyles have come to symbolically represent the link between liberalization, development, and nationhood (Fernandes 2006), and are realized on the back of state policies, for instance in the form of urban restructuring.

Liberalization encouraged uneven growth and widened existing gaps between Indian states, classes, castes, and gendered populations. Neoliberal policies that cut back on welfare left the huge majority of India's population vulnerable to the fluctuations of the market with fewer state resources to protect access to education and healthcare, credit, services, and employment. But in post-liberalization India, neither the state nor resistance to the effects of liberalization can be understood without taking transnational discourses, institutions, and networks into account (Gupta 1995).

Further reading: Corbridge and Harriss 2000; Fernandes 2006; Gupta 1995; Khilnani 1997.

—HENRIKE DONNER, *Senior Lecturer in Social Anthropology, Oxford Brookes University*

— .•. —

Litigation

L itigation refers to the carrying on of a legal contest through a judicial process. For South Asianists, this has emerged as a rich site for studying the interaction between state and society.

While dispute resolution systems existed in precolonial regimes, they were decentralized, and the state deferred to local authority on most questions. The colonial state, with its investment in creating a rule of law, displaced local authorities through new courts and formal procedures. Litigation became central to the creation of the colonial state. British legal procedure was based on the normative idea of equality; it understood relationships in contractual terms, sought to arrive at a specific decision, and saw a dispute as a discrete problem (Cohn 1987b). Indian society was not premised on equality or contract between individuals, but sought to locate them within a network of social relationships. Indigenous forms of dispute resolution postponed clear-cut decisions and aimed at compromise. Cohn argues that this made courts the site of a direct clash of the values between British and Indian society. Indians used the courts as a form of speculation or gambling. Given the cost and time involved, litigation was often a threat, rather than a method of resolving disputes. With the demilitarization of society, litigation became the new battleground and a form of public entertainment (Cohn 1987b: 573). This view was shared by colonial administrators who sought to police the 'lying, litigious native' by increasing court fees, punishing perjury, and changing evidentiary practices (Raman 2012). While ethnographic and empirical scholarship has come to challenge the reality of the 'litigious Indian', suggesting that levels of litigiousness were low given the population, it is recognized that legal consciousness plays a greater role in comparison to other Asian countries (Moog 1993; Galanter 2009; Mendelsohn 1981).

The gap between colonial courts and the society it sought to regulate provided opportunities for litigation to be used as a tactic. Litigants, who were disempowered under traditional systems, found new spaces to manoeuvre and challenge traditional authority, be it Muslim women challenging the authority of their fathers, or lay members contesting priestly authority, in the process reinscribing and creating new forms of status and knowledge (Sharafi 2009).

The relative autonomy of the judicial system also brought out the tensions implicit in the 'rule of law claims' made by the colonial state, which created a field of contestation between the executive and the judiciary. This tension continued after Independence, with the Constitution enabling greater access to courts and stronger remedies against state action. In the first two decades after Independence, with Congress domination of legislatures, the courts emerged as the primary site for opposition against the government. By the 1960s, not only was litigation against the state on the rise, the government was losing 40 per cent of the cases as well (Gadbois 1970). The Emergency (1975–7) led to the courts diluting in its aftermath (1977–9) requirements for legal standing before the judiciary and encouraged public interest litigation (PIL), that is encouraged individuals to bring in cases on behalf of those who could not represent themselves (Baxi 1982). Through PIL, the courts created new rights, checked executive discretion, and administered welfare programmes, thus forcing scholars to reconceptualize the role of the judiciary in a democracy (Sathe 2002).

Further reading: Baxi 1987; Cohn 1987b; Galanter 1993; Moog 1993; Raman 2012.

—ROHIT DE, *Assistant Professor, Department of History,*
Yale University

— .•. —

Malabar

The term 'Malabar' was used by Arab writers from the tenth century CE onwards to denote the region of southwest India that lies between the Western Ghats and the Arabian Sea. Today, the region constitutes the state of Kerala which was created in 1956 from the merger of Malabar district, part of the British Madras Presidency from 1800, and the erstwhile princely states of Cochin and Travancore further south (Menon 1991: 9–10, 291, 311).

From the thirteenth century, European writers referred to the whole of Kerala, as well as sometimes the coastal belt up to Mumbai in the north and bordering on the Tamil country to the east, as Malabar (Yule and Burnell 1996: 539–42). The word probably derives from *Malavaram* ('the hilly country') in Malayalam, a Dravidian language that became distinct from Tamil by the end of the first millennium CE (Menon 1991: 17; George 1968: 1–9).

Malabari became synonymous with *Malayali*, the latter being the term favoured by Malayalam-speakers. Famed for its spices, especially pepper and cardamom, Malabar was historically associated with Hindu matrilineal groups, notably the Nairs (a landowning martial caste), and strong local traditions of Syrian Christianity and Islam dating from the first millennium CE (Bayly 1989: 243–57; Miller 1992: 39–51). In the twentieth century, the state's politics attracted particular attention as the Communist Party built up a strong following in the 1930s and 1940s, attaining a springboard for success in the first elections in Kerala in 1957 (Nossiter 1982). Communist and Congress-led governments have alternated in the state ever since, as Kerala has become known for its high levels of social development (Jeffrey 1992) and labour migration (especially to the Persian Gulf) (Zachariah and Rajan 2009).

Further reading: Bayly 1989; George 1968; Jeffrey 1992; Menon 1991; Miller 1992; Nossiter 1982; Yule and Burnell 1996; Zachariah and Rajan 2009.

—JAMES CHIRIYANKANDATH, *Senior Research Fellow, Institute of Commonwealth Studies, University of London*

Mandal Commission

The Mandal Commission is post-Independence India's most politically charged effort to extend its reservations regime. In 1978, the then prime minister Morarji Desai (1896–1995) assigned B.P. Mandal (1918–82) to head a five-member Commission to devise a policy in accordance with the provisions of Article 340 of the Indian Constitution for the 'welfare of the Backward Classes'. The Mandal Commission Report (1980) recommended 27 per cent reservation for the so-called Other Backward Classes (OBCs) in central government institutions based on eleven criteria of socioeconomic deprivation, in addition to the existing reservation of 22.5 per cent of positions in education and employment for Scheduled Castes and Tribes (GOI 1980).

Prime Minister V.P. Singh's (1931–2008) decision to implement the Report in 1989 provoked widespread upper-caste protest, including violent riots orchestrated by the Bharatiya Janata Party (BJP), and led to the fall of the Janata government in November 1990. However, the Supreme Court ruled in favour of the Report's constitutionality in 1993, in the landmark lawsuit, now known as the Indra Sawhney v. Union of India case. In September 1991, Prime Minister P.V. Narasimha Rao's (1921–2004) Congress government announced support for the Report, together with 10 per cent for poorer members of the upper castes and non-Hindu minorities (Dudley-Jenkins 2003).

The history of reservations in India can be traced to the (colonial) history of non-Brahmanism. The administration of Mysore first used the term 'Backward Class' in 1918 to categorize everyone who was *not* Brahmin; the Baroda and Kolhapur Princely States had instituted policies to curb Brahmin dominance in the late nineteenth century; Madras had caste quotas for bureaucratic recruitment from 1916, and Bombay's State Committee Report (1930) included reservations for socially and economically 'backward' groups (Rao 2009). Efforts in the post-Independence period date from the 1953 Backward Classes Commission headed by Kaka Kalelkar (1885–1981), though this Commission's recommendations were discredited for emphasizing caste separation. By 1965, individual states had been advised to develop their own socioeconomic indices for affirmative action policies (Galanter 1984).

The Mandal Commission's Report has renewed debates about the salience of caste as a political identity, while posing ongoing definitional dilemmas about what constitutes 'backwardness,' and the legal means to resolve it.

Further reading: Dudley-Jenkins 2003; Galanter 1984; Jaffrelot 2003; Rao 2009.

—ANUPAMA RAO, *Professor of History, Barnard College, Columbia University*

— ••• —

Manuvad

Manuvad describes the philosophy of descent-based hierarchy and occupational segregation that is supposed to be articulated in Manu's *Dharmashashtra* or *Manava-dharmashashtra* (dated between 200 BCE–200 CE), a Sanskrit text, also referred to as the 'Laws of Manu', that takes the form of a discourse between Manu, the progenitor of mankind, and a group of seers.

However, given that caste society predates Manu, he was not really a 'law-giver', but a theorist and ideologue of a system that had, in all probability, already been extant for centuries. In fact, it is the *Purusa Sukta*, the ninetieth hymn of the Tenth Book of the *Rig Veda*, which articulates the fourfold division of society that is fundamentally theoretical, and which diverges from the empirical history of caste formation anywhere on the subcontinent (Doniger 1991).

Though idealized and incompletely instantiated, caste hierarchy is typically reinforced by invoking the *Manava-dharmashashtra*, a text defined by the multiple interpretive traditions that have grown around it. Typically associated with the regulation of social intercourse between castes, and codification of punishments for their infraction, the *Manava-dharmashashtra*'s elaborate description of forbidden unions suggests some anxiety with regard to the possibility of regulating caste identity through daily conduct (one of the *Manusmriti*'s canonical commentators is Kane 1930, 1946, 1968; furthermore see Doniger 1991, Olivelle 1999).

B.R. Ambedkar (1891–1956) and Kanshiram (1934–2006), among others, have criticized *Manuvad* as an ideology that secures upper-caste privilege. B.R. Ambedkar, during the Mahad *satyagraha*, famously burned on 25 December 1927 those sections of the *Manava-dharmashashtra* that withheld scriptural knowledge from Dalits and women.

Today, in addition to *Manuvad*, the more commonly used term, *Manuvadi*, describes a proponent of status-based inequality who typically espouses a commitment to the discourse and practice of 'merit', while criticizing the contemporary reservations regime, which undertakes social and economic redistribution through caste-based affirmative action. Both terms, *Manuvad* and *Manuvadi*, have been revivified with the rise of the Bahujan Samaj Party (BSP) in Uttar Pradesh (Jaffrelot 2003). They essentially function as a political shorthand for describing the interlinkage of caste (identity) with power, on the one hand, and the social hegemony that upper castes exercise in everyday life, on the other.

Further reading: Ambedkar 1989; Doniger 1991; Kane 1968; Kanshiram 1982; Olivelle 1999.

—ANUPAMA RAO, *Professor of History, Barnard College,*
Columbia University

— •◦• —

Maoist Movement (Naxalites)

One of the world's longest-running insurgencies, India's Maoist movement has its roots in Naxalbari village in West Bengal when, in 1967, peasants attacked local landlords, forcibly occupied land, burned records, and cancelled old debts. This was no 'spontaneous' peasant uprising, but marked the revolutionary line of armed peasant struggle organized by communist radicals under Charu Mazumdar (1918–72), the son of a progressive Bengali landlord family whose father was a freedom fighter. These radicals felt that the transition to socialism could not be achieved by the parliamentary means and 'peaceful co-existence' of communism and capitalism that Nikita Khrushchev (1894–1971) had chosen for the Communist Parties of the Soviet Union at the time. The Chinese Communist Party hailed the Naxalbari rising as the 'Spring Thunder over India' and Mazumdar tried to spread the struggles across the country, founding the 'Communist Party of India (Marxist-Leninist)' [CPI (ML)] in 1969. A separate group of radicals, who later became the 'Maoist Communist Centre' (MCC), did not join the CPI (ML) but also took a similar revolutionary line. These parties analysed India as semi-feudal and semi-colonial and adopted Chairman Mao's (1893–1976) strategy of a protracted people's war that was supposed to spread from the rural areas to the cities. The immediate task of the party thus became the organization of a united four-class alliance of the proletariat, the peasantry, the petty bourgeoisie, and the national bourgeoisie in armed struggle to seize power in what they called a 'new democratic revolution', establish socialism, and ultimately foster a communist society.

The struggles of these revolutionaries spread to the forested and hilly tracts of Srikakulam in Andhra Pradesh, Koraput in Orissa, and the plains of Bhojpur in Bihar and Birbhum in West Bengal. But the 1970s saw massive police repression by Indira Gandhi's (1917–84) Congress-led government. Many leaders were killed or imprisoned, and Charu Mazumdar died in police custody in 1972. Against the backdrop of the repressive regime, some revolutionaries tried to build up their strength once more in the late 1970s: 'CPI (ML) Party Unity' was formed in 1978 by a small group of previously imprisoned Naxalites, and they built strongholds in the plains of central Bihar; similar motives led to the formation of 'CPI (ML) People's War Group' in Andhra Pradesh in 1980. Over the years, various groups attempted mergers and, significantly, in 1998 the People's War Group and Party Unity combined to form the 'Communist Party of India (Marxist-Leninist) People's War'. This set the stage for the most important merger to date between the former MCC and People's War who, in September 2004, united to form the 'Communist Party of India (Maoist)'.

Since the 1990s, in particular, the Maoists have increasingly run a parallel government in guerrilla zones that they would like to turn into liberated bases (where the Indian state will not be present at all). These are areas in remote parts of the forests and hills of Chhattisgarh, Jharkhand, Orissa, West Bengal, Andhra Pradesh, and Bihar that are predominantly inhabited by Adivasis, India's indigenous peoples. These are lands which are also rich in mineral reserves of coal, iron ore, and bauxite in particular, but where land sales and transfers are difficult because of colonial laws protecting Adivasis. It is perhaps then no coincidence that, as India liberalized its economy and signed Memorandums of Understanding (MoUs) endorsing the sale of Adivasi lands to multinational corporations keen on harvesting these minerals, in 2006 prime minister Manmohan Singh (b. 1932) declared the Maoists the greatest single internal security threat that the country faced, and mounted a military offensive of an unprecedented scale to 'wipe them out' from these remote but mineral-rich regions. In Chhattisgarh, as part of a 'purification hunt' called the *Salwa Judum*, villagers were even armed by the police and instructed to kill their neighbours (see Indian Citizens' Initiative [ICI] resolution 2006). The application of criminal laws, public security acts, and anti-terror legislation in these 'terrorist areas' means that suspected Maoists are arrested on little or no evidence, causing severe infringements of civil rights, and many have been murdered and then presented as killed in an 'encounter'—India's infamous 'encounter killings'. In the remote rural areas of central and eastern India, the security forces act with impunity and the violence of the state is experienced as random and inexplicable. Meanwhile, the 'People's Liberation Guerrilla Army' of the Indian Maoists is growing.

The question of how and why such insurgencies spread has been crucial for scholarship on peasant insurgency all over the world. In India, media and government reports have often depicted the ordinary villagers as either forced into Maoist action or as rational economic peasants bene-fiting in some monetary and developmental way from the revolutionaries. Scholars, journalists, and activists have gone deeper to explore the moral appeal of the Maoists, namely how their struggles for the poor against caste oppression, land alienation, and better wages have attracted the masses (for instance Bhatia 2000; Chakravarti 2007; Chowdhry 2012; Kunnath 2012; Navlakha 2012; Pandita 2011; Roy 2011). There may, however, also be a range of other important factors involved—such as the relations of intimacy that the Maoists have been able to create and sus-tain in their strongholds (Shah 2013). As the Maoists become one of the most hotly contested issues of Indian politics, we are increasingly seeing a proliferation of journalistic reports as well as academic analysis based on secondary sources with some minimal primary data. However, many of these accounts remain speculative and superficial as, in fact, there has been very little sustained research into the processes of social transforma-tion in the Maoist revolutionary heartlands.

Further reading: Banerjee 1984; Government of India [GOI] 2008; Independent Citizen's Initiative [ICI] 2006; Shah 2011; Shah and Pettigrew 2011.

—ALPA SHAH, *Reader, Department of Anthropology, London School of Economics and Political Science, University of London*

— ••• —

Metro

A contraction of 'metropolis', the term 'metro' is generally used in the South Asian context to designate the largest cities of the region. In India, the four main colonial cities—Mumbai,

New Delhi, Chennai, and Kolkata—are usually designated as the four big metros. In recent years, however, Hyderabad (Deccan), Bengaluru, Ahmedabad, Pune, Surat, and Chandigarh are often added to this list, taking into consideration both their increasing populations and also their rising economic stature. Karachi and Lahore used to be the big metros of Pakistan, though now Faisalabad, Rawalpindi, and Hyderabad (Sind) also often make the list. Dhaka is Bangladesh's one giant metro.

In general, it is the former colonial cities that were established as ports, and as financial and governmental centres of the colonial economy which have continued to dominate the South Asian urbanscape. This was particularly true in the Nehruvian period, that is the first four decades after Indian Independence from British rule in 1947, with large-scale immigration dominating growth in the big metros (Prasad et al. 2009). In the last two decades, however, regional cities have also become large attractors, testifying to their increasing economic clout. The latter are sometimes referred to as 'regional metros', highlighting their non-colonial origins. The two are also often designated as 'Tier I' and 'Tier II metros', with the implication of an additional 'Tier III metros' that are emerging (Thakur 2010).

Besides size, metro also designates a distinctive culture in South Asia. In the Nehruvian period, the identities of India's metros were closely aligned to their rural hinterlands. At this time, Indian metros were usually portrayed by Hindi language cinema as places of immigration and opportunity for the rural poor. Satyajit Ray's *Apu* trilogy (1955–9) and Yash Chopra's *Deewar* (1975) are classic examples of this narrative. More recently, Hindi cinema has investigated the autonomous urban culture of Indian cities, as for instance in Rakeysh Omprakash Mehra's *Delhi-6* (2009), Anurag Kashyap's *Dev.D* (2009), and Kiran Rao's *Dhobi Ghat* (2011). Popular literature identified with metros usually explores them on their own terms. Suketu Mehta's *Maximum City* (2004) on Mumbai, and Ravi Vasudevan's *Pirate Modernity* (2009) on subcultures in Delhi, are two examples of academic readings on Indian metros. Vikram Chandra's *Love and Longing in Bombay* (1997) and *Sacred Games* (2007) as well as Gregory David Roberts' *Shantaram* (2004) showcase novels exploring the social and cultural fabric of Mumbai.

The colonial metros are generally considered more cosmopolitan (both on a national and international scale) than the regional metros, although such distinctions are often vociferously challenged. Following the establishment of neoliberal economic policies in 1991, India's metros (both colonial and regional) have actively attempted to market themselves as autonomous economic and cultural entities, distinct from their states and hinterlands. One such attempt has been the creation of the 'Indian Premier League' (IPL) franchises, most of which advertise themselves and are directly associated with the metros of their origin. The IPL metros are Chennai, Delhi, Kochi, Kolkata, Mumbai, and Bengaluru.

At the same time, however, there has been a 'regionalist' backlash against the cosmopolitanism of the metros, as, for instance in Mumbai with the 'Mumbai for Maharashtrians' campaign of the Shiv Sena, a pro-native regional party. The changing of the colonial names of most of the metros (from Bombay to Mumbai, Calcutta to Kolkata, Madras to Chennai, Bangalore to Bengaluru, Poona to Pune) can be seen as a part of the ongoing tussle among Indian metros regarding their cosmopolitan or regional identities. The IPL team, Royal Challengers Bangalore, famously chose to associate itself with the colonial name of its host city. At the same time, the Punjab Kings XI and the Deccan Chargers chose to align themselves with their region rather than their metro.

In popular parlance, metro of late is generally used to refer to the rapid mass-transit systems that are currently being deployed in the larger metros of India. The Kolkata metro, started in 1984, is the oldest of these. Chennai also built a small single-line metro in 1987. Delhi currently has the most extensive metro network with six completed lines. Additional metros are currently being built in Bengaluru, Jaipur, Chennai, Pune, and Hyderabad (Singh 2011).

Further reading: Chalana 2010; Huyssen 2008; Shaw 2007.

—VIKRAMADITYA PRAKASH, *Professor of Architecture,*
University of Washington

—— •◆• ——

Middle Class

Since the mid-1980s, one of the more noticeable symptoms of the process of social and economic liberalization in India has been an obsessive public cultural concern with the category 'middle class'. Especially the English-language metropolitan media have routinely and anxiously dissected the size, scope, desires, and politics of the Indian middle classes. Several contemporary concerns have thus been brought into critical juxtaposition: the rise of Hindu nationalism, consumerist liberalization, as well as the pluralization and fragmentation of national politics (Fernandes 2006; Rajagopal 2001). Commentary on this juxtaposition has been marked by a great deal of anxiety about the relationship between, on the one hand, normative discourses of political practice and, on the other, more corporeal and affective dimensions of contemporary public life.

The transformation of the middle class in India describes a shift, in the 1970s and 1980s, from a Nehruvian civil service–oriented salariat, short on money but long on institutional perks, to a bewildering array of new, entrepreneurial groups. This shift was precipitated by the salary hikes following the 1973 Pay Commission, the Green Revolution, remittances from the Gulf and, more broadly, the complex of reforms collectively known as liberalization (Baviskar and Ray 2011). The displacement of the 'old' Nehruvian middle class and its nationalist–modernizing vision is often linked to a mounting illiberality and incivility in politics, a crass new consumerism, and a disorienting fragmentation of the national imaginary.

A product of European political history, the category 'middle class' may seem ill-suited to capture the dynamics of contemporary Indian life, let alone its precolonial foundations. The Indian middle class, however it is measured, remains a minority; it has never been able to establish itself as politically hegemonic in independent India (Chatterjee 1998).

The term 'middle class' covers a staggering diversity of socioeconomic and cultural situations, further separated by language, religion, and social position. Although seemingly impossible to define, the category itself has become an important marker of identification, aspiration, and critique in contemporary Indian public culture.

The middle classes are the main addressees of the national media, and at the core of every political party's campaigning strategies, as their elites—united by their (variable) relationship to the English language and to the educational and administrative machinery—dominate and control the judiciary, the civil service, the election commission, and the media.

Middle class consumerist 'culture' is associated with greed, political impatience (often expressed as a longing for authoritarian government), and contempt for the less fortunate, who, in contrast to middle-class self-perceptions of industriousness and decency, are invariably figured as lazy, dirty, and encroaching. Alongside the 'big' and 'old-fashioned' national issues of economic development, general education, and poverty allevia-tion, the focus here is on pavement encroachments, garbage, and traffic congestion (Anjaria and McFarlane 2011).

The 'new' middle classes have apparently transcended both 'traditional scruples' and 'colonial hang-ups'. Their consuming desires are at one with their political impatience. In the vaunted immediacy of the global market, they find a model for good governance with which to counter the cor-ruption and venality to which conventional politics appear to have been reduced (Mazzarella 2006, 2010). While this move may be seen as a healthy sign of burgeoning grassroots civil engagement, it involves violence against the poor, most notably in its manifestation as urban 'beautification' (also known as slum clearance).

The middle class cult of immediation also takes the form of an apparently contradictory blend of technocratic rationalism and cultural–religious chauvinism. The 1980s and 1990s saw the cheek-by-jowl juxta-position of Bangalorean/Hyderabadi silicon dreams with a surge in mass media-fuelled religious rioting. This same period saw the emergence of a powerful new mass-mediated idiom of Indianness on television and in Hindi cinema that was at once globally savvy and often culturally conser-vative: a commercial public culture that is perhaps the closest thing to a truly national contemporary Indian culture. Both Hindu nationalism and this shared popular culture bring a corporeal, affective density to public life. While the urban poor constitute at once the material support and the paradigmatic social Other to the cosmopolitan middle class, ironically, the provincial and rural middle classes are its intimate enemies. Chief among their crimes is a refusal to transcend local, regional concerns.

A Tocquevillean idealization of Euro-American civic culture is often held up as a disapproving mirror to the realities of Indian middle-class lives. Mired in patronage, status-assertion, and personalized particularism, the political modernity of the Indian middle class is, in this reflection, always embarrassingly incomplete.

Further reading: Anjaria 2011; Baviskar 2011; Chatterjee 1998; Fernandes 2006; Mazzarella 2006, 2010; Rajagopal 2001.

—WILLIAM MAZZARELLA, *Professor, Department of Anthropology, University of Chicago*

— ·◆· —

Monsoon

Originally an Arabic word (*mausim*) traceable to its sixteenth-century usage by Arab sailors, the monsoon refers to the seasonal change in the winds of the tropics and sub-tropics between the Persian Gulf, India, and Zanzibar. India experiences both the Northeast monsoon where northeasterly winds bring dry weather during October and May and the Southwest monsoon where winds bring wet weather from Southeast Asia during June and September. The latter, known as the 'Indian Summer monsoon' is believed amongst scientists to result from the differential heating of the Tibetan High Plateau, where rising warm air spreads southwards towards the Equator to create the easterly jet stream, a powerful poleward flow of air that picks up moisture on its northwestward course across the Indian Ocean to bring rains to the subcontinent.

The characteristic unpredictability and high variability of the monsoon poses a significant challenge to Indian agriculture and the livelihood of the majority of Indians. Over 70 per cent of annual rainfall, and most foodgrain production, occurs during the Southwest monsoon, with rainfall highly concentrated in the northeastern states of Assam and West Bengal. Famines in 1877, 1889, and 1918 were primarily a consequence of bad monsoons, as were the droughts of 1965–6, which resulted in emergency food imports and later government-led projects to provide funds and expertise to expand the use of irrigation, bore wells, fertilizers, and high-yielding wheat varieties, ushering in the Green Revolution. Whilst control over water supply has improved, most farmers rely on traditional methods such as diversifying crop varieties to adapt to varying moisture conditions and observing the *karwand* and *heever* (types of thorny bushes) for green shoots that indicate the onset of rains. Accurate monsoon prediction remains elusive despite satellite-based meteorological data, given the sheer complexity of modelling the factors that determine the timing and intensity of rainfall.

The monsoon has intricately shaped Indian culture and society. The rise and decline of the Indus Valley Civilization has been attributed to shifts in monsoon patterns. Relief from the heat and the promise of good harvests, wealth, fertility, and joy are common literary themes associated with the monsoon. Parjanya, the God of Rain in the *Rig Veda*, symbolizes prosperity. Bursting monsoon rains serve as the backdrop to the scenes of eroticism and forlorn love between Krishna and Radha, the celebrated lovers of Hindu mythology, a tradition continued in Bollywood cinema and modern literature, such as Tagore's *Gitanjali*. Conversely, the sixteenth-century tradition of Hindi poetry known as *Barahmasa* (lit. 'songs of the twelve months'), which also appears in Punjabi in the Granth Sahib, portrays the monsoon as a time of difficulty and uncertainty, as do many colonial and western narratives of disaster and misery from flooding. The monsoon has inspired musical repertoires such as the raga Megha-Malhar ('cloud festival'), architectural theories for situating temples in the *Vastushastra*, and Mughal palace designs that maximize the coolness from the rain. Many religious and cultural festivals centre around the monsoon, such as Naga Pancami, where Hindus offer milk to *nagas* ('snake deities') and paint their images on doorways for protection from snakes seeking refuge from flood waters.

Further reading: Das 1995; Fein and Stephens 1987; Frater 2005; Katiyar 1987; Yasuda and Shinde 2004.

—MARTIN MENSKI, *Senior Associate, Clifford Chance LLP,*
Washington, DC

Mughal/Mughlai

The Mughal emperors were a Sunni Muslim dynasty of Turko-Mongol descent who ruled over much of the Indian subcontinent from Babur's (1483–1530) conquest of Delhi in 1526 until 1858 when the British ousted the last emperor, Bahadur Shah Zafar (1775–1862), for his role as figurehead of the 1857 Indian Rebellion. The heyday of the empire is usually considered to extend from the accession of the third 'Great Mughal' emperor, Akbar (1542–1605), in 1556 to the death in 1707 of the sixth emperor, Aurangzeb Alamgir (1618–1707). By the reign of Muhammad Shah (1702–48, r. 1719–48), the Mughal emperors' geopolitical power had diminished virtually to the environs of Delhi; but their nominal sovereignty and cultural influence, particularly in the arts, literature, and architecture, continued to hold significant sway across India until the end of the empire, especially in regional successor states like Awadh and Hyderabad. The terms 'Mughal' (literally 'Mongol') and 'Mughlai' (meaning 'of or pertaining to the Mughals') may thus refer either to the historical empire or to its cultural and artistic inheritance (Richards 1995: xv–2; Steingass 1957: 1281–2).

The Mughal emperors were technically not 'Mughal' by ethnicity, but Timurid—Babur, the first 'Mughal' emperor (r. 1526–30), was directly descended from the Central Asian conqueror Timur (Tamerlane), and inherited in full the Turko-Persian courtly and military traditions of the Timurid dynasties of Central Asia. Forced to flee his ancestral seat in Samarqand, Babur became ruler of Kabul in 1504, only to set his sights on the far-richer prize of Delhi, which he conquered in 1526. His successor, Humayun (1508–56, r. 1530–56), spent most of his reign in exile in Iran, and returned to Delhi in 1555, heavily influenced by Persian court culture. Humayun's son, Akbar (r. 1556–1605), enjoyed nearly fifty years on the throne, in the process becoming the greatest and most liberal of the Mughal emperors. It was Akbar who consolidated Mughal rule in the subcontinent through military conquest and alliances, infrastructural improvements, new systems of revenue collection, and the institution of a centralized bureaucratic hierarchy of official service. Culturally, Akbar fostered interreligious dialogue between Hindus, Muslims, and Christians, and rapprochement between Persianate and Indic cultural traditions, patronizing musicians, poets, and painters from both. Key to this cultural confluence were perceived affinities between local Rajput and Mughal cultures of governance and warfare, on the one hand, and Sufi and *bhakti* expressions of devotional love, on the other (Metcalf and Metcalf 2006: 14–20; Richards 1995: 1–3).

This Indo-Persian hybridity became the enduring hallmark of Mughal culture and aesthetics. Akbar's successors, Jahangir (1569–1627, r. 1605–27) and Shah Jahan (1592–1666, r. 1628–58), followed in his footsteps, slowly increasing Mughal dominions while perfecting Mughal cultural expressions, especially in painting, architecture, and gardens. Under Aurangzeb Alamgir (r. 1658–1707) the empire was pushed to its greatest geographic extent, but this overstretch of the empire's resources, coupled with Alamgir's alienating Islamic orthodoxy, led to the virtual collapse of Mughal power in the years following his death (Richards 1995: 290–1). The eighteenth century saw the *de facto* rule of Delhi successively pass from Nadir Shah, who sacked Delhi in 1739, to the Afghans, the Marathas, and, finally, the British in 1803 (Metcalf and Metcalf 2006: 1–2). At the same time, there was a resurgence of autonomous regional power that saw cities like Lucknow and Hyderabad, both ruled by ex-Mughal houses, flourish as new centres of late Mughal-style in culture and the arts.

The Mughals' greatest artistic legacy lies in the exquisite miniature paintings and architectural masterpieces executed during the empire's heyday. Mughal painting owes much to the Persian tradition of book illustration, but by the mid-seventeenth century a receptivity to Rajput painting and, to a lesser extent, European styles had transformed Mughal miniature painting into a highly refined art with a bias towards narrative and historical subjects, meticulous attention to detail in depiction of both nature and manmade objects, accuracy in portraiture; and use of expensive luxury materials. Equally emblematic are the architectural masterpieces of the Mughal golden age, especially Shah Jahan's major works of the mid-seventeenth century: wholesale renovations of Delhi, Agra, and Lahore, the Shalimar Garden (Lahore); and the Taj Mahal, the fabled tomb of his third wife, Mumtaz Mahal (1593–1631). All of these are remarkable for their symmetry and exquisite stone carving and decorative inlay (Asher 1992; Beach 1992).

The Mughal emperors and nobility were also dedicated connoisseurs of Persian and classical Hindi poetry, and the Urdu *ghazal* (form of poetry in rhyming couplets) reached its peak of perfection under the eighteenth- and nineteenth-century Mughal emperors and the Nawabs of Awadh, under whom Mughal cultural practices flourished right through the nineteenth century despite diminishing political potency. Some of the later Mughal emperors are justly famed for significant cultural achievements, such as Muhammad Shah's patronage of new tastes in music and painting, and the poetry of Shah Alam II (1728–1806, r. 1759–1806) and Bahadur Shah Zafar (1775–1862, r. 1837–58) (Alam 2004; Busch 2011; Pritchett 1994). The last Nawab of Awadh, Wajid Ali Shah (1822–1887, r. 1847–56), likewise made serious contributions to North Indian music and dance as an important theorist, song lyricist, and choreographer (Sharar 1975: 138, 146). Hints of authentic Mughal style can still be sensed today in the rich dishes of Mughlai cuisine in Hyderabad and Lucknow, with their emphasis on spice, fruits, nuts, meat, and bread; in the traditional dress worn by descendants of the old courtly elite in Lucknow and Hyderabad; and in the *darbari* or 'courtly' style of performance maintained by hereditary exponents of Hindustani music.

Further reading: Beach 1992; Richards 1995; Schimmel 2004; Sharar 1975; Spear 1973.

—KATHERINE BUTLER SCHOFIELD, *Professor of Music,*
King's College London, University of London

— ••• —

Muslim Religious Reform Movements

Muslim religious reform is a prominent aspect of modern India's religious landscape, as of its history more generally. The movements advocating and inculcating religious reform—today and historically—are not of a piece, however. They vary as much in their scope, scale, and religious disposition—from extremely orthodox to what some consider heretical—as in the regional, sectarian, and class bases of their constituents. This article, therefore, provides a representative rather than comprehensive overview of the more historically significant Muslim religious reform movements in modern India, beginning in the eighteenth century.

Two political processes that mark India's eighteenth-century history provided an important impetus for religious reform: the devolution of Mughal imperial power and, from mid-century, the establishment and consolidation of British colonial rule. Muslim religious reformers were extremely troubled by the demise of Muslim empire and the expansion of Christian colonial political power in India. Until 1858, however, many Muslim intellectuals and theologians—but not all—were able to take some solace in continuing Mughal, and thus Muslim, sovereignty, if not political power over India. The Faraizi movement exemplifies a Muslim religious reform movement produced both in and by this historical context, as it does one of the earliest anti-colonial movements in the subcontinent.

As their name suggests—*farz* is the Arabic term for 'religious obligation'—the Faraizis called for a return to the fundamentals of Islam. The movement was started by Shariat Allah (ca. 1781–1840), who initiated it among Muslim peasants in his native East Bengal. The Faraizi emphasis on fundamentals as well as on giving up Sufi saint worship and reforming marriage and funerary customs suggests the influence of Wahhabism on Shariat Allah, a movement that similarly promoted a return to the fundamentals of Islam which was at the time taking hold in the Arabian peninsula. Shariat Allah had been exposed to the teachings of Muhammad ibn Abd al-Wahhab (1703–92) during his twenty-year residency in Mecca, where he had stayed on after completing the *haj* ('pilgrimage to Mecca' required of all Muslims) as a young man. Upon his return to British Bengal in the early nineteenth century, Shariat Allah's advocacy was simultaneously religious and political. He argued that Muslims should not perform communal prayer as they did not have a Muslim ruler. His son, Dudu Miyan (1819–62), under whom the movement thrived, took this argument one step further and declared India *dar al-harb* ('abode of war') due to British colonial rule. The movement gained traction among the East Bengal Muslim peasantry in the second quarter of the nineteenth century, as much for its reformist message as for its anti-landlordism, but waned in the early twentieth century (Choudhury 2001).

The Faraizi was not the only religious movement of its time to take an unaccommodating stance towards colonialism on religious (and economic) grounds, or to declare British-controlled territory in India *dar al-harb*. Sayyid Ahmad of Rae Bareilly (1786–1831) did the same, but took a more militant approach to returning India to *dar-al-Islam* ('abode of Islam'). Trained by a prominent lineage of theologians in Delhi (the descendants of Shah Walliullah, 1703–62), Ahmad's religious training also included initiation into three Sufi orders: the Naqshbandi, Qadiri, and Chishti. Ultimately, he would achieve recognition as one of the leading *ulema* ('clerics'; sing.: *alim*) of Delhi. With that authority, Ahmad advocated reforms at the popular level—of common rituals and practices around weddings and deaths, for example. He also wrote on theology, emphasizing the transcendent unity of God and identifying three threats from within Islam that undermined this belief:'false' Sufism, Shiism, and popular customs. While he castigated Muslims for their participation in such activities, he targeted the British as the principal threat to Muslims in India and committed himself to eradicating their rule through military means, referring to his endeavour as a jihad. His effort in taking up arms was surely audacious. It was also a dismal failure, however, and in 1831 Ahmad was killed in battle (Jalal 2000).

Muslim reform proliferated in the late nineteenth century as Muslims contended with the demise of Mughal sovereignty, the institution of British Crown rule, and developments in other religious communities. While Muslim reformers by and large shared the view that their political fate had befallen Muslims because of religious and moral decay in the community at large, they differed in their notions of how to correct this. The Deoband, Ahmadiyya, and Tablighi Jamaat movements are three divergent responses to this late colonial period (1858–1947). The founders of the Deoband movement responded to the eradication of Muslim sovereignty in India (in 1858) by focusing on the moral uplift of the Muslim community. The leaders of the movement were *ulema* who saw the salvation of India's Muslims in this group. To this end, they started a seminary in the North Indian town of Deoband in 1867 to train *ulema* (Metcalf 1982). The reformed Sunni Islam taught at the seminary emphasized the 'revealed' over the 'rational' sciences—that is, the Quran and particularly *hadith* ('sayings of the prophet Muhammad' which, with accounts of his daily practice, constitute the major source of guidance for Muslims apart from the Quran) over all else. It advocated doing away with what were deemed un-Islamic practices, particularly popular rituals at births, deaths, and marriages. Although Sufism was an integral feature of the movement—many Deoband *ulema* simultaneously served as Sufi spiritual guides—the movement denounced particular kinds of Sufi devotion, such as prostration at a saint's tomb, that it interpreted as approaching *shirk*, or associating any being or thing too closely with God. It also refused the notion of the Sufi saint as an intermediary with God (a key distinction from a parallel Muslim movement: the Barelvi). The seminary and its teachings had a broad impact, both through branch schools that were set up across India and because students came from across India and returned to their native places to propagate Deoband's reformed Islam. The Deoband movement began as self-consciously inward-looking and apolitical, focusing solely on reforming Muslim religious practice through the creation of a reform-minded *ulema*. It would be transformed in the early twentieth century, however, as Deoband *ulema* began to actively participate in anti-colonial activities and India's nationalist movement (Minault 1982).

The Ahmadiyya movement epitomizes a rather different response to the late colonial context. Mirza Ghulam Ahmad (late 1830s–1908) established the movement in the Punjab in 1889, in a regional context of vibrant competition between Muslim, Hindu, Sikh, and Christian reform and missionary movements for adherents (Friedmann 1989). Ahmad offered his followers a charismatic leader who claimed status as both a messiah and a *mahdi*, or rightly guided one, and ultimately as that of a prophet as well (leading some, both then and now, to see the movement as heretical for challenging the Sunni doctrine that Muhammad is the ultimate prophet). Ahmad and his movement gained immediate notoriety in the Punjab due to his heated public debates with members of other religious groups, including Christian missionaries, Sunni *ulema*, and leaders of the prominent contemporary Hindu and Sikh reform organizations, the Arya Samaj and the Singh Sabha, respectively. Historically, Mirza Ghulam Ahmad and the Ahmadiyya movement are best remembered for their role in the contentious religious atmosphere of late nineteenth century North India, in which religious identities were being reforged, often in competition and confrontation with one another. This obfuscates two important aspects of the movement's later history, however: The first is that this was a vibrant movement that gained many adherents. Although there are no precise statistics on the size of the Ahmadiyya community, estimates suggests that the Ahmadiyya population today is likely to be about ten million people (Human Rights Watch 2005). Secondly, in more recent times, they have suffered overt discrimination for their beliefs. The Ahmadiyya were officially declared non-Muslims by the Pakistani state in 1974, for example, and are persecuted in a number of Muslim countries (Human Rights Watch 2005). In contrast, the Indian state has largely protected their rights by recognizing the Ahmadiyya as Muslims.

Given Ahmadiyya doctrine, the organization might rightly be described as a revival, as well as a reform movement. The same is true of the Tablighi Jamaat (the society for 'inviting'/'conveying'), another movement that emerged in the context of late colonial India. Maulana Muhammad Ilyas (1885–1944) established the organization in a context of religious competition in 1920s North India. The immediate catalyst was a Hindu 'reconversion' campaign targeting Muslims in the area of Mewat, south-west of Delhi. Ilyas's encounter with members of the targeted community, who were largely humble labourers, convinced him that formal education and schooling would have only limited success in influencing them. Rather, he initiated a method of practical learning in which Muslims taught and preached to one another; and he insisted that participating in such activity was incumbent upon all Muslims, not just a select few (such as the *ulema*). The doctrine of the Jamaat crystallized into a rather straightforward 'six points': the attestation of faith; canonical prayer; knowledge and ritual remembrance of God; respect towards all Muslims; sincerity; and volunteering time for *tabligh* ('inviting'/'conveying'). The movement relied (and relies) on this last tenet for its propagation, ideally seeking from its members one day a week, one three-day period a month, one forty-day period a year, and one four-month tour at least once in a lifetime. On this basis, it has been exceptionally successful in disseminating its message of proper Muslim comportment and practice, and is the most widespread Muslim proselytizing, or *dawa* organization in the world today (Metcalf 2004).

Muslim religious reform in India since 1947 is largely marked by continuities with late colonial developments. The Deoband seminary, for instance, continues to be one of the most significant institutions voicing opinions on Muslim religious matters. Sufi shrines remain popular institutional sites of devotion, as does the concern among some Muslims to ensure that devotion at shrines is not 'excessive', that it should not approach *shirk*. One transformation brought about by 1947 and worth noting is in the activity of the Jamaat-e-Islami, a political organization of *ulema* started by Maulana Maududi (1903–79) in 1941 on the basis of a religious philosophy with immense political implications. Maududi was trained as an *alim* in the Deoband tradition and had as a young man been an active member of the Jamaat-e Ulema-e Hind, a political organization that actively supported the Indian National Congress and championed the idea of 'composite nationalism', or a nationalism that incorporated people of all religious faiths. Maududi became increasingly disenchanted with nationalism in the 1930s, however, and evolved a radical critique of the democratic nation state, the very thing that nationalists of all stripes were fighting for. His critique rested on the idea that Muslims could not accept the sovereignty of man over God. The former, sovereignty of man (the people), was, of course, foundational to the political discourse and theory of the state espoused by Indian nationalists. In its place, Maududi called for an Islamic state that would enshrine the sovereignty of God over all (Nasr 1996).

With the partition of India in 1947, Maududi and most of his followers migrated to Pakistan where they attempted to construct their Islamic state (with limited, but significant results). This did not mean the dissolution of the Jamaat-e-Islami in India, though, and it remained a significant institution there. In its postcolonial Indian guise, the Jamaat-e-Islami has abandoned the notion of an Islamic state. Rather, it has evolved a position committing itself to a secular, democratic India as the most fertile environment for Muslims to pursue a properly pious life. One might see the Jamaat-e-Islami's evolving philosophy as just the latest in a long line of strategies employed by Muslim reformers in modern India, some of which have been outlined here.

Further reading: Ahmad 2009; Ahmed 1981; Choudhury 2001; Friedmann 1989; Human Rights Watch 2005; Jalal 2000; Jones 1989; Metcalf 1982, 2004; Minault 1982; Nasr 1996.

—FARINA MIR, *Associate Professor, Department of History, University of Michigan*

— ••• —

Nationalism

Nation' and 'nationalism' made their appearance in Indian political discussions in the English language between the sixth and eighth decades of the nineteenth century, gradually replacing their commonly used predecessor term, 'native'. The legitimating potential of claiming to be a nation was not lost on an Indian political elite that was linked into European and British public debates, political theory, and history. Initially the basis of a claim to a greater share in representative government, a national claim came with time to justify a demand for popular sovereignty and eventual statehood for India. The central oppositional category against which the nation was defined was alien or colonial rule, although attempts to harmonize an Indian nationalism with a qualified belonging to a wider British imperial polity were also central to the language of Indian politics.

It is important to distinguish between the words used in political language as intended legitimation, and the ideas they refer to. The question of translatability enters into the equation: Indian languages did not have equivalents which were readily adaptable to the new expression of collective identity which were far less flexible, and indeed in some cases sought to impose collective belonging to the nation, than existing vocabulary allowed for. Pre-existing words referred more to 'fuzzy' than to 'enumerated' communities (Kaviraj 1992), and depending on the audience addressed, *qaum, jati, rashtra*, and so on, were used as imperfect translations that had to be naturalized, but continued to bear the connotations of their older, and other, usages alongside the newer ones. That the nation was largely imagined, debated, and theorized in English, even when written about in Indian languages, remains evident in most cases, as the writers' self-conscious referring back to English, or to other European languages via English, shows. A standardization of translational practices for words in the independent state's vocabulary had to await national Independence.

Nationalism also remained a concern of an emerging all-India middle class that sought to control the economic and social spaces of the state-to-be. Among this emerging middle class, subgroups competing for dominance in this anticipated state also contested the parameters and boundaries of belonging to the nation, attempting to exclude those they sought to disempower in an eventual state. At the same time, academic writing on an Indian nation (which was itself part of the nationalist movement) sought to buttress claims to independence and statehood, as well as to produce various versions of a nationhood, projected into the past as well as the future, serviceable for a new state. Nationalism was used to refer to a loyalty to India as a whole, used in opposition to 'communalism', sectional or sectarian loyalty to a (usually religious) identity that was less than national. 'Communal' was seldom used as self-description, and more as attempted delegitimation.

The early years of the invocation of nationalism in the service of anti-colonial politics were based on defining the practical, spatial, and cultural parameters of a nation, and watching the struggles for national unification in Italy and Germany. What should a nation do—build up its economic strength through protection of infant industries through tariffs, as recommended by Friedrich List (1789–1846) (Chandra 1966; Goswami 2004), or follow Giuseppe Mazzini (1805–72) in finding the soul of a nation (Banerjea 1925)? By the late nineteenth century, the word 'national' was used to describe organizations, as part of their names (the Indian National Conference, the Indian National Congress), and the idea of 'national awakening' was widely discussed by intellectuals. The need for 'national industries' and 'national education' had begun to be institutionalized by the turn of the century, and found a focal point in the campaign against the Partition of Bengal from 1905 onwards. Widely referred to as *swadeshi*, which translates as 'of our own country', this is the closest word in Indian languages that came to connote the national, though the *desh* in question (which could mean 'village', 'place of birth', or 'locality') was not clearly defined. *Swaraj* ('self-rule' or 'independence') avoided the question of the collective self that was to be the nation (Gandhi 1938).

The principle of 'national self-determination' was not, however, acknowledged as the central guiding principle of the international state system until after World War I, when the Bolshevik revolutionaries Vladimir Lenin (1870–1924) and Leon Trotsky (1879–1940) proclaimed it as a principle, and the US president, Woodrow Wilson (1856–1924), could offer no less in his principles for remodelling the world after the war (Manela 2007; Mayer 1963). At this point, what had been in the nineteenth century a radical innovation in thinking about states and sovereignty became tamed by its official anointment. The divergence between the principle and the practice remained stark. The formula of 'trusteeship' that the League of Nations (and the United Nations thereafter) adopted to deal with not-yet-nations was a reminder that the criteria of nation-hood were in the custody of outsiders with a coercive power that relied on more than concepts.

'National' in India still invoked the collective that was yet to be. From the 1920s, imperial administrators as well as native intellectuals and aca-demics spoke of 'nation-building', following the official British rhetoric of impending self-rule in 'nations ripe for self-government'. The question of who belonged and who did not to an entity called India became urgent in connection with British claims that divergent and antagonistic 'com-munities' could not be considered a nation, and against the backdrop of communal tensions between Hindus and Muslims, in particular. Nationalism thus invoked race, civilization, and often the religious com-munity alongside the sense of belonging to a future nation state. It also mobilized European debates on Aryanism and eugenics in search of the healthy national body (Zachariah 2005: 242–52). The tautological nature of national claims is obvious—that the nation and state must be congruent; therefore the state-to-be must be defined in terms of the nation that justifies it. International discourse on what a nation is and should be—the standard of legitimation for the staking of claims to ter-ritorial sovereignty—conspired with the idea of the one nation–one state model that was promoted.

Definitions came with contestations, and varieties of Indian nation had various ethnic and religious inflections. The normative importance of the national notwithstanding, it was descriptively vague. The national unit being sought was in turn Bengali (Hindu, upper caste and male), Marathi, and so on, with sectional or regional ideas of the nation simply projected onto the rest of India. The search for the essence of the nation and its national genius lent itself easily to organicist ideas of the ancient-and-modern nation that must be purged of its 'impurities' to realize itself once again. In such arguments, the 'Hindu' past was to be the Hindu future, and since Muslims, in particular, and other minorities, in general, had their loyalties and sacred imagination tied to other places, only Hindus could be true nationals (Golwalkar 1938; Savarkar 1989 [1928]). In some arguments, 'Hindu' was a confused but crucial category—geographical, cultural, religious, ancient civilization, sacred soil and earth, birth, culture, and way of life—all at the same time. A struggle by outcastes, excluded from Hindu normative hierarchies, and by Muslims not to be included in such definitions of national belonging led logically enough to counter-claims to different nationalisms. By the 1920s, the theory of the 'Aryan invasion' of India was used to argue that Hindu upper castes were for-eigners to the nation (Irschick 1969), and by the 1940s Muslim leaders sought to organize around the idea that South Asian Muslims were not a minority but a separate and distinct nation (Jalal 1985).

The version of nationalism that the new Indian state adopted after independence and partition was, however, a broad and inclusive one, invoking a cultural continuity with the past that went beyond sectari-anism. Articulated by the left wing of a nationalist movement that saw the end of imperialist rule as an interim goal on the road to socialism, it regarded nationalism as obsolete at its very moment of realization (Nehru 1946). It relied, however, on asserting an Indian nationalism rather than describing it, and on asserting a collective goal for the nation, now identified with the state, in development (Zachariah 2009). As nationalism, seen as a composite culture of belonging in which all persons within the borders of the state could (and ought to) participate, became the language of political legitimation, exclusions from national belonging on the grounds of more sectarian definitions of the nation were difficult to articulate legitimately in public. Such a nationalism was so inclusive as to be unusable to distinguish citizens of India from citizens of other countries—which is precisely what made it so attractive in a state with so diverse a population, in which any discussion on national belonging would lead to making explicit the actual or potential exclusions that any nationalism must have. Forms of exclusion were now more implicit than explicit, with nonetheless serious practical implications. Indeed, forcible inclusion, as in the case of parts of the northeast of India (Nehru 1959), or Kashmir from the 1980s, was often more of a contentious issue.

Post-Independence India has tended to frame its arguments about national belonging more around 'secularism' and 'communalism' or 'sepa-ratism' than by the term 'nationalism', at least until the 1990s, when the overthrow of the obligatorily secular understanding of nationalism in India and the rise of Hindutva definitions of national belonging forced a more nuanced understanding of nationalism into being, as potentially (Basu et al. 1993) or inherently (Zachariah 2011) exclusionary, and the terms 'religious nationalism' (van der Veer 1994) or 'Hindu nationalism' (Jaffrelot 1996) were coined to engage with the new phenomenon.

The retrospective teleology of the nation-state that is so much a part of historiographical tradition has led to the keyword 'nationalism' being inadequately questioned in the Indian context, with historians from very early on as partisans for a national ideology. Partially critical voices have never abandoned the urge to advocate versions of nationalism that they are willing to support, and to describe other versions as exclusionary, sectarian, or 'communal'. A more nuanced view might have seen 'communalism' as a nationalism with the wrong unit of loyalty from the perspective of the Indian state, or the Indian state-to-be.

Further reading: Banerjea 1925; Gandhi 1938; Kaviraj 1992; Nehru 1946; Zachariah 2011.

—BENJAMIN ZACHARIAH, *Senior Research Fellow, Karl Jaspers Centre for Advanced Transcultural Studies, Heidelberg University*

— ·•· —

New Social Movements

In the Indian context, the term 'new social movements' refers to those collective movements that emerged from the late 1960s onwards, in the wake of the outbreak of the Naxalite insurgency in 1967. The designation of these movements as 'new' derives from the political conjuncture in which they emerged, the social groups and issues they mobilized around, and the strategies and forms of organization they developed to pursue their goals.

Significant examples of India's new social movements are the Shramik Stri Mukti Sangathana, which championed the rights of Adivasi women in rural Maharashtra, the Kerala Fishworkers' Forum which organized poor fisherfolk in Kerala against the depredations wrought on their livelihoods by mechanized trawling, and the Chhattisgarh Mines Shramik Sangh, which mobilized Adivasi mineworkers in erstwhile eastern Madhya Pradesh. These movements can be designated as 'new' in three different ways.

First, new social movements signalled the emergence of *a new conjuncture* in Indian politics. Following the repression of the CPI-led Telengana uprising in 1951, the early postcolonial era in India was characterized by the relative acquiescence of poor and marginalized social groups to the Nehruvian project of developmentalist nation-building. The rise of new social movements was expressive of the unravelling of the Nehruvian project, which ultimately culminated in the Emergency (1975–7) and the electoral victory of the Janata Party in 1977 (Omvedt 1993).

Second, new social movements crystallized around *social groups and issues* that had been relatively peripheral in left politics since independence in 1947. New social movements such as the Dalit Panthers, the Jharkhand Mukti Morcha, and the Self-Employed Women's Association (SEWA) brought Dalits, Adivasis, and women working in the informal sector to the centre of political mobilization in a way that the parliamentary left, with its focus on building a worker–peasant alliance, had not done. Moreover, new social movements were instrumental in politicizing issues that had hitherto not been considered relevant to left-wing politics in India, chief among them being the environment (through movements such as the Chipko Andolan), development-induced displacement (through movements such as the Narmada Bachao Andolan), and gender-based violence (the autonomous women's movement) (Vanaik 1990).

Third, new social movements pursued *strategies of organizing and mobilizing* that departed from prevailing repertoires of contention on the left in India in a number of ways. First of all, new social movements maintained a distinct distance from political parties and electoral politics, preferring instead to mobilize subaltern social groups outside the parliamentary domain. Second, new social movements were generally sceptical of working in and through the state, as the state was perceived to be a centralizing force that deprived marginalized and subaltern social groups of the possibility to participate in decision-making processes. Finally, mobilization often proceeded through voluntary and localized grassroots groups that aimed to augment community-level participation and decision-making in mobilizing processes (Kamat 2002).

New social movements remained a political force in India throughout the 1980s, and in the 1990s—in the context of the implementation of neoliberal reforms—concerted efforts were made to build nation-wide links between movements mobilizing in different fields. These efforts ultimately culminated in the formation of the National Alliance of People's Movements (NAPM) in 1996, which today consists of more than two hundred movements across India.

Critics argue that India's new social movements reached an impasse in the 1990s, evidenced most clearly in the inability to halt the momentum of market-oriented reforms and Hindu communalism. An alternative and more positive assessment of the achievements of India's new social movements would point out that many of the recent advances in the field of rights-based legislation—for example, the Right to Information Act (2005), the National Rural Employment Guarantee Act (2005), and the Forest Rights Act (2005)—would not have been possible without their persistent mobilization. Nevertheless, the contemporary scenario appears to be one in which new social movements are losing ground to, on the one hand, non-governmental organizations and, on the other hand, the armed Maoist insurgency in India's 'Red Corridor'.

Further reading: Guha 1989; Nilsen 2010; Rangan 2000; Ray and Katzenstein 2005; Shah 2004.

—ALF GUNVALD NILSEN, *Associate Professor, Department of Sociology, University of Bergen*

— •◦• —

Nehruvian

The term 'Nehruvian' is used in a temporal as well as an ideological–political sense: thus, Nehruvian *era* as well as Nehruvian *thought* or *politics*. In both cases, the semantic community is limited to an English-speaking, scholarly, policy and public intellectual elite.

As a temporal signifier, Nehruvian refers to the period 1947–64, when Jawaharlal Nehru (1889–1964) served as the interim prime minister and subsequently the first prime minister of independent India. A more expansive temporal definition might extend the period to 1969 when Nehru's daughter Indira Gandhi (1917–84) assumed prime ministerial office and effected a series of decisive and deliberate policy and ideological transformations. The term has been applied retrospectively, and it is difficult to find instances of its usage during the eponymous era.

While Nehru is usually the foundational figure in discussions of the Nehruvian era, the formative role of numerous other individuals, institutions, and social–historical forces in shaping this historical moment is also acknowledged. These include both supporters as well as adversaries of Jawaharlal Nehru. For instance, a description of Nehruvian India could plausibly include the role of defence minister and close ally V.K. Krishna Menon (1896–1974) and of home minister Vallabhai Patel (1875–1950), who frequently disagreed with and opposed Nehru's policies and worldview (Guha 2007).

Discussions of the Nehruvian era are generally event-centric: they focus on and privilege specific and discrete episodes or events during this period. Among the key events are the Partition of British India into the sovereign nation-states of India and Pakistan; the drafting and adoption of the Indian Constitution with its distinctive commitment to state-directed social reform and modernization; the first three general elections of the postcolonial period; the incorporation of independent princely states into the Indian union to create a singular territorial sovereignty for the new nation-state; the elaboration of linguistic federalism and the adoption of a multilingual official language policy; the introduction and implementation of the first two Five-Year Plans for the national economy and the broader and ongoing project of national economic planning. Significant activities and events that unfolded in a wider, international arena during these years included two wars with Pakistan (1948, 1965) and one with China (1962); and the emergence and consolidation of the Bandung Bloc of Third World nation-states that adhered, albeit unevenly, to a doctrine of nonalignment in the bipolar global theatre of Cold War politics.

The Nehruvian era was also replete with challenges, setbacks, defeats, and disappointments. A more comprehensive recounting of this moment in history includes as well events such as unprecedented levels of mass migration, displacement, and violence in the wake of Partition; acute food shortages; popular, class-based, and ethno-national mobilizations against central governmental authority in Telangana, Tamil Nadu, and

Maharashtra; Nehru's dismissal of the popularly elected communist government of the state of Kerala in 1959; and the imprisonment of Kashmiri political leader Sheikh Abdullah (1905–82) (Guha 2007).

All these discrete episodes may be enfolded within a larger narrative of postcolonial nation-state formation as the emblematic and primary project of the Nehruvian era. Involving both identitarian and institutional coordinates, or the production and legitimization of a new national identity and new institutions and laws following the formal end of colonial rule in August 1947, the Nehruvian national project grappled with the distinctive dilemma of postcolonial sovereignty: how to assert both continuity and distance from the colonial (which was equally the anti-colonial, nationalist) past; how to demobilize a mass population and redefine state–society relations around the normative imperative of civil obedience rather than disobedience; how to align the historically opposed formations of national community and state authority.

The resulting project of Nehruvian nation-state formation had distinctive ideological and material dimensions, and it is these that are referenced in the second sense of the term 'Nehruvian'. As an ideological–political term 'Nehruvian' refers to a wide variety of themes apparently endorsed by Jawaharlal Nehru and related to the conduct of political, social, cultural, and economic life. These include: secularism; civic nationalism, and the embrace of subnational diversity; a centrally planned 'command' or *dirigiste* economy with an emphasis on heavy industrial growth; state-led social and cultural modernization; developmentalism; the promotion of 'scientific temper' and a demonstrable fascination with scientific and technological accomplishments and artefacts; and a nonaligned foreign policy. Although all these themes are commonly characterized as Nehruvian, it is worth remembering that not all received explicit articulation by Nehru, nor were they formalized as part of a coherent ideology or worldview. Nehru's political thought underwent considerable changes over time, and the notion of a singular and immutable Nehruvian ideology is thus largely ahistorical.

Since the late 1980s, a historical conjuncture marked by the rise of Hindu nationalism and the liberalization of the Indian economy, the public use of the term 'Nehruvian' has acquired a pronounced and deliberate normative edge. For instance, while some scholars and public intellectuals praise Nehruvian secularism for its superior political and ethical commitments, others highlight its inadequacies and failures. Discussions of Nehruvian economic policy reveal similar normative polarizations between proponents of free market economies and supporters of social welfare and socialist alternatives. Yet another variant of the normative debate addresses the character of the Nehruvian state, with considerable critical attention directed towards the bureaucratic, 'top-down,' and 'high-modernist' constitution of the Nehruvian state.

A presumption of radical disjuncture informs these normative discussions, with Nehruvian India relegated to an increasingly distant and distinct past that has little in common with present national realities. However, such a distinction may be overstated. There are significant institutional and ideological affinities and continuities between 'old' and 'new' India; hence the pronouncement of the death of Nehruvian India may be somewhat premature.

Further reading: Bhargava 1999; Brecher 1959; Kaviraj 2005; Khilnani 1997; Roy 2007; Rudolph and Rudolph 1968; Thapar 1991.

—SRIRUPA ROY, *Professor of State and Democracy,*
Centre for Modern Indian Studies, Göttingen

— .•. —

Nonalignment

The word 'nonalignment' has a two-fold historical resonance. On the one hand, it refers to a set of ideas that underpinned the foreign policy of independent India, especially during the prime ministerial years of Jawaharlal Nehru (1947–64). On the other hand, it tends to be associated with the Non-Aligned Movement (NAM), a political grouping that was formally launched in 1961 and was closely associated with the idea of the Third World. The history of the idea of nonalignment is further complicated by the fact that successive Indian governments have constantly claimed allegiance to it in the conduct of their foreign policy. Moreover, the NAM continues to exist today although the Cold War context in which it was born has long since passed.

Whatever its subsequent vicissitudes, nonalignment initially took shape as the response of a newly independent country that attained freedom under unpropitious international circumstances. As the vice-president of the Interim Government, Jawaharlal Nehru (1889–1964) stated in a radio broadcast in September 1946: 'We propose, so far as possible, to keep away from the power politics of groups aligned against one another, which have led in the past to world wars and which may again lead to disasters on an even vaster scale' (cited in Raghavan 2010: 10). Nehru's speech can be read as a response to another famous speech made earlier by Winston Churchill (1874–1965), which warned of an iron curtain descending on Europe and which warned of the onset of the Cold War and the need to make firm choices. By contrast, Nehru indicated that independent India would seek to navigate its own way through the shoals of international politics.

From the outset, Nehru stressed that nonalignment embodied pragmatism as much as principle. It was, he observed, 'not a wise policy to put all our eggs in one basket [...] purely from the point of view of opportunism [...] an independent policy is the best' (cited in ibid.). Later, Nehru increasingly couched nonalignment in the language of morality. This deservedly laid him open to the charge of a gap between his rhetoric and action. Yet it bears emphasizing that nonalignment in Nehru's conception was geared towards advancing India's interests as much as promoting a set of values.

At its core the idea of nonalignment as conceived of by Nehru comprised three principles: first, the importance of retaining the capacity for independent judgement and action on the international stage; second, the avoidance of military alliances and arms races; third, working towards a more just and equitable international order. In pursuit of these, Nehru espoused a series of causes: anti-colonialism, anti-racism, a concerted move away from economic under-development, and the building of ever-widening areas of peace.

In practice, Nehru's own record on each of these aspects of nonalignment was mixed. India did take an independent stance on the major problems of the times: Korea, Laos, Vietnam, Congo, and so forth. Yet, Nehru's determination to take a measured stance on such issues led him to tarry in his criticism of the actions of great powers, namely of the United Kingdom and France over Suez and the Soviet Union over Hungary (Gopal 1979/1983). Nehru also managed to hold India clear of formal alliances, but the defeat against China forced him to look for military support from the West. The ensuing arrangement, he realized, considerably diluted this principle.

Lastly, Nehru remained a votary of Afro-Asian solidarity, although he developed reservations about the institutions that were coming into being. Speaking at the Asian Relations Conference organized in New Delhi in early 1947, Nehru said: 'For too long we of Asia have been petitioners in Western courts and chancelleries. That story must now belong to the past. We propose to stand on our own feet and to cooperate with all others who are prepared to cooperate with us. We do not intend to be the playthings of others' (cited in Chand 1993: 251). At the Afro-Asian Conference in Bandung in 1955, Nehru played a prominent role. But he was troubled both by the presence of countries that were formally aligned to one of the superpowers as well as by the lack of fidelity among many leaders to the ideas of democracy and individual freedom. By the time the founding conference of NAM was held in Belgrade in 1961, Nehru was unenthusiastic about the idea of a third, nonaligned 'bloc'. This not only struck him as an oxymoron, but he felt that the era of classic colonialism was at an end and that the real dangers lay in superpower rivalry and the possibility of nuclear war.

As it happened, the NAM far outlived the original idea of nonalignment, but its subsequent incarnations would have certainly surprised Jawaharlal Nehru.

Further reading: Datta 2005; K.S. Pavithran 2007; Ministry of External Affairs 1982; Rauch 2008.

—SRINATH RAGHAVAN, *Senior Fellow, Centre for Policy Studies, New Delhi*

— .•. —

NRI

It is estimated that there are roughly 20 million persons of Indian descent living abroad, of which some of the largest concentrations are in the USA, Canada, United Kingdom, South Africa, as well as the United Arab Emirates and Saudi Arabia (Report of the High Level Committee [RHCL] 2001). India is one of but a few countries to have a specialized and popularized acronym to refer to its expatriates: 'NRI', or 'Non-Resident Indian', is the most common colloquial term used by those in India to refer to Indian citizens living abroad, although it is rarely used by diasporic Indians to describe themselves. Other terms like *desi*, 'overseas Indian', 'expatriate Indian', and 'PIO' ('Person of Indian Origin') are also used, although less frequently. *Desi* colloquially refers to persons of Indian origin and is used in the diaspora as a form of personal identification. It is used by persons from other parts of the Indian subcontinent as well. 'PIO' is often colloquially seen as synonymous with the term 'NRI', as both refer to those Indians residing outside India; however, it carries a different set of political, historical, and cultural implications.

The term 'NRI' was previously applied to a citizen of India living abroad for business and, according to Margaret Walton-Roberts (2004: 58), emerged in the 1970s as the result of banking initiatives marketed to Indians abroad in an effort to encourage their investment. The 1973 Foreign Exchange Regulations Act defines NRI and PIO, as does the RHLC from 2001, referenced earlier (Reserve Bank of India [RBI]). In the wake of the sweeping economic reforms of the 1990s, the period of liberalization in India, the NRIs were elevated to a new status of importance, their relationship to India defined and valued almost entirely in financial and economic terms. Special incentives were created to attract the investment and remittances of middle- and upper-middle class NRIs; by doing so, NRIs were positioned as necessary to the economic success of the nation (Mankekar 1999: 745–46). The term 'NRI' is loaded with the economic underpinnings of its origins, and the perception in India that they find immense financial success abroad, a view reflected in popular culture. The cultural resonance of NRI is, therefore, much broader than its economic implications.

In December 2003, the Indian parliament passed a bill to grant to persons of Indian origin what is now known as OCI, or Overseas Citizenship of India (UNHCR 2004). This is not the same as dual citizenship, in that they may not retain or obtain an Indian passport, but it does increase the rights of the holder. The aim of such a bill was to make travel to India easier, to permit business investment, and to forge a greater sense of belonging amongst the Indian diaspora. An important incentive for acquiring OCI is that holders receive a special visa in their passport allowing them lifelong multiple entries into India for any period.

Further reading: Dickinson and Bailey 2007; Kalra et al. 2005; Lall 2001; Mani and Varadarajan 2005; Walton-Roberts 2004.

—SARAH JOSHI, *Birkbeck College, University of London*

—— •◦• ——

Panchayati Raj

The idea of *panchayati raj* ('self-governing village assemblies') owes its origin to the system that prevailed in India for a long time under which villages were to a great extent self-governing. According to Dharampal (1972), a perusal of early (late eighteenth and early nineteenth century) British colonial records leaves little doubt that in most parts of India villages (and perhaps also towns) possessed an organized institutional framework that looked after the civic, administrative, and political needs of the community, and was endowed with the necessary powers and resources to perform the various tasks. These institutions of village self-governance decayed and disintegrated under British rule, particularly due to most of the produce being expropriated as land tax by the rulers. British initiatives regarding the establishment of village panchayats in the last decades of the nineteenth century and the first decades of the twentieth were undertaken primarily for the purpose of enhancing administrative efficiency. The village panchayats that came into existence as a result of these policy decisions were in no way related to the self-governing institutions of earlier times (Dharampal 1972).

The idea of *panchayati raj* in the sense of self-governing villages constituted a crucial and integral part of Mohandas Karamchand Gandhi's (1869–1948) conception of *swaraj* (Gandhi 1999). Notwithstanding this, in the initial drafts of the Constitution, *panchayati raj* did not find any mention. It was only after a large number of members of the Constituent Assembly had expressed their disaffection at the absence of any provision for *panchayati raj* that an Article to the effect that the State would take steps to organize village panchayats and endow them with such powers and authority as might be necessary to enable them to function was added to the Directive Principles of State Policy. The Seventy-third Amendment to the Constitution (1992) was enacted to enshrine in it certain basic and essential features of *panchayati raj* as it is envisaged today. The most important of the provisions of the amendment include constitution of panchayats at village and other levels; direct elections to all seats in panchayats at the village and intermediate level, if any; reservation of seats for the Scheduled Castes and Scheduled Tribes in proportion to their population; and reservation of not less than one-third of the seats for women.

One rationale for *panchayati raj* institutions is straightforward, namely decentralization of power. It is, however, important to distinguish the objective of decentralization of power from the objective of establishment of *gram raj* ('village rule'), wherein the village is conceptualized as a community, an organic entity, rather than an ensemble of individuals (Dharampal 1962: 9–13, foreword by Jayaprakash Narayan). For Gandhi, *panchayati raj* meant *gram raj*; and not merely decentralization of power. The governmental initiatives with respect to *panchayati raj* have not come up to these expectations. The reason possibly lies in the fact that 'development' in the modern sense is inherently power-centralizing and, consequently, is impeded by institutions that tend to decentralize power. It is in this sense that the Gandhian insight of there being a close relationship between the choice of technology and the possibilities and exercise of freedom assumes importance (Gandhi 1938).

Further reading: The Constitution of India (Seventy-third Amendment) Act 1992; Dharampal 1962, 1972; Gandhi 1938 [1909], 1999.

—SATISH K. JAIN, *Centre for Economic Studies and Planning, School of Social Sciences, Jawaharlal Nehru University, New Delhi*

—— ·•· ——

Pandit

Pandit (also pundit) derives from Sanskrit *pandita*, meaning 'wise' or 'learned.' Typically pandits are male Brahmin scholars in the Hindu tradition.

The intellectual practice and cultural identity of the pandit centres on the creation, reproduction, and exposition of scriptural and classical learning as embodied in the Sanskrit tradition. Pandits are typically associated with skills of oral transmission and memorization and are lauded for their ability to accurately pass on vast amounts of knowledge from teacher to student, generation to generation. Pandits are also associated with a range of scholarly practices: exegesis and commentary; philosophical analysis and hermeneutics; verbal exposition and public debate; and the explication of social, legal, and religious norms.

Unlike other Brahmin religious experts who are involved in ritual exchanges, the pandit ideally avoids the service of divine images on behalf of human worshippers. While pandits may accept gifts (*dakshina*) from their students, these gifts are not thought to compromise the independence and purity of the pandits' lifestyle. They are 'prestige intellectuals' whose purity and learning attract the support of wealthy patrons, but whose prestige depends upon the maintenance of ritual and social independence (Pollock 2001: 5).

Becoming a pandit involves eight to twelve years of study in such areas as grammar, rhetoric, philosophy, logic, law, and theology. Traditionally, study begins at the age of eight, when the pupil takes up residence at the home of his teacher. The teacher provides food, shelter, and lessons, while the student performs daily chores in addition to his studies. Such schools, established on lands gifted to Brahmin families by local rulers or landowners, are known by a variety of names (*pathshala, tol, chatushpathi*).

Acquisition of Sanskrit often commences with rote learning and memorization. Students early on master a traditional lexicon like the *Amarakosha* ('immortal treasure/casket/dictionary'). Study then turns to specific fields, such as grammar (*vyakarana*), exegesis (*mimamsa*), logic (*nyaya*), and rhetoric (*alamkara*). Along the way, students gain proficiency in composition and commentarial skills and may acquire a miscellany of aphorisms, poetry, and didactic fables. Depending on the training of their teacher, students might specialize in one or more of the Vedic collections, in Hindu law, or in other specialized disciplines. To acquire mastery students often accompany their teachers to ceremonies where their learning is tested in debate (*shastravichara* or *tarkayuddha*). A formal examination marks the end of study, leading to conferral of a title (*upadhi*).

Sanskrit learning and pedagogy were profoundly transformed during the modern era, which occasioned a shift from oral and manuscript practices to the printing of Sanskrit texts and the reform of curricular practices. While pandits helped mediate Sanskrit knowledge to the West, in time they were marginalized by the discipline of modern Indology (Rocher 2007). Nonetheless, pandits were neither unprepared for the challenges created by colonialism nor were they unwilling to adapt to changing circumstances (Hatcher 2005). Today, the norms of pandit training have expanded to include standardized curricula, regular examinations, and the conferral of academic degrees (see Sinha 1993).

Further reading: Cenkner 1982; Dalmia 1996; Dodson 2002; Hatcher 1996, 2005; Kumar 1998; Michaels 2001; Minkowski 2001; Parry 1985; Pollock 2001; Rocher 1995, 2007; Sarasvati 1975; Sinha 1993.

—BRIAN A. HATCHER, *Professor and Packard Chair of Theology,*
Department of Religion, Tufts University, Medford

—— •◦• ——

Partition

In its most commonly understood sense, Partition refers to the division of the erstwhile British Raj into two separate nation states, India and Pakistan, in 1947. The impact of Partition, however, went far beyond this demarcation of political boundaries and included large-scale migration and uprooting of minorities, the fissuring of social and cultural identities, the division of families across newly erected national borders, and the transformation of cities and urban spaces.

The roots of Partition lay in the idea that Muslims of the Indian subcontinent were culturally distinct. Two leading Muslim intellectuals, Sayyid Ahmad Khan (1817–98) and Muhammad Iqbal (1877–1938), contended that Muslims must safeguard their distinct identity and protect their interests as a minority to avoid being submerged by an overwhelming non-Muslim majority population. The All-India Muslim League (est. 1906) demanded that Muslims be given separate electorates to ensure that they were represented in sufficient strength in elected bodies. Accepted by the British in 1909, this demand helped institutionalize the political separateness of Muslims. From 1937 onwards, Mohammed Ali Jinnah (1876–1948), popularly described as *Quaid-i-Azam* ('Supreme Leader') and 'Founder' of Pakistan, spearheaded the campaign for a separate Pakistan to provide a 'homeland' for Muslims. Jinnah's leadership came at a critical juncture in the face of heightened Muslim concerns about safeguarding their interests and protecting their minority status, as the British signalled their intention to end their rule and transfer power to Indians. A key phase in Jinnah's campaign was triggered by Congress's refusal after the 1937 provincial elections to form coalition ministries with the Muslim League. Intractable differences over power-sharing arrangements led Jinnah to realize that separate electorates had not been enough to safeguard Muslim interests (Talbot and Singh 2009: 31–6). Moreover, Congress rule in seven key provinces during 1937–9, which Jinnah characterized as inaugurating 'Hindu rule', further estranged the League.

On 23 March 1940, at its Lahore session, the Muslim League adopted the Pakistan Resolution, demanding that 'the areas in which the Muslims are numerically in a majority, as in the northwestern and eastern zones of India, should be grouped to constitute Independent States in which the constituent units shall be autonomous and sovereign' (Jalal 1985: 58). Jinnah did not elaborate whether the new formation would be part of a federal structure, or constituted a blueprint for sovereign Muslim state-hood. The historian Ayesha Jalal (1985) has argued that the demand was intended to be a bargaining counter vis-à-vis the British and Congress to secure a better deal for the Muslims prior to the transfer of power. Having raised the demand for Pakistan, Jinnah was faced with the chal-lenge of uniting Muslims into one political bloc. Acutely aware of the deep divide among the subcontinent's Muslims, he employed the slogan of 'Islam in danger' and used religious symbols and imagery to mobilize mass support. He also insisted during negotiations with the British and Congress that he be recognized as the 'sole spokesman' of the Muslims (Jalal 1985). Towards the end of World War II, reconciliation efforts were made between Congress and Muslim League, but talks between Mohandas Karamchand Gandhi (1869–1948) and Jinnah, held in 1944, failed, as did British attempts at mediation. In 1946, the Cabinet Mission Plan made a desperate attempt to accommodate both Congress and Muslim League and to avoid the creation of a separate Muslim state by proposing autonomy for the Muslim-minority provinces and minimal central control (Talbot and Singh 2009: 40–1). However, the Plan failed to satisfy both parties.

In September 1946, an Interim Government took office, led by Jawaharlal Nehru (1889–1964) as prime minister, with the Muslim League accepting two cabinet positions. But Congress and Muslim League continued to pull in different directions. On 20 February 1947, British Prime Minister Clement Attlee (1883–1967) announced that he was committed to handing over power to a 'responsible Indian government' within 18 months. To carry out this mission, Lord Louis Mountbatten (1900–79) was appointed Viceroy of India in April 1947. After dis-cussions with a range of political leaders, Mountbatten concluded that Jinnah's demand for a separate Muslim state could no longer be resisted (Mansergh 1981–2).

Mountbatten formulated a blueprint for the transfer of power, known as the 3 June 1947 Plan, which conceded, in principle, the demand for Pakistan: the Muslim-majority provinces of Bengal and Punjab, in view of their large non-Muslim populations, would be divided. A commission would demarcate the boundaries, based upon the religious composition of population, transport infrastructure, and 'other factors' (Tan and Kudaisya 2000: ch. 3). Mountbatten speeded up the timetable and set 14–15 August 1947 as the dates for the transfer of power. The boundary commission, chaired by Cyril Radcliffe (1899–1977), began its work in the summer of 1947 (Talbot and Singh 2009: 44–6). Although Radcliffe was singularly responsible for the boundaries that would divide India and Pakistan, he was unfamiliar with boundary-making and also totally unaware of the complexities of the territories he was about to divide. Moreover, it was not clear what 'contiguous majority areas' meant—a district, a *thana* ('police circle'), or a *tehsil* ('subdivision of a district'). In short, what was the unit of territory to be partitioned? Further, there was the issue of the relative weightage assigned to the three criteria of demography, 'contiguous areas', and 'other factors'. The commission's plans for the demarcation of boundaries were not published, as it was feared that widespread communal violence might erupt in protest. The Radcliffe Boundary Award was announced only after Independence ceremonies had ended. The impact of this delay was momentous: by keeping everybody guessing about the exact boundary line, and by not giving the governments of the two new states enough time to make arrangements to provide the necessary security of life and property during the mutual transfer of population in the newly created border areas, the Award contributed greatly to the violence and disorder that followed, particularly in Punjab. The Boundary Award was seen as particularly disappointing by the Muslim League. The Sikhs were also bitterly disappointed as the division of Punjab ensured that the community, concentrated in the central divisions of Lahore and Jalandhar, was split down the middle. Further, some of their sacred pilgrim centres now lay within Pakistan (Tan and Kudaisya 2000: ch. 4).

Communal violence erupted on a large scale as minorities caught on the wrong side of the border decided to abandon their homes, creating waves of refugees in a panic-stricken exodus. Hindus and Sikhs fled from Pakistan and Muslims from western, northern, and eastern India left for East and West Pakistan. It is estimated that over 18 million people on both sides of the border were eventually uprooted. The boundary-demarcation exercise and the new borders led to many problems. For example, in Punjab, many canals were cut off from their headworks on the rivers, thus damaging the integrity of the province's irrigation system. In Bengal, roads and railways were disrupted. Protracted conflicts arose over water-sharing between India and East Pakistan (later Bangladesh) and valuable opportunities were lost in harnessing the Ganges and Brahmaputra rivers for the benefit of over 400 million people living in their basins. The circumstances that led to Partition did not improve the plight of minority communities—the *mohajirs* ('Muslims who seek refuge to escape religious persecution') in Sind (Pakistan), Biharis in Bangladesh, Muslims in India. But perhaps the bitterest legacy of Partition has been the deadlock over Kashmir and the arms race between India and Pakistan, with both neighbours having acquired nuclear weapons.

Further reading: Jalal 1985; Khan 2007; Mansergh 1981–2; Talbot and Singh 2009; Tan and Kudaisya 2000, 2008; Zamindar 2007.

—GYANESH KUDAISYA, *Associate Professor, South Asian Studies Programme, National University of Singapore*

— •◦• —

Plantation Labour

Modern plantations were set up as agro-industries in several parts of the Indian subcontinent during colonial rule. In nineteenth century India, indigo, tea, rubber, and coffee emerged as the most significant plantation products. These plantation enterprises were monopolized by British capital and produced for the world market. Tea plantations in Assam were the first and the biggest plantation industry to be opened up by British capital. They were arguably the largest employer of migrant labour; by the end of the nineteenth century, the industry could mobilize over a million emigrants from Bihar, Bengal, and Orissa to work on these plantations. As indentured labour, they were employed under a contractual penal system with statutory fixed minimum monthly wages, number of hours, and an obligation to labour for the duration of the contract, which ranged from three to five years. Most of these 'protective' norms provided by labour legislations were flouted by the industry with impunity.

In this short article, the focus will be on the initiation, development, and functioning of tea plantations. In the wake of tension over opium smuggling and the ensuing supply difficulties with China, tea plantations were set up in Assam in 1840 as an alternative. Beginning with a combination of joint-stock companies and individual proprietors, the tea industry, from 1870 onwards, came under the monopolistic control of the corporate world of British Managing Agency houses in Calcutta with their headquarters in the United Kingdom. In 1948, the Indian Tea Association, the apex body of the Indian tea industry, represented 92 per cent of tea acreage in Assam and 78 per cent in the province of Bengal. At the all-India level, thirteen leading agency houses of Calcutta controlled over 75 per cent of the total tea production in 1939 (Behal 2007).

Characteristically, plantation labour and managerial personnel were made to compulsorily reside within the tea estates. Unlike the production in China, which was predominantly based on the use of peasant household labour, Assam plantations adopted labour-intensive production methods from 1840s onward. Almost entirely based on manual labour, the cultivation process went through seasonally different stages: site selection and clearance; production and seed sowing; establishing nurseries; transplanting; digging, weeding, and hoeing; pruning and, finally, plucking. After plucking, the green leaf was processed by withering, rolling, fermenting, drying and firing, sorting, heating and packaging. The manufacturing process, initially manual, was mechanized over time employing about 10 per cent of the total labour force residing in the plantations (Griffith 1967).

The frenetic pace of expansion from the 1860s onwards generated a huge demand for plantation labour. Having failed to coerce the local communities to work on the plantations, the planters began importing migrant labour; in the catchment areas, the term *arakatti* ('the private labour recruiter') acquired special significance and notoriety.

Under the indenture regime, plantation life of the labouring communities was marked by below-subsistence wages (which were often supplemented in kind), physical and sexual coercion, illegal confinement, disease, malnutrition, low reproduction, and a high mortality rate. To discipline and tame the migrants, the planters adopted a strategy of immobilizing tens of thousands within the spatial confines of isolated plantation enclaves. Their vast size and geographical locations within heavily forested areas were found conducive to organize labour life in the confinement of *bastis* ('coolie residences'), which were kept under surveillance (Behal 1992).

Within the confines of this isolated geographical space, the planters established a social hierarchy where the British planter occupied an omnipotent position of almost absolute authority. Resident communities of managers, clerks, overseers, and labourers spoke diverse languages which were not understood by everyone. A special vocabulary evolved in which keywords like *budda sahib* ('senior manager'), *chhota sahib* ('assistant manager'), *mem-sahib* ('wife of the manager'), *coolie* ('labourer'), *khansama* ('cook'), snd so on, connoted the nature of power relationships mediated through this social hierarchy in everyday life on the plantations.

Percival Griffiths (1967: 376), the official historian of the Indian tea industry, rationalized that the nature of labour relations on the Assam tea plantations was benevolently paternalistic. However, contemporary colonial officials, fully supportive of the British capitalist venture in Assam, and Indian nationalists were less sanguine in their assessment; both considered the indentured labour regime in Assam to be an arbitrary evil and an abnormal system (Behal 2010). While to the colonial officials this was the necessary price to be paid for private British enterprise to develop the resources of a 'distant' and 'backward' province, the nationalists condemned this as slavery.

Further reading: Behal 2007, 2010; Behal and Mohapatra 1992; Griffiths 1967.

—RANA P. BEHAL, *Professor of Modern Indian History,*
Deshbandhu College, University of Delhi

Political Economy

A single definition of the term 'political economy' does not exist (Groenewegen 1987). Having evolved over time and being used in various ways, the concept presents both a method of study and connotes a specificity in time and space: A precursor of the *term* 'economics', political economy is now taken as a sub-theme of the *discipline* of 'economics', though the former has broader implications. Given that the concept of social science implies a unity between various academic disciplines—history, sociology, economics, and political science—political economy per se represents this more closely than economics does.

Different schools of thought have used the term differently. Karl Marx (1818–83) criticized the classical economists' (for example, David Ricardo [1772–1823]) use of the concept political economy, which saw capitalism as a natural phenomenon with fixed and stable laws, as ahistorical. According to Marx (1894), capitalism as a result of the development of social relations was neither permanent nor 'natural'. Yet, he took his point of departure from classical economists who arrived at their understanding of the dynamics of capitalism on the basis of changing social relationships. Marx, hence, recognized the essence of social science analysis in the interlinkages between politics, history, economics, and sociology.

To avoid confusion, analysts need to specify the manner in which they are using the term 'political economy'. Here, it will be used in the classical sense of a holistic analysis relevant to the Indian economy. Further, it cannot be based on borrowed categories of analysis due to the space–time specificity of social science analysis. In this context, it may be pointed out that there are vast differences between the historical evolution of Indian and western societies due to the diametrically opposite economic changes that the two have witnessed over the last two and a half centuries.

During the colonial period (1757–1947), the drain of wealth led to the dissipation of potential economic surplus generated in the colonies to the advantage of the colonial powers who diverted the flow of capital to their own benefit. Thus, the trajectory followed by India during this period and subsequently has been vastly different to that of the West. These historical conditions need to be heeded in an analysis of India's contemporary political economy (Kumar 2013). Independence in 1947 did not lead to a radical departure since the inherited attitudes and economic structures that determined much of the post-Independence dynamics were conditioned by colonization.

Colonial rule left India with a weak and inadequate physical and social infrastructure, backward industrial and agricultural development (Dutt 1963), and a leadership that was 'feudal' in its outlook. The 'divide-and-rule' strategy employed by the colonizers instrumentalized India's heterogeneity to create and deepen a communal divide that led to the division of the country in 1947 and, subsequently, to the breakdown of complementarities across contiguous areas (Sridhar 2008), leading to a succession of wars between the two neighbours, India and Pakistan, and, concomitantly, to a diversion of resources from development projects.

Mohandas Karamchand Gandhi's (1869–1948) ideas of development from below, based on village republics (Gandhi 1909) were rejected by modernists like Jawaharlal Nehru (1889–1964) even before Independence. India's ruling elite, in its colonized mindset and its self-centredness, ignored Indian reality in its economic analysis. For instance, the important issues of a growing black economy (incomes that are not reported to the direct tax authorities and often not reflected in national income) and caste as a dominant factor in social and political matters have remained marginal in political and economic analysis, since borrowed western ideas and models do not incorporate them.

Due to a paucity of knowledge-generation over two centuries, India became heavily dependent on western ideas that were adopted on a large scale. At Independence, its elite was largely western-trained and had adopted western modernity as its goal. After Independence, the separation between the ruling elite and the common people created deliberately by colonial rule was widened. The western path of development chosen by the post-Independence state intensified the marginalization of the common people.

It was assumed that development would follow a European pattern, with a modernized advanced sector elevating and thus reducing the extent of the backward sector (Lewis 1954). The idea of a 'trickle-down' effect which was supposed to facilitate an automatic and natural dissemination of the benefits of modernization from one sector to another supported this model. But while the latter may have worked during the development process in the West since it had colonies, including the Americas, to send its surplus labour to, this is not the case for contemporary modernizing postcolonial economies.

India, following this strategy, went in for showpiece large dams and industrial plants that led to a mass displacement of the rural population which often had no choice but to migrate to urban slums. Furthermore, the borrowing of technology meant that India did not develop its own technological base and has remained dependent on the import of technology. Rather than reaping the benefits from an 'advantage of a late start', due to the possibility of jumping stages of technological development, India experienced a distinct 'disadvantage of a late start' (Kumar 2013).

Yet, India at Independence was also distrustful of the imperial powers and western hegemonic designs. Consequently, the ruling elite, affirming a western orientation even as it called for self-sufficiency, was plagued by confusion and contradiction. At a strategic level, India allied with the Soviets while simultaneously still aspiring to copy the West European model (Kumar 2013). These confusions led to an economic crisis in 1991 as the Soviet system weakened after the mid-1970s.

The leadership of the national movement realized that the principal problems of Indians—poverty, illiteracy, ill health, and so on—in the pre-Independence period were a result of colonial rule. The system and not the individual were to blame for the nation's ills. Thus, it was accepted that the solution to the basic problems of the people lay in the collective; hence a large role was given to the state to solve the basic problems facing the country. Indian capitalists accepted their weakness in terms of capital and technology and suggested that an independent India needed a strong public sector to develop the rudiments of the economy that could then provide a base for their growth (Thakurdas 1944). National capital knew it could not face foreign competition and needed protection from foreign goods. The notion of 'infant industry' was invoked and protection afforded to Indian goods (Kumar 2013).

India adopted the concept of a 'mixed economy' with a strong public sector to create infrastructure—both of the social and physical kind. Reservation for small-scale and cottage sectors (Industries [Development and Regulation] Act, 1951) as well as affirmative action for the downtrodden were introduced on grounds of equity (on the basis of Article

15[4], Constitution of India). The policy paradigm gave the appearance of a socialistic pattern of development, but it was in reality a state-led capitalist path with the public sector supporting the growth of the private sector. The former could not generate the resources for its self-sustained development and remained dependent on the state.

Instead of a socialistic path of development being initiated, there was rapid growth of monopolies, rising disparities, sickness in the public sector, growing corruption and black economy, and alienation of the people, all of which created political and social problems. Thus, the country experienced one crisis after another—the severe drought of 1966–7, the Naxalite movement in 1967, the Nav Nirman and JP (Jayaprakash Narayan) movements in the early seventies followed by the Emergency in 1975, the recurrent economic shocks with each oil crisis in 1973, 1979–80, and 1989–90 (Kumar 2013). This necessitated loans from the IMF and the World Bank, and the capitulation to their dictates resulted in the penetration of international finance capital in India's decision-making.

From the mid-1960s onwards, forms of production changed from backward agriculture with small-scale production using traditional technologies to modern farming based on imported Green Revolution technology, leading to mechanization and to casualization of labour. The former dominance of agriculture in the GDP has since given way to a predominance of the service sector. Thus, India's following a classical development path has led to the marginalization of the vast majority which still remains entrenched in agriculture. These trends are a consequence of India being a late entrant into the world of technological development, where it has also not been able to make much of an original contribution.

India's economy is characterized by primitive capitalism with extreme forms of exploitation both through the white and the black economies (Kumar 2013). Pervasive corruption has augmented the criminalization of society and marginalized the poor. The drain of wealth has thus continued after the British departure and the country, in spite of its development, remains short of resources.

After 1991, India rapidly opened up to global influences: policy-making underwent a U-turn—a paradigm shift. Now, individuals themselves, not the collective, are held responsible for their problems and, as a consequence, individuals have to deal directly with the mechanisms of the free market in order to solve their problems such as poverty, unemployment, or illiteracy. The state, corrupted by the private sector, is considered inefficient and has retreated in favour of the market. India has been set on a path of 'growth at any cost' with marginalized sections and the environment having to bear the burden (Kelly and D'Souza 2010).

In brief, to understand India's political economy, a historical, social, and political, besides an economic, analysis is required. Further, given India's unique circumstances, its history, diversity, and the rapid changes it has undergone, a political economy approach also entails that methodology and models cannot be copied from alien western contexts as has happened since the 1990s, but must be developed in line with Indian specificities.

Further reading: Dutt 1963; Gandhi 1909; Groenewegen 1987; Kelly and D'Souza 2010; Kumar 2013.

—ARUN KUMAR, *Sukhamoy Chakravarty Chair, Professor,*
Centre for Economic Studies and Planning, School of Social Sciences,
Jawaharlal Nehru University, New Delhi

— ⋅•⋅ —

Postcolonialism

Postcolonialism' refers primarily to a study of the historical experience of colonial rule over a large part of the world by European powers, including especially the literary and cultural discourse produced by the colonized subjects as a result of that experience. Secondarily, the term signifies a set of resistant or 'contrapuntal' reading practices applicable equally to canonical texts of English literature such as Shakespeare's *The Tempest* or Jane Austen's *Mansfield Park*.

The beginning of postcolonial discourse is traced to Edward Said's *Orientalism* (1978), though the term does not actually occur in that book, and its founding trinity of theorists comprises, besides Said (1935–2003),

Gayatri Chakravorty Spivak (b. 1942) and Homi K. Bhabha (b. 1949). Whereas Said's seminal contribution was to highlight the nexus between Orientalist knowledge and imperial power, Spivak (1999) has focused on the repression of the subaltern (in the figure equally of an Indian queen and a destitute tribal woman), while Bhabha (1994) has explored the psychological effects of colonization as manifested through mimicry and hybridity. The intellectual genealogy of these theoretical developments derives from Michel Foucault (1926–84), Antonio Gramsci (1891–1937), Frantz Fanon (1925–61), and Jacques Derrida (1930–2004), among others.

The parameters of postcolonial studies were set in two crucially delimiting ways in an early and widely circulated handbook, *The Empire Writes Back: Theory and Practice in Postcolonial Literatures* (1989), by Bill Ashcroft, Gareth Griffiths, and Helen Tiffin. They proposed that the term 'postcolonial' be interpreted to encompass not only the period after the independence of a colony (as etymology and common sense would suggest) but the longer time-span beginning with the moment of colonial intervention. While this nicely encompassed the whole seamless history of white colonies such as Australia, New Zealand, and Canada, it served to erase the radical emancipatory rupture that independence brought to colonies in Asia and Africa.

Also, Ashcroft et al. laid down that only literature written in the colonies in the colonizer's language, English, may be considered to be postcolonial, which included nearly all the writing from the white colonies while leaving out the vast majority of works written during the colonial and postcolonial period in an inveterately multilingual country such as India. A further exclusion has followed through which diasporic Anglophone writers from the former colonies, still writing about the home countries that they have left behind, are seen to represent their 'imaginary homelands' to a metropolitan readership or, in an alternative formulation, to narrate their nations, while writers in Indian languages still living in the post-colony are only rarely translated, and hence are omitted from this discourse.

On all these grounds, Salman Rushdie (b. 1947) has come to be recognized as probably *the* emblematic postcolonial writer, with other younger writers who grew up in his shadow, such as Amitav Ghosh (b. 1956) and Arundhati Roy (b. 1961), also marking the Indian contribution to postcolonial literature. Earlier Indian writers in English, from Mulk Raj Anand

(1905–2004) and R.K. Narayan (1906–2001) to Anita Desai (b. 1937) and Nayantara Sahgal (b. 1927), who were once counted among eminent 'Commonwealth' writers, have undergone a relative eclipse, especially after Rushdie's polemical argument in his essay '"Commonwealth Literature" Does Not Exist' (Rushdie 1991).

Postcolonialism early established a distinct presence for itself in the American academy where Said taught, and Spivak and Bhabha continue to teach. The British scholar Robert Young (who, too, now teaches in America) has, in his insightful historical account of the process of decolonization, sought to extend the scope of postcolonial studies by giving it a 'tricontinental' perspective, by including in his discussion non-British colonies such as Algeria and Cuba as well (Young 2001). A recent compendium seeks to widen the discourse by including rubrics such as 'Postcolonial Translations' and 'Anthropology and Postcolonialism' (Chew and Richards 2010).

In the Indian academy, Postcolonialism remains yet another of the many critical or theoretical movements that arise in the West and are after a little lag duly imported—with the paradoxical difference that (unlike Postmodernism or Cultural Studies) this new discourse was intended to give a voice precisely to the peoples of a former colony such as India. An early Indian book to address the subject contains a range of essays by academics who appear to look askance at this metropolitan discourse of resistance and indeed to resist it rather than identify with it (Trivedi and Mukherjee 1996).

Further reading: Bhabha 1994; Chew and Richards 2010; Said 1978; Spivak 1999; Trivedi and Mukherjee 1996; Young 2001.

—HARISH TRIVEDI, *Former Professor of English,*
University of Delhi

—— •◦• ——

Poverty

U nidimensional (money-metric) poverty assessment requires the specification, in monetary units, of a poverty line whose job it is to distinguish the poor and non-poor segments of a population. Once the poverty line has been fixed, the extent of poverty in a society can be measured in terms of a number of indices, of which the most widely employed index is the so-called headcount ratio, or proportion of the population below the poverty line.

India has had a long history of engagement with the poverty line, ably reviewed by T.N. Srinivasan (2007). Yet, how and where should the poverty line be fixed? The present author (Subramanian 2012) suggests that official efforts at identifying a poverty line for India have been deeply disappointing. The point at issue boils down to the most appropriate 'space' in which invariance of the poverty norm employed must be sought. Official Indian approaches (see GOI 1993, for instance) have required that for poverty comparisons to be meaningful the commodity bundle underlying the poverty line should be held fixed. Amartya Sen (1983) has persuasively argued that the poverty norm employed ought to be invariant in the space of 'human functionings', so that the poverty line is amenable to determination as the monetary cost of achieving a specified list of minimally satisfactory states of being and doing (such as adequate nutrition, health, mobility, shelter, and literacy). In this view, the money-metric poverty line can vary, in terms of resources (commodity bundles or 'real incomes'), across individuals and contexts. A 'functionings'-based approach of this nature is, arguably, conceptually sound but difficult to implement, while the opposite is true of 'resources'-based approaches.

Typically, official methodologies of identification in India have tended to conform to resources-based approaches in a manner that, in turn, has tended to soft-pedal magnitudes and to fast-track rates of reduction of poverty. The credibility of these official methodologies has been seriously called into question by Utsa Patnaik's (2004) demonstration that a plausible variation on their theme is actually compatible with a trend of *increasing*, rather than declining, poverty rates (the latter being the official version of the poverty story in India). It should be noted that even the official headcount ratio estimate of 37 per cent for India in 2004–5 implies the existence of over 400 million poor persons in the country. Overall, it would be fair to suggest that there has been no more than a plodding decline in money-metric poverty in India.

Loosely speaking, multidimensional approaches to the quantification of deprivation assess poverty directly in the space of human functionings. Jayaraj and Subramanian (2009) is an example of an effort in this regard. The authors analyse the magnitudes and trend of a consolidated 'multidimensional headcount ratio' of poverty that is sensitive to the range (or number of dimensions) of deprivation. Their method is an application of a measure of social exclusion earlier proposed by Chakravarty and d'Ambrosio (2006). Jayaraj and Subramanian employ National Family Health Survey data for 1992–3 and 2005–6 to construct a picture of multidimensional deprivation in India across its states and over time. The authors consider eight specific dimensions of functioning, revolving around the possibility of access to drinking water, sanitation, shelter, education, health, mobility, and elementary recreation. Bihar, Madhya Pradesh, Rajasthan, Uttar Pradesh, Orissa, and West Bengal unsurprisingly emerge as amongst the most deprived states of the Indian Union. While there has unquestionably been a reduction in multidimensional deprivation between 1992–3 and 2005–6, the magnitude of such deprivation, even as late as 2005–6, is of a considerably higher order than is suggested by official estimates of unidimensional poverty. Apart from anything else, the number of individuals in considerable or severe deprivation—counted as those who are deprived in at least five of the eight dimensions considered—is a staggering 472 million in 2005–6.

India's much-celebrated growth of per capita income in the last couple of decades has been accompanied by a substantial widening of absolute inequality. Concentrated affluence, in this scheme of things, coexists with dispersed impoverishment. India, by all accounts, is both a low-tax and high-evasion country. It is a cause for dismay that the state's increasing emphasis on neoliberal reform has been purchased at the cost of minimally redistributive anti-poverty policy. Such a policy orientation could be based on slightly more stringent insistence on tax-compliance and enhanced direct taxation (not least of wealth and corporate profit) to finance elementary social security provisioning (such as old-age pension, survivor benefit, maternity assistance, and accident relief—for details, see Guhan 1993); a reasonably functioning Public Distribution System

(PDS) for food and essential commodities; decent wages in publicly sponsored employment programmes; investment in essential infrastructure for the promotion of basic human capabilities in the dimensions of nutrition, health, education, sanitation, shelter, and mobility; and land reform. These failures of positive freedom (or the freedom to achieve valued capabilities) are compounded by the failures of negative freedom (or freedom from restraint and coercion), as reflected in routine transgressions of elementary rights (in cases of rape, custodial deaths, caste atrocities, communal riots, and public theft in the form of political and bureaucratic corruption). The burden of deprivation falls with disproportionate severity on identifiable sections of the population: females, Dalits, people of rural origin, and religious minorities. The analytical categories of positive freedom, negative freedom, and group-related discrimination in the distribution of these freedoms thus provide a useful conceptual framework for the study of deprivation in India.

It is undeniable that the weight of history and an unjust international economic order have had a very large role to play in causing and perpetuating India's poverty, as reflected in the consequences of colonialism, unfair global trade practices, the conditionalities imposed by supranational financial institutions, the burdens of strife and international debt, and the capriciousness and niggardliness of international aid flows. Notwithstanding this, any reasonable account of the phenomenon of poverty in India must—despite official statistics or elitist aspirations to the contrary—stand as a severe moral indictment of Indian society and the Indian state alike.

Further reading: Chakravarty and d'Ambrosio 2006; Guhan 1993; Jayaraj and Subramanian 2009; Patnaik 2004; GOI 1993; Sen 1983; Srinivasan 2007; Subramanian 2012.

—S. SUBRAMANIAN, *Professor of Economics, Madras Institute of Development Studies, Chennai*

—— ••• ——

Qawm

The Muslim 'community' emerged in India during the nineteenth century as a direct consequence of colonial rule. With the destruction of royal and aristocratic forms of power in British territory, these indigenous sources of profane authority were displaced by religious ones, which for the first time stood free of the formers' tutelage (Devji 2007a). In other words, it was the Muslim community's separation from political authority that made it a religious entity in the modern sense. Yet, by freeing Islam of such profane elements, the secular politics of colonialism freed it from all inherited forms of authority, making the Muslim community a site of competition between different groups of divines and laymen. The birth of this new collectivity was signalled by its adoption of a name unknown to history, with Muslims in the nineteenth century calling themselves a *qawm*, an Arabic word meaning something like a tribe or people that had rarely been used to describe religious groups in the past (Devji 2007b). Eventually, this word would become an equivalent for the equally novel term 'nation' in South Asia. Notwithstanding their reference to ties of kith and kin in other contexts, neither community nor *qawm* was used to describe local forms of Muslim belonging, being deployed instead to represent the disparate, dispersed, and merely demographic collection of Queen Victoria's Muslim subjects (Devji 2007b).

The Muslim 'community' or *qawm* emerged, then, during the colonial period as a new kind of sociological category, one derived at least in part from the new forms of enumeration and classification put in place by the British in India. Administrative measures like taking a census to reserve a proportion of seats for religious groups in those administrative bodies that were open to Indians, or to determine who fell under Muslim personal law, proved crucial in the making of a Muslim *qawm*. But Muslims themselves inhabited this community in different ways. Indeed, it soon became the site of great struggles between Muslim groups in northern India, primarily Sunni clerics and their relatives among the laity. Both these groups belonged to the same class of minor landholders, administrators, and bureaucrats, all Urdu-speaking, who had been liberated by colonial rule from the kings and nobles they had once served. Fully conscious of their independence, these men called themselves *sharif* ('well-born'), and set out to recast Islam in their own image, thus lending the *qawm* some substance as an ethnic category. It was the laymen who set the terms of debate in this struggle, and especially those who gathered under the 'reformist' and pro-British banner of the Aligarh Movement, whose project to modernize Muslims was named after a town in the United Provinces that was home to its great institutions, the Mohammedan Anglo-Oriental College (later Aligarh Muslim University) and the Mohammedan Educational Conference (Lelyveld 1978). Aligarh was also the base of the movement's founder and guiding spirit, the influential modernizer Sayyid Ahmad Khan (1817–98).

During the nineteenth century, this new community was anchored by the rival institutions of both reformers and traditionalists, as well as being addressed and represented in the outpouring of pamphlets, journals, and books produced by these groups (Metcalf 1982). It was not until 1909, however, that the community became a formal political actor, when the British introduced limited franchise to India, with legislative seats being reserved along religious lines, thus producing a separate Muslim electorate (Robinson 1974). But this meant that the North Indian Muslims who had dominated the debate on the community's future suddenly became a minority among their coreligionists, whose superior numbers they finally had to acknowledge by handing leadership to the Punjabi landlords, Bengali trades unionists, and Gujarati merchants who came together in the Muslim League. The word *qawm*, of course, eventually came to refer to India's Muslims as a nation represented by the League, though this did not happen until after the 1937 elections, when Mohammad Ali Jinnah (1876–1948) first put forward his 'two-nation theory' and in 1940 called for the creation of Pakistan. But even with the rise of the Pakistan Movement in the 1940s, this term and its English equivalent, community, continued being used for Muslims in a non-national sense. In today's India, for example, the Muslim minority is still called both a *qawm* and a community, as indeed are all religious groups despite the fact that *qawm* is also the word for nation. The non-political history of the Muslim community, then, continues to exist alongside its nationalist past, lending this collectivity great depth and complexity.

Further reading: Devji 2007a, 2007b; Lelyveld 1978; Metcalf 1982; Robinson 1974.

—FAISAL DEVJI, *University Reader in Modern South Asian History,*
Oxford University

— ·•· —

Quit India Movement

Also known as the August Revolution (*August kranti*), the Quit India Movement was the third all-India mass movement against British rule initiated by the Indian National Congress (the first two mass movements were the Non-Cooperation Movement and the Civil Disobedience Movement). The slogans 'Quit India' and 'Do or Die' (*karenge ya marenge*) indicated that it was meant to be the final effort to push the British out of India. Although the movement failed in terms of its stated objective, it has become a celebrated event in the autobiography of the independent Indian nation state.

Launched by Mohandas Karamchand Gandhi (1869–1948) and the Congress in Bombay on 8 August 1942, the movement can only be understood in the context of World War II. After the Japanese conquest of much of Southeast Asia, including Burma, a Japanese invasion of India seemed imminent. The Congress wished to avoid such a catastrophe, which the British presence in India seemed certain to invite. Negotiations in March 1942 with a British government mission headed by Stafford Cripps (1889–1952), on the issue of how much government power could be conceded to the Congress, had failed completely; though the Cripps Mission offered the Congress Dominion status after the war was over, the Congress wanted power immediately, as an Allied victory seemed unlikely.

The government's priority was the war against the Japanese, who frightened it much more than the Congress Party ever did. In a bid to forestall a mass movement, it arrested the Congress leaders pre-emptively on 9 August 1942. The result of the arrests was an eruption of anti-government protests in the cities, followed a couple of weeks later by a rural rebellion against colonial state power. Railway lines were uprooted, telegraph lines cut, police outposts attacked, and government buildings burnt. While such incidents occurred in many parts of India, the largest affected area lay in the United Provinces and Bihar. Here, British power collapsed temporarily, and the restoration of government authority required the deployment of the army. Elsewhere, in isolated cases, like Midnapur in Bengal and Satara in Maharashtra, parallel governments were established, and sporadic terrorist activities continued into 1944. On the whole, however, the main force of the Quit India Movement was extinguished within two to three weeks.

Compared to the previous movements, the Quit India Movement was remarkably different: shorter in duration, violent, lacking an established leadership, and occurring in a war context. As Gandhi and the Congress Working Committee were incarcerated, the movement occurred in Gandhi's name rather than under his guidance.

Recounted as a year of extraordinary nationalist bravery against the British, 1942 in another perspective can be seen as a year of unprecedented fear, when the looming Japanese threat prompted many people to withdraw their money from banks and to flee to parts of India they considered safe from invasion. Nationalist history has tended to replace narratives of fear with those of courage. We may also reflect that had the British been evicted from India in 1942, at the time of maximum nationalist effort, Indian nationalist history-writing would have had a more satisfying and neater story to tell.

Further reading: Hutchins 1971; Niblett 1957; Pandey 1988.

—INDIVAR KAMTEKAR, *Associate Professor, Centre for Historical Studies, Jawaharlal Nehru University, New Delhi*

— ••• —

Race

Ethnographers divide South Asia's population into groups such as Proto-Australoid, Mediterranean/Dravidian, Nordic, Negrito, Mongoloid, and western Brachycephal, all regarded as migrants, though early hominids lived in South Asia. The divisions depend on supposed physical characteristics and speculation. Similarly, race, ethnicity, and nationality are constructed amidst unreliable physical markers. They reflect a human need to belong, identifying with ancestors and kin, and then social groups. All are inherited.

Nationalities as *people*, in the modern sense, imply a citizenship of birth, over time though not for everyone in each generation (Herder 1989). Unlike the ancient distinction between city and citizen, nationalities derive from subjecthood, and then 'popular sovereignty', but may persist beyond the confines of the state; hence joint nationality and multinational nations. Ethnicity too implies descent, above common language, mores, beliefs, or institutions. Most of all, race relies on birth not homogeneity, despite theories about history or culture. Even 'mixed race', frequently pejorative, implies the prior existence of separate races. Biological inheritance supposedly transmits unchanged—like divine revelation for religious fundamentalists, or Sanskrit texts (usually) for Hinduism (Doniger 2009). Thence arise the pathologies of 'scientific' racism: hierarchies of civilization, eugenics, and 'final solutions'.

Prejudice against other peoples for their supposedly intrinsic character is widespread if not universal. But the genealogy of race theory implies that prejudice is not identical over time, or at any one moment. Dean Mahomet's *Travels* (1793–4) described the 'people of India' as 'peculiarly favoured by Providence' and 'possessed of all that is enviable in life', and so 'still more happy in the exercise of benevolence and good-will to each other, devoid of every species of fraud or low cunning' (Fisher 1997: 34). Many eighteenth-century Europeans disagreed, but they shared the idea that environment mattered more than inherent qualities; the Abbé Dubois (ca. 1766–1848), for example, focused on customs and beliefs of the Hindu 'nation'. It was left to a footnote in the English translation casually to attribute caste (defined by Dubois as 'different tribes or classes') to a 'difference of colour between the Aryan Brahmins and the aboriginal inhabitants' (Dubois 1906: 14), referring to the supposed meaning of the word *varna*, following in particular the ideas of French nineteenth-century ethnographers.

Some social scientists were greatly taken with this equation of 'race' and 'caste': treating ancient prejudice as biological as well as acquired pollution. Reviewing Herbert Risley's *Tribes and Castes of Bengal* (1891–2), J.F. Hewitt extolled its 'historic importance' for accurately classifying 'the almost unchanged representatives of some of the principal races' of Vedic India (Hewitt 1893: 237). G.S. Ghurye, *Caste and Race in India* (1932), often reprinted, stressed the original endogamy and fixed professions of castes as evolving but self-regulating institutions—claims traceable to Megasthenes in the third century BCE. Ghurye did quote J.C. Nesfield (1855) who regarded Indians as a single race, denying that racial distinctions were a basis for caste. Ghurye also criticized the fallibility of Risley's anthropometry (since no caste has a uniform physical type). But Ghurye was wedded to a history of racial influx, separation, and mixing: Aryans were 'long-headed and fine-nosed'; aboriginal Indians broad-nosed; Brahmans descended from Aryans who tried to keep themselves apart. Thereby, race was the core of caste's practice and purpose.

The development of more general identities also resembles a prehistory of race. During the first millennium CE, India's scattered agrarian settlements and polities relied on dharma, warfare, and kinship. Identities were expressed in sacred sites and allegiances—*bhakti*, Sufism, temples, and shrines—as well as kingdoms. Shared ideas, customs, and rituals distinguished Indians from other peoples, not unlike the way practices and aptitudes supposedly differentiate races. From many encounters (invasion, travel, trade), some Indians recognized their distinct identity, if only as people of their own place. They imagined themselves as civilizations struggling against natural and supernatural forces, against *mlecchas* ('barbarians'), invaders, and hillmen—primeval struggles repeated throughout history (Basham 1956; Thapar 2003).

Regional identities also coalesced, during the second millennium, while 'Indian' identity continued to evolve. Quasi-ethnic local labels appeared, notably for speakers of languages that now had a full range of elite and literary purposes, where Sanskrit had once served. For the Mughals, too, the categories Afghan, Turk, Persian, infidel, and *ashraf* ('noble', 'gentry') and convert, were racial *in idiom*, as were some South Asian terms for 'Muslim', such as 'Turkic'.

Such indigenous allegiances, evolving under political influence, were powerful and not invented in modern times, as some (Inden 1990) have claimed. The British adopted (did not impose) South Asian identities, arguably even stereotypes such as 'martial' race (Robb 2011: 167). On caste, they echoed their Brahmin allies' exaggerated reliance on the laws of Manu. On religion, they heard earlier as well as current demands for orthodoxy and separatism.

Yet these categories were not races as they would later be defined. From the later nineteenth century, Hindus and Muslims became not only different in religion, but distinct, unitary cultures and interests ('tribes'). Caste was more rigidly defined by occupation, endogamy, and solidarity—legacies of British-Indian jurists from the late eighteenth century. Thus the British helped reconfigure generic groups, such as the Rajputs of Tod's *Annals* (1829, 1832), or the so-called criminal tribes. Marathas, originally regional inhabitants, came to be a caste or service elite, and then were celebrated as proto-national resisters, with Shivaji (1630–80) as an ideal Hindu king. 'Dravidians', identified by Thurston (1909) from crude anthropometry, were the first of many to be regarded as original inhabitants, possibly responsible for the Indus Valley civilization until overrun by migrant Indo-Europeans. The 1931 Census, inheriting the habit of demeaning 'country-born' Indians, pictured migrants mixing with indigenous populations, bearing knowledge: agriculture from the Mediterranean; metalworking from Mesopotamia.

These views were polemical. Since Robert Caldwell's *Comparative Grammar* (1856), Dravidian, for example, has been recognized as a major language group. But linguists deny any necessary correlation of race and language, and stress mutual influences between languages, as from Dravidian to Indo-European forms and vocabulary. Meanwhile, DNA and Y chromosome investigations—modern science's substitute for anthropometry, with similar problems about averages and interpretation—suggest that two ethnic strands (one older than the other) existed between 60 thousand and 40 thousand years ago; but afterwards a single hybrid South Asian population emerged. Genetically, Dravidians are not distinct from most South Asians.

At Independence in 1947, therefore, a 'single' people or rather several contiguous cultures and ethnicities were divided. The avowedly secular

Indian state permitted a conflation of 'Hindu/Sikh' with 'Indian' when it came to people 'stranded' in Pakistan by the Partition; and similar distinctions still exist in India's visa and immigration policy. Already, Indians, including Mohandas Karamchand Gandhi (1869–1948) and, differently, Jawaharlal Nehru (1889–1964), had extolled the particular virtue of Indic traditions and peoples, accommodating nationalism to race theories. Even eugenics had been fashionable for a time, amidst concerns about population growth and physical prowess, inspiring some Hindus to promote mass child-bearing as a weapon against allegedly fecund or predatory Muslims (Gupta 2002).

Today, unthinking confusions of religion, nationality, and race are everywhere. 'India exhibits an immense society of racial elements ranging from the highest grade of civilization to the lowest,' wrote Radhey Shyam Chaurasia in a *History of Ancient India* (2008: 5). Current websites explore the 'Scythic origins of Rajputs', or the 36 'royal races' of India. Nationalists, separatists, and other identity politicians each lay claim to their own narratives, cultural symbols, and political rights, striving for solidarity, claiming territory or privileges, inventing exclusory not pluralistic histories. Such groups assert their quasi-ethnic basis and character, unlike the supporters of class interest or political ideology, who may have similar goals, or join in the same national rituals. The separate 'nationalisms' claim political recognition, as quasi-ethnic entities; examples include Gurkhas, Bhils, Nagas, and a host of other hill peoples. Such arguments also led to the subdivision of Indian states, the secession of Bangladesh, the disputes over Kashmir or within Sri Lanka, and other tensions involving Hindus, Muslims, and Sikhs, or Dalits and Adivasis. At the macro-level, echoing the virtual deification of Shivaji, the Vishwa Hindu Parishad (VHP) has set up the god Ram, on a selective reading, as ideal ruler over a common homeland and defender of the national race. VHP 'nationalism' is pitched against Muslims, as alien invaders and iconoclasts, symbolized by Babar (1483–1531) in the case of the disputed mosque/temple at Ayodhya (Ludden 1996).

Tourism, communications, migration, and globalization, also make race identities more visible. Unlike early Hindus in Southeast Asia, but like earlier nationalists who backed Indians in East and South Africa and the plantation colonies, South Asians of the modern diaspora generally profess a separate ethnic identity while accepting citizenship in their new countries. East African South Asians, denied a right of 'return' by

India, moved to the UK as British subjects; their ethnic (not necessarily national) markers mostly remained 'Asian' or 'Indian'. India now welcomes 'back' wealthy 'Indians' from overseas. Meanwhile, the upsurge of Saudi Wahhabism intensifies some South Asians' identification with Pakistan as well as with forms of universal Islam. These allegiances are not just the afterlife of atavistic loyalties—in the sports arena or political debates. Many migrants are more avid and rigid than South Asia's inhabitants, espousing ideal forms of their inherited culture and identity. Some of the most ruthless supporters of Khalistan (an independent Sikh homeland) lived in the USA, Canada, or Europe. Sri Lanka's Tamil militants were sheltered by Tamils in India and backed by 'expatriate' organizations in the West. Such solidarities are quasi-racial. They persist while daily life, education, and even culture and language are shared less and less between emigrants and the South Asians 'at home'.

Thus are complex fallacies promoted. 'Hinduism', despite recurring features and the potential to produce unified sects, is not a single organized religion. As a political entity 'India' is not 'Hindu'. Unlike 'Indian', therefore, 'Hindu' is not a nationality, let alone a race (Ludden 1996). Nor is race fixed while caste can change (when *jatis* merge or gain economic and political power). On the one hand, caste *is* hard to lose and, on the other, race can be porous and ambiguous. Both terms are contingent social constructs not physical conditions. They require politics and ideology to give them effect. This is equally true not only for those who regard Hindus as a distinct ethnicity and a single religion, but also for many other linguistic, sectional and regional identities that purport to be racial in character or basis, such as the 'low castes', Dalits and Adivasis who, from the early twentieth century, claimed the status of original inhabitants.

Further reading: Chadda 1997; Doniger 2009; Dumont 1970; Inden 1990; Phadnis 1989; Robb 1995; Trautmann 1997, 2006; Washbrook 1982.

—**PETER ROBB**, *Research Professor of the History of India, SOAS, University of London*

— .◆. —

Radicalism

Radicalism refers to an individual's or group's agenda of transforming profoundly the social, political, or cultural landscape of a society. Defined in opposition to more moderate approaches to change, radicalism has a number of dimensions that can, but do not always, go together. Radicalism can indicate especially far-reaching transformative goals; it can imply the support of 'extreme' methods, such as violence; and it can express itself in the demand for a very rapid pace of change.

Historically, the term 'radicalism' developed out of European Enlightenment thought and was, for most of the nineteenth and twentieth centuries, connected to a specifically modern idea of a progressive movement towards a better future. Indian activists appropriated and reformulated certain elements of European notions of radicalism, while rejecting others. In the twentieth century, there also were instances of direct cooperation between European and Indian radicals, such as Indians working together with European revolutionary parties or with the Irish liberation movement (Gandhi 2006; O'Malley 2008; van der Veer 2001: 55–82).

In India, a radical outlook in an Enlightenment sense can be first observed among the reformers of the nineteenth-century Bengal Renaissance who aimed at modernizing religious and social norms. Ram Mohan Roy (1772–1833), for instance, favoured educational reform; he tried to purge Indian society of what he saw as 'superstitious' traditions, such as child marriage and *sati* ('the self-immolation of a widow on her husband's funeral pyre'); and he propagated a 'reformed', monotheistic form of religiosity (Bayly 1998: 155–7). At the same time, these social reformers were less radical in the political sphere, usually accepting colonial rule as such. From the late nineteenth century onwards, in contrast, radicalism took on a more explicitly nationalist meaning. However, this went together with abandoning much of the desire for social change that had characterized the earlier generation, as the new leaders attempted to create a national identity by protecting an inherently Indian sphere of cultural and spiritual values from European intrusion (Chakrabarty 2006; Chatterjee 1993a).

In the early twentieth century, political radicalism was exemplified by activists who were called 'extremist' by the colonial authorities. They defined themselves against the more 'moderate' first generation of the Indian National Congress (founded in 1885). Inspired by, among other issues, their opposition to the partition of Bengal in 1905, political leaders such as Bal Gangadhar Tilak (1856–1920) were the first ones to pursue the goal of speedy, full independence. Some among this generation of radicals were willing to use violent and terrorist means to achieve their goals, setting them apart from moderates who were content with a more limited form of self-government, accepted a slower pace of progress, and were opposed to violence (Chakrabarty 2006: 9–11).

Active in India from 1915 onwards, Mohandas Karamchand Gandhi (1869–1948) and his followers reshaped the political landscape, combining views that had thus far been seen as 'moderate' with 'radical' ones. Like other radicals, Gandhi was in favour of confronting the colonial state directly. However, he strictly opposed the use of violence. While Gandhi's followers saw this stance as an inherently radical one, aiming at overcoming a never-ending cycle of violence, some 'extremist' opponents attacked his approach as weak and accommodationist. This 'extremist' opposition, centred, above all, around the Bengal terrorist movement of the first decades of the twentieth century, may have been important in convincing the colonial state to settle for partial cooperation with the more 'moderate' Gandhi (Heehs 1998). Moreover, Gandhi was also attacked by social radicals. In the view of the leader of the Untouchable movement, Bhimrao Ambedkar (1891–1956), Gandhi did not go far enough in his efforts to overcome caste discrimination. Meanwhile, people on the Communist Left, such as Manabendra Nath Roy (1887–1954) in the 1920s, argued in favour of a proletarian revolution, and were willing to use collective violence if it was necessary to achieve their goal of a classless society (Ambedkar 1945; Roy 1926).

After Independence in 1947, radicalism was often defined against the secularist, reformist programme of the dominant Congress Party (Gopal 2005). Communists, especially strong in West Bengal and Kerala, worked from inside the Indian parliamentary system, pressing for more far-reaching economic and social change. The radical Maoist Naxalite insurgents, in contrast, have been challenging the Indian state in parts of eastern India from the late 1960s onwards, using violent means. At the same time, radical religious groups are willing to 'remake' society on their own terms. Radical Hinduism became much more prominent after 1980, as exemplified by anti-Muslim riots and the increasing influence of the Bharatiya Janata Party (BJP). Such religious radicals rejected the Enlightenment tradition that had long been associated with the term 'radicalism'.

Further reading: Chakrabarty 2006; Chatterjee 1993a; Heehs 1998; van der Veer 2003.

—DANIEL BRÜCKENHAUS, *Assistant Professor of History,*
Beloit College, Wisconsin

— •◆• —

Raj

The word *raj* means sovereignty or rule in Sanskrit and many other Indian languages. It is linked to the terms *raja* ('king') and *rajya* ('polity' or 'statecraft'). In precolonial India, *raj* denoted a particular style of rule, for instance, *dharmaraj* ('virtuous and dutiful rule'). Today, the term is used in English with a qualifying term to describe a particular kind of governance—*permit raj, gunda raj, panchayati raj*. It describes the polity and lineage of kingly ruled Indian states, Darbhanga Raj, for example. With only the definite article ('the Raj'), it is now used to describe the concentration of British political power in the Indian sub-continent under colonial rule, particularly after the Crown assumed direct sovereignty over British India in 1858.

Today, the Raj is a phrase that often conveys a particular idea of British rule: a fusty, old-fashioned sense of order, rooted in the attempt to establish rigid hierarchical distinctions within and between social groups. Taken over to sell products that want to indicate their quality by Indian marketeers, hundreds of British Indian restaurants are so styled (Buettner

2009). The USA's largest Ayurvedic retreat, opened in Iowa in 1993, is called 'The Raj' too. The phrase was used occasionally to talk about British imperialism in India in the first half of the twentieth century: *Life Magazine*'s editorial for its Indian Independence edition was entitled 'Farewell to the Raj' (*Life* 1947: 34).

As a way of talking about the culture and political life of British power in India, the Raj was a postcolonial invention, popularized as a result of the wave of British Raj nostalgia that emerged in the 1970s and 1980s, and which was presaged by the publication of Paul Scott's *Jewel in the Crown* in 1964 and subsequent novels which were later filmed in 1984 (Scott 1964; Moore 1990). This use of the term indicates the stabilization of British storytelling about British imperialism in India after the end of British rule there, and the acceptance of a particular high Tory conception of empire throughout both British and Indian society.

From the late eighteenth century, Raj or Raje were used in English texts to talk about Indian polities. The phrase 'Company Raj' or 'Raj of the Company' emerged in the 1800s, and then only 'British Raj' and 'the Raj' during the 1857 rebellion. The first text to refer to the 'British Raj' in English was the translation of a text published initially in Gujarati and Marathi during the rebellion by the Bombay Parsi, Dosabhoy Framjee. Published alongside a work on Parsi history (1861), Framjee's text, *The British Raj Contrasted with Its Predecessors*, celebrated British rule as British power seemed most vulnerable (Framjee 1858). Framjee criticized pre-British regimes with a standard trope about eastern despotism, but tried to challenge the authoritarian practice of British sovereignty with Indian idioms of ethical rule that emphasized the continual interaction between British officers and their Indian subjects through a processes of dialogue, complaint, and appeal.

The vicissitudes of the term 'Raj' mark an important shift in the way the British imagined their power, from a view that privileged administrative practice to an assumption of formal sovereign authority. Its use after 1857 demonstrates the emergence of a British desire to rule as sovereigns possessed fully of the symbolic trappings of absolute authority. Talking about British rule as a Raj denoted its ultimate paramount power, whose apex lay with the Queen in London—denoted Empress of India from 1877. So, for example, the phrase 'British Raj' was first uttered in Parliament during the debate on Benjamin Disraeli's Royal Titles Bill, and then only used with any frequency in the debate over the India Act (House of Commons

Debate, 1876, Vol. 228: 75–164). In Indian languages, 'Raj' emerged to describe British rule long after institutions of colonial governance had been established. In Bengali, before 1858, for example, it was far more common to talk about Company or British *sashan* ('administration') than Raj.

Yet, at the same time, as Framjee's early use of the word shows, the use of an Indian term for a British form of rule implied an Indian complicity in the practice of colonial administration. It is for this reason that it appears so infrequently in nationalist texts critical of British rule, which emphasized the absence of a partnership between Indians and Europeans, and the illegitimacy of British power. 'British Raj' was a phrase spoken only nine times in the Constituent Assembly debates after Independence. Positively or negatively, 'Raj' was attached far more frequently to forms of rule seen as indigenous—'Panchayati Raj' and 'Hindu Raj' were spoken about far more frequently (IP 1946–50).

The fate of the word 'Raj' indicates both the growth of a gap between the understanding of symbolic authority and everyday administrative power, and also the difference in the way people in Britain and in India have understood the character of colonial rule during the past century and a half.

Further reading: Bayly 1990; Cannadine 2001; Framjee 1858; Scott 1964; Yang 1989.

—JON E. WILSON, *Senior Lecturer in South Asian History,*
King's College, University of London

—— .•. ——

Religion

Definitions of the term 'religion' and the academic study of religions in modern India are not only connected to the history of colonialism and of the postcolonial Indian Republic, but also to debates on modernity and modernization. The multilayered (academic, political, legal, and so on) manner in which the term 'religion' was applied to Indian society had far-reaching consequences for the self-perception of the members of various religious communities and for the shape of religious pluralism in India. The discourse on religion both mirrors and produces multifaceted intercultural encounters and hegemonic claims in colonial as well as postcolonial India.

Seen from a historical perspective, the emergence of religion as an abstract term as well as its objectification as a separate realm of social and cultural practice is a characteristic feature of the modern age. Emerging in seventeenth-century Europe, religion had by the nineteenth century become a generic term for the empirical manifestations of 'religions' (Harrison 1990). What was subsumed under this abstract term had been referred to earlier, in India as well as in Europe, by a variety of words covering religious beliefs, norms, communities, and organizations (such as norm, scripture, sect, of which Sanskrit equivalents are dharma, *agama, sampradaya*). The term 'religion', then, referred to a 'universal' form of human thinking and acting to be studied cross-culturally. As a consequence, later in the nineteenth century a new discipline emerged, the 'science of religion', confirming the idea that religion is a specific experiential, conceptual, practical, social, and/or cultural realm. In recent postcolonial studies, the genealogy of the term 'religion' is critically analysed as being rooted in the history and structure of western imperialism (Asad 1993). The application of the term is criticized (Fitzgerald 1997) and seen as being connected to strategies of colonial subjugation which aim to establish ideological control through concepts, classifications, and taxonomies. It is argued that the term 'religion' tends to fundamentally distort the social and cultural realities to which it is applied and its usefulness for the study of Indian religions is questioned (King 1999; Fitzgerald 2005).

According to conventional modernization theories, religion emerged as a separate social domain as a result of the paradigmatic 'functional differentiation' of society in different autonomous sectors (Luhmann 2013). Once constituted as a separate sector, religion functions according to its own systemic requirements, similar to law, art, or science. This process is often interpreted as exemplifying secularism, that is, the strict separation of politics and religion. Secularism, in turn, is closely connected to an increasing individualization of religious practice. Religion has come to be considered a 'private matter'. However, this view has also been criticized as a simplification because modernization processes are not homogenous but multiple. Modern societies across the globe do not simply become secular, but also witness the emergence of new religious movements and the embedment of religions in the workings of modern society, that is, in mass media, public mobilization, market economies, legal frameworks, and so on (Hefner 1998). This embedment can also be seen in the multilayered debates on religion in modern India, in which not only members of religious communities articulate their respective understandings, but also politicians, judges, journalists, or artists (Beyer 2003). Religion in modernity is thus not just a privatized, separate sector, but emerges in pluralized, multi-sited forms. One aspect of this situation is the formation of fundamentalist groups propelling religious homogeneity and envisioning a reinstatement of what is construed as the 'traditional' union between society and religion. As a consequence, the idea and place of secularism in India has been subject to debate and critical analysis (Madan 1987, 1993).

Pluralization and objectification of religion is also reflected in academic studies of religion in modern India. Religion is studied in various academic disciplines using a variety of perspectives based on different types of definition (Dobbelaere and Lauwers 1973). It can be said that 'the intellectual construct "religion" is to a large measure constituted by the methods which are supposed to elucidate it' (Harrison 1990: 14). A variety of disciplinary perspectives is employed, ranging from scholars of text-oriented disciplines (History, Indology, and so on.) to comparative and empirical studies of religion in particular social settings by anthropologists, sociologists, and so on. While most of these disciplines are well established in Indian universities, there are virtually no departments focusing on the 'study of religions'. This points to the fact that religion has become a highly debated, sensitive issue in modern India (Kumar 2004).

One reason for this lies in the colonial 'genealogy' of the application of the term 'religion' in India. When the term 'religion' was employed by early oriental scholars and Christian missionaries, its normative implications structured their view of Indian traditions. The notion of religion was at this time heavily influenced by Protestant Christian ideas of religion based on a holy book and a defined set of principles of faith and morality (Oddie 2006). The emergence of the term 'Hinduism' as the designation for religious traditions based on Sanskrit texts and administered by the Brahmin elite within the framework of the caste system can be regarded as an epic example of the impact of colonial ideologies. The idea of 'Hinduism' as a distinct religion reduced traditional religious pluralism—based on adherence, for instance, to a local or regional cult, particular ritual practices, or teaching traditions—to a 'single' religion. The Sanskrit word 'dharma' became the standard translation for religion (Halbfass 1999). Since then, how to define and represent Hinduism has been a matter of debate. Attempts to unify Hinduism as Hindu dharma or *sanatana dharma* ('eternal law') by postulating a core set of texts and essential doctrines or by creating an institution that represents all Hindus still constitutes an important aspect of the debates on religion in India today (for example, Vishwa Hindu Parishad, see Jaffrelot 2001). Hinduism was constructed in a unifying way, for instance, by Swami Vivekananda (1863–1902) as a tolerant 'universal religion' (King 1999) or, in nationalist circles (Vinayak Damodar Savarkar [1883–1966], for instance), as the religion of the Hindus, the Hindus being those who solely represent the Indian nation (Jaffrelot 1996). Others, such as Mohandas Karamchand Gandhi (1869–1948), advocated pluralism as the characteristic feature of Hinduism and emphasized individual experiences and capacities rather than adherence to doctrines. Academic attempts to define Hinduism mirror this situation in offering a variety of definitions (Llewllyn 2005).

The application of the term 'religion' also had repercussions for all the other religions in India that were construed as monolithic and separate religions, and designated as Islam, Buddhism, Sikhism, Jainism, or Zoroastrianism, rather than being referred to as regional and local traditions or to individual doctrinal schools (Gottschalk 2013). The quest for unification and centralized forms of representation is a typically modern feature of religious self-assertion as can be seen not only in the case of Hinduism, but also in Muslim (Shaikh 1989) and Sikh communities (Madan 1997; Ballard 1999). This process was also reinforced by colonial policies (in particular by the Census operations from 1861 onwards) which made religion an administrative category and a basis for the claims of social groups to political influence and occupational opportunities (Jones 1981). Indians were asked to identify themselves as belonging to one particular religion. In this way distinct, quantifiable religious identities were created and accorded majority or minority status at a political level. This process continued in the Censuses carried out after Independence (Bhagat 2001). Religion became the basis of the self-perception of social groups and of the emergence of fixed and distinct 'religious' communities replacing the 'fuzziness' (Kaviraj 1995) of their former embedment in various local or regional contexts. Although the awareness of religious differences and 'communal' views was also present in precolonial India, religious plurality was negotiated within sociopolitical and local frameworks (Bayly 1985). With the objectification of religion as a marker of social identity, communalism became a characteristic feature of the political and social landscape of modern India (Pandey 1990).

In the process, religion started to be related to modern social issues, such as common welfare, social justice or freedom of the individual, with religions being measured according to their contribution to societal progress. From the mid-nineteenth century onwards, calls for the reform of religious traditions (or even the abolition of certain practices) were voiced. At a doctrinal level, religious teachers and theologians reflected on the historicity of sacred texts and their teachings and adapted them to modern standards. At the centre of these debates were, firstly, forms of religion-based social discrimination against women (such as widow burning, child marriage, exclusion from education, and so on) and of the subaltern classes (for example, the inequality ingrained in caste hierarchy and 'untouchability'). Secondly, practices deemed superstitious or auto-destructive (for example, possession cults and hook-swinging, Oddie 1996) were considered as signs of religious backwardness and were denounced as having no place in a modern, enlightened society. In response, calls for change as well as admonishments to retain the age-old traditions were voiced within religious communities. This resulted not only in the typically modern tension between 'traditional' and 'modern', but also in multiple constructions of 'tradition', a development mirrored in new religious movements and organizations, 'reformist', 'conservative', 'orthodox', 'fundamentalist', and so on, emerging in all the religious traditions of India (Baird 1981; Madan 1997). Long-standing religious pluralism was transformed by these changes since the self-reflexivity and tradition-building that unfolded in the different communities went along with an increased awareness of the religious 'other' and of the importance of representing oneself with 'one voice' in public arenas. In this connection, debates on gender equality and the status of women constituted an important element. Women, on the one hand, were construed as markers of religious values who needed to be protected from 'outside' intrusions (Chatterjee 1982); on the other hand, in nationalist discourse, for instance, they turned into defenders of tradition and joined militant religious organizations (Sarkar and Butalia 1995; Sethi 2002). At the same time, religions were, in feminist thought for instance, identified as agents prolonging age-old structures of discrimination that needed to be changed (Kishwar 1998).

In these debates, political and legal frameworks of both the colonial and postcolonial Indian state play a crucial role. The modern Indian state is defined by its secularism, which implies 'neutrality towards all religions' and 'freedom of religion' on the basis of its constitutional principles (equality, and so on; Art. 25, Constitution of India). This means that representatives of particular religions cannot disregard constitutional norms by claiming allegiance to higher, transcendent values, and that the state has the right to interfere in religious matters when constitutional rights or principles are violated. The Constitution also includes definitions of, and special provisions for, individual religions. On this basis, religion is transformed into a legal category and made subject to court rulings. Particular constitutional provisions were made in the case of the 'Hindu' religion. In this connection, Buddhists, Jains, and Sikhs were defined as 'Hindus' (Article 25, Expl. 2), and the state reserved the right to provide for reform and the 'throwing open of Hindu religious institutions of a public character to all classes and sections of Hindus' (Art. 25, 2b). In reaction to these interventions, 'Hindu' groups have filed lawsuits against their legal classification (Smith 1993). Differences between religions exist also with regard to 'personal law' (marriage, divorce). To date, there is no Civil Code applicable to all Indians (Baird 1993, Larson 2007). Hindu 'personal law' was codified in a series of Bills enacted in the 1950s on the basis of secular principles. Thus, rules from the traditional Hindu law-books (*Dharmashastra*) were disregarded when, for instance, divorce was legalized. However, other religious communities, such as Muslims or Christians, were granted the right to adhere to their religious canons when regulating divorce, adoption, or inheritance. This situation was regarded, especially by fundamentalist Hindu groups, as an example of state-sanctioned discrimination against the 'majority religion' and has repeatedly provoked massive political campaigns, as for instance in the Shah Bano divorce case in the 1980s. Feminist groups viewed this as deferring the implementation of equal citizenship for women in the name of religious freedom or minority rights (Mullaly 2004). However, as Hindu fundamentalist groups used such instances against the secular state and for propagating a greater Hinduization of the state, it became difficult for feminist groups 'to challenge the discriminatory practices of religious minorities lest this added further support to the Hindu right' (Mullaly 2004: 673).

Apart from the emergence of religion as a legal category, politicization can be seen as a characteristic feature of the enactment of religion in public arenas of modern India. Once thought to be constituted and objectified as a separate domain by the dominant political discourse, religion(s) enter(s) the political realm with a vengeance. Influential religious leaders, such as Gandhi, have insisted that religion must not and cannot be separated from politics because religion must be the foundation of all advancement (Gandhi 1997). From a different perspective, fundamentalist groups argue that religion must be propagated as the central element of the nation or the community. Furthermore, communalism and fundamentalism can be seen as typically modern forms of the politicization of religion resulting in intolerance and violent conflicts.

At all levels at which religions participate in the dynamics of modern society, the mass media play an important role. They have been skilfully employed by religious groups in order to disseminate and popularize their message (Babb and Wadley 1995). Modern India witnesses a continuous proliferation of religious images, music, films, and TV channels, as well as a steady supply of religious services via the new media (for example, Internet worship). This results, on the one hand, in the decline and homogenization of local traditions and a 'thinning' of religion (Kaviraj 1995). On the other hand, it testifies to an expanded presence of religious symbols pervading the public sphere, pointing to the multiple embedment of religion in the structures of modern society. While this may be interpreted as proof that secularism in India is a 'dream of a minority' (Madan 1987: 748), it can also be seen as pointing to the complex histories and polyvalent configurations of modernity in India. Religion plays a prominent role in this constellation. The multifaceted political, legal, and intellectual debates and the plethora of academic studies demonstrate that the unique religious pluralism that has historically and structurally shaped the subcontinent is deeply embedded as well as contested in the modern, global age.

Further reading: Babb and Wadley 1995; Baird 1981; King 1999; Madan 1997.

—ANGELIKA MALINAR, *Professor, Department of Indian Studies, University of Zurich*

— .•. —

Sahitya

O ver the past two centuries, *sahitya* (or, equivalently, *sahityam*) has emerged as the term most commonly used in the Indian languages to designate 'literature' in the modern sense.

Like its counterpart in English, *sahitya* in this sense refers generally and variously to the whole body of written compositions in a particular language or set of languages, or of writings produced in a given nation, region, or historical period. It also designates literary production in its entirety; the body of writing valued for its aesthetic qualities and effects; and texts of any kind in manuscript or in print. Used with a qualifier, it may also signify written composition in a specific form or genre, on a particular subject, or in a particular field or discipline. Thus, in languages ranging from Hindi and Bengali to Marathi and Malayalam, phrases such as *bharatiya sahitya* and *vishwa sahitya* denote 'Indian literature' and 'world literature', respectively; *loka sahitya* means 'folk literature'; and *adhunika sahitya* refers broadly to 'modern literature'. Many of the modern Indian languages also use words derived from *sahitya* to name related objects or phenomena: *sahitya-kara*, literally 'maker of literature', for example, is employed widely for 'writer' or 'author'; whereas *sahitya-alochana* is the formal rubric for 'literary criticism'.

Sahitya, however, is not a modern term, and its primary meanings in the Indian languages are not borrowed from its equivalents in the European languages. It is originally a Sanskrit word, probably coined in the fifth century, early in India's classical period (ca. 400–1200 CE). Grammatically, it is a substantive adjective that serves as a noun; in Sanskrit, its lexical form is *sahityam*, in the neuter gender. It is derived from *sa* + *hita*, where the prefix designates 'with, together or along with', and *hita* means 'that which is beneficial, advantageous, good, fit, proper, salutary'. *Sahitya* is, therefore, something of mutual benefit to both elements in a combination, or both parties in a transaction; and its abstract meaning therefore emphasizes the idea of a good or advantageous association.

At a basic level, classical Sanskrit poetics suggested that literature, as the repository of finely crafted texts, is the site where 'signifier' and 'signified' (*shabda* and *artha*) join together to their greatest aesthetic advantage. At a more complex level, it linked the concept of *sahitya* to its theory of authorship and audience, in which the *kavi* ('poet' or 'visionary') is the paradigmatic composer of a verbal artefact, whose goal is to communicate emotions and ideas to a *rasika* ('a connoisseur of the arts'). The ideal of success in this transaction is an ethical one, in which the *rasika* proves to be the poet's *sahridaya* ('a companion of the heart'), and the communication between them turns out to be *sa-hita*, of mutual benefit. Oral as well as written compositions, which comprise the fabric of *sahitya* or literature, thus become the ground upon which author and auditor or reader interact, creating a bond that spiritually nourishes both of them.

Sahitya is also not the only term for literature that modern Indian cultures have inherited from the classical period. The earlier and encompassing conception is that of *kavya*, 'poetry' in the most general sense as sublime verbal composition or emotionally and rhetorically heightened discourse, whether in verse or prose or a mixture of both, and whether 'only in words' (*shravya kavya*) or 'in words accompanied by performance and spectacle' (*drshya kavya*). The still broader category, not tied to aesthetic value, is that of *vangmaya*, discourse, 'that which is made of words', which includes all forms of expression and communication in a language, whether oral or written, literary or non-literary. Today, in languages such as Hindi, Marathi, and Bengali, all three terms resonate together in the category of 'literature'.

Further reading: Chari 1990; Dharwadker 1993; Dimock 1974; Pollock 2003, 2006.

—VINAY DHARWADKER, *Professor of Languages and Cultures of South Asia, University of Wisconsin-Madison*

———— ••• ————

Samachar

*S*amachar is a relatively recent loanword from Sanskrit (McGregor 1993). R.S. McGregor's *Oxford Hindi–English Dictionary* defines the word as follows: 'Proceeding, practice or behaviour; state, condition', and lists its uses: '1. an occurrence. 2. (often pl.) news, information; for example, *kya samachar hai*, what is the news?' (McGregor 1993: 986). Sanskrit words for news include *vartta*, under which the following entry can be found: 'an account of anything that has happened, tidings, report, rumour, news, intelligence, story of or about. Monier-Williams gives an example of the word's usage, "kya vartta", "what is the news?"' (Monier–Williams 1999 [1899]: 945, 1143, 1159). Another word used in this sense is *samdesa* (meaning 'communication of intelligence, message, information, errand, direction, command').

Vartta, and to a lesser extent *samdesa*, continue to be used in this sense. For instance, the Hindi arm of the news agency United News of India (UNI) is called Univarta; and *Sandesh* is the name of a newspaper in Gujarat.

The contemporary importance of the word *samachar* is shaped by the linguistic Sanskritization that developed in North India during the nineteenth century, to eliminate words presumed as foreign, or to exclude them from authoritative speech.

The colloquial equivalent for news in North India today, *khabar*, has Arabic and Persian roots (Wehr 1980: 260–1). Hans Wehr's Arabic dictionary defines *khabar* in terms of imperial practices of information and intelligence allied to politics and governance, but the more common reference nowadays is to an everyday perspective rather than to state pronouncements. 'Kya khabar?' is a more frequent colloquial form in North India, for example, than 'kya samachar?' In South India, however, *samachar* is used colloquially to denote news.

We should note that the translation of a concept, that is, from news to *samachar*, points to the translation of a set of practices as well. Three features of news as a western institution deserve notice in this context. Firstly, it is identified with a widespread culture of print literacy. Second, the communication of news is assumed to be objective and transparent when subject to professional strictures. The attendant implication that readers should be able to judge matters for themselves points back to the assumption of a generally prevalent literacy. Third, the ultimate anchor of professional news judgement is the presumed neutrality of the state, as the ultimate court of appeal. When significant numbers of readers or viewers perceive the state to be biased, however, news media can become partisan, and claim to redress such bias.

A colonial history of governance could not provide the context in which the above conditions obtained. For example, transparency about the social conditions of its production might have lent a subversive quality to news in the colonial era. In practice, the difficulty was resolved through an audience that was stratified by language. Jawaharlal Nehru (1889–1964) described the English press in India in 1936 as follows:

> A reader of the newspapers would hardly imagine that a vast peasantry and millions of workers existed in India or had any importance. The British-owned Anglo-Indian newspapers were full of the doings of high officials; English social life in the big cities and in the hill stations was described at great length with its parties, fancy-dress balls and amateur theatricals. Indian politics, from the Indian point of view, were almost completely ignored by them, even the Congress sessions being disposed of in a few lines on a back page. They were not considered news of any value except when some Indian, prominent or otherwise, slanged or criticised the Congress and its pretensions. Occasionally there was a brief reference to a strike, and the rural areas only came into prominence when there was a riot. Indian newspapers tried to model themselves on the

Anglo-Indian ones but gave much greater prominence to the nationalist movement. (Nehru 1936: 48)

The fact that English was spoken by a tiny minority was concealed by equating the language community, principally the British, with India as a whole. We might say that the terms 'news' and 'samachar' each referred to distinct strata of Indian society, although they each claimed to stand for the country as a whole.

Since Independence, the influence of the English language media has increased, while English is still spoken only by a small fraction of the population. Simultaneously, however, following the linguistic reorganization of states, the influence of Indian languages has also increased enormously. For example, of the ten largest circulating newspapers, only one, the *Times of India*, is in English. Still, Indian language papers, including Hindi media, continue to be considered regional. Further, they command far lower advertising rates. The widespread resort to English as a means of social mobility, as affording an access to technical expertise, and as a link language with global connectivity, reinforces this dominance.

With the exponential growth of electronic communications, Indian language media have gained considerably in their influence vis-à-vis English language media, although the latter are likely to retain their advantage as portals to and symbols of a larger world in a way that Indian languages cannot. The irony is that the very assurance of English-language speakers of their leadership function renders them insular in ways that are not always true of their vernacular counterparts.

Further reading: McGregor 1993; Monier-Williams 1999 [1899]; Nehru 1936; Wehr 1980.

—ARVIND RAJAGOPAL, *Professor of Media, Culture, and Communication, New York University*

— .•. —

Samaj

amaj, the modern Hindi word for 'society', is derived from the Sanskrit *samaja*, namely, 'arisen together', 'born equal', or 'co-produced'. It refers to a community of people, bound together by some principle of social cohesion.

While in standard and official Hindi, *samaj* means 'society' or the social totality, in narrower, more specific contexts it can also indicate communities defined by caste, religion, region, historical era, or some other vector of identity. The word could refer to Indian society (*bharatiya samaj*) and western society (*pashcimi* or *pashcatya samaj*) as very large groupings; it could also refer to the community of all Hindus (*hindu samaj*), all Brahmins (*brahma samaj*), all South Indians (*dravid samaj*), all backward castes (*dalit-bahujan samaj*), all those living in modern times (*adhunik samaj*), and so on. It implies not only some properties or features in common, but also a coherence or adherence that obtains between members of the group—a shared culture.

Derived from *samaj* is the adjective *samajik*, literally 'social' or 'societal'; hence *samajik parivartan*, 'social change' or 'social transformation'. The term for 'socialism' is *samajvad* ('the ideology associated with the social'), while *samajvadi* means 'socialist' or 'espousing socialism'. *Samaj* is generally included in a variety of terms dealing with social topics like *samaj sudhar*, meaning 'social uplift' or 'social betterment', *samaj seva*, meaning 'social service', and so on. These forms are all commonly used in postcolonial India. The word *samaj* occurs in Urdu as well (so *musalman samaj*, 'Muslim society').

Religio-cultural sects bearing the designation *samaj* that arose between the 1830s and the 1870s include the Arya Samaj, Brahmo Samaj, Prarthana Samaj, and Satyashodhak Samaj, running the gamut from orthodox to reformist, upper caste to lower caste, spreading all across northern India (Uttar Pradesh, Bihar, Punjab), western India (Maharashtra, Gujarat) and eastern India (Bengal). Together, these 'sects' transformed the face of caste society, giving rise to modern Hinduism as well as to non-Brahmin, Dalit, Dravidian, Phule-Ambedkarite, and other protest movements.

The term *samaj* was closely connected to socialism and socialist ideology which spread in India in the years preceding World War I and became a complicated ecosystem, with connections to different left-wing ideologies, including Gandhianism and even, at one extreme, to National

Socialism via Subhash Chandra Bose (1897–1945). A number of social movements in India call themselves *samajvadi*, by which they mean not strictly 'socialist' so much as 'people-oriented', 'broad-based', 'progressive', and committed to social change. Prominent socialist thinkers and political leaders include Narendra Dev (1889–1956), Jawaharlal Nehru (1889–1964), Rammanohar Lohia (1910–67), Jayaprakash Narayan (1902–79), and J.B. Kripalani (1888–1982). Socialists, at first housed within the Congress-led anti-colonial national movement, gradually broke away after Independence. In the mid-century, progressive thinkers experimented with a mix of Gandhian, Marxist, Ambedkarite, and socialist ideas, producing a uniquely Indian cocktail lacking any equivalent in western politics, thereby broadening the meaning of *samaj* as well as *samajvadi*.

In 1976, during the Emergency, the then Prime Minister Indira Gandhi (1917–84) added the word 'socialist' to the Preamble of the Indian Constitution. India, which had hitherto been a 'sovereign democratic republic', then became a 'sovereign *socialist secular* democratic republic'. The word 'socialist' here implies 'social and economic equality', reinforcing the equal citizenship, equal rights, and equality of opportunity present in the very definition of the Indian nation state. India was thereby presented as a *samaj* in the sense stated at the outset.

The Samajwadi Party (Socialist Party), founded in 1992 and led by Mulayam Singh Yadav (b. 1939) in Uttar Pradesh (UP), representing the interests of 'other backward castes' (OBCs) and Muslims, describes itself as a 'democratic socialist party'. Its arch-rival, the Bahujan Samaj Party (Party of the Majority of the People), founded by Kanshiram (1934–2006) in 1984 and led by Mayawati (b. 1956) since 2003, represents Scheduled Castes and Tribes, Dalit-Buddhists, and OBCs in Uttar Pradesh. Both parties illustrate the way in which *samaj* and *samajvadi* are positive but also slightly vacuous (that is, ideologically meaningless) monikers in the contemporary political lexicon.

Further reading: Chatterjee 2011; Hardiman 2007; Guha 2007, 2012; Gupta 2006; Tagore 1921, 1951; Vajpeyi 2009, 2012.

—ANANYA VAJPEYI, *Centre for the Study of Developing Societies,*
New Delhi

— •••• —

Samvad

The traditional Indian practice of *vada* denoted a rule-governed debate that involved two parties, one of whom would be declared victor by a presiding authority. For Patton (2004), *samvad* initially signifies a loose, indigenous genre in Sanskrit epic literature which was incorporated into philosophical thought. In some cases, these epic dialogues provided occasions to explore moral options. A particularly famous dialogue takes place between Gargi and Yajnavalkya in the *Brihadaranyaka Upanishad* in which the sage articulates the idea of the imperishable Brahman ('the absolute'). Another famous story is about the philosopher Shankara's (788–820 CE) dialogue with the *Mimamsa* philosopher, Madan Misra, whom he defeats. The latter's wife, Ubhaya Bharati, however, challenges his knowledge of eros as he is an ascetic; hence, in order to answer Ubhaya's questions about man–woman relations Shankara enters the king's body, and finally succeeds in having his philosophical pre-eminence recognized.

Samvad presented an alternative to violent modes of theological and philosophical argument. In some cases, *samvad* appeared in a polemical form, as in Swami Dayanand Sarasvati's (1824–88) *Shastrartha* with Christian missionaries. It has been used in dance as in the playful exchange between Radha and Krishna in the *Radha Madhava Samvadam*, and has also been invoked by projects on interfaith dialogue.

Two contemporary Indian philosophers, Daya Krishna (1924–2007) and Ramchandra Gandhi (1937–2007), took *samvad* beyond the binary of dialogue and *vada*-like debate. Instead they introduced an exercise of thought in which participants were to understand different positions in order to arrive at a deeper self-understanding (Mayaram 2013).

Ramchandra Gandhi emphasizes the *samvad* between *advaita* ('nondualist philosophy'), Buddhism, and subcommunities of Adivasis as well, as present in the advaitic and gendered metaphoric space of Sita's kitchen in Ayodhya (Gandhi 1994). He postulates an alternative to Cartesian thought, arguing that self-consciousness is a mode of being, not a mode of knowing. The foundation of all human communication lies in the act of addressing, when human beings recognize themselves as selves, whereby the very act of addressing summons the self, the individual soul, to self-awareness. Thus the self/soul itself is constituted dialogically (Gandhi 1976).

Daya Krishna initiated several intellectual *samvads* between scholars trained in western philosophy and in Indian traditions. These were held at Poona, Tirupati, Varanasi, and in Kashmir with scholars trained in Sanskrit, and at Hyderabad and Lucknow with scholars of Arabic and Persian. The volume of the Poona seminar (1983), comprising sections in both English and Sanskrit, has been described as a genuine instance of 'comparative philosophy' and as one of the first efforts to establish a *samvad* with scholars of *Nyaya* and *Mimamsa* (the philosophical schools of Logic and Vedic exegesis, respectively) (Krishna 1991). Another effort was made to relate *samvad* with the treatises on dharma, *artha*, and *natya* ('ethics', 'economy', and 'aesthetics') (Krishna 1987).

Further reading: Gandhi 1976, 1994; Krishna 1987, 1991; Mayaram 2013; Patton 2004.

—SHAIL MAYARAM, *Senior Fellow, Centre for the Study of Developing Societies, New Delhi*

— ·•· —

Sanskrit

S anskrit can be considered from three interrelated perspectives: as an Indo-European language, as a South Asian language, and as a world language. In 1784, Sir William Jones (1746–94) famously proposed that Latin, Greek, and Sanskrit shared a common origin (Jones 1799). This theory of a common ancestor language ('Proto-Indo-European') accounts for the structure of most of the languages of modern Europe and North India, as well as large parts of Central Asia. Sanskrit, as the best-attested early derivative of the proto-language, has proven to be the linchpin for determining the grammatical and lexical features of the reconstructed ancestor, as well as for gathering some inkling of the culture of its speakers (Watkins 2000: vii–xxxv; West 2007: 1–26).

Sanskrit provided the irreplaceable medium through which the literate civilizations of southern Asia were expressed. It is the language of the scriptures of the Hindu religion, as well as much of the literature of the Jains and Buddhists. Sanskrit's productivity is owed in large part to the grammar attributed to Panini, who lived in what is now Afghanistan in the fourth century BCE. This formed a description of a refined register of Panini's own spoken dialect in less than 4,000 algebraic rules (Cardona 1997). It provided an unwavering standard that enabled Sanskrit to act as a timeless, placeless language throughout a region extending far beyond the borders of India, into Southeast and Central Asia (Pollock 2006).

For millennia, men and (some) women scattered far across the Eurasian landmass participated in the order inaugurated by Panini. Part of this dissemination was owed to a religious community—the Buddhists—and their gradual decision to use this versatile and far-travelling language, despite the Buddha's alleged prohibitions (Norman 1997: 59ff, 95–112). Sanskrit thus played a crucial role in the cultures of East and Inner Asia. Sanskrit's reception in the West continues this story up to our own times. It is impossible to imagine the work of Johann Wolfgang von Goethe (1749–1832), Ralph Waldo Emerson (1803–82), Friedrich Wilhelm Nietzsche (1844–1900), or James Joyce (1882–1941) without the influence of Sanskrit's colonial reception, while the modern discipline of linguistics is the result of the western project of assimilating Sanskritic language science.

Further reading: Burrow 1965; Clay Sanskrit Library 2005–2009; Pollock 2006; Trautmann 1997; West 2007.

—**WHITNEY COX**, *Associate Professor, University of Chicago*

Science

cience has been integral to modern Indian history. The word itself
is of European origin, derived from the Latin *scientia* ('knowledge')
but it has acquired distinct meanings and definitions in India.
Science has had two broad meanings in modern Indian history. On the
one hand, it has represented European Enlightenment, modernity, and
westernization. On the other, the adoption of western scientific ideas
has stimulated efforts to identify scientific and rational traditions within
Indian culture and antiquity. The deep engagements with these two in
India has led to both the internalization of ideas of science in the Indian
economy, everyday lives, culture, and society, as well as its redefinition.

European natural history—the study of plants, animals, minerals, and
climatic theories—was introduced in India in the late seventeenth century
by surgeons, botanists, and missionaries. Over the next two hundred and
fifty years, science became one of the foundations of Indian modernity
and the nation state. It helped in the study and exploitation of flora, fauna,
and natural resources. Science also facilitated the introduction of technologies such as the telegraph and the railways, as well as the inventions
of traditional and alternative science and medicine, and contributed to the
declaration of the Scientific Policy Resolution (SPR 1958) as one of the
foundations of the newly formed Indian nation state.

In the nineteenth century, the British colonial government established
many scientific institutions and surveys such as the Geological Survey of
India (GSI), established in 1851, the Indian Meteorological Department
(IMD) (1875), the Botanical Survey of India (BSI) (1890), and the
Indian Agricultural Research Institute (IARI) in Pusa (Bihar) in 1903.
These were set up primarily to serve the economic needs of the colonial
state and exploit India's natural resources through scientific research.

A new involvement with science in India developed at the end of the
nineteenth century, when educated Indians sought to locate European scientific ideas and principles within Indian culture as well as to adopt them
for the country's economic and social progress. The first effort towards
institutionalizing Indian interest in western science was Mahendra Lal
Sircar's (1833–1904) Indian Association for the Cultivation of Science

(IACS), founded in 1876. The Indian Institute of Science (IISc) was established in 1909 with a grant from the businessman and philanthropist Jamsetji N. Tata (1839–1904). The Indian Science Congress Association, established in 1914, provided a broad platform to scientists on which to exchange ideas (Chakrabarti 2004).

These institutes provided the scope for Indian independent and innovative research. Jagadish Chandra Bose (1858–1937) demonstrated that non-living objects responded in the same manner to external stimuli as living beings and challenged the conventional conceptual boundaries between the two (Bose 1902). He explained this as the scientific confirmation of the ancient Vedic philosophy of monism and as an expression of modern Indian science—a blend of western metaphysics with Indian spirituality. Chandrasekhara V. Raman (1888–1970) discovered that light scattered from a transparent medium includes wavelengths shifted from that of the incident radiation. Raman experimented with a mercury arc to replace the sun as his radiation source, which demonstrated that discrete lines were observable and could be photographed (Raman 1928). This phenomenon came to be known as the 'Raman Effect'. In 1930, he became the first Indian scientist to receive the Nobel Prize.

Historians have explained the history of colonial science in India in two different ways. Some have seen science as a 'western' or colonial tradition imposed on India and used by the colonial state to exploit natural resources (Nandy 1990; Kumar 1995). Others have explored the more nuanced redefinition and absorption of western science within India (Raina and Habib 2004; Prakash 1999). From the 1920s, nationalists believed that science could play a critical role in the making of the nation state. Jawaharlal Nehru (1889–1964) was inspired by the economic and scientific achievements of the Soviet Union. A group of prominent scientists such as S.S. Bhatnagar (1894–1955), P.C. Mahalanobis (1893–1972), M.N. Saha (1893–1956), and Homi J. Bhabha (1909–66) shared this vision of planned growth through the application of science and technology. Together, they formulated the close links between science and the state in eradicating poverty, malnutrition, and underdevelopment. World War II led to the constitution of the Council for Scientific and Industrial Research (CSIR), established in 1942, whose main function was to promote, guide, and coordinate scientific and industrial research.

After Independence, the government undertook an initiative of linking large-scale investment in scientific research with national developmental plans. By 1950, several prominent laboratories under the CSIR were inaugurated, including the National Chemical Laboratory (NCL, 1947), National Physical Laboratory (NPL, 1950), and the Central Food Technology Research Institute (CFTRI, 1950). Other major state-funded agencies were also established such as the Department of Atomic Energy (DAE, 1954) and the Defence Research and Development Organisation (DRDO, 1958). The SPR, published by the government on 13 March 1958, declared that the key to prosperity was in the creation and adoption of new scientific techniques to harness the country's natural resources and generate capital (SPR 1958).

This ushered in the era of 'Big Science', characterized by large numbers of scientists working with well-defined goals and plans, and large financial investments by the state. The CSIR laboratories investigated sectors identified as the keys to national progress—food, energy, drugs, and industrial production. It involved massive investments by the government and led to a revolution in production, particularly in industrial goods and food crops.

However, this focus on large-scale research and production came under criticism from scholars and activists who pointed out that this often created regional economic and social disparities and environmental devastation (Shiva 1991). The general criticism of Big Science in India has been that it has alienated science from the needs of the common people (Mukherjee 1955; Abraham 1996; Visvanathan 2005).

Beyond the major state-sponsored and industry-oriented investments in science, the latter has been part of the search for alternative modes of development in Indian society. Mohandas Karamchand Gandhi (1869–1948) produced a critique of modern civilization and scientific modernity in his *Hind Swaraj* (1909). Gandhi pointed out that large-scale industries were inherently dehumanized and thereby de-socialized (Gandhi 1958: vol. 48, 403–6). Shiv Visvanathan argues that by doing so, Gandhi's stance was not 'anti-science'; he did not reject modern science but sought 'to create a technological and scientific conscience for Nehru's India' (Visvanathan 1998: 43).

There have been other attempts at developing social movements around science in India as well. Since the 1950s, People's Science Movements have encouraged mass participation in science-related development plans and policies. These, along with several non-governmental organizations (NGOs) and environmental groups have generated critiques of state-sponsored science and technology projects, and developed technologies that are less capital intensive and geared towards the needs of artisans, women, and farmers (Kumar 1984).

Modern India has been an amphitheatre of science and it has found diverse meanings and applications here, starting from William Jones' (1746–94) application of Sanskrit nomenclature for Indian plants to the Green Revolution aided by high-yielding variety crops and intensive cultivation. In India, science has also faced some of its greatest challenges and critiques. Despite this rich history of and major investments in science over several centuries, a large section of Indians remain without its benefits and in poverty.

Further reading: Arnold 2000; Chakrabarti 2004; Kumar 1995; Nandy 1980; Prakash 1999.

—PRATIK CHAKRABARTI, *Senior Lecturer in History,*
University of Kent

— •◦• —

Secularism

Secularism was an inextricable part of the Indian nationalist self-conception at Independence (1947) and has remained central to subsequent debates about citizenship and belonging in the postcolonial state. It signified all that was enlightened and integrative about a modern society. The Indian Constitution enshrined freedom of religion as one of the core principles of the new state. Crucially, the practice of religion was to be personal and private. Secularism was defined through and against 'communalism': a politics of a religious identity that many saw as the assertion of sectarianism in the public sphere. In fact, Jawaharlal Nehru (1889–1964) held communalism responsible for social fragmentation and, ultimately, for the creation of Pakistan (Nehru 1958: 74).

The rise of Hindu nationalism from the late 1980s prompted widespread alarm, and this 'crisis' rekindled a debate on secularism in India. The debate turned on the binary oppositions of secularism and communalism, modernity and tradition. Liberal scholars asked how such religious hatred could take root in a secular society (Ganguly 2003; Gopal 1993; Malik and Vajpeyi 1989; Tambiah 1998). Many believed that secularism and modernization had failed. Deeply troubling has been the targeting of religious minorities—Muslims and Christians—through the argument that they do not properly belong. The debate on secularism in contemporary India has had little to do with religion in a theological sense or with the separation of religion and politics. Rather, at its core lies the question of how a minority community can legitimately assert its presence within India's liberal democracy and how, in turn, the Indian state recognizes and accommodates social difference within a broader national identity (Bhargava 2010; Bajpai 2010; Tejani 2007; Nigam 2000; Chandhoke 1999; Mahajan 1999; Chatterjee 1994).

The term 'secular' saw brief and sporadic mention through the latter half of the nineteenth century. For instance, Wood's Educational Dispatch of 1854 laid down that government education should be 'exclusively secular', as it would not promote religious education but rather introduce Indians to scientific and rational thought. In the early years of the Indian National Congress, it was argued that whatever their religious background, members would be able 'to represent each other in the discussion of political questions' and 'in the discussion of public secular affairs' (Smith 1963: 88). Thus, 'secular' here represented a non-religious, civic arena for debate.

It is significant that the term 'secularism' only became part of wider Indian political discourse after 1947. Historically, the colonial state had not remained separate from religious communities: it intervened in disputes, legislated on custom, and managed and taxed religious institutions that were under its jurisdiction. Its rhetoric was not a separation of religious and political institutions but of 'non-interference' in the customs and traditions of Indians. It sought to stand as a neutral adjudicator, to uphold rather than alter traditions. Thus, neither was the term used, nor was secularism practised. India's postcolonial state retained this 'equidistance' from religious institutions rather than separation from them

(Copland 2010; Luthera 1964; Smith 1963). Rajeev Bhargava has called this position one of 'principled distance' (Bhargava 2010).

It was 'nationalism' that signified before Indian Independence what secularism came to mean after. Since the late 1920s, nationalism was seen as a unifying ideal and a counter to the politics of communalism (Pandey 1992). Liberal nationalists termed the demands for separate Muslim recognition 'communalism', which was seen to undermine a broader 'national' unity (Jalal 1997). For Nehru, a national identity defined around religion was a contradiction in terms. Liberal democracies by their very definition protected minorities, religious or otherwise, with regard to their rights and freedoms. Moreover, they provided a forum for citizens to debate the issues of the day as individuals rather than as communal blocs. Any assertion of an identity smaller than that of the nation, especially if it were religious, Nehru argued, would be utterly destructive (Nehru 1972: 119–33). After 1947, this relation between the nation and its minorities came to be called secularism, lying at the heart of India's postcolonial identity.

While India only declared itself a secular republic in 1976, secularism was written into the Constitution from the outset. It guaranteed: (1) freedom of religion to individuals as well as religious communities; (2) equality of citizenship, that is, no discrimination on grounds of religion and no communal electorates, although there were reservations in public employment and education for Scheduled Castes and Scheduled Tribes; and (3) separation of state and religion, that is, no state promotion of religion and no religious education in government schools. Article 25(1) of the Constitution guarantees freedom of religion. However, Article 25(2) allows the state to intervene in religious practices seen to impede social welfare or equality. Thus, Article 25(2) entitled the state to open temples to untouchable castes for worship, regulate financial administration of Hindu religious institutions, and outlaw the practice of dedicating young girls (*devadasis*) to temple deities.

Members of the Constituent Assembly argued that there was a conflict between protecting the rights of Indian society's most vulnerable individuals and determining where the boundary between the 'social' and the 'religious' lay. Bhimrao Ambedkar (1891–1956), the architect of the Constitution, argued that in India the definition of what constituted religion covered 'every aspect of life from birth to death. There is nothing which is not religion [...]' (IP, *Constituent Assembly Debates*, vol.

VII, 1946–50: 781). A definition of religion should be limited to beliefs and ceremonies which are 'essentially religious' (IP, *Constituent Assembly Debates*, vol. VII, 1946–50: 781). However, the Supreme Court supported a broader definition: 'what constitutes the essential part of a religion is primarily to be ascertained with reference to the doctrines of that religion itself' (Smith 1963: 106–7). In general, it can be held that the Indian Constitution provided for the state's interventionist role in matters of religion (Copland 2010; Chiriyankandath 2000).

There are four distinct strands to the debate on secularism in India. The first is the classic liberal position whose proponents saw the rise of Hindu nationalism as a failure of secularism. Religion had not taken its rightful place in the private lives of individuals, and it was Indians' excessive attachment to their primordial identities that prevented the emergence of a civic ideal (Engineer 2003; Verma 1990; Chatterji 1984). However, not all defenders of secularism support the modernization model. Some, taking the position that Mohandas Karamchand Gandhi (1869–1948) was best known for, argue that secularism was not a western concept but one with deep roots in India (Parekh 1989: ch. 4). Hindu dharma, with its accommodative, 'tolerant' character, accepted the numerous migrant tribes that had come into India over millennia and made them culturally 'Hindu'. Indian civilization thus had an indigenous concept of secularism—*sarva dharma samabhava*—the idea that all religions are equal.

Second is the argument that secularism is a western ideal and thus inappropriate for India. Indian religious traditions, argue T.N. Madan (1987) and Ashis Nandy (1988), never generated a separation of secular and sacred spheres, and any attempt to do so would damage their cultural fabric. Moreover, those who argued that religion should be separated from politics 'ignored the fact that religion itself could be a powerful resource in the struggle against religious extremism' (Madan 1987: 747–59). For Nandy, secularism in India represented a form of imperialism (Nandy 1988: 177–94).

Third is the position that any recognition of religious minorities is 'pseudo-secularism' (Talreja 1996). This was the charge that Hindu nationalist organizations brought against the Congress in the early 1990s, arguing that this so-called secular party was pandering to Muslims. Reservations for minorities in state institutions and concessions to Muslim opinion such as in the case of Shah Bano (1985) were evidence of pseudo-secularism, for a properly secular state would treat all as equal before the law (Copland 2010: 142; Chiriyankandath 2000: 14).

Finally, the fourth position is represented by Bhargava who argues that Indian secularism was a 'multi-value' doctrine: it sought to promote the liberal ideal of 'tolerance' but was also 'explicitly tied to citizenship rights, including the rights of religious minorities' (Bhargava 2007: 47). Thus, although the Constitution allowed for the state to intervene in the practices of religious communities, these were measures that sought to enhance the democratic nature of the state and did not undermine the authenticity of Indian secularism (Bhargava 2007: 41). It is these values of egalitarianism, democracy, and citizenship that Indian secularism represented, and they need to be recovered.

In India, secularism has been at the centre of debates around national identity and the legitimate place that minority communities have in forging this identity.

Further reading: Bhargava 1998, 2010; Chandhoke 1999; Chatterjee 1994; Needham and Sunder Rajan 2007; Tejani 2007.

—SHABNUM TEJANI, *Senior Lecturer in the History of Modern South Asia, SOAS, University of London*

—— ·•· ——

Self-Respect Movement

Would *paracceri* (a physically segregated colony outside the boundary of a caste Hindu village for the oppressed castes) be a part of the motherland?' Pandit Iyotheedasar's question in 1907 to nationalist politics expressed the rage felt against the humiliation meted out by Brahmanism. Reconstructing a Buddhist past as the original Dravidian culture, which the Aryan Brahmin had displaced,

Iyotheedasar initiated a tradition that would fundamentally alter subsequent Tamil political consciousness.

From the early years of the twentieth century, the non-Brahmin movement framed a language of rights as signifying levels of oppression and subordination, wealth and poverty, knowledge and ignorance. Its political instrument, the Justice Party's (established in 1917) forays into politics could not resolve the contradictions in espousing justice in a polity divided by caste. Limited by urban sensibilities, the non-Brahmin movement could not engage with the oppressive relation between the non-Brahmin dominant castes and the labouring *adidravidas* ('original inhabitants of Dravidian land'). Emerging from the same political context, Periyar E.V. Ramaswamy (1879–1973) broke ties with the Congress to form in 1925 the Self-Respect Movement that would define the ethos of an alternative nation and community founded on empowerment through Self-Respect and rationalism.

Self-Respect meant restoring the dignity wrenched away from the socially oppressed by Brahmanism. The practice of untouchability was central to caste, so its eradication was a prerequisite for the abolition of caste. Through engagement with the ideals of socialism in the 1930s, the Self-Respecters attempted to theorize freedom in the context of caste Hindu society as the realization of equal rights. Women were also oppressed under Brahmanical patriarchy; their liberation was sought through ideals of love which resulted in 'Self-Respect marriage' as a revocable social contract.

The formation of the Dravidar Kazhagam (Dravidian Organization) in 1944 transformed the movement into a political one that envisioned a new republic, a new Dravidian nation comprising communities bound by rationality and freedom. Through propaganda and acts of subversion like burning the *Manusmriti* and temple entry, they countered the Congress and the imposition of Hindi. Through Self-Respect, a limited non-Brahmin project was transformed into an ideal for creating a new subjectivity in history.

Further reading: Aloysius 1998; Geetha and Rajadurai 1998; Irshick 1969; Nambi 1980; Pandian 2007.

—D. SENTHIL BABU, *Department of Indology, French Institute of Pondicherry*

— ·•· —

Seven Sisters

On 7 February 1944, Sir Robert Reid (1883–1964) addressed a meeting of the Royal Society of Geographers in London and began to explain the complicated landscape of Assam where he had just served as a governor (1937–42). The territory he discussed at length was the hill region that sequestered the colonial province of Assam. Reid was making a plea for the British government to consider creating a Crown Colony in the regions inhabited by communities that had always been subjected to light-touch colonial administration and who lived along the frontier of colonial Assam and Burma.

Following the transfer of power to Indian rule in 1947, the province was carved up into federal units that were part of the Indian Union. The first reorganization was in 1951, when colonial frontier tracts were amalgamated to form the North-East Frontier Agency (NEFA). By 1956, the Government of India had begun to nationalize NEFA by easing out Assamese political officers and introducing Hindi as the medium of instruction in schools (Chaliha 1958). This led to protests by the Asom Sahitya Sabha (Assam Literary Society), a civic literary body of valley-based intellectuals and public figures who felt that these attempts were aimed at marginalizing the role of Assamese, both as a link language and as integral members of the political society in the region. Thereafter, Nagaland was created as a state within the Indian Union in 1963 and was followed by the creation of Mizoram as a Union Territory in 1971 (later upgraded to a state in 1987) and the state of Meghalaya, comprising the Khasi-Jaintia and Garo Hills districts, in 1973.

One of the ostensible reasons for the reorganization of Assam was the alienation expressed by political parties and individuals in the hills. They felt that the imposition of Assamese as the state language as well as the lack of developmental activities in the hills were detrimental to their democratic aspirations for autonomy. Sections of Assamese civil society, however, felt that they needed to retain some sense of organic solidarity with the newly formed states and their peoples. It is not clear who began to use the phrase 'Seven Sisters' first, but what is certain is that it gained currency after the formation of the state of Meghalaya in 1973 (Deka 2008).

Assamese intellectuals like Hare Krishna Deka (b. 1943) attribute the phrase to journalist Jyoti Prasad Saikia (1927–2006) who became Assam Chief Minister Sarat Sinha's (1914–2005) press secretary in 1976 (Deka 2008). Sinha had just shifted his capital from Shillong to Guwahati which was accompanied by a crisis that would persist into contemporary times. Border disputes between Assam and the newly formed states had led to an increase in skirmishes that involved the respective state police personnel, insurgents, and even civil society actors.

However, the term 'Seven Sisters' is not only synonymous with political engineering, but also has some resonance with the romance of unity amongst the different communities of the region. Assam's foremost singer and cultural icon, Bhupen Hazarika (1925–2011) often referred to the Seven Sisters, especially during the 1970s and later during the height of militant Assamese nationalism in the 1990s (Baruah 2005). He sang songs (admittedly not composed by him) about undivided Assam being the mother of the Seven Sisters who were married away, thereby fragmenting the unity of the house. Such emotional appeals and exhortations of unity were apparently aimed against the Indian state's frequent threats of dismembering Assam and fomenting problems between the different ethnic communities in the region.

These appeals belie the disconnect that exists in peoples' interactions with the Indian state and its advocates in the region. Of greater interest is the manner in which the Seven Sisters' theme is able to diffuse political opposition to large-scale developmental projects, despite the obvious impact on the environment and livelihoods of citizens living within the composite region. When added together, the idea of Seven Sisters remains an intriguing attempt at engineering an identity that can be appropriate both for the state as well as for disparate non-state actors. Equally, it remains a phrase that remains orphaned by the dearth of political investment that is required to make it a meaningful alternative to the geographical designation of Northeast India.

Further reading: Baruah 2005; Chaliha 1958; Deka 2008; Sarma 2008.

—SANJAY (XONZOI) BARBORA, *Tata Institute of Social Sciences, Guwahati*

Strategic Enclave

The term 'strategic enclave' was first used in order to distinguish between India's nuclear weapons and ballistic missile complexes, and its conventional defence industries (for example, ordnance, tank, shipbuilding, and aircraft factories). As the original article put it, India's nuclear and missile programmes are 'strategic' because they are 'the most advanced technological means towards the goal of national security' [...] [and form] an 'enclave' because 'institutionally, spatially, and legally, the high technology sectors of space and nuclear energy are distinct and different from the existing structure of the Indian military-security complex' (Abraham 1992: 233). The term has morphed from its original analytic-taxonomic definition to become a shorthand for the scientists and engineers who man India's ballistic missile and nuclear weapons complexes as well as the analysts and commentators who debate India's military policies and grand strategy. That strategic enclave now typically refers primarily to people, not machines, is significant. Abraham (2009) argues that it implies the formation of a self-conscious national security public sphere seeking closer conformity and linkages with a homologous global discourse.

One of the most distinctive features of India's nuclear weapons and ballistic missile programmes is the strategy adopted to acquire critical and rare technologies from abroad. Both began as peaceful programmes that later developed military capabilities. The institutional bifurcation of global nuclear and missile technology control regimes into peaceful and military components allowed civilian agencies for nuclear power (Department of Atomic Energy) and space (Department of Space) legitimately to acquire blueprints, expertise, and components that were later adapted for military purposes. The success of this strategy comes from the inherent ambivalence of nuclear and space technologies, glossed in the literature as 'dual use' (Abraham 2010). To begin with, this was not a deliberate strategy of illicit technology acquisition, but became one with time and circumstances.

Another mark of distinction is the relative technological success of the nuclear and missile programmes when compared to the huge cost overruns, delays, and performance problems of the conventional defence industries' prestige projects: the Light Combat Aircraft, Main Battle Tank, Advanced Light Helicopter, and nuclear-powered submarine. Demonstrable achievement in advanced military technologies is seen as a necessary condition for achieving a long-standing ambition of the Indian political elite, namely, admission to the most exclusive 'clubs' of the international community, the pinnacle of which is a permanent seat in the UN Security Council. The strategic enclave (in its latter, interest-group sense) derives no small measure of its institutional power from its presumed ability to help achieve this widely held elite desire.

Finally, it should be noted that the spatial segregation that is central to the concept of the strategic enclave is qualitatively different from the neoliberal production of divided space in India today. The strategic enclave epitomizes the struggle of the early postcolonial state to create zones of technological modernity whereas its development project could be fully realized. Where once the separation of the modern, scientific, and progressive from the rest of India was driven by the postcolonial desire to create a national imaginary of a possible and desirable *future*, today's division of the globalized and the locally bound reflects middle class demands to live *coevally* as do their counterparts in the First World.

Further reading: Abraham 1992, 2009, 2010.

—**ITTY ABRAHAM**, *Associate Professor,*
National University of Singapore

— •◦• —

Subaltern

The shift in the meaning of the term 'subaltern' from a lower position in the army to a position characterized by *subalternity*—a term now pointing to the position in society of an individual who stands outside hegemonic power structures inherent in it—is associated with the Marxist theorist Antonio Gramsci (1891–1937). Its widespread intellectual currency is associated with Subaltern Studies, a series of volumes brought out by an editorial collective during the period 1982 to 2005.

Initially, the Subaltern Studies Group came together under the leadership of Ranajit Guha (b. 1922). Guha's article, 'The Prose of Counterinsurgency' (*Subaltern Studies* II, Guha 1983), was a virtual manifesto for Subaltern Studies. His *Elementary Aspects of Peasant Insurgency in Colonial India* had analysed over one hundred cases of peasant rebellion in British India between 1783 and 1900 in an effort to theorize subaltern insurgency (Guha 1983). Building on Gramsci's thesis of hegemony as the source of legitimacy, Guha argued that British colonialism in India involved 'dominance without hegemony' (*Subaltern Studies* IV, Guha 1985). Of the two dominant elites in India, the British colonial rulers and the Indian bourgeois nationalists, the former established dominance through coercion while the latter, 'spawned and nurtured by colonialism' (Guha 1997), led a passive nationalist movement to succeed in gaining political power. Both groups represented dominance without hegemony, as the state's juridical power was not derived from the consent of the people and did not depend on their moral and cultural persuasion. What has been missing from Indian colonial and nationalist historiography is the parallel story of the Indian subaltern masses who constituted an autonomous domain of anti-colonial and anti-bourgeois politics.

Guha asked the question about 'the contributions made by people on their own', independent of the elite, to the making and development of this nationalism (Guha 1982: 3). The subaltern was described as a 'perspective' or 'the small voice' of history, yielding fragmentary narratives, indicative of lifeworlds and subjectivities regarded as constituents of an alternative history. It was different from the Annales School's 'history from below'— an approach which emphasized *mentalité* and 'social history', focusing on ecological and demographic explanations. While E.P. Thompson (1963) saw the working class in terms of plebeian consciousness, and much ferment had been produced as a consequence of feminist interventions and peasant studies, Subaltern Studies, David Ludden asserts, reinvented subalternity: 'Domination, subordination, hegemony, resistance, revolt, and other old concepts could now be subalternized' (Ludden 2002: 16).

Subaltern historiography, as Dipesh Chakrabarty argues, necessarily entailed a 'relative separation of the history of power from any universalist histories of capital, a critique of the nation state and of nationalism and interrogated the relationship between power and knowledge, hence of history as a form of knowledge [...].' In these differences, he points out, 'lay the beginnings of a new way of theorizing the intellectual agenda for postcolonial histories' (Chakrabarty 2002: 8).

Its originality, Ludden comments, lay in its effort 'to rewrite the nation outside the state-centred national discourse and the power of colonial power/knowledge' (Ludden 2002: 19). This involved the exploration of new archives since subaltern pasts are hidden and usually inhabit the terrain of memory rather than history. Appearing in practices and genres that are oral, dramatic, and vernacular, they represent an experienced, lived history with its complex mix of sacrality and secularity.

In her influential essay 'Can the Subaltern Speak?' Gayatri Spivak raised the epistemic question of representation, claiming that the subaltern is incapable of speaking in terms of its own discourse or forms of knowledge, and is instead always represented by the professional. This entailed the colonization of the subaltern subject who is therewith condemned to muteness (Spivak 1988).

Subaltern Studies challenged both historicism and the idea of the political that entailed a 'pre-political', identified in the practices of subaltern actors. Even if its construction of the political emphasized bourgeois, pre-bourgeois, and the secular, Subaltern Studies also take into account a non-secular which is not conceptualized as 'archaic' or primitive à la Hobsbawm (Chakrabarty 2000). As Guha rightly observed, the militant movements of India's rural masses were highly political, even if the capitalist development in agriculture, which—outside of Subaltern Studies—has often been claimed to be a precondition for political resistance, had never taken place (1983: 5–6). In addition to the Subaltern Studies volumes, a substantial and diverse body of knowledge about the subaltern has been produced outside Subaltern Studies. The concept of the subaltern has also been used to understand diverse historical contexts in Africa and Latin America.

An early argument criticizing the autonomy of subaltern politics was acknowledged by Chakrabarty's characterization of subalternity as 'the composite culture of resistance to and acceptance of domination and hierarchy' (*Subaltern Studies* IV, 1985: 364–76). Critics see it as 'anarchist' and even fascist, given the serious attention paid to subaltern community and belief. Others have pointed out the rigidity of the elite/subaltern binary, coupled with its elitism in empowering the professional who speaks for the subaltern. Jim Masselos refers to 'the subaltern [...] [as] a creation, a reification of historians' which 'combines a polarized social category with the mentality of opposition' (the equivalence of subordination and resistance) and which is distinct from 'real' subaltern people (Masselos 1992). Criticism of the 'literary turn', which was launched by Gayatri Chakravorty Spivak in the mid-1980s and followed, amongst others, by Sudipta Kaviraj, Amitav Ghosh, and Gyan Prakash (Ludden 2002), suggests the appropriation of subaltern politics by postcolonial theory and cultural studies. It has been pointed out that a cultural critique of colonialism is not adequate, as subalternity must be located within structures of global capitalism.

Nonetheless, there has been a relationship between the subaltern and democracy manifest in the way in which new subaltern classes and groups have been incorporated into Third World public spheres, including peasants, tribals, industrial workers, and others. Their histories have become a tool of citizenship enabling a deeper understanding and striving for a better future for subaltern peoples. In the last three decades, a mainstreaming of the subaltern has taken place: having started as an extremely influential approach in the discipline of history, the concept now also exercises a substantial impact on other disciplines of the social sciences and humanities.

Further reading: Chakrabarty 2002; Guha 1982–9, 1983, 1988; Ludden 2002; Spivak 1988.

—SHAIL MAYARAM, *Senior Fellow, Centre for the Study of Developing Societies, New Delhi*

Sufi

In Arabic, the term 'Sufi' was used since the early ninth century to denote a 'wearer of wool' (*suf*), in reference to the ascetic tendencies of early Muslim pietists. With the emergence of a school of mystical theorists in Iraq and Khurasan (historical region covering present-day Afghanistan, parts of Iran and Turkmenistan) in the tenth century, the term became more widely used for the social description of an emergent renunciant movement and for the theoretical denotation of an ideal psychological type.

By the eleventh century at the latest, both usages of the term were introduced to South Asia when the term featured in the Persian *Kashf al-Mahjub* of al-Hujwiri (Abul Hassan Ali Ibn Usman al-Jullabi al-Hajvery al-Ghaznawi [ca. 990–1075]), who had migrated to Lahore from Ghazna. By the period of the Delhi Sultanate, 'Sufi' continued to be employed in such formative texts as the *Fawaid al-Fuad* that recorded the teachings of Nizam al-Din Awliya of Delhi (1238–1325). However, in these Persian texts as well as in later texts in Urdu and other vernaculars, 'Sufi' was only one term among a larger lexicon of labels, such as *arif* ('gnostic'), *baba* ('father', 'master'), *bozorg* ('great one'), *darwish* ('itinerant renouncer'), *faqir* ('[spiritual] pauper'), *murshid* ('guide'), *pir* ('father', 'master'), *shaykh* ('elder', 'master') or *wali* ('friend of God', 'saint'). In both discourse and practice, such terms enjoyed more widespread usage than 'Sufi' itself. In their implicit hints at social relationships—*darwish*es and *faqir*s require patrons; *baba*s, *pir*s, and *murshid*s require disciples—this fuller lexicon connected living Sufi holy men and dead Sufi saints to traditions of shrine veneration and patronal relationships which were of central importance to South Asian Muslims.

In South Asia, as in other Muslim regions, the followers of such Sufi holy men have pursued mystical and/or devotional practices such as chanting (*zikr*), meditation (*muraqaba*), pilgrimage (*ziyara*), and listening to music (*sama*). In theory (though not necessarily in practice), such practitioners have been initiated into one or more of the Sufi *tariqa*s ('pathways, orders') from the thirteenth century onwards, the most influential of which include the many sub-lineages of the Chishtiyya, Naqshbandiyya, and Qadiriyya. However, South Asia has also developed its own distinctive forms of Sufi practice, such as the celebration of the saintly wedding (*urs*) and the music of *qawwali*. The popular appeal of localized spiritual and festive traditions has often drawn followers from Hindu caste groups, with Hindus sometimes becoming formal Sufis without conversion to Islam (Dahnhardt 2002).

The prominence of the term 'Sufi' relative to the fuller lexicon used in South Asian languages is partly due to the term's adoption into early colonial discourse on Islam. Early formative accounts of the Sufis (or 'Soofies') include those of William Jones (1746–94) in his 1792 'On the Mystical Poetry of the Persians and Hindus', John Malcolm (1769–1833) in his 1815 *History of Persia*, and Lieutenant James William Graham in his 1819 'Treatise on Sufiism [*sic*], or Mahomedan Mysticism' in the *Transactions of the Literary Society of Bombay*. Such colonial accounts wavered between idealization and denigration, with the term 'Sufi' itself often set aside for freethinking poets and mystics (usually long-deceased), leaving the adapted wider lexicon of 'dervish', 'fakeer', and 'peer' as disparaging synonyms for contemporary charlatans and imposters. From the mid-nineteenth century, Muslim reformers drew this critique into their own attack on customary forms of South Asian Islam. These ambivalent usages of the Sufi lexicon continue to shape South Asian Muslim discourse in English and the regional languages to this day.

Further reading: Dahnhardt 2002; Ernst and Lawrence 2002; Ewing 1997; Frank 1984; Green 2012; Rizvi 1978–83.

—NILE GREEN, *Professor of History, Department of History, University of California, Los Angeles*

—— ••• ——

Swadeshi

Swadeshi is a foundational concept of modern Indian political-economic thought and practice. A neologism of the early twentieth century, it was a *portmanteau* construction that joined two distinct terms—*swa* or 'self' and *desh* or 'territory'—to signal a new collective nationalist meaning.

Often translated as 'of one's own nation', the concept gained popular resonance during the eponymous Swadeshi Movement (1905–8), the first attempt to mobilize and incorporate the 'masses' within elite nationalism in early twentieth-century Bengal (Sarkar 1973). The movement radicalized and popularized the economic critique of colonialism, first advanced in the late nineteenth century, in multiple and overlapping social, cultural, and political-economic domains. More specifically, it fused together a universal conception of a collective national economy with a particular vision of an autonomous national collective. This fusion of *swadeshi* with its most significant cognate term *swaraj* (in its various meanings as 'autonomy', 'freedom', 'independence') established the ground for a concrete and durable linkage between state, economy, territory, and nation within popular anti-colonial imagination. The movement spawned an enduring repertoire of idioms and practices that informed subsequent nationalist mass-mobilization campaigns, especially the Gandhian movement of Non-Cooperation in the early 1920s (Bayly 1986: 285–328; Guha 1988: 100–50). This repertoire included the valorization of indigenous industry and handicrafts; the fostering of national practices of consumption and production; and the proliferation of philosophical, aesthetic, and political-economic discourses that upheld autonomy, self-reliance, and sacrifice as a collective normative and political ideal.

There is robust debate about the meaning and trajectory of the Swadeshi Movement. Various historians have emphasized its failure to incorporate the peasantry (Sarkar 1973), the deployment of caste-based forms of social coercion (Guha 1988: 100–50), and the way conceptions of political-economic autonomy framed a Hindu-centred vision of nationhood (Goswami 2004: 242–77). But there is also a general consensus that it was a profoundly generative moment for the collective authoring of new practices of cultural, socioeconomic, and philosophical modernism (Bayly 1986; Sarkar 1973; Goswami 2004). Rabindranath Tagore (1861–1941), the philosopher-poet of the early phase of the movement, provided an influential and eloquent elaboration of a Swadeshi Samaj or an 'autonomous national society'. The most significant iteration of this vision in the post-Swadeshi era was provided by Gandhi (1869–1948) and his programme of mass mobilization that sought to empower popular visions of a self-reliant economic collective forged from below (Chatterjee 1993a: 85–130; Markovits 2004: 56–77).

Although initially employed within the nationalist movement, the concept 'swadeshi' continues to shape postcolonial debates about the value of state-directed versus communitarian models of economic planning and of urban-centred industrialization versus a village-centred fostering of an alternative political economy. *Swadeshi* acquired renewed salience in the post-1991 era of political-economic reforms with diverse politicians, technocrats, and social movements claiming its mantle and seeking to fix a single, authoritative meaning. The dual imperative of *swadeshi* and *swaraj*, the ideal of an autonomous national economy and democratic representation, remains a central referent of ongoing social struggles and debates about the political economy of nationhood.

Further reading: Bayly 1986; Goswami 2004; Guha 1988; Sarkar 1973.

—MANU GOSWAMI, *Associate Professor, Department of History,*
New York University

— ·•· —

Swaraj

In its initial usage during the freedom struggle, *swaraj*, a Hindi word that literally means 'self-rule', connoted the idea of India being ruled by Indians rather than being under British colonial subjugation; and for large numbers of people this remained the predominant, if not the exclusive, meaning of the term throughout the freedom movement. But soon after its usage became current, the expression acquired new layers of meanings, and the concept became a quasi-embodiment of the ensemble of ideas inspiring and underlying the Independence movement.

The most important exposition and enrichment of the idea of *swaraj* was put forward by Mohandas Karamchand Gandhi (1869–1948) in *Hind Swaraj* (1909). For Gandhi, the replacement of British rulers by Indian rulers, but keeping the system erected by the British intact, did not constitute *swaraj*. He emphasized the necessity of discarding British colonial institutions for the attainment of *swaraj*. The reason was not that the institutions were developed in England, and not in India; rather, according to him, the very nature of these institutions made them inimical to the idea of self-rule. Moreover, he was of the opinion that British institutions had a negative influence not only on India, but on Britain as well (Gandhi 1909).

In making this insightful point, Gandhi broke new ground by connecting the possibilities for realizing desirable social goals with institutional structures. As the notions of independence and *swaraj* are intimately connected with the idea of freedom and liberty, Gandhi in *Hind Swaraj* asserted by implication that the goal of freedom at the societal level required an appropriate set of social institutions. He further claimed that traditional Indian institutions were particularly suitable viewed from this perspective. Although during the Independence struggle *swaraj* and *swadeshi* were intimately connected, at a purely conceptual level *swaraj* does not imply *swadeshi*. What *swaraj* requires is a set of social institutions that will be conducive to the idea of self-rule, the place of origin of the institutions being of no consequence. Gandhi's emphatic approval of indigenous institutions was, to a great extent, due to his belief in their superiority from the perspective of self-rule (Gandhi 1909, 1999).

There is one other sense, quite distinct from the one discussed above, in which the expression *swaraj* is used by Gandhi: regardless of how oppressive a rule might be, to the extent an individual is willing to suffer rather than to submit to tyranny and injustice, to that extent he has attained his personal *swaraj* (Gandhi 1909). While the notion of *swaraj* discussed in relation to societal organization is collective and external in nature, this notion of *swaraj*, at once moral and self-sacrificial, is both personal and internal. This personal notion of *swaraj* is related to the idea of *satyagraha* or 'nonviolent civil disobedience' in a natural way. From a reading of *Hind Swaraj* it seems that for Gandhi the two notions of *swaraj* were inextricably linked to each other.

Further reading: Gandhi 1909, 1999; Dharampal 2003; Misra 2007.

—SATISH K. JAIN, *Centre for Economic Studies and Planning, School of Social Sciences, Jawaharlal Nehru University, New Delhi*

—— •◦• ——

Theosophy

The Theosophical Society (hereafter TS) was founded in New York in 1875 by the Russian émigrée Helena Petrovna Blavatsky (1831–91) and the American lawyer Henry Steel Olcott (1832–1907). In 1879, the founders moved to India where, in 1882, the new Society established its headquarters at Adyar, near Madras (now Chennai). The only test of admission to the TS was agreement with its 'First Object': 'to form a nucleus of the Universal Brotherhood of Humanity without distinction of race, creed, sex, caste or color' (Dixon 2001: 3–4). The Society did not officially endorse any particular teachings or dogmas, but from early on it developed a distinctive set of teachings which was widely understood as theosophy.

According to these teachings, which were most fully developed in Blavatsky's massive two-volume *The Secret Doctrine* (1888), the universe was 'One Life' that evolved to self-realization through a complicated series of cosmic cycles. The evolution of spirit into matter and back to spirit took place via the laws of karma (often referred to as the 'law of cause and effect') and reincarnation (Dixon 2001: 46–8). Blavatsky's *The Secret Doctrine* was, as its subtitle claimed, the synthesis of science, religion, and philosophy, and most theosophists followed Blavatsky in arguing for the fundamental agreement between 'ancient wisdom' and modern sciences and religions (Dixon 2001: 4). In a significant reorientation of the western esoteric tradition which helped to popularize the image of a 'mystical East', they argued that the 'divine wisdom' which was theosophy had been best preserved in the great spiritual traditions of Asia, and especially in India (Bevir 1994: 756, 764).

According to Blavatsky, the real founders of the Society were the 'Mahatmas', members of an occult hierarchy located in remote Tibet which included advanced souls from throughout the world (Dixon 2001: 18, 25). The sometimes awkward relationships between theosophists and these mysterious 'Mahatmas' allowed for a complex reimagining of relationships between colonizer and colonized, as prominent Anglo-Indians attempted to reconcile their own sense of themselves as representatives of the British Raj with spiritual deference to those they perceived as their 'racial' inferiors (Viswanathan 2000: 2–3). British theosophists thus occupied an ambiguous position in relationship both to India and to the British Empire, imperialist in orientation even as they criticized empire and identified with India. On her arrival in India in 1893, for example, Annie Besant (1847–1933), who became President of the TS in 1907, worked to assimilate herself to Indian culture, becoming involved in movements for the revival of Hinduism alongside both conservative Hindus and Hindu reformers; she was actively involved in educational reform and from 1913 abandoned her earlier compromises with orthodox Hinduism to call for an end to child marriage and the seclusion of women, the expansion of women's education, and the reform of the caste system alongside her commitment to Indian self-government (Anderson 1994: 566–7, 571–5).

The TS was closely associated with the Indian nationalist movement, and members of the Society played an important role in the formation of the Indian National Congress (INC), which first met in Bombay in 1885 (Dixon 2003: 70). When the Congress met in Calcutta in 1917, Besant was elected its first woman president. A year earlier, with support from the network of theosophical lodges across India, Besant had founded an all-India Home Rule League; in 1917 she was interned by the Madras government (along with her colleagues at the journal *New India*, which Besant had launched in 1914) for her nationalist activities. While Besant's vision of Home Rule—a self-governing India within the British Empire—was displaced in the 1920s by the Gandhian vision of *swaraj* or 'self-rule' (Dixon 2003: 67–8, 73), the TS played a critical role in the cultural, political, and spiritual encounter between Britain and the subcontinent for at least half a century.

Further reading: Anderson 1994; Bevir 1994; Dixon 2001, 2003; Viswanathan 2000.

—JOY DIXON, *Associate Professor, University of British Columbia, Vancouver*

— .•. —

Unani Medicine

*T*ibb or *hikmat* ('medicine', 'discernment') is a stream of medical knowledge that has been cultivated and practised within Indo-Muslim milieux in the Indian subcontinent. Since the nineteenth century it has been commonly qualified in India as *[y]unani* ('Greek' in Arabic, Persian, and Urdu) *tibb* or Unani medicine. The textual legacy of *tibb* in India, from the fourteenth century, provides evidence of significant local and regional variations, marked changes over time, as well as the transregional traffic of people, texts, substances, and ideas. From this perspective, the contemporary demarcations between 'systems' of indigenous medicine with their discrete histories need to be understood as the outcome of historical processes that have taken shape during and since colonial times.

The waning of Mughal power and the collapse of local patronage systems in the eighteenth and nineteenth centuries, in the face of European military, political, and economic assertion, put an end to the recruitment of *hakims* ('practitioners') from centres of learning in what are now Afghanistan, Iran, and the Central Asian Republics, and brought about changes in patterns of education, transmission, and textual production (Speziale 2010; Alavi 2008; Azmi 2004). The implications for *tibb* brought about by these changes, and those that came about through more sustained contact with newly circulating European medical knowledge and practice during the nineteenth century, have been variously interpreted.

A conventional understanding is that Unani medicine underwent a 'decline' as a consequence of the lack of support of indigenous medicine by colonial authorities, which, in turn, precipitated a revival. Quaiser (2001) proposed the significance of resistance among practitioners of Unani medicine to colonial western medicine in order to create a new and legitimate sphere of practice. Attewell (2007) emphasized the negotiation of authority in the formation of Unani medicine as a system itself. Alavi (2008) sees a fading of what she considers to be Persian styles of writing about medicine and health, ethics, and comportment, in favour of a scientized Arabic that adhered more closely to the foundational formulations of Galen (129–ca. 200) and Ibn Sina (980–1037) and that was produced within physician family lineages. In this way, she argues for a scientization of Unani medicine that does not foreground, and is prior to, the role usually ascribed to the increasing authority of colonial medicine from the late nineteenth century. Speziale (2010), while noting the decrease of Iranian physicians employed at the Mughal courts in the eighteenth century, and concurring with the changing loci of textual production, points rather to new impulses in the composition of Persian (not Arabic), and later Urdu, texts on medicine among Sufi lineages in Delhi during the late eighteenth century (Speziale 2010: 56–64). His arguments concerning the prominent role of members of Sufi orders in the transmission of Unani medicine, which increases over the eighteenth and into the nineteenth centuries, also run counter to a common strain of thought about the separation of Galenic ('unani') medicine from religious disciplines (Rahman 1997).

The mobilization of Unani medicine as an emblem of elite Muslim culture and as a repository of valuable healing knowledge, with its own rational pedigree and claims to science, took place through the initiatives of influential family lineages from the late nineteenth century as well as through nascent state support following legislative reforms in 1919. The coming of Independence to India (1947) did not radically reshape the priorities of the new nation states to provide comparatively cheap health provision through the institutionalization of Unani medicine and Ayurveda, in which they were clearly subordinated to the biomedical establishment. The Indian Medicine Central Council Act of 1970 sought to standardize the education and registration of practitioners, while a government body to coordinate research in Unani medicine was set up in 1978. New forms of hybridized Unani medicine have been produced through these initiatives, through commoditization and through the harnessing of print and other media. Today, specific regimental therapies, pulse and urine diagnosis, and the home production of Unani preparations found in the pharmacopeia, such as electuaries, pastes, powders, and decoctions, are no longer a typical feature of Unani medicine—they are not taught at length in institutional settings, and are only cultivated and practised within family lineages that have adequate resources to do so.

Further reading: Alavi 2008; Attewell 2007; Azmi 2004; Bode 2008; Quaiser 2001; Rahman 1987; Speziale 2010; Zillurrahman 1994.

—GUY ATTEWELL, *Researcher, French Institute of Pondicherry*

— •◦• —

Vegetarianism

Though it is commonplace to regard Hindus as vegetarian and India as the land of vegetarianism from time immemorial, historical scholarship and social fact call these axioms into question; the very meaning of vegetarianism has been, and continues to be, a matter of contestation and of historical and regional variation.

Harappans (3300–1300 BCE), like the Vedic Aryans (1700–500 BCE) who succeeded them in northern India, were carnivorous, as were the Dravidian civilizations of southern India. The *Vedas* and the *Brahmanas*, the earliest of the Sanskrit sacred texts, list dozens of animals deemed fit for divine sacrifice, hospitality, and human consumption. The religious epics, the *Ramayana* and the *Mahabharata*, the *Arthashastra*, Panini's Sanskrit grammar, and the medical treatises of Sushruta and Charaka (legendary authors of two classical texts of Ayurveda, codified in the first centuries CE) also provide evidence of the consumption of animals by members of all castes in the Hindu social order. In his analysis of the Ayurvedic medical tradition, Francis Zimmermann (1987) underlines the importance, especially in royal and military contexts, of therapeutic remedies derived from the hunting, slaughter, and consumption of animals.

However, Zimmerman also notes the equivocal character of Ayurvedic prescription, which is recognized as impure and immoral, even if therapeutic (1987: 171). A similar ambivalence is registered in the *Dharmashastra* (the later Hindu 'lawbooks'), particularly in the *Manusmriti* (200 BCE–200 CE). The thirty verses of the *Manusmriti* devoted to meat-eating situate it explicitly with respect to *jati/varna* ('caste') and ritual norms. Brahmins, Manu says (in *The Laws of Manu*, ch. 5, verses 26–44), may eat meat consecrated in sacrifice, and they may subsist on otherwise forbidden flesh when necessary to preserve life. But best of all is the practice of ahimsa.

The advocacy of a renunciatory alimentary ethic among Brahmins was the result of a great centuries-long social transformation in northern India, starting in the sixth century BCE. The combined influence of the heretical sects, Buddhism and Jainism, led to the eventual demise of Vedic animal sacrifice and to the broad dissemination of vegetarianism. It was in Emperor Asoka's reign (269–32 BCE) that Buddhist doctrines of ahimsa found their greatest efflorescence and impact (Thapar 2002: 174–208 passim). Asoka's principles, as defined in his rock edicts and the pillar edicts, expressed themselves in a concern for all living things and an aversion to killing. He abandoned the royal hunt, criticized blood sacrifices, and curtailed the cooking of meat in the royal kitchen, though he neither banned hunting outright nor insisted upon the vegetarianism of his subjects (Thapar 2002: 201–3).

Even more far-reaching than Buddhism in its impact upon the diet of caste Hindus was Jainism which emerged concurrently with Buddhism. Simultaneously sympathizing with the suffering of the sacrificial beast and guarding against the possibility of being eaten in turn in another life, ascetic and lay Jains began by the early medieval period to express ahimsa in a predominantly dietary form (Sutherland 1997: 8; Laidlaw 1995: 155). Prohibited foods also included vegetables and fruits whose consumption involved any potential violence, unboiled or unfiltered water (which harboured countless minute life forms), onions and garlic (considered 'hot' or passion-inducing according to Ayurvedic norms), and honey. The most complete (if rare) abjuration of violence in cooking and eating was manifested in *sallekhana/samadhi maran*, a controlled wasting away through fasting that approached the sacral status of sacrifice; several Jain renouncers and lay people are said to have ended their lives in this manner (Laidlaw 1995: 161).

Jainism's commitment to vegetarianism eventually established itself as the dietary norm among many (though not all) Brahmin communities and several non-Brahmin caste Hindu communities in the subcontinent, though in a less exacting form. Among the best known of modern Jains was Raychandbhai Mehta (1867–1901), distinguished for his spiritual exercises and asceticism, as well for his role as Mohandas Karamchand Gandhi's (1869–1948) counsellor on diet and *brahmacharya* ('male celibacy'). Indeed, Gandhi's distinguished career in gastro-politics, including vegetarianism, is clarified enormously by situating it in the history of the Jain dietary and ascetic practice (Alter 2000).

Historically, vegetarianism has been relatively rare among the subcontinent's Christian and Muslim communities; it is likewise a common practice only among a few Sikh sects such as the Namdharis (founded as a reform movement in the nineteenth century). Among caste Hindus, abstention from meat always has been inextricable from the eater's *jati/varna* status, gender, *ashram*, or stage in the human life cycle, regional origin, state of bodily health, personal disposition, and other contingencies (such as travel or famine). In general, married and unmarried caste Hindu women are more likely than men to be vegetarian and to function as custodians of alimentary purity. Widows in most instances are subjected to a rigorously ascetic regimen, of which vegetarianism is a part.

Dietary practices, however, are far from being fixed. Large-scale transformations in diet are often associated with the process denominated as 'Sanskritisation' by M.N. Srinivas (1989). This process of vertical mobility within the *jati/varna* hierarchy is defined as the means by which a lower-ranked caste, tribe, or other community emulates the customs, rituals, beliefs, ways of life, and even the caste denomination of a higher, particularly a *dvija* ('twice-born') caste. In the Brahmin and Vaishya models of Sanskritization, a turn to vegetarianism and teetotalism is common; this is not true of the Kshatriya model. In fact, Kancha Ilaiah, the Dalit critic of Brahmanical Hinduism, has suggested, only partly sardonically, that the turn to meat and alcohol among the previously vegetarian be characterized as 'Dalitisation' rather than 'Sankritisation' (Ilaiah 2010: 87–8).

No account of vegetarianism in the subcontinent can ignore the historical and ongoing controversy around cow slaughter and cow protection. The cow emerged for newly emergent middle-class Hindu males in late nineteenth-century northern and central India as a sacred symbol of the Hindu nation requiring protection from the violence of non-Hindus (Gupta 2001: 213–21; Pandey 1983). Since 1947, several Indian states have instituted bans upon cow slaughter. Such moves are clearly directed against the beleaguered Muslim minority in India, but they also have a potential impact upon beef-eating Dalit, Christian, and tribal communities. An issue such as this one underlines the fact that the abjuration of meat, or of some kinds of meat, is by no means straightforward or even non-violent. Vegetarianism in the subcontinent, and particularly in India, continues to be marked by conflict and ambivalence.

Further reading: Achaya 1994; Alter 2000; Laidlaw 1995; Srinivas 1989; Zimmermann 1987.

—PARAMA ROY, *Professor of English, Department of English, University of California, Davis*

— .•. —

Zenana

Z enana is an Anglicization of the Persian *zanaana*, from *zan* (plural *zanaan*), meaning 'woman' (Steingass 1996 [1892]: 623). The Persian language was brought to India from Iran in the ninth century and soon became the preferred language of the Muslim elite. In the sixteenth century, under the Mughals, it became the principal administrative and literary language and the medium of polite public discourse within the higher social strata of society. Over time, Persian vocabulary and styles of expression were increasingly incorporated into the local Hindavi language of northern India, creating a new *lingua franca* that came to be known as Urdu (Alam 1998).

The word *zanaana* was used in Urdu as both adjective and noun, meaning 'female, feminine [...] effeminate', as well as 'a woman, a eunuch' (Platts 1988 [1884]: 618). By extension, it also designated the 'women's apartments' of an upper-class residence (Platts 1988: 618) or any space set aside temporarily for the sole use of women at a gender-segregated gathering, such as a wedding (nowadays the English loanword 'ladies' is widely used instead).

The word 'zenana' was brought into English via travel writers, missionaries, and British officials and in India came to be restricted largely to its 'architectural' sense, referring to a set of rooms occupied by the unmarried daughters, daughters-in-law, wives, concubines, and female slaves of an aristocratic male householder. Over time, it acquired a distinctly negative connotation, as a place where women were confined by their menfolk, living in complete seclusion, unseen by outsiders, and rarely, if ever, permitted to leave. It was imagined as a dark, dank, and unhealthy space, its inhabitants languishing in idleness, unable to exercise their bodies or their minds, reduced to passing their time in gossip, backbiting, intrigue, and deviant sexual indulgences (for example, Das 1932 [1929]). Since almost no male Britishers and few females ever saw first-hand how women really lived within the walls of the zenana, it inevitably became an object of fascination and fantasy.

Some of the rare British woman travellers to gain admission to royal zenanas wrote accounts that were avidly consumed by an eager public (for example, Parlby 1850). 'Zenana missions' also sent British women into the homes of upper-class women, ostensibly to teach reading and writing, but also to inspire their pupils to become exemplary wives and mothers in the Christian Victorian mode (Kent 1999). Some of these western visitors discovered that zenana life had certain positive features: opportunities for close female bonding, frequent festive gatherings, and playful amusements (for example, Meer Hassan Ali 1917 [1832]; Diver 1909). But most found their negative preconceptions reinforced and wrote accordingly (cf. Ghose 1998; Nair 1990; Sen 2002).

Elite Indians no longer strictly seclude women as they once did, and the morbid curiosity and fantasizing about the zenana that once prevailed in the West has mostly dissipated. Today, the word is rarely used and has a decidedly archaic connotation.

Further reading: Alam 1998; Das 1932 [1929]; Diver 1909; Ghose 1998; Kent 1999; Meer Hassan Ali 1917 [1832]; Nair 1990; Parlby 1850; Platts 1988 [1884]; Sen 2002; Steingass 1996 [1892].

—SYLVIA VATUK, *Professor Emerita, Department of Anthropology,*
University of Illinois, Chicago

Bibliography

Abraham, Itty. 1992. 'India's "Strategic Enclave": Civilian Scientists and Military Technologies', *Armed Forces and Society*, Vol. 18, No. 2, pp. 231–52.

———. 1996. 'Science and Power in the Postcolonial State', *Alternatives*, Vol. 21, No. 3, pp. 321–39.

———. 2009. 'Introduction: Nuclear Power and Atomic Publics', in Itty Abraham, ed., *South Asian Cultures of the Bomb: Atomic Publics and the State in India and Pakistan*, pp. 1–19. Bloomington.

———. 2010. '"Who's Next?" Nuclear Ambivalence and the Contradictions of Non-Proliferation Policy', *Economic and Political Weekly*, Vol. 45, No. 43, pp. 48–56.

Achaya, K.T. 1994. *Indian Food: A Historical Companion*. Delhi.

Aggarwal, Neil. 2008. 'Kashmiriyat as Empty Signifier', *Interventions*, Vol. 10, No. 2, pp. 222–35.

Agha, Shahid Ali. 1998. *The Country without a Post Office*. New York.

Agnes, Flavia. 2005. 'Politicization of Personal Laws: A Study of Colonial India', in Bharati Ray, ed., *Women of India: Colonial and Post Colonial Periods*, pp. 3–25. History of Science, Philosophy and Culture in Indian Civilization, Vol. 9, Part 3. New Delhi.

Ahluwalia, Sanjam. 2008. *Reproductive Restraints: Birth Control in India, 1877–1947*. Ranikhet.

Ahmad, Aziz. 1964. *Studies in Islamic Culture in the Indian Environment*. Oxford.

———. 1967. *Islamic Modernism in India and Pakistan, 1857–1964*. London.

Ahmad, Irfan. 2009. *Islamism and Democracy in India: The Transformation of the Jamaat-e-Islami*. Princeton.

Ahmed, Rafiuddin. 1981. *The Bengal Muslims, 1871–1906: A Quest for Identity*. New York.

Ahuja, Ravi. 2009. *Pathways of Empire: Circulation, 'Public Works' and Social Space in Colonial Orissa, c. 1780–1914*. New Delhi.

Alam, Muzaffar. 1998. 'The Pursuit of Persian: Language in Mughal Politics', *Modern Asian Studies*, Vol. 32, No. 2, pp. 317–49.

———. 2004. *The Languages of Political Islam: India1200–1800*. Chicago/Delhi.

Alavi, Hamza. 1972. 'Kinship in West Punjabi Villages', *Contributions to Indian Sociology*, Vol. 6, No. 1, pp. 1–27 [N.S.].

Alavi, Seema. 2008. *Islam and Healing: Loss and Recovery of an Indo-Muslim Medical Tradition, 1600–1900*. Delhi.

Ali, Shaheen S. and Rukhshanda Naz. 1998. 'Marriage, Dower and Divorce: Superior Courts and Case Law in Pakistan', in Farida Shaheed, Sohail A. Warraich, Cassandra Balchin, and Aisha Gazdar, eds, *Shaping Women's Lives, Laws, Practices and Strategies in Pakistan*, pp. 107–42. Lahore.

al-Kulayni al-Razi, Abu Jafar Mohammad ibn Yaqub ibn Ishaq, 1978. *al-Kafi*. Tehran/Karachi.

Allen, James de Vere. 1980. 'A Proposal for Indian Ocean Studies', *Historical Relations across the Indian Ocean: The General History of Africa, Studies and Documents*, Vol. 3. Paris.

Alley, Kelly D. 2002. *On the Banks of the Ganga: When Wastewater Meets a Sacred River*. Vancouver.

Aloysius, G. 1998. *Religion as Emancipatory Identity: A Buddhist Movement among the Tamils under Colonialism*. New Delhi.

Alter, Joseph. 2000. *Gandhi's Body: Sex, Diet, and the Politics of Nationalism*. Philadelphia.

Alvi, Anjum. 2001. 'The Category of the Person in Rural Punjab', *Social Anthropology*, Vol. 9, No. 1, pp. 45–63.

———. 2007. 'India and the Muslim Punjab: A Unified Approach to South Asian Kinship', *Journal of the Royal Anthropological Institute*, Vol. 13, No. 3, pp. 657–78 [N.S.].

Ambedkar, Bhimrao R. 1945. *What Congress and Gandhi Have Done to the Untouchables*. Delhi.

———. 1979. 'Untouchability, the Dead Cow and the Brahmin', in *Collected Works of B.R. Ambedkar*, Vol. 7, pp. 185–207.

———. 1989. 'The Annihilation of Caste', in *Dr. Babasaheb Ambedkar, Writings and Speeches*, Vol. 1, pp. 25–96. Bombay.

———. 1990a. 'What Congress and Gandhi Have Done to the Untouchables', in *Dr. Babasaheb Ambedkar, Writings and Speeches*, Vol. 9, pp. 1–387. Bombay.

——— 1990b. 'The Untouchables: Who Were They and Why They Became Untouchables?' in *Dr Babasaheb Ambedkar, Writings and Speeches*, Vol. 12, pp. 232–82. Bombay.

Amin, Shahid. 1984. 'Gandhi as Mahatma: Gorakhpur District, Eastern UP, 1921–1922', in Ranajit Guha, ed., *Subaltern Studies*, Vol. 3, pp. 1–61. Delhi.

Amin, Sonia. 1996. *The World of Muslim Women in Colonial Bengal, 1876–1939*. Leiden.

Anderson, Benedict. 1983. *Imagined Communities*. London.

Anderson, Nancy. 1994. 'Bridging Cross-Cultural Feminisms: Annie Besant and Women's Rights in England and India, 1874–1933', *Women's History Review*, Vol. 3, No. 4, pp. 563–80.

Anjaria, Jonathan S. and Colin McFarlane, eds. 2011. *Urban Navigations: Politics, Space and the City in South Asia*. New Delhi.

Annadurai, C.V. 1948. *Radiovil Anna*. Tiruchirapalli.

Anthony, David. 2007. *The Horse, the Wheel, and Language*. Princeton.

Appadurai, Arjun. 1986. 'Is Homo Hierarchicus?' *American Ethnologist*, Vol. 13, No. 4, pp. 745–61.

———. 1988. 'Putting Hierarchy in Its Place', *Cultural Anthropology*, Vol. 3, No. 1, pp. 36–49.

Appadurai, Arjun and Carol Breckenridge. 1995. 'Public Modernity in India', in Carol Breckenridge, ed., *Consuming Modernity: Public Culture in a South Asian World*, pp. 1–22. Minneapolis.

Arberry, Arthur J. 1942. *An Introduction to the History of Sufism*, pp. 8–15. London.

Arnold, David. 1993. *Colonizing the Body: State Medicine and Epidemic Disease in Nineteenth Century India*. Berkeley.

———. 2000. *Science, Technology, and Medicine in Colonial India*. Cambridge.

Arunima, G. 1992. 'Colonialism and the Transformation of Matriliny in Kerala, Malabar 1850–1940'. Dissertation, electronic resource. Cambridge.

———. 2003. *There Comes Papa: Colonialism and the Transformation of Matriliny in Kerala, Malabar, c. 1850–1940*. Hyderabad.

Asad, Talal. 1993. *Genealogies of Religion: Discipline and Reasons of Power in Christianity and Islam*. Baltimore.

———. 2006. 'French Secularism and the "Islamic Veil Affair"', *The Hedgehog Review*, pp. 92–106, http://www.iasc-culture.org/THR/archives/After Secularization/8.12IAsad.pdf [last accessed on 5 August 2013].

Ashcroft, Bill, Gareth Griffiths, and Helen Tiffin. 1989. *The Empire Writes Back: Theory and Practice in Postcolonial Literatures*. London.

Asher, Catherine. 1992. *Architecture of Mughal India*. New Cambridge History of India Series, Vol. 1, No. 4. Cambridge.

Attewell, Guy. 2007. *Refiguring Unani Tibb: Plural Healing in Late Colonial India*. Hyderabad.

Azmi, Altaf A. 2004. *History of Unani Medicine in India*. Delhi.

Babb, Lawrence A. 1981. 'A Glancing: Visual Interaction in Hinduism', *Journal of Anthropological Research*, Vol. 37, pp. 387–401.

Babb, Lawrence A. and Susan S. Wadley, eds. 1995. *Media and Transformation of Religion in South Asia*. Philadelphia.

Bagchi, Amiya Kumar. 1972. *Private Investment in India1900–1939*. Cambridge: Cambridge University Press.

Bailey, Frederick G. 1957. *Caste and the Economic Frontier: A Village in Highland Orissa*. Manchester.

Baird, Robert D. 1993. 'On Defining "Hinduism" as a Religious and Legal Category', in Robert D. Baird, ed., *Religion and Law in Independent India*, pp. 41–58. Delhi.

———, ed. 2009 [1981]. *Religion in Modern India*. Delhi.

Bairy, Ramesh. 2010. *Being Brahmin, Being Modern*. New Delhi.

Bajpai, Rochana. 2011 [2010]. *Debating Difference: Group Rights and Liberal Democracy in India*. Oxford/Delhi.

Bakshi, Rajni. 1986. *The Long Haul: The Bombay Textile Workers Strike of 1982–83*. Mumbai.

Ballard, Roger. 1994. *Desh Pardesh: The South Asian Presence in Britain*. London.

———. 1999. 'Panth, Kismet, Dharma te Qaum: Continuity and Change in Four Dimensions of Punjabi Religion', in Pritam Singh and Shinder Singh Thandi, eds, *Punjabi Identity in a Global Context*, pp. 7–37. Oxford.

Bandyopadhyay, Sekhar. 2009. *Decolonization in South Asia: Meanings of Freedom in Post-Independence West Bengal, 1947–52*. London/New York.

Banerjea, Surendranath. 1925. *A Nation in Making*. London.

Banerjee, Madhulika. 2009. *Power, Knowledge, Medicine: Ayurvedic Pharmaceuticals at Home and in the World*. New Delhi.

———. 2007. 'Sacred Elections', *Economic and Political Weekly*, Vol. 42, No. 17, pp. 1556–62.

Banerjee, Sumanta. 1984. *India's Simmering Revolution: The Naxalite Uprising*. London.

———. 1989. *The Parlour and the Streets*. Calcutta.

Banerjee-Dube, Ishita, ed. 2008. *Caste in History*. Delhi.

Bangha, Imre. 2010. 'Rekhta: Poetry in Mixed Language', in Francesca Orsini, ed., *Before the Divide: Hindi and Urdu Literary Culture*, pp. 21–83. New Delhi.

Bari, M.A. 1965. 'A Nineteenth-Century Muslim Reform Movement in India', in George Makdisi, ed., *Arabic and Islamic Studies in Honour of Hamilton A.R. Gibb*, pp. 84–102. Leiden.

Barnett, Marguerite R. 1976. *The Politics of Cultural Nationalism in South India*. Princeton.

Baruah, Sanjib. 2005. *Durable Disorder: Understanding the Politics of Northeast India*. New Delhi.

Basu, Chandranath. 1892. *Hindutva*. Calcutta.

Basu, Srimati. 2001. *She Comes to Take Her Rights: Indian Women, Property, and Propriety*. New Delhi.

———, ed. 2005. *Dowry and Inheritance*. London.

Basu, Tapan, Pradeep Datta, Sumit Sarkar, Tanika Sarkar, and Sambuddha Sen. 1993. *Khaki Shorts, Saffron Flags: A Critique of the Hindu Right*. Delhi.

Bates, Crispin. 1995. *Race, Caste and Tribe in Central India—The Early Origins of Indian Anthropometry*. Edinburgh.

———. 2007. *Subalterns and Raj: South Asia since 1600*. London.

Bates, Crispin and Gavin Rand, eds. 2013. *Mutiny at the Margins: New Perspectives on the Indian Uprising*, Vols 1–4. New Delhi.

Baviskar, Amita and Raka Ray, eds. 2011. *Elite and Everyman: The Cultural Politics of the Indian Middle Classes*. London.

Baxi, Upendra. 1987 [1982].'Taking Suffering Seriously: Social Action Litigation in the Supreme Court of India', in Neelan Tiruchelvam and Radhika Coomaraswamy, eds, *The Role of the Judiciary in Plural Societies*, pp. 32–60. New York.

Bayly, Christopher A. 1983. *Rulers, Townsmen and Bazaars: North Indian Society in the Age of British Expansion, 1770–1870*. New Delhi.

———. 1985.'The Pre-History of Communalism? Religious Conflict in India, 1700–1860', *Modern Asian Studies*, Vol. 19, No.2, pp. 177–203.

———. 1986. 'The Origins of Swadeshi (Home Industry): Cloth and Indian Society', in Arjun Appadurai, ed., *The Social Life of Things: Commodities in Cultural Perspective*, pp. 285–328. Cambridge..

———. 1990a. *The Raj. India and the British, 1600–1947*. London.

———. 1990b. *Indian Society and the Making of the British Empire*. Cambridge.

———. 1996. *Empire and Information: Intelligence Gathering and Social Communication in India, 1780–1870*. Cambridge.

———. 1998. *Origins of Nationality in South Asia: Patriotism and Ethical Government in the Making of Modern India*. Oxford.

Bayly, Christopher A. and Sanjay Subrahmanyam. 1988. 'Portfolio Capitalists and the Political Economy of Early Modern India', *Indian Economic and Social History Review*, Vol. 25, No. 4, pp. 401–24.

Bayly, Susan. 1983.'The History of Caste in South Asia', *Modern Asian Studies*, Vol. 17, No. 3, pp. 519–27.

———. 1989. *Saints, Goddesses and Kings. Muslims and Christians in South Indian Society, 1700–1900*. Cambridge.

———. 1999. *Caste, Society and Politics in India: From the Eighteenth Century to Modern Age*. Cambridge.

Beach, Milo C. 1992. *Mughal and Rajput Painting*. Cambridge.

Beaglehole, Timothy H. 1966. *Thomas Munro and the Development of Administrative Policy in Madras, 1792–1818*. Cambridge.

Behal, Rana P. 2007. 'Power Structure, Discipline and Labour in Assam Tea Plantations under Colonial Rule', in Rana P. Behal and Marcel van der Linden, eds, *India's Labouring Poor: Historical Studies, c. 1600–2000*, pp. 143–72. Delhi.

———. 2010. 'Coolie Drivers or Benevolent Paternalists? British Tea Planters in Assam and the Indenture Labour System', *Modern Asia Studies*, Vol. 44, No. 1, pp. 29–51.

Behal, Rana P. and Prabhu P. Mohapatra. 1992. 'Tea and Money versus Human Life': The Rise and Fall of the Indenture System in the Assam Tea Plantations, 1840–1908', in E. Valentine Daniel, Henry Bernstein, and Tom Brass, eds, *Plantations, Proletarians and Peasants in Colonial Asia*, pp. 145–61. London.

Belsare, M.B. 1904. *An Etymological Gujarati–English Dictionary*. Ahmedabad.

Benei, Véronique. 2002. 'Missing Indigenous Bodies: Educational Enterprise and Victorian Morality in the Mid-Nineteenth Century Bombay Presidency', *Economic and Political Weekly*, Vol. 37, No. 17, pp. 1647–54.

———. 2008. *Schooling Passions: Nation, History and Language in Contemporary Western India*. Stanford. [Indian Edition: 2009. *Schooling India: The Forging of Hindu and Muslim Citizens*. New Delhi.]

Berger, Peter L. 1967. *The Sacred Canopy*. Boston.

Berger, Rachel. 2013. *Ayurveda Made Modern: Political Histories of Indigenous Medicine in North India, 1900–1955*. Basingstoke.

Berreman, Gerald D. 1971. 'The Brahmanical View of Caste', *Contributions to Indian Sociology*, Vol. 5, No. 1, pp. 16–23 [N.S.].

Béteille, André. 1966. *Caste, Class and Power: Changing Patterns of Social Stratification in a Tanjore Village*. Berkeley.

———, ed. 1969. *Social Inequality*. Harmondsworth.

———. 1987. 'Homo Hierarchicus, Homo Equalis', in André Béteille, *The Idea of Natural Inequality and Other Essays*, pp. 33–53. Delhi.

———. 1992a. *Society and Politics in India: Essays in a Comparative Perspective*. Delhi.

———. 1992b. *The Backward Classes in Contemporary India*. Delhi.

———. 1996. 'Caste in Contemporary India', in Christopher J. Fuller, ed., *Caste Today*, pp. 150–79. Delhi.

———. 2002. 'Hierarchical and Competitive Inequality', *Sociological Bulletin*, Vol. 51, No.1, pp. 3–27.

Bevir, Mark. 1994. 'The West Turns Eastward: Madame Blavatsky and the Transformation of the Occult Tradition', *Journal of the American Academy of Religion*, Vol. 62, No. 3, pp. 747–67.

Beyer, Peter. 2003. 'Conceptions of Religion: On Distinguishing Scientific, Theological, and "Official" Meanings', *Social Compass*, Vol. 50, No. 2, pp. 141–60.

Bhabha, Homi K. 1994. *The Location of Culture*. London.

Bhagat, R.P. 2001. 'Census and the Construction of Communalism in India', *Economic and Political Weekly*, Vol. 36, Nos 46–7, pp. 4352–56.

Bhargava, Rajeev. 1995. 'Religious and Secular Identities', in Upendra Baxi and Bhiku Parekh, eds, *Crisis and Change in Contemporary India*, pp. 317–49, New Delhi.

———, ed. 1998. *Debates on Indian Secularism*. New Delhi.

———, ed. 1999. *Secularism and Its Critics*. New Delhi.

———. 2007. 'The Distinctiveness of Indian Secularism', in T.N. Srinivasan, ed., *The Future of Secularism*, pp. 54–9. New Delhi.

———. 2010. *The Promise of India's Secular Democracy*. Oxford.

Bhatia, Bela. 2000. *The Naxalite Movement in Central Bihar*. Cambridge.

Bhattacharya, Debraj. 2004. 'Kolkata "Underworld" in the Early 20th Century', *Economic and Political Weekly*, Vol. 39, No. 38, pp. 4276–82.

Bhattacharya, Sanjoy. 2006. *Expunging Variola: The Control and Eradication of Smallpox in India, 1947–1977*. New Delhi/London.

———, ed. 2007. *Rethinking 1857*. New Delhi.

Bhattacharya, Sanjoy and Rajib Dasgupta. 2007. 'A Tale of Two Global Health Programs: Smallpox Eradication's Lessons for the Antipolio Campaign in India', *American Journal of Public Health*, Vol. 99, No. 7, pp. 1176–84.

Bhattacharya, Sanjoy, Mark Harrison, and Michael Worboys. 2005. *Fractured States: Smallpox, Public Health and Vaccination Policy in British India, 1800–1947*. New Delhi/London.

Bhattacharya, Sibesh C. 2010. *Understanding Itihasa*. Shimla.

Bhattacharya, Tithi. 2005. *Sentinels of Culture*. Delhi.

Bhave, Vinoba. 1965. *Sulabha Gramadana*. Varanasi.

———. 1996. *Vinoba Sahitya*, Vol. 16. Wardha.

Bhide, Amita. 2008. 'Resettlement or a Silent Displacement?' in *Mumbai Reader*, ch. 17, Urban Design Research Institute (UDRI). Mumbai.

Bilgrami, Akeel. 2003. 'Gandhi, the Philosopher', *Economic and Political Weekly*, Vol. 38, No. 39, pp. 4159–65.

Bilimoria, Purushottama. 1998. 'Indian Religious Traditions', in David E. Cooper and Joy A. Palmer, eds, *Spirit of the Environment: Religion, Value and Environmental Concern*, pp. 1–14. London/New York..

———. 2010. 'The Idea of Hindu Law', *Journal of the Oriental Society of Australia*, Vol. 43, 2011, pp. 103–30.

Bilimoria, Purushottama, Joseph Prabhu, and Renuka Sharma, eds. 2007. *Indian Ethics, Classical and Contemporary Challenges*, Vol. 1. Aldershot/Burlington.

———, eds. [Forthcoming.] *Indian Ethics, Gender, Justice and Ecology*, Vol. 2.

Birla, Ritu. 2009. *Stages of Capital: Law, Culture and Market Governance in Late Colonial India*. Durham NC/London.

Blavatsky, Helena P. 1988. *The Secret Doctrine: The Synthesis of Science, Religion, and Philosophy*, Vols 1–2. London/Pasadena [Facsimile].

Blunt, Alison. 2005. *Domicile and Diaspora: Anglo-Indian Women and the Spatial Politics of Home.* Hoboken, New Jersey.

Bode, Maarten. 2008. *Taking Traditional Medicine to the Market: The Modern Image of the Ayurvedic and Unani Industry, 1980–2000.* Hyderabad.

Borthwick, Meredith. 1984. *The Changing Role of Women in Bengal, 1849–1905.* Princeton.

Bose, Jagadis C. 1902. *Response in the Living and Non-Living.* London.

Brass, Paul. 1974. *Language, Religion and Politics in North India.* Cambridge.

Brecher, Michael. 1959. *Nehru: A Political Biography.* New York.

Brentjes, Helga. 1964. *Die Imamatslehren im Islam nach der Darstellung des al-Ash'ari.* Berlin.

Brimnes, Niels. 2007. 'Vikings against Tuberculosis: The International Tuberculosis Campaign in India, 1948–1951', *Bulletin of the History of Medicine*, Vol. 81, No. 2, pp. 407–30.

Brinkmann, Mankel. 2009. 'Fighting World Hunger on a Global Scale: The Rockefeller Foundation and the Green Revolution in Mexico', http://www.rockarch.org/publications/resrep/brinkmann.pdf [last accessed on 15 August 2013].

Bronkhorst, Johannes and Madhav Deshpande, eds. 1999. *Aryan and Non-Aryan in South Asia: Evidence, Interpretation and Ideology.* Cambridge.

Brugmann, Jeb. 2009. *Welcome to the Urban Revolution: How Cities Are Changing the World.* New Delhi.

Bryant, Edwin and Laurie Patton, eds. 2005. *The Indo-Aryan Controversy: Evidence and Inference in Indian History.* London/New York.

Bughart, Richard. 1978. 'Hierarchical Models of Hindu Social System', *Man*, Vol. 18, No. 4, pp. 635–53.

Buitenen, Johannes A.B. van, ed. and transl. 1981. *The Bhagavadgita in the Mahabharata: Text and Translation.* Chicago.

Burrow, Thomas. 1965. *The Sanskrit Language.* London.

Busch, Allison. 2011. *Poetry of Kings: The Classical Hindi Literature of Mughal India.* New York.

Butcher, Melissa. 1999. 'Parallel Texts: The Body and Television in India', in Christiane Brosius and Melissa Butcher, eds, *Image Journeys: Audio-Visual Media and Cultural Change in India*, pp. 165–98. New Delhi.

Buettner, Elizabeth. 2009. 'Chicken Tikka Masala, Flock Wallpaper, and "Real" Home Cooking: Assessing Britain's "Indian" Restaurant Traditions', *Food and History*, Vol. 7, No. 2, pp. 203–29.

Calder, Norman. 1984. 'The Significance of the Term *Imam* in Early Islamic Jurisprudence', *Zeitschrift für die Geschichte der arabisch-islamischen Wissenschaften*, Vol. 1, pp. 253–64.

Caldwell, Robert. 1856. *A Comparative Grammar of the Dravidian or South Indian Family of Languages.* London.

Cannadine, David. 2001. *Ornamentalism. How the British Saw Their Empire.* London.

Caplan, Lionel. 2003. *Children of Colonialism: Anglo-Indians in a Postcolonial World.* London.

Cardona, George. 1988. *Panini: His Work and Its Traditions—Background and Introduction,* Vol. 1. Delhi.

Carroll, Lucy. 1978. 'Colonial Perceptions of Indian Society and the Emergence of Caste(s) Associations', *Journal of Asian Studies,* Vol. 37, No. 2, pp. 233–50.

———. 1983. 'Law, Custom and Statutory Reform: The Hindu Widows Remarriage Act of 1856', *Indian Economic and Social History Review,* Vol. 20, No. 4, pp. 363–88.

Cenkner, William. 1982. 'The Pandit: The Embodiment of Oral Tradition', *Zeitschrift für Religions—und Geisteswissenschaf,* Vol. 34, No. 2, pp. 118–29.

Cernea, Michael M., ed. 1999. *The Economics of Involuntary Resettlement: Questions and Challenges.* Washington D.C.

Chadda, Maya. 1997. *Ethnicity, Security and Separatism in India.* New York.

Chakrabarti, Pratik. 2004. *Western Science in Modern India: Metropolitan Methods.* New Delhi.

Chakrabarty, Bidyut. 2006. 'Radicalism in Modern Indian Social and Political Thought: Nationalist Creativity in the Colonial Era', in Vrajendra R. Mehta and Thomas Pantham, eds, *Political Ideas in Modern India: Thematic Explorations,* pp. 3–25. New Delhi.

Chakrabarty, Dipesh. 1992. 'Of Garbage, Modernity and the Citizen's Gaze', *Economic and Political Weekly,* Vol. 27, Nos 10–11, pp. 541–46.

———. 2001. 'Clothing the Political Man: A Reading of the Use of Khadi/White in Indian Public Life', *Postcolonial Studies,* Vol. 4, No. 1, pp. 27–38.

———. 2002. *Habitations of Modernity: Essays in the Wake of Subaltern Studies.* Chicago.

Chakrabarty, Dipesh, Rochana Majumdar, and Andrew Sartori, eds. 2007. *From the Colonial to the Postcolonial: India and Pakistan in Transition.* New Delhi.

Chakravarti, Sudeep. 2007. *Red Sun: Travels in Naxalite Country.* New Delhi.

Chakravarti, Uma. 1998. *Rewriting History: The Life and Times of Pandita Ramabai.* Oxford.

Chakravarti, Uma and Preeti Gill, eds. 2007 [2001]. *Shadow Lives: Writings on Widowhood.* Delhi.

Chakravarty, S.R. and C. D'Ambrosio. 2006. 'The Measurement of Social Exclusion', *Review of Income and Wealth,* Vol. 52, No. 3, pp. 377–98.

Chalana, Manish. 2010. 'Slumdogs vs. Millionaires: Balancing Urban Informality and Global Modernity in Mumbai, India', *Journal of Architectural Education,* Vol. 63, No. 2, pp. 25–37.

Chaliha, Parag D., ed. 1958. *The Outlook on NEFA*. Jorhat.

Chandavarkar, Rajnarayan. 1994. *The Origins of Industrial Capitalism in India: Business Strategies and the Working Classes in Bombay, 1900–1940*. Cambridge.

Chandhoke, Neera. 1999. *Beyond Secularism: The Rights of Religious Minorities*. New Delhi.

Chandra, Bipan. 1966. *The Rise and Growth of Economic Nationalism in India: 1889–1905*. New Delhi.

———. 1984. *Communalism in Modern India*. New Delhi.

———. 2003. *In the Name of Democracy: The JP Movement and Emergency*. New Delhi.

Chandra, Kanchan. 2004. *Why Ethnic Parties Succeed: Patronage and Ethnic Head-Counts in India*. Cambridge.

Chapple, Christopher K. 2007. 'Action Oriented Morality in Hinduism', in Purushottama Bilimoria, Joseph Prabhu, and Renuka Sharma, eds, *Indian Ethics, Classical Traditions and Contemporary Challenges*, Vol. 1, pp. 351–62. Aldershot/Burlington.

Chari, V.K. 1990. *Sanskrit Criticism*. Honolulu.

Charlesworth, Neil. 1982. *British Rule and the Indian Economy 1800–1914*. London.

Chatterjee, Indrani, ed. 2004. *Unfamiliar Relations: Family and History in South Asia*. New Delhi.

Chatterjee, Nandini. 2011. *The Making of Indian Secularism: Empire, Law and Christianity, 1830–1960*. Basingstoke.

Chatterjee, Partha. 1989. 'The Nationalist Resolution of the Woman's Question', in Kumkum Sangari and Sudesh Vaid, eds, *Recasting Women. Essays in Colonial History*, pp. 233–54. New Delhi.

———. 1993a. *Nationalist Thought and the Colonial World: A Derivative Discourse*. Minneapolis.

———. 1993b. *The Nation and Its Fragments: Colonial and Postcolonial Histories*. Princeton.

———. 1994. 'Secularism and Toleration', *Economic and Political Weekly*, Vol. 29, No. 28, pp. 1768–77.

———. 1995. 'The Disciplines of Colonial Bengal', in Partha Chatterjee, ed., *Texts of Power: Emerging Disciplines in Colonial Bengal*, pp. 1–29. Minneapolis.

———. 1998 [1997]. *A Possible India: Essays in Political Criticism*. New York [New Delhi].

———. 2011. *Lineages of Political Society: Studies in Postcolonial Democracy*, pp. 94–126. New York.

Chatterji, Probhat C. 1984. *Secular Values for Secular India*. New Delhi.

Chaudhuri, Kirti N. 1999 [1985]. *Trade and Civilisation in the Indian Ocean: An Economic History from the Rise of Islam to 1750*. Cambridge.

Chaudhuri, Maitrayee. 1995. 'Citizens, Workers, Emblems of Culture: An Analysis of the First Plan Document on Women', *Contributions to Indian Sociology*, Vol. 29, Nos 1–2, pp. 211–34.

———, ed. 2004. *Feminism in India*. New Delhi/London.

———. 2010. 'Nationalism Is Not What It Used to Be: Can Feminism Be Any Different? A View from India', *Nivedini: Journal of Gender Studies*, Vol. 16, pp. 120–45.

———. 2011 [1993]. *The Indian Women's Movement: Reform and Revival*. New Delhi.

———. 2012. 'Feminism in India: The Tale and Its Telling', *Revue Tiers Monde*, No. 209, January–March 2012, pp. 19–36.

Chaurasia, Radhey S., 2008. *History of Ancient India: Earliest Times to 1200 AD*. Delhi.

Chew, Shirley and David Richards, eds. 2010. *A Concise Companion to Postcolonial Literature*. Chichester.

Chiriyankandath, James. 2000. 'Creating a Secular State in a Religious Country: The Debate in the Indian Constituent Assembly', *Commonwealth and Comparative Politics*, Vol. 38, No. 2, pp. 1–24.

Choudhary, Subharansu. 2012. *Let's Call Him Vasu*. New Delhi.

Choudhury, Nurul. 2001. *Peasant Radicalism in Nineteenth Century Bengal: The Faraizi, Indigo, and Pabna Movements*. Dhaka.

Chowdhry, Prem. 1994. *The Veiled Women: Shifting Gender Equations in Rural Haryana*. Delhi.

———. 2009 [2007]. *Contentious Marriages, Eloping Couples: Gender, Caste, and Patriarchy in Northern India*. New Delhi.

Chouhan, T.R., Indira Jaising, and Claude Alphonso Alvares. 1994. *Bhopal: The Inside Story—Carbide Workers Speak Out on the World's Worst Industrial Disaster*. New York.

Clark, Matthew. 2006. *The Dashanami-Samnyasis: The Integration of Ascetic Lineages into an Order*. Leiden.

Cleaver, Harry M. Jr. 1972. 'The Contradictions of the Green Revolution', *The American Economic Review*, Vol. 62, Nos 1–2, pp. 177–86.

Cohen, Lawrence. 1995. 'The Pleasures of Castration: The Postoperative Status of Hijras, Jankhas and Academics', in Paul R. Abramson and Steven D. Pinkerton, eds, *Sexual Nature, Sexual Culture*, pp. 276–304. Chicago.

Cohn, Bernard S. 1987a. 'Notes on the History of the Study of Indian Society and Culture', in Bernard S. Cohn, ed., *An Anthropologist among the Historians and Other Essays*, pp. 136–72. Delhi.

———. 1987b. 'Some Notes on Law and Change in North India', in Bernhard S. Cohn, *An Anthropologist Among Historians and Other Essays*, pp. 554–74. Delhi.

Cohn, Bernard S. 1996. *Colonialism and Its Forms of Knowledge: The British in India*. Princeton.

Connelly, Mathew. 2008. *Fatal Misconception: The Struggle to Control World Population*. Cambridge.

Copland, Ian. 1993.'Lord Mountbatten and the Integration of the Indian States: A Reappraisal', *The Journal of Imperial and Commonwealth History*, Vol. 21, No. 2, pp. 385–408.

———. 1998.'The Integration of the Princely States: A "Bloodless Revolution?"', in Donald Anthony Low and Howard Brasted, eds, *Freedom, Trauma, Continuities: Northern India and Independence*, pp. 153–74. New Delhi/ Thousand Oaks/London.

———. 2010.'What's in a Name? India's Tryst with Secularism', *Commonwealth and Comparative Politics*, Vol. 48, No. 2, pp. 123–47.

Corbridge, Stuart and John Harriss. 2000. *Reinventing India: Liberalization, Hindu Nationalism and Popular Democracy*. London.

Creel, Austin. 1977. *Dharma in Hindu Ethics*. Columbia.

Crone, Patricia. 2004. *God's Rule: Government and Islam: Six Centuries of Medieval Islamic Political Thought*. Cambridge.

Crook, Nigel, ed. 1996. *The Transmission of Knowledge in South Asia: Essays in Education, Religion, History and Politics*. Delhi.

Daftary, Farhad. 1990. *The Isma'ilis: Their History and Doctrines*. Cambridge.

Dahl, Robert. 2000 [1998]. *On Democracy*. New Haven/London.

Dahnhardt, Thomas. 2002. *Change and Continuity in Indian Sufism: A Naqshbandi-Mujaddidi Branch in the Hindu Environment*. Delhi.

Dalmia, Vasudha. 1996.'Sanskrit Scholars and Pandits of the Old School: The Benares Sanskrit College and the Constitution of Authority in the Late Nineteenth Century', *Journal of Indian Philosophy*, Vol. 24, pp. 321–37.

———. 1997. *The Nationalization of Hindu Traditions: Bharatendu Harischandra and Nineteenth-Century Banaras*. Delhi.

Dalrymple, William. 2006. *The Last Mughal: The Fall of a Dynasty: Delhi 1857*. London.

Dangle, Arjun, ed. 1992. *Poisoned Bread*. New Delhi.

Daniel, E. Valentine. 1984. *Fluid Signs: Being a Person the Tamil Way*. Berkeley.

Das, Frieda Hauswirth. 1932 [1929]. *Purdah: The Status of Indian Women*. London.

Das, Prosad K. 1995. *The Monsoons*. New Delhi.

Das, Suranjan and Jayanta K. Ray. 1996. *The Goondas: Towards a Reconstruction of the Calcutta Underworld*. Calcutta.

Das, Veena. 1977. *Structure and Cognition*. Delhi.

———. 1995. *Critical Events: An Anthropological Perspective on Modern India*. New Delhi.

Dashopanishadah (The Ten Upanishads). 1937. Anandashrama Edition (https://
ia601704.us.archive.org/2/items/Anandashram_Samskrita_Granthavali_
Anandashram_Sanskrit_Series/ASS_106_Dasopanishadah_-_SS_
Marulkar_1937.pdf) [last accessed on 23 July 2013].

Dasgupta, Surendranath. 1922 [1932]. *A History of Indian Philosophy*, Vols 1–2.
Cambridge.

Dayanand, Saraswati. 1875. *Satyarth Prakash*. Benares.

Deka, Harekrishna. 2008. 'North-East in Fragments and Invention of a
Metaphor', in Chandan K. Sarma, ed., *Souvenir: North-East India History
Association (29th Annual Session)*, pp. 101–13. Dibrugarh.

Deliège, Robert. 1997. 'At the Threshold of Untouchability: Pallars and Valaiyars
in a Tamil Village', in Christopher J. Fuller, ed., *Caste Today*, pp. 65–92. Delhi.

Desai, G.H. 1898. *Gujaratno Arvichin Itihas*. Ahmedabad.

Devji, Faisal. 2007a. 'Apologetic Modernity', *Modern Intellectual History*, Vol. 4,
No. 1, pp. 61–76.

———. 2007b. 'A Shadow Nation: The Making of Muslim India', in Kevin Grant,
Philippa Levine, and Frank Trentmann, eds, *Beyond Sovereignty: Britain,
Empire and Transnationalism, 1860–1950*, pp. 126–45. London.

Dharampal. 1962. *Panchayati Raj as the Basis of Indian Polity: An Exploration into
the Proceedings of the Constituent Assembly*. New Delhi.

———. 1972 [1971]. *The Madras Panchayat System*, Vol. 2. Delhi.

———. 2003. *Understanding Gandhi*. Mapusa.

Dharampal and T.M. Mukundan. 2002. *The British Origin of Cow-Slaughter
in India: With Some British Documents on the Anti-Kine-Killing-Movement
1880–1894*. Mussoorie.

Dharampal-Frick, Gita. 1994. *Indien im Spiegel deutscher Quellen der frühen
Neuzeit (1500–1750): Studien zu einer interkulturellen Konstellation*. Tübingen.

———. 1995. 'Shifting Categories in the Discourse on Caste: Some Historical
Observations', in Vasudha Dalmia and Heinrich von Stietencron, eds,
*Representing Hinduism: The Construction of Religious Traditions and National
Identity*, pp. 82–100. New Delhi.

Dharampal-Frick, Gita and Katja Götzen. 2011. 'Interrogating Caste and Race
in South Asia', in Manfred Berg and Simon Wendt, eds, *Racism in the Modern
World: Historical Perspectives on Cultural Transfer and Adaptation*, pp. 192–
212. New York.

Dhareshwar, Vivek. 1993. 'Caste and the Secular Self', *Journal of Arts and Ideas*,
Nos 25–6, pp. 115–26.

Dhareshwar, Vivek and R. Srivatsan. 1996. 'Rowdy Sheeters: An Essay on
Subalternity and Politics', *Subaltern Studies*, Vol. 9, pp. 201–231. Delhi.

Dharwadker, Vinay. 1993. 'Orientalism and the Study of Indian Literatures', in
Carol Appadurai Breckenridge and Peter van der Veer, eds, *Orientalism and the
Postcolonial Predicament: Perspectives on South Asia*, pp. 158–85. Philadelphia.

Dickinson, Jen and Adrian J. Bailey. 2007. '(Re)membering Diaspora: Uneven Geographies of Indian Dual Citizenship', *Political Geography*, Vol. 26, No. 7, pp. 757–74.

Dimock, Edward C. Jr. and Edwin Gerow. 1974. *The Literatures of India: An Introduction*, pp. 115–43. Chicago.

Dirks, Nicholas B. 1987. *The Hollow Crown: Ethnohistory of an Indian Kingdom*. Hyderabad.

———. 1989. 'The Original Caste: Power, History and Hierarchy in South Asia', *Contributions to Indian Sociology*, Vol. 23, No. 1, pp. 59–101.

———. 1993. 'Colonial Histories and Native Informants: Biography of an Archive', in Carol Appadurai Breckenridge and Peter van der Veer, eds, *Orientalism and the Postcolonial Predicament: Perspectives on South Asia*, pp. 279–313. Philadelphia.

———. 2001. *Castes of Mind: Colonialism and the Making of Modern India*. Princeton.

Diver, Maud. 1909. *The Englishwoman in India*. London.

Dixon, Joy. 2001. *Divine Feminine: Theosophy and Feminism in England*. Baltimore.

———. 2003. 'Of Many Mahatmas: Besant, Gandhi, and Indian Nationalism', in Harold Coward, ed., *Indian Critiques of Gandhi*, pp. 67–86. Albany.

D'Monte, Darryl. 2002. *Ripping the Fabric: The Decline of Mumbai and Its Mills*. New Delhi.

Dobbelaere, Karel and Jan Lauwers. 1973. 'Definition of Religion: A Sociological Critique', *Social Compass*, Vol. 20, No. 4, pp. 535–51.

Dodson, Michael. 2002. 'Re-presented for the Pandits: James Ballantyne, 'Useful Knowledge,' and Sanskrit Scholarship in Benares College during the Mid-Nineteenth Century', *Modern Asian Studies*, Vol. 36, No. 2, pp. 257–98.

Doniger, Wendy. 2009. *The Hindus: An Alternative History*. New York.

Doniger, Wendy and Brian King Smith, trans and eds. 1991. *The Laws of Manu*. London.

D'Souza, Rohan. 2006. *Drowned and Dammed: Colonial Capitalism and Flood Control in Eastern India*. Oxford.

Dubash, Navroz K. 2002. *Tubewell Capitalism: Groundwater Development and Agrarian Change in Gujarat*. New Delhi.

Dubois, Abbe J.A. 1906. *Hindu Manners, Customs and Ceremonies*, Henry King Beauchamp, trans. Oxford.

Dudley-Jenkins, Laura. 2003. *Identity and Identification in India: Defining the Disadvantaged*. London/New York.

Dumont, Louis. 1970 [1966]. *Homo Hierarchicus: The Caste System and Its Implications*. London [Paris].

Durkheim, Emile. 1965. *The Elementary Forms of Religious Life*, Joseph Ward Swain, trans. New York.

Dutt, Romesh C. 1901. *The Economic History of India under Early British Rule: From the Rise of the British Power in 1757 to the Accession of Queen Victoria in 1837*, Vol. 1. London.

———. 1903. *The Economic History of India in the Victorian Age: From the Accession of Queen Victoria in 1837 to the Commencement of the Twentieth Century*, Vol. 2. London.

Dwyer, Rachel. 2000. *All You Want Is Money, All You Need Is Love*. London.

———. 2005. *100 Bollywood Films*. London.

———. 2011. 'Zara hatke!: The New Middle Classes and the Segmentation of Hindi Cinema', in Henrike Donner, ed., *A Way of Life: Being Middle-Class in Contemporary India*, pp. 184–208. London.

Dwyer, Rachel and Christopher Pinney, eds. 2001. *Pleasure and the Nation: The History, Politics and Consumption of Public Culture in India*. New Delhi.

Echanove, Matias and Rahul Srivastava. 2008. 'The Tool-House', in *Mumbai Reader 2008*, ch. 21, Urban Design Research Institute (UDRI). Mumbai.

———. 2010. 'The Village Inside', in Lynne Elizabeth and Stephen Goldsmith, eds, *What We See: Advancing the Observations of Jane Jacobs*, pp. 135–151. New York.

———. 2012. 'The High Rise and the Slum: Speculative Urban Development in Mumbai', in Nancy Brooks, Kieran Donaghy and Gerrit-Jan Knaap, eds, *The Oxford Handbook of Urban Economics and Planning*, pp. 789–813. New York.

Eck, Diana L. 1981. *Darsan: Seeing the Divine Image in India*. Chambersburg.

Eckerman, Ingrid. 2005. *The Bhopal Saga—Causes and Consequences of the World's Largest Industrial Disaster*. Hyderabad.

Edwardes, Stephen M. 1909–1910. *Gazetteer of Bombay City and Island*, Vols 1–2. Bombay [Reprint: The Government of Maharashtra, 1977–8].

Emeneau, Murray. 2012. 'India as a Linguistic Area', *Language*, Vol. 32, No. 1, pp. 3–16.

Engineer, Ashghar Ali. 2003. *Communal Challenge and Secular Response*. Delhi.

Ernst, Carl W. and Bruce B. Lawrence, eds. 2002. *Sufi Martyrs of Love: The Chishti Order in South Asia and Beyond*. New York.

Ewing, Katherine P. 1997. *Arguing Sainthood: Modernity, Psychoanalysis, and Islam*. Durham NC.

Farquhar, John N. 1915. *Modern Religious Movements in India*. New York.

Fein, Jay S. and Pamela. L. Stephens, eds. 1987. *Monsoons*. Washington, D.C.

Fernandes, Leela. 2006. *India's New Middle Class: Democratic Politics in an Era of Economic Reform*. Minneapolis.

Fisher, Michael H. 2004a [1997]. *The Travels of Dean Mahomet: An Eighteenth-Century Journey through India*. Edited with an Introduction and Biographical Essay. Berkeley.

———. 2004b. 'Becoming and Making "Family" in Hindustan', in Indrani Chatterjee, ed., *Unfamiliar Relations: Family and History in South Asia*, pp. 95–121.

Fitzgerald, Timothy. 1997. 'A Critique of "Religion" as a Cross-Cultural Category', *Method and Theory in the Study of Religion*, Vol. 9, No. 2, pp. 91–110.

———. 2005. 'Problems with "Religion" as a Category for Understanding Hinduism', in J.E. Llewllyn, ed., *Defining Hinduism: A Reader*, pp. 171–202. London.

Forrester, Duncan B. 1980. *Caste and Christianity: Attitudes and Policies on Caste of Anglo-Saxon Protestant Missions in India*. London.

Foucault, Michel. 2002 [1969]. *The Archaeology of Knowledge*, Alan Mark Sheridan Smith, trans. London.

Framjee, Dosabhoy. 1858. *The British Raj, Contrasted with Its Predecessors*. London.

———. 1861. *The Parsees*. London.

Frank, Tamar. 1984. '"Tasawwuf is...": On a Type of Mystical Aphorism', *Journal of the American Oriental Society*, Vol. 104, No. 1, pp. 73–80.

Frater, Alexander. 2005. *Chasing the Monsoon: A Modern Pilgrimage through India*. Basingstoke.

Freitag, Sandra B. 1990. *Collective Action and Community: Public Arenas and the Emergence of Communalism in North India*. Oxford.

Friedmann, Yohanan. 1989. *Prophecy Continuous: Aspects of Ahmadi Religious Thought and Its Medieval Background*. Berkeley.

Frykenberg, Robert E. 1999. 'India to 1858', in Robin William Winks, ed., *Historiography: The Oxford History of the British Empire*, Vol. 5, pp. 194–21. Oxford.

Fuller, Christopher J. 1977. 'British India or Traditional India? An Anthropological Problem', *Ethnos*, Vol. 42, pp. 92–121.

———. 1984. *Servants of the Goddess: The Priests of a South Indian Temple*. Cambridge.

Gadbois, George. 1970. 'Indian Judicial Behavior', *Economic and Political Weekly*, Vol. 5, No. 3, pp. 149–66.

Gabrieli, F. 2013. 'Adab', *Encyclopaedia of Islam Online*, Second Edition (http://www.encquran.brill.nl/entries/encyclopaedia-of-islam-2/adab-SIM_0293?s.num=0) [last accessed on 5 August 2013].

Galanter, Marc. 1984. *Competing Equalities: Law and the Backward Classes in India*. Delhi.

———. 1993. *Law and Society in Modern India*. New Delhi.

———. 2009. '"To the Listed Field...": The Myth of Litigious India', *Jindal Global Law Review*, Vol. 1, No. 1, pp. 65–79.

Gandhi, Dharma V., ed. 1976. *Era of Discipline:Documents on Contemporary Reality*. New Delhi.

Gandhi, Leela. 2006. *Affective Communities: Anticolonial Thought, Fin-de-Siècle Radicalism, and the Politics of Friendship*. Durham NC/London.

Gandhi, Mohandas K. 1938 [1909]. *Hind Swaraj or Indian Home Rule*. Ahmedabad [Phoenix Natal].

Gandhi, Mohandas K. 1969 [1927]. *An Autobiography or the Story of My Experiments with Truth*. Ahmedabad.

———. 1997. *Hind Swaraj and Other Writings*, Anthony J. Parel, ed. Cambridge.

———. 1999. *Collected Works of Mahatma Gandhi* (CD-ROM). New Delhi.

———. 1958–1994. *The Collected Works of Mahatma Gandhi*, 1–100 Vols. New Delhi.

———. 1999. *The Collected Works of Mahatma Gandhi*, 1–89 Vols. New Delhi. [Electronic version.]

Gandhi, Nandita. 1996. *When the Rolling Pins Hit the Streets: Women in Anti-Price Movement in Maharashtra*. New Delhi.

Gandhi, Ramchandra. 1976. *The Availability of Religious Ideas*. London.

———. 1994. *Sita's Kitchen*. New Delhi.

Ganguly, Sumit. 2003. 'The Crisis of Indian Secularism', *Journal of Democracy*, Vol. 14, No. 4, pp. 11–25.

Ganeri, Jonardon. 2001. Philosophy in Classical India: The Proper Work of Reason. London.

———. 2009. 'Intellectual India: Reason, Identity, Dissent', *New Literary History*, Vol. 40, pp. 247–63.

Ganeri, Jonardon. 2011. *The Lost Age of Reason: Philosophy in Early Modern India*. Oxford.

Ganti, Tejaswini. 2004. *Bollywood: A Guidebook to Popular Hindi Cinema*. London.

Gayer, Laurent. 2009. 'The Khalistan Militias: Servants and Users of the State', in Laurent Gayer and Christophe Jaffrelot, eds, *Armed Militias of South Asia: Fundamentalists, Maoists and Separatists*, pp. 237–57. London/New York.

Geetha, V. 2004. 'Periyar, Women and an Ethic of Citizenship', in Maitrayee Chaudhuri, ed., *Feminism in India*, pp. 156–74. New Delhi.

Geetha, V. and S.V. Rajadurai. 1998. *Towards a Non-Brahmin Millennium From Iyothee Dass to Periyar*. Calcutta.

Gell, Alfred. 1998. *Art and Agency: An Anthropological Theory*. Oxford.

George, Karimpumannil M. 1968. *A Survey of Malayalam Literature*. London.

Ghose, Indira. 1998. *Women Travellers in Colonial India: The Power of the Female Gaze*. New Delhi.

Ghosh, Durba. 2008. *Sex and Family in Colonial India: The Making of Empire*. Cambridge.

Ghosh, Suresh C. 1995. *The History of Education in Modern India, 1757–1986*. New Delhi.

Ghosh, Vishwajyoti. 2010. *Delhi Calm*. Delhi.

Ghurye, Govind S. 1932. *Caste and Race in India*. London.

Gibb, Hamilton. 1962. 'Islamic Biographical Literature' in Bernard Lewis and P.M. Hold, eds, *Historians of the Middle East*. London.

Gidumal, Dayaram. 1892. *Behramji M. Malabari: A Biographical Sketch*. London.

Gilmartin, David. 1988. *Empire and Islam: Punjab and the Making of Pakistan.* Berkeley.

———. 1994. 'Scientific Empire and Imperial Science: Colonialism and Irrigation Technology in the Indus Basin', *The Journal of Asian Studies*, Vol. 53, No. 4, pp. 1127–49.

Golwalkar, Madhav S. 1938. *We, or Our Nationhood Defined.* Nagpur.

Gombrich, Richard. 1975. 'Ancient Indian Cosmology' in Carmen Blacker and Michael Loewe, eds, *Ancient Cosmologies*, pp. 110–42. London.

Gopal, Priyamvada. 2005. *Literary Radicalism in India. Gender, Nation and the Transition to Independence.* London/New York.

Gopal, Sarvepalli. 1993. *Anatomy of a Confrontation: The Rise of Communal Politics in India.* London.

Goswami, Manu. 2004. *Producing India: From Colonial Economy to National Space.* Chicago.

Gottschalk, P. 2013. *Religion, Science, and Empire: Classifying Hinduism and Islam in British India.* Oxford.

Govindan, Padma and Aniruddhan Vasudevan. 2011. 'The Razor's Edge of Oppositionality: Exploring the Politics of Rights-based Activism by Transgender Women in Tamil Nadu', in Arvind Narrain and Alok Gupta, eds, *Law Like Love: Queer Perspectives on Law*, pp. 84–112. New Delhi.

Grant, David. 1793. *Sermons, Doctrinal and Practical.* Edinburgh/Newcastle.

Green, Nile. 2012. *Sufism: A Global History.* Oxford.

Greenough, P. 1995. 'Intimidation, Coercion and Resistance in the Final Stages of the South Asian Smallpox Eradication Campaign, 1973–1975', *Social Science and Medicine*, Vol. 4, No. 5, pp. 663–45.

Grewal, Manraj. 2004. *Dreams after Darkness: A Search for a Life Ordinary under the Shadow of 1984.* Delhi.

Grewal, J.S. and Indu Banga. 2000. 'Pakistan, Khalistan and Partition', in Amrik Singh, ed., *The Partition in Retrospect*, pp. 159–77. Delhi.

Grierson, George A. 1903–1922. *Linguistic Survey of India.* Calcutta.

———. 1909. 'Bhakti-Marga,' in James Hastings, ed., *Encyclopaedia of Religion and Ethics*, Vol. 2, pp. 539–51. Edinburgh.

Griffiths, Percival. 1967. *The History of the Indian Tea Industry.* London.

Groenewegen, Peter. 1987. 'Political Economy and Economics', in John M. Eatwell, M. Milgate, and P. Newman, eds, *The New Palgrave Dictionary of Economics*, Vol. 3, pp. 904–7. London.

Grove, Richard H. 1996a. *Green Imperialism: Colonial Expansion, Tropical Island Edens and the Origins of Environmentalism, 1600–1860.* Cambridge.

———. 1996b. 'Indigenous Knowledge and the Significance of South-West India for Portuguese and Dutch Constructions of Tropical Nature', *Modern Asian Studies*, Vol. 30, No. 1, pp. 121–44.

Guha, Ramachandra. 1989. *The Unquiet Woods: Ecological Change and Peasant Resistance in the Himalaya*. Oxford.

———. 2001. 'The Prehistory of Community Forestry in India,' *Environmental History*, Vol. 6, No. 2, pp. 213–38.

———. 2003. *The Last Liberal and Other Essays*. Ranikhet.

———. 2007. *India after Gandhi: The History of the World's Largest Democracy*. London.

———. 2010. *Makers of Modern India*. New Delhi.

Guha, Ranajit. 1963. *A Rule of Property for Bengal*. Paris.

———, ed. 1982–9. *Subaltern Studies: Writings on South Asian History and Society*, Vols 1–9. New Delhi.

———. 1983. *Elementary Aspects of Peasant Insurgency in Colonial India*. Delhi.

———. 1997 [1988]. 'Discipline and Mobilize', in *Dominance without Hegemony: History and Power in Colonial India*, pp. 69–120. Cambridge MA.

Guha-Thakurta, Tapati. 1995. 'Recovering the Nation's Art', in Partha Chatterjee, ed., *Texts of Power: Emerging Disciplines in Colonial Bengal*, pp. 63–92. Minneapolis.

Guhan, Sanjivi. 1993. 'Social Security for the Poor in the Unorganized Sector: A Feasible Blueprint for India', in Kirit S. Parikh and R. Sudarshan, eds, *Human Development and Structural Adjustment*, pp. 203–31. Chennai.

Gupta, Akhil. 1995. 'Blurred Boundaries: The Discourse of Corruption, the Culture of Politics, and the Imagined State', *American Ethnologist*, Vol. 22, No. 2, pp. 375–402.

Gupta, Akhil and Aradhana Sharma, eds. 2006. *The Anthropology of the State: A Reader*. Malden/Oxford/Victoria.

Gupta, Charu, ed. 2002 [2001]. *Sexuality, Obscenity, Community: Women, Muslims, and the Hindu Public in Colonial India*. New York [Delhi].

———. 2001. 'The Cow as Mother', in Charu Gupta, ed., *Sexuality, Obscenity, Community: Women, Muslims, and the Hindu Public in Colonial India*, pp. 213–21. New Delhi.

Gupta, Dipankar. 1992. 'Hierarchy and Difference: An Introduction', in Dipankar Gupta, ed., *Social Stratification*, pp. 1–21. Delhi..

———. 2000. *Interrogating Caste: Understanding Hierarchy and Difference in Indian Society*. New Delhi.

———, ed. 2004. *Caste in Question: Identity or Hierarchy*, Contributions to Indian Sociology, Occasional Studies 12. New Delhi.

Gupta, Pamila, Isabel Hofmeyer, and Michael Pearson, eds. 2010. *Eyes across the Water: Navigating the Indian Ocean*. Pretoria.

Gupta, Swarupa. 2007. 'Samaj, Jati and Desh: Reflections on Nationhood in Late Colonial Bengal', *Studies in History*, Vol. 23, No. 2, pp. 177–203.

Guru, Gopal. 1993. 'Dalit Movement in Mainstream Sociology', *Economic and Political Weekly*, Vol. 28, No. 14, pp. 570–3.

Guru, Gopal and V. Geeta. 2000. 'New Phase of Dalit-Bahujan Intellectual Activity', *Economic and Political Weekly*, Vol. 35, No. 3, pp. 130–4.

Habib, Irfan. 1995. 'Colonisation of the Indian Economy', in Irfan Habib, *Essays in Indian History: Towards a Marxist Perception*, pp. 296–335. New Delhi.

Halbfass, Wilhelm. 1988. *India and Europe: An Essay in Understanding*. Albany.

Halm, Heinz. 2004. *Shiism*. Edinburgh.

Hansen, Thomas B. 1999. *The Saffron Wave: Democracy and Hindu Nationalism in Modern India*. Princeton.

Hardgrave, Robert. L. Jr. 1964–1965. 'The DMK and the Politics of Tamil Nationalism', *Pacific Affairs*, Vol. 37, No. 4, pp. 396–411.

Hardiman, David. 1987. *The Coming of the Devi: Adivasi Assertion in Western India*. Oxford.

———. 2003. *Gandhi in His Time and Ours*. New Delhi.

———. 2007 [2006]. *Histories for the Subordinated*. New York [New Delhi].

———. 2007. 'Purifying the Nation: The Arya Samaj in Gujarat 1895–1930, *Indian Economic and Social History Review*, Vol. 44, No. 1, pp. 41–66.

———. 2008. *Missionaries and Their Medicine: A Christian Modernity for Tribal India*. Manchester.

Hardtmann, Eva-Maria. 2009. *The Dalit Movement in India: Local Practices, Global Connections*. New Delhi.

Harrison, Peter. 1999 [1990]. *'Religion' and the Religions in the English Enlightenment*. Cambridge.

Harriss, John. 2002. 'Whatever Happened to Cultural Nationalism in Tamil Nadu? A Reading of Current Events and the Recent Literature on Tamil Politics', *Commonwealth and Comparative Politics*, Vol. 40, No. 3, pp. 97–117.

Hartung, Jan-Peter. 2004. *Viele Wege und ein Ziel: Leben und Wirken von Sayyid Abu l-Hasan 'Ali al-Hasani Nadwi, 1914–1999*. Würzburg.

Harvey, David. 2003. *The New Imperialism*. New York.

Hasan, Mushirul. 1979. *Nationalism and Communal Politics in India*. New Delhi.

Hatcher, Brian. 1996. 'Indigent Brahmans, Industrious Pandits: Bourgeois Ideology and Sanskrit Pandits in Colonial Calcutta', *Comparative Studies of South Asia, Africa and the Middle East*, Vol. 16, No. 1, pp. 15–26.

———. 2005. 'What's Become of the Pandit? Rethinking the History of Sanskrit Scholars in Colonial Bengal', *Modern Asian Studies*, Vol. 39, No. 3, pp. 683–723.

Hawes, Christopher J. 1996. *Poor Relations: The Making of a Eurasian Community in British India, 1773–1833*. London.

Hawley, John Stratton. [Forthcoming.] *India's Real Religion: The Idea of the Bhakti Movement*. Cambridge MA.

Hayden, Cori. 2003. *When Nature Goes Public: The Making and Unmaking of Bio-Prospecting in Mexico*. Princeton.

Hayes, Richard. 1988. *Dignaga on the Interpretation of Signs*. Dordrecht.

Heehs, Peter. 1998. *Nationalism, Terrorism, Communalism: Essays in Modern Indian History*. Oxford.

Heesterman, Johannes C. 1959. 'Reflections on the Significance of *Dakshina*', *Indo-Iranian Journal*, No. 3, pp. 241–58.

———. 1985. *The Inner Conflict of Tradition: Essays in Indian Ritual, Kingship and Society*. Chicago.

Hefner, Robert W. 1998. 'Multiple Modernities: Christianity, Islam, and Hinduism in a Globalizing Age', *Annual Review of Anthropology*, Vol. 27, pp. 83–104.

Heller, Patrick. 2000. 'Degrees of Democracy: Some Comparative Lessons from India', *World Politics*, Vol. 52, No. 4, pp. 484–519.

Hewitt, J.F. 1893. 'The Tribes and Castes of Bengal, by Herbert H. Risley, Vols I and II, Ethnographic Glossary, Vols I and II, Anthropometric Data', *Journal of the Royal Asiatic Society*, Vol. 25, No. 2, pp. 237–300.

Hiriyanna, Mysore. 1949. *The Essentials of Indian Philosophy*. London.

Hocart, Arthur M. 1950. *Caste a Comparative Study*. London.

Hodges, Sarah. 2008. *Contraception, Colonialism and Commerce: Birth Control in South India, 1920–1940*. London.

Hodson, Harry V. 1969. *The Great Divide: Britain–India–Pakistan*, Part 4. London.

Houben, Jan. 1995. *The Sambandha-Samuddesa and Bhartrhari's Philosophy of Language*. Groningen.

Human Rights Watch. 2005. *Breach of Faith: Persecution of the Ahmadiyya Community in Bangladesh*. http://www.hrw.org/reports/2005/06/15/breach-faith [last accessed on 17 February 2013].

Hutchins, Francis G. 1971. *Spontaneous Revolution: The Quit India Movement*. Delhi.

Huyssen, Andreas. 2008. *Other Cities, Other Worlds: Urban Imaginaries in a Globalizing Age*. Durham NC.

Ilaiah, Kancha. 1996. *Why I Am Not a Hindu: A Sudra Critique of Hindutva Philosophy, Culture and Political Economy*. Calcutta.

———. 2010. *The Weapon of the Other: Dalitbahujan Writings and the Remaking of Nationalist Thought*. New Delhi.

Inden, Ronald. 1986. 'Orientalist Constructions of India', *Modern Asian Studies*, Vol. 20, No. 3, pp. 401–40.

———. 1990. *Imagining India*. Oxford.

Irschick, Eugene F. 1969. *Politics and Social Conflict in South India: The Non-Brahman Movement and Tamil Separatism, 1916–1929*. Berkeley.

———. 1994. *Dialogue and History: Constructing South India 1795–1895*. Berkeley.

Izutsu, Toshihiko. 1965. *The Concept of Belief in Islamic Theology: A Semantic Analysis of Iman and Islam*. Tokyo.

Jaffrelot, Christophe. 1996. *The Hindu Nationalist Movement and Indian Politics, 1925 to the 1990s: Strategies of Identity-Building, Implantation and Mobilisation, with Special Reference to Central India*. London.

———. 2001. 'The Vishva Hindu Parishad: A Nationalist but Mimetic Attempt at Federating the Hindu Sects', in Vasudha Dalmia, Angelika Malinar, and Martin Christof, eds, *Charisma and Canon: Essays on the Religious History of the Indian Subcontinent*, pp. 388–412. Oxford.

———. 2003. *India's Silent Revolution: The Rise of the Lower Castes in North India*. Delhi/New York/London.

———. 2005. *Dr Ambedkar and Untouchability: Analysing and Fighting Caste*. London.

———. 2011. *Religion, Caste and Politics in India*. London.

Jaffrelot, Christophe and Sanjay Kumar, eds. 2009. *Rise of the Plebeians? The Changing Face of Indian Legislative Assemblies*. New Delhi.

Jaffrey, Zia. 1996. *The Invisibles: A Tale of the Eunuchs of India*. New York.

Jalal, Ayesha. 1985. *The Sole Spokesman: Jinnah, the Muslim League and the Demand for Pakistan*. Cambridge.

———. 1995. *Democracy and Authoritarianism in South Asia*. Cambridge.

———. 1997. 'Exploding Communalism: The Politics of Muslim Identity in South Asia', in Sugata Bose and Ayesha Jalal, eds, *Nationalism, Democracy and Development: State and Politics in India*. New Delhi.

———. 2000. *Partisans of Allah: Jihad in South Asia*. Boston.

Jambuvijayaji, Sri Muni, ed. 1961. *Vaisheshikasutras of Kanada, with the Commentary of Candrananda*. Baroda. [Critical Edition.]

Jayal, Niraja Gopal. 1999. *Democracy and the State: Welfare, Secularism and Development in Contemporary India*. Delhi.

Jayal, Niraja Gopal, ed. 2001. *Democracy in India*. Delhi.

Jayaraj, Dhairiyarayar and Subramanian Sreenivasan. 2009. 'A Chakravarty-D'Ambrosio View of Multidimensional Deprivation: Some Estimates for India', *Economic and Political Weekly*, Vol. 45, No. 6, pp. 53–65.

Jeffrey, Craig, Patricia Jeffrey, and Roger Jeffery. 2004. '"A Useless Thing!" or "Nectar of the Gods?" The Cultural Production of Education and Young Men's Struggles for Respect in Liberalizing North India', *Annals of the Association of American Geographers*, Vol. 94, No. 4, pp. 961–81.

Jeffrey, Robin. 1992. *Politics, Women and Well-Being: How Kerala Became 'a Model'*. Basingstoke.

———. 2010. *India's Newspaper Revolution*. New Delhi.

Jha, Dwijendra N. 2004. *The Myth of the Holy Cow*. London.

Jha, Ganganath, ed. and trans. 1939. *Gautama's Nyayasutras, with Vatsyayana-Bhasya*. Poona.

Jha, N. and Rajaram, N.S. 2000. *The Deciphered Indus Script: Methodology, Readings, Interpretations*. New Delhi.

Jivaka. 1959. 'The Buddha and His Dhamma', *Mahabodhi*, No. 68, pp. 58–9 [book review].

John, Mary. 2004. 'Gender and Development in India, 1970s–1990s: Some Reflections on the Constitutive Role of Contexts', in Maitrayee Chaudhuri, ed., *Feminism in India*, pp. 52–68. New Delhi.

Johnson, William J. 1995. *Harmless Souls*. Delhi.

Jondhale, Surendra and Johannes Beltz, eds. 2004. *Reconstructing the World: B.R. Ambedkar and Buddhism in India*. New Delhi.

Jones, Kenneth W. 1981. 'Religious Identity and the Indian Census', in Gerald Norman Barrier, ed., *The Census in British India: New Perspectives*, pp. 73–102. New Delhi.

———. 1994 [1989]. *Socio-Religious Reform Movements on British India*. Delhi [Cambridge].

Jones, William. 1794. *Institutes of Hindu Law, or, The Ordinances of Manu, according to the Gloss of Culluca: Comprising the Indian System of Duties, Religious and Civil, Verbally Translated from the Original Sanskrit, with a Preface*. Calcutta.

———. 1799. 'The Third Anniversary Discourse, on the Hindus', in G.G. Robinson and J. Robinson, *Works*, Vol. 1, pp. 19–34, London.

Jordens, Joseph. 1998 [1978]. *Dayananda Sarasvati: His Life and Ideas*. New Delhi.

Kabir, Ananya J. 2009. *Territory of Desire: Representing the Valley of Kashmir*. Minneapolis/New Delhi.

Kadam, Manohar. 1995. *Narayan Meghaji Lokhande*. Mumbai.

Kalra, Virinder S., Raminder Kaur, and John Hutnyk. 2005. *Diaspora and Hybridity*. London.

Kamtekar, Indivar. 2002. 'The Shiver of 1942', *Studies in History*, Vol. 18, No. 1, pp. 81–102 [reprinted in Kaushik Roy, ed. 2006. *War and Society in Colonial India*, pp. 330–57. Delhi.].

Kane, Pandurang V. 1930. *History of Dharmashastra: Ancient and Medieval Religious and Civil Law in India*, Vol. 1. Poona.

———. 1946. *History of Dharmashastra: Ancient and Medieval Religious and Civil Law in India*, Vol. 3. Poona.

———. 1968. *History of the Dharmashastra: Ancient and Medieval Religious and Civil Law in India*, Vol. 5. Poona.

Kanshiram. 1982. *The Chamcha Age—The Era of the Stooges*. New Delhi.

Karnik, V.B. 1967. *Strikes in India*. Mumbai.

Katiyar, Vidya S. 1987. *The Indian Monsoon and Its Frontiers*. New Delhi.

Kaur, Amarjit. 2006. 'Indian Labour, Labour Standards, and Workers' Health in Burma and Malaya, 1900–1940', *Modern Asian Studies*, Vol. 40, No. 2, pp. 393–444.

Kaur, Ravinder. 2004. 'Across-Region Marriage: Poverty, Female Migration, and the Sex Ratio', *Economic and Political Weekly*, Vol. 39, No. 25, pp. 2595–603.

Kaviraj, Sudipta. 1986. 'Indira Gandhi and Indian Politics', *Economic and Political Weekly*, Vol. 21, Nos 38–9, pp. 1697–708.

———. 1992. 'The Imaginary Institution of India', in Partha Chatterjee and Gyanendra Pandey, eds, *Subaltern Studies: Writings on South Asian History and Society*, Vol. 7, pp. 1–39. Delhi.

———. 1995. 'Religion, Politics and Modernity', in Upendra Baxi and Bhikhu Parekh, eds, *Crisis and Change in Contemporary India*, pp. 295–316. New Delhi.

———. 2000. 'Democracy and Social Inequality', in Francine Frankel et al., eds, *Transforming India: Social and Political Dynamics of a Democracy*, pp. 89–119. Delhi.

———. 2002. 'Ideas of Freedom in Modern India', in Robert H. Taylor, ed., *The Idea of Freedom in Asia and Africa*, pp. 97–142. Stanford.

———. 2005. 'On The Enchantment of the Indian State', *European Journal of Sociology*, Vol. 46, pp. 263–96.

Keer, Dhananjay. 1988. *Veer Savarkar*. Bombay.

Kelly, Michele and Deepika D'Souza, eds. 2010. *The World Bank in India: Undermining Sovereignty, Distorting Development*. New Delhi.

Kent, Eliza. 1999. 'Tamil Bible Women and the Zenana Missions of Colonial South India', *History of Religions*, Vol. 39, No. 2, pp. 117–49.

Keppley-Mahmood, Cynthia. 1996. *Fighting for Faith and Nation: Dialogues with Sikh Militants*. Philadelphia.

Kessinger, Tom G. 1974. *Vilyatpur: 1848–1968*. Berkeley.

Khagram, Sanjeev. 2004. *Dams and Development*. New York.

Khalfaoui, Moezz. 2008. *L'Islam Indien: Pluralité ou Pluralisme. Le cas d'al-Fatawa al-Hindiyya*. Frankfurt.

Khan, Yasmin. 2007. *The Great Partition: The Making of India and Pakistan*. New Haven.

Khare, Arvind, Madhu Sarin, N.C. Saxena, Subhabrata Palit, Seema Bathla, Farhad Vania, and M.Satyanarayana. 2000. *Joint Forest Management: Policy, Practice and Prospects: India Country Study*. New Delhi/London.

Khilnani, Sunil. 1997. *The Idea of India*. London.

———. 2007. 'The India Project', *Architectural Design*, Special Issue: Made in India, Vol. 77, No. 6, pp. 12–15.

Kidambi, Prashant. 2007. *The Making of an Indian Metropolis: Colonial Governance and Public Culture in Bombay, 1890–1920*. Aldershot.

King, Christopher. 1994. *One Language, Two Scripts: The Hindi Movement in Nineteenth-Century North India*. New York/New Delhi.

King, Richard. 1999. *Orientalism and Religion: Postcolonial Theory, India and the Mystic East*. London.

Kinra, Rajeev. 2011. 'This Noble Science: Indo-Persian Comparative Philology, c. 1000–1800 CE', in Yigal Bronner, Whitney Cox, and Lawrence McCrea, eds, *South Asian Texts in History: Critical Engagements with Sheldon Pollock*, pp. 359–85. Ann Arbor.

Kishwar, Madhu. 1998. *Religion in the Service of Nationalism and Other Essays.* Delhi.

Kohli, Atul, ed. 2001. *The Success of India's Democracy.* Cambridge.

Konermann, Lutz, Rob Appleby, and Farida Pacha. 2010. *Slum for Sale*, CH/D [80 min., 1:1.85, DolbySR; documentary film on the Dharavi redevelopment].

Kothari, Rajni. 1970. *Caste in Indian Politics.* Hyderabad.

Kripilani, Manjeet. 1997. 'The Business Rajahs', *Businessweek*, International Edition, 14 April 1997, http://www.businessweek.com/1997/15/b352210. htm [last accessed on 15 August 2013].

Krishna, Daya, ed. 1987. *India's Intellectual Traditions: Attempts at Conceptual Reconstructions.* Delhi.

Krishna, Daya and A.M. Ghose. 1987. *Contemporary Philosophical Problems: Some Classical Indian Perspectives.* Pune.

Krishna, Daya, A.M. Ghose, et al., eds. 1991. *Samvada: A Dialogue between Two Philosophical Traditions.* New Delhi.

Kshirsagar, Ramchandra K. 1994. *Dalit Movement in India and Its Leaders: 1857–1956.* New Delhi.

Kumar, Arun. 2011 [1913]. *Indian Economy since Independence: Tracing the Dynamics of a Disrupted Society.* New Delhi.

Kumar, Dharma. 1998. *Colonialism, Property and the State.* New Delhi.

Kumar, Deepak. 1995. *Science and the Raj: 1857–1905.* Delhi.

Kumar, Krishna. 1984. '"People's Science" and Development Theory', *Economic and Political Weekly*, Vol. 19, No. 28, pp. 1082–4.

———. 1991. *Political Agenda of Education: A Study of Colonialist and Nationalist Ideas.* New Delhi/London.

Kumar, Nita. 1998. 'Sanskrit Pandits and the Modernisation of Sanskrit Education in the Nineteenth to Twentieth Centuries', in William Radice, ed., *Swami Vivekananda and the Modernization of Hinduism*, pp. 36–60. Delhi.

Kumar, Prakash. 2012. *Indigo Plantations and Science in Colonial India.* Cambridge.

Kumar, Pratap. 2004. 'A Survey of New Approaches to the Study of Religion in India', in Peter Antes et al., eds, *New Approaches to the Study of Religion*, Vol. 1, pp. 127–45. Berlin.

Kunnath, George J. 2012. *Rebels from the Mud Houses: Dalits and the Making of the Maoist Revolution in Bihar.* Delhi.

Kuz'mina, Elena. 2007. *The Origin of the Indo-Iranians.* Leiden.

Laidlaw, James. 1995. *Riches and Renunciation: Religion, Economy, and Society among the Jains.* Oxford.

Laidlaw, James. 2000. 'A Free Gift Makes No Friends', *The Journal of the Royal Anthropological Institute*, Vol. 6, No. 4, pp. 617–34.

Lall, Marie-Canne. 2001. *India's Missed Opportunity: India's Relationship with the Non-Resident Indians*. Aldershot.

Landes, David. 1998. *The Wealth and Poverty of Nations*. London.

Larson, Gerald J., ed. 2007. *Religion and Personal Law in Secular India: A Call to Judgement*. Bloomington.

Lelyveld, David. 1978. *Aligarh's First Generation*. Princeton.

———. 1993. 'The Fate of Hindustani: Colonial Knowledge and the Fate of a National Language', in Carol Appadurai Breckenridge and Peter van der Veer, eds, *Orientalism and the Postcolonial Predicament: Perspectives on South Asia*, pp. 189–214. Philadelphia.

Liechty, Mark. 2003. *Suitably Modern: Making Middle-Class Culture in a New Consumer Society*. Princeton NJ.

LIFE Magazine, 18 August 1947. Editorial: *Farewell to the Raj*.

Lochtefeld, James G. 2004. 'The Construction of the Kumbha Mela', *South Asian Popular Culture*, Vol. 2, No. 2, pp. 103–26.

Lorenzen, David N., ed. 2004. *Religious Movements in South Asia, 600–1800*. Delhi.

Ludden, David. 1993. 'Orientalist Empiricism: Transformations of Colonial Knowledge', in Carol Appadurai Breckenridge and Peter van der Veer, eds, *Orientalism and the Postcolonial Predicament: Perspectives on South Asia*, pp. 250–78. Philadelphia.

———, ed. 1996. *Contesting the Nation: Religion, Community and the Politics of Democracy in India*. Philadelphia.

———. 2002. 'A Brief History of Subalternity', in David Ludden, ed., *Reading Subaltern Studies: Critical History, Contested Meaning, and the Globalisation of South Asia*, pp. 1–40. Delhi.

Luhmann, Niklas. 1984. *Religious Dogmatics and the Evolution of Societies*. New York.

———. 2013. *Systems Theory of Religion*. Stanford.

Maclean, Kama. 2008. *Pilgrimage and Power: The Kumbh Mela in Allahabad, 1765–1954*. New York.

MacMunn, George Fletcher. 1933. *The Martial Races of India*. London.

Madan, Triloki N. 1987. 'Secularism in Its Place', *Journal of Asian Studies*, Vol. 46, No. 4, pp. 747–59.

———. 1993. 'Whither Indian Secularism?' *Modern Asian Studies*, Vol. 27, No. 3, pp. 667–97.

———. 1997. *Modern Myths, Locked Minds: Secularism and Fundamentalism in Modern India*. Delhi.

Madelung, Wilferd. 1961. 'Das Imamat in der frühen ismailitischen Lehre', *Der Islam*, Vol. 37, pp. 43–135.

Mahajan, Gurpreet. 1999. *Minority Identities and the Nation-State*. New Delhi.

Malik, Yogendra K. and Dhirendra K. Vajpeyi. 1989.'The Rise of Hindu Militancy: India's Secular Democracy at Risk', *Asian Survey*, Vol. 23, No. 3, pp. 308–25.

Malleson, George B. 1857. *The Mutiny of the Bengal Army: An Historical Narrative*. London.

Mallory, James P. 1989. *In Search of the Indo-Europeans: Language, Archaeology, and Myth*. London.

Manela, Erez. 2007. *The Wilsonian Moment: Self-Determination and the International Origins of Anticolonial Nationalism*. Oxford.

Mani, Lata. 1989. 'Contentious Traditions: The Debate on Sati in Colonial India', in Kumkum Sangari and Sudesh Vaid, eds, *Recasting Women: Essays in Colonial History*, pp. 88–120, New Delhi.

———. 1998. *Contentious Traditions: The Debate on Sati in Colonial India*. Berkeley.

Mani, Bakirathi and Latha Varadarajan. 2005. 'The Largest Gathering of the Global Indian Family: Neoliberalism, Nationalism, and Diaspora at Pravasi Bharatiya Divas', *Diaspora*, Vol. 14, No. 1, pp. 45–73.

Mankekar, Purnima. 1999a. *Screening Culture, Viewing Politics: An Ethnography of Television, Womanhood and Nation in Postcolonial India*. Durham NC.

———. 1999b.'Brides Who Travel: Gender, Transnationalism, and Nationalism in Hindi Film', *Positions*, Vol. 7, No. 3, pp. 731–61.

Mansergh, Nicholas et al., eds. 1971. *Constitutional Relations between Britain and India: The Transfer of Power, 1942–47, Quit India, 30 April–21 September 1942*, Vol. 2. London [1–12 Vols].

———, eds. 1981–2. *Constitutional Relations between Britain and India: Transfer of Power. The Mountbatten Viceroyalty: Formulation of a Plan, 22 March–30 May 1947*, Vol. 10. London [Vols 1–12].

———, eds. 1982. *Constitutional Relations between Britain and India: Transfer of Power, 1942–47. The Mountbatten Viceroyalty: Announcement and Reception of the 3 June Plan, 31 May–7 July 1947*. Vol. 11. London [Vols 1–12].

———, eds. 1983. *Constitutional Relations between Britain and India. Transfer of Power 1942–7. The Mountbatten Viceroyalty: Princes, Partition and Independence, 8 July–15 August 1947*, Vol. 12. London [Vols 1–12].

Marcelin, Tonye M. 2010. *Intellectual Property, Community Rights and Human Rights: The Biological and Genetic Resources of Developing Countries*. Abingdon/New York.

Markovits, Claude. 1983. *Indian Business and Nationalist Politics*. Cambridge.

———. 1985. *Indian Business and Nationalist Politics, 1931–39: The Indigenous Capitalist Class and the Rise of the Congress Party*. Cambridge: Cambridge University Press.

———. 2004. *Un-Gandhian Gandhi: The Life and Afterlife of the Mahatma*. London.

Marx, Karl. 1894. *Capital*, Vol. 3. New York.

Masselos, Jim. 1990. '"The Magic Touch of Being Free": The Rituals of Independence on 15 August', in Jim Masselos, ed., *India: Creating a Modern Nation*, pp. 37–53. New Delhi.

———. 1992. 'The Dis/appearance of Subalterns: A Reading of a Decade of Subaltern Studies', *South Asia*, Vol. 15, No. 1, pp. 105–25.

Matilal, Bimal Krishna. 1986. *Perception: An Essay on Classical Indian Theories of Knowledge*. Oxford.

———, ed. 1989. *Moral Dilemmas in the Mahabharata*. Shimla.

———. 1990. *The Word and the World: India's Contribution to the Study of Language*. Delhi.

Mayaram, Shail, ed. 2013. *Philosophy as Samvad and Svaraj: Dialogical Meditations on Daya Krishna and Ramchandra Gandhi*. New Delhi.

Mayer, Adrian C. 1960. *Caste and Kinship in Central India*. London.

Mayer, Arno. 1963 [1959]. *Wilson vs Lenin: Political Origins of the New Diplomacy 1917–1918*. New Haven.

Mazzarella, William. 2003. *Shoveling Smoke: Advertising and Globalization in Contemporary India*. Durham NC.

———. 2006. 'Internet X-Ray: E-Governance, Transparency, and the Politics of Immediation in India', *Public Culture*, Vol. 18, No. 3, pp. 473–505.

———. 2010. '"Beautiful Balloon": The Digital Divide and the Charisma of New Media in India', *American Ethnologist*, Vol. 37, No. 4, pp. 783–804.

McCrea, Lawrence and Parimal Patil. 2010. *Buddhist Philosophy of Language in India: Jnanasrimitra on Exclusion*. New York.

McGregor, R.S., ed. 1993. *The Oxford Hindi-English Dictionary*. New Delhi/Oxford.

McLane, John. 1993. *Land and Local Kingship in Eighteenth-Century Bengal*. Cambridge.

McMillen, Christian and Niels Brimnes. 2010. 'Medical Modernization and Medical Nationalism: Resistance to Mass Tuberculosis Vaccination in Postcolonial India, 1948–1955', *Comparative Studies in Society and History*, Vol. 52, No. 1, pp. 180–209.

McPherson, Kenneth. 1995. *The Indian Ocean: A History of People and the Sea*. Delhi.

Medick, Hans and David Sabean, eds. 1984. *Interest and Emotion: Essays on the Study of Family and Kinship*. Cambridge.

Meer Hassan Ali. 1917 [1832]. *Observations on the Mussulmauns of India: Descriptive of Their Manners, Customs, Habits, and Religious Opinions, Made during a Twelve Year Residence in Their Immediate Society*, second edition, edited with Notes and an Introduction by W. Crooke. London.

Mehta, Vinod. 1977. *The Sanjay Story*. Bombay.

Mendelsohn, Oliver. 1981. 'The Pathology of the Indian Legal System', *Modern Asian Studies*, Vol. 15, No. 4, pp. 823–63.

Menon, Alappat S. 1991. *A Survey of Kerala History*. Madras.

Menon, Meena and Neera Adarkar. 2004. *One Hundred Years, One Hundred Voices: The Millworkers of Girangaon: An Oral History*. Calcutta.

Menon, Meena, R. 2012. 'Land for Mumbai's Millworkers', *Economic and Political Weekly*, Vol. 47, No. 29.

Menon, Vapal P. 1956. *The Story of the Integration of the Indian States*. Bombay.

Menski, Werner, ed. 1998. *South Asians and the Dowry Problem*. Stoke-on-Trent.

Metcalf, Barbara D. 1982. *Islamic Revival in British India: Deoband 1860–1900*. Princeton.

———, ed. 1984. *Moral Conduct and Authority: The Place of Adab in South Asian Islam*. Berkeley/Los Angeles.

———. 2004. 'Tablighi Jama'at', in Richard C. Martin, ed., *Encyclopedia of Islam and the Muslim World*, Vol. 2, pp. 671–2. New York.

———. 2006. *Islamic Contestations: Essays on Muslims in India and Pakistan*. Oxford.

Metcalf, Barbara D. and Thomas R. Metcalf. 2006. *A Concise History of Modern India*. Cambridge.

Metcalf, Thomas R. 1994. *Ideologies of the Raj*. Cambridge.

Mgbeoji, Ikechi. 2005. *Global Biopiracy: Patents, Plants, and Indigenous Knowledge*. Toronto.

Michaels, Axel. 2001. *The Pandit: Traditional Scholarship in India*. Delhi.

Mill, James. 1858 [1817]. *The History of British India*. London.

Miller, Roland E. 1992. *Mappila Muslims of Kerala: A Study in Islamic Trends*. Hyderabad.

Minault, Gail. 1982. *The Khilafat Movement: Religious Symbolism and Political Mobilization in India*. New Delhi.

Minkowski, Christopher. 2001. 'The Pandit as Public Intellectual: The Controversy over Virodha Inconsistency in the Astronomical Sciences', in Axel Michaels, ed., *The Pandit: Traditional Scholarship in India*, pp. 80–96. Delhi.

Misra, A.M. 2000. '"Business Culture" and Entrepreneurship in British India, 1860–1950', *Modern Asian Studies*, Vol. 34, No. 2, pp. 333–48

Misra, Rameshwar P. 2007. *Hind Swaraj: Gandhi's Challenge to Modern Civilization*. Delhi.

Mizutani, Satoshi. 2011. *The Meaning of White: Race, Class, and the 'Domiciled Community' in British India 1858–1930*. Oxford.

Mohammed, K.K. 1989. 'Bazars in Mughal India', *Islamic Culture*, Vol. 58, No. 3, pp. 60–76.

Mohanty, Jitendranath. 2007. 'Dharma, Imperatives, and Tradition: Toward an Indian Theory of Moral Action', in Purushottama Bilimoria et al., eds, *Indian Ethics: Classical Traditions and Contemporary Challenges*, Vol. 1, pp. 57–68. Aldershot/Burlington.

Momen, Moojan. 1985. *An Introduction to Shi'i Islam: The History and Doctrines of Twelver Shi'ism*. New Haven/London.

Monier-Williams, Monier. 1976 [1899]. *A Sanskrit–English Dictionary: Etymologically and Philologically Arranged with Special Reference to Cognate Indo-European Languages*. Delhi.

Moog, Robert. 1993. 'Indian Litigiousness and the Litigation Explosion: Challenging the Legend', *Asian Survey*, Vol. 33, No. 12, pp. 1136–50.

Moore, Robin. 1990. *Paul Scott's Raj*. London.

Morris-Jones, Wyndraeth Humphreys. 1962. 'India's Political Idioms', in Cyril Henry Philips, ed., *Politics and Society in India*, pp. 133–54. New York.

Mosse, David. 2003. *The Rule of Water: Statecraft, Ecology and Collective Action in South India*. Oxford.

Mukharji, Projit. 2009. *Nationalizing the Body: The Medical Market, Print and Daktari Medicine*. London.

Mukherjee, Aditya.'Empire: How Colonial India Made Modern Britain', *Economic and Political Weekly*, Vol. 45, No. 50, pp. 73–82.

Mukherjee, J.M. 2010.'Development and Utilisation of Scientific Talent in India', *Science and Culture*, Vol. 21, 1955, pp. 198–200.

Mukherjee, Rudrangshu. 2001 [1984]. *Awadh in Revolt, 1857–1858*. New Delhi.

———. 2005. *Mangal Pandey: Brave Martyr or Accidental Hero?* New Delhi.

Mukherjee, S.N. 1987. 'Bhadralok and Their Dals—Politics of Social Factions in Calcutta, c. 1820–1856', in Pradip Sinha, ed., *The Urban Experience— Calcutta: Essays in Honour of Professor Nisith R. Ray*, pp. 39–58. Calcutta.

Mullaly, Siobhan. 2004. 'Feminism and Multicultural Dilemmas in India: Revisiting the Shah Bano Case', *Oxford Journal of Legal Studies*, Vol. 24, No. 4, pp. 672–92.

Murugkar, Lata. 1994. *Dalit Panther Movement in Maharashtra*. London.

Muslim, ibn al-Ḥajjaj, al-Qushayri. 1987. *Sahih Muslim*. Beirut.

Nair, Janaki. 1990. 'Uncovering the *Zenana*: Visions of Indian Womanhood in Englishwomen's Writings, 1813–1940', *Journal of Women's History*, Vol. 2, No. 1, pp. 26–50.

Nambi, Arooran K. 1980. *Tamil Renaissance and Dravidian Nationalism, 1905–1944*. Madurai.

Nanda, Serena. 1990. *Neither Man nor Woman: The Hijras of India*. Belmont CA.

Nandi, Sugata. 2010.'Constructing the Criminal: Politics of Social Imaginary of the Goonda, 1919–23', *Social Scientist*, Vol. 38, Nos 3-4, pp. 37–54.

Nandy, Ashis. 1980. *Alternative Sciences: Creativity and Authenticity in Two Indian Scientists*. New Delhi.

———. 1988.'The Politics of Secularism and the Recovery of Religious Tolerance', *Alternatives*, Vol. 8, pp. 177–94.

Nandy, Ashis, ed. 1990. *Science, Hegemony, and Violence: A Requiem for Modernity.* Delhi.

———, ed. 1998. *The Secret Politics of Our Desires: Innocence, Culpability and Indian Popular Cinema.* New Delhi.

Naoroji, Dadabhai. 1901. *Poverty and Un-British Rule in India.* New York.

Nargolkar, Vasant. [N.D.] *The Creed of Saint Vinoba.* Bombay.

Narrain, Arvind and Alok Gupta, eds. 2011. *Law like Love: Queer Perspectives on Law.* New Delhi.

Nasr, Syed V. 1996. *Mawdudi and the Making of Islamic Revival.* New York.

Natarajan, J. 1955. *History of Indian Journalism.* New Delhi.

Navlakha, Gautam. 2012. *Days and Nights in the Heartland of Rebellion.* New Delhi.

Nayar, Kuldip. 2012. *Beyond the Lines: An Autobiography.* Delhi.

Needham, Anuradha Dingwaney and Rajeshwari R. Sunder, eds. 2007. *The Crisis of Secularism in India.* Durham NC.

Nehru, Jawaharlal. 1945. *Glimpses of World History: Being Further Letters to His Daughter, Written in Prison, and Containing a Rambling Account of History for Young People.* London.

———. 1947 [1936]. *An Autobiography.* London.

———. 1958 [1949]. *Jawaharlal Nehru's Speeches, September 1946–May 1949,* Vol. 1. New Delhi.

———. 1959. 'Preface', in Verrier Elwin, *A Philosophy for NEFA,* pp. xv–xvii. Shillong.

———. 1972. *Selected Works of Jawaharlal Nehru,* S. Gopal, ed., Vol. 8. New Delhi.

———. 1989 [1946]. *The Discovery of India.* New York.

Nelson, Robert S., ed. 2000. *Visuality Before and Beyond Renaissance.* Cambridge.

Netting, Robert M., Richard R. Wilk, and Eric J. Arnould, eds. 1984. *Households: Comparative and Historical Studies of the Domestic Group.* Berkeley.

Newman, John H. 1890 [1845]. *An Essay on the Development of Christian Doctrine.* London [New York].

Niblett, Robert H. 1957. *The Congress Rebellion in Azamgarh, August to September 1942.* Allahabad.

Nigam, Aditya. 2000. 'Secularism, Modernity, Nation: Epistemology of the Dalit Critique', *Economic and Political Weekly,* Vol. 35, No. 48, pp. 4256–68.

Ninan, Sevanti. 2007. *Headlines from the Heartland.* New Delhi.

Norman, Kenneth R. 1997. *A Philological Approach to Buddhism: The Bukkyo Kyokai Lectures 1994.* London.

Nossiter, Thomas J. 1982. *Communism in Kerala: A Study in Political Adaptation.* London.

Novetzke, Christian L. 2008. *Religion and Public Memory: A Cultural History of Saint Namdev in India.* New York.

Nyayadarsanam with Vatsyayana's Bhasya, Uddyotakara's Varttika, Vacaspati Misra's Tatparytika and Visvanatha's Vrtti, Critically edited with notes by Amarendramohan Tarkatirtha and Narendra Chandra Vedantatirtha. Calcutta 1936.

Oddie, Geoffrey A. 1996. *Popular Religion, Elites and Reform: Hook-Swinging and Its Prohibition in Colonial India, 1800–1894.* New Delhi.

———. 2006. *Imagined Hinduism: British Protestant Missionary Constructions of Hinduism, 1793–1900.* New Delhi.

O'Hanlon, Rosalind and David Washbrook. 1991. 'Histories in Transition: Approaches to the Study of Colonialism and Culture in India', *History Workshop Journal,* Vol. 32, No. 1, pp. 110–27.

Oldenburg, Veena. 2002. *Dowry Murder: The Imperial Origins of a Cultural Crime.* New Delhi.

———, ed. and trans. 1998. *The Early Upanisads: Annotated Text and Translation.* New York.

———. 1999. *The Dharmasutras.* Oxford.

———, ed. 2005. *Manu's Code of Law: A Critical Edition and Translation of the Manava-Dharmashastra.* Oxford.

Olivelle, Patrick. 2009. *Dharma: Studies in Its Semantic, Cultural and Religious History.* Delhi.

O'Malley, Kate. 2008. *Ireland, India and Empire. Indo-Irish Radical Connections, 1919–1964.* Manchester/New York.

O'Toole, Marie-Therese and Anthony Copyley. 2003. 'Secularising the Sacred Cow: The Religious Reforms and Hindu Nationalism', in Antony Copley, ed., *Hinduism in Public and Private: Reform, Hindutva, Gender, and Sampraday,* pp. 84–109. Delhi.

Omvedt, Gail. 1996. *Dalit Visions: The Anti-Caste Movement and the Construction of an Indian Identity.* New Delhi.

Orsini, Francesca. 2002. *The Hindi Public Sphere: Literature in the Age of Nationalism.* New Delhi.

———. 2012. 'How to Do Multilingual Literary History? Lessons from Fifteenth- and Sixteenth-century Century North India', *Indian Economic and Social History Review,* Vol. 49, No. 2, pp. 225–46.

Ostergaard, Geoffrey. 1985. *Nonviolent Revolution in India.* New Delhi.

Ostergaard, Geoffrey and Melville Currell. 1971. *The Gentle Anarchists: A Study of the Leaders of the Sarvodaya Movement for Non-violent Revolution in India.* Oxford.

Pandey, Gyanendra, ed. 1988. *The Indian Nation in 1942.* Calcutta.

———. 1992 [1990]. *The Construction of Communalism in Colonial North India.* New Delhi.

———. 1993. 'Rallying around the Cow: Sectarian Strife in the Bhojpuri Region, c. 1888–1917', in Ranajit Guha, ed., *Writings on South Asian History and Society.* Subaltern Studies. Vol. 2, pp. 60–129. New Delhi.

Pandeya, R.C., ed. 1967. *Ishvarakrishna: Sankhyakarika, Yuktidipika*. Delhi.

Pandian, M.S.S. 2007. *Brahmin and Non Brahmin: Genealogies of the Tamil Political Present*. New Delhi.

Pandita, Rahul. 2011. *Hello Bastar: The Untold Story of India's Maoist Movement*. Manipal.

———, ed. 1991. *Communalism: History, Politics and Culture*. New Delhi.

———, ed. 1999. *The Concerned Indian's Guide to Communalism in India*. New Delhi.

Parekh, Bhiku. 1989. *Gandhi's Political Philosophy: A Critical Examination*. Basingstoke.

Parlby, Fanny P. 1850. *Wanderings of a Pilgrim in Search of the Picturesque: During Four-and-twenty Years in the East—with Revelations of Life in the Zenana*. London

Parry, Jonathan P. 1979. *Caste and Kinship in Kangra*. London.

———. 1985. 'The Brahmanical Tradition and the Technology of the Intellect', in Joanna Overing, ed., *Reason and Morality*, pp. 200–25. New York.

Patel, Tulsi, ed. 2005. *Family in India: Structure and Practice*. New Delhi.

Patnaik, Utsa. 2004. 'The Republic of Hunger', *Social Scientist*, Vol. 32, Nos 9–10, pp. 9–35.

Patton, Laurie L. 2004. 'Samvada as a Literary and Philosophical Genre: An Overlooked Resource for Public Debate and Conflict', *Evam: Forum on Indian Representations*, Vol. 3, Nos 1–2, pp. 177–90.

Pearse, Andrew. 1980. *Seeds of Plenty, Seeds of Want: Social and Economic Implications of the Green Revolution*. Oxford.

Pearson, Michael N. 2000. 'Consolidating the Faith: Muslim Travellers in the Indian Ocean World', *UTS Quarterly: Cultural Studies and New Writing*, Vol. 6, No. 2, pp. 6–13.

Perlin, Frank. 1978. 'Of White Whale and Countrymen in the Eighteenth Century Maratha Deccan: Extended Class Relations, Rights and the Problem of Rural Autonomy under the Old Regime', *Journal of Peasant Studies*, Vol. 5, No. 2, pp. 173–237.

Phadnis, Urmila. 1989. *Ethnicity and Nation-building in South Asia*. New Delhi.

Pingree, David. 1990. 'The Puranas and Jyotihshastra: Astronomy', *Journal of the American Oriental Society*, Vol. 110, No. 2, pp. 274–80.

Pinney, Christopher. 1997. *Camera Indica: The Social Life of Indian Photographs*. Chicago.

Piramal, Gita. 1997. *Business Maharajas*. New Delhi/London.

Plate, Brent S., ed. 2002. *A Crosscultural Reader in Religion, Art and Visual Cultures*. New York.

Platts, John T. 1988 [1884]. *A Dictionary of Urdu, Classical Hindi and English*. New Delhi.

Pocock, David. 1973. *Mind, Body and Wealth*. Oxford.

Pollock, Sheldon. 2001. 'The New Intellectuals in Seventeenth-Century India', *Indian and Economic Social History Review*, Vol. 38, No. 1, pp. 3–31.

———, ed. 2003. *Literary Cultures in History: Reconstructions from South Asia*. Berkeley.

———. 2006. *The Language of the Gods in the World of Men: Sanskrit, Culture, and Power in Premodern India*. Berkeley.

———. 2011. 'Crisis in the Classics', *India's World, Social Research: An International Quarterly*, Vol. 78, No. 1, pp. 21–48 [special issue].

Prakash, Gyan. 1990. 'Writing Post-Orientalist Histories of the Third World: Perspectives from Indian Historiography', *Comparative Studies in Society and History*, Vol. 32, No. 2, pp. 383–408.

———. 1999. *Another Reason: Science and the Imagination of Modern India*. Princeton.

Preston, Lawrence W. 1988. *The Devs of Cincvad: A Lineage and the State in Maharashtra*. Cambridge.

Prasad, Archana. 2004. *Environmentalism and the Left: Contemporary Debates and Future Agendas in Tribal Areas*. New Delhi.

Prasad, Bimla. 2001. *Foundations of Muslim Nationalism*. New Delhi.

Prasad, Rajiva, M.N. Singh, K.C. Das, Kamla Gupta, and R.B. Bhagat. 2009. 'Migration to Greater Mumbai Urban Agglomeration: A Study of Characteristics of Principal Migrants and Their Social Linkages', *Demography India*, Vol. 38, No. 2, pp. 319–34.

Prashad, Vijay. 1996. 'Emergency Assessments', *Social Scientist*, Vol. 24, Nos 9–10, pp. 36–68.

Pritchett, Frances. 1994. *Nets of Awareness: Urdu Poetry and Its Critics*. Berkeley.

Quaiser, Neshat. 2001. 'Politics, Culture and Colonialism: Unani's Debate with Doctory', in Biswamoy Pati and Mark Harrison, eds, *Health, Medicine and Empire: Perspectives on Colonial India*, pp. 317–55. Delhi.

Rahman, Fazlur. 1987. *Health and Medicine in the Islamic Tradition: Change and Identity*. New York.

Raina, Dhruv and Irfan Habib. 2004. *Domesticating Modern Science: A Social History of Science and Culture in Colonial India*. New Delhi.

Raj, Kapil. 2003. 'Circulation and the Emergence of Modern Mapping: Great Britain and Early Colonial India, 1764–1820', in Claude Markovits, Jacques Pouchepadass, and Sanjay Subrahmanyam, eds, *Society and Circulation: Mobile People and Itinerant Cultures in South Asia, 1750–1950*, pp. 23–54. New Delhi.

Rajadhyaksha, Ashish. 2003. 'The "Bollywoodization" of the Indian Cinema: Cultural Nationalism in a Global Arena', *Inter-Asia Cultural Studies*, Vol. 1, No. 4, pp. 25–39.

Rajagopal, Arvind. 2001. *Politics after Television: Hindu Nationalism and the Reshaping of the Public in India*. Cambridge.

Rajan, Nalini, ed. 2005. *Practising Journalism*. New Delhi.

———. 1999. 'Bhopal: Vulnerability, Routinization, and the Chronic Disaster', in Anthony Oliver-Smith and Susanna Hoffman, eds, *The Angry Earth: Disaster in Anthropological Perspective*, pp. 257–78. New York.

———. 2002. 'Missing Expertise, Categorical Politics, and Chronic Disasters: The Case of Bhopal', in Susanna Hoffman and Anthony Oliver-Smith, eds, *Catastrophe and Culture: The Anthropology of Disaster*, pp. 237–60. Santa Fe.

———. 2006. *Modernizing Nature: Forestry and Imperial Eco-Development 1800–1950*. Oxford.

Rajaram, Navaratna S. and David Frawley. 1994. *Vedic Aryans and the Origins of Civilization: A Literary and Scientific Perspective*. Quebec.

Raman, Bhavani. 2008. *Document Raj: Scribes and Writing under Early Colonial Rule in Madras, 1771–1860*. Michigan.

———. 2012. *Document Raj: Writing and Scribes in Early Colonial South India*. Chicago: University of Chicago Press.

Raman, Chandrasekhara V. 1928. 'A New Radiation', *Indian Journal of Physics*, Vol. 2, pp. 388–98.

Ramanujan, A.K. and Edwin Gerow. 1974. 'Indian Poetics', in Edward C. Dimock Jr. et al., *The Literatures of India: An Introduction*, pp. 115–43. Chicago.

Ramaswamy, Sumathi. 1993. 'En/Gendering Language: The Poetics of Tamil Identity', *Comparative Studies in Society and History*, Vol. 35, pp. 683–725.

———. 1997. *Passions of the Tongue: Language Devotion in Tamil India, 1891–1970*. Berkeley.

Ranade, Mahadev Govind. 1902. *Religious and Social Reform: A Collection of Essays and Speeches*, M.B. Kolasker, ed. Bombay.

Rangarajan, Mahesh. 2001. *India's Wildlife History: An Introduction*. Delhi.

Rangaswamy, Nimmi. 2004. 'Making a Dravidian Hero in Confronting the Body: The Politics of Physicality in Colonial and Post-colonial India', in James H. Mills and Satadru Sen, eds, *Confronting the Body: The Politics of Physicality in Colonial and Post-Colonial India*, pp. 135–45. London.

Rao, Anupama. 2009. *The Caste Question: Dalits and the Politics of Modern India*. Berkeley.

Rao, Mohan. 2004. *From Population Control to Reproductive Health: Malthusian Arithmetic*. New Delhi.

Rashid, Omar. 2013. 'Over Three Crore Devotees Take the Dip at Sangam', *The Hindu*, Kumbh Nagri/Allahabad, 11 February, http://www.thehindu.com/todays-paper/tp-national/over-three-crore-devotees-take-the-dip-at-sangam/article4401726.ece [last accessed on 3 March 2013].

Ray, Rajat K., ed. 1992. *Entrepreneurship and Industry in India, 1800–1947*. New Delhi.

Ray, Rajat K. 2002. *The Felt Community: Commonalty and Mentality before the Emergence of Indian Nationalism*. New Delhi.

Reddy, Gayatri. 2005. *With Respect to Sex: Negotiating Hijra Identity in South India*. Chicago.

Rege, Sharmila. 2004.'Dalit Women Talk Differently: A Critique of "Difference" and Towards a Dalit Feminist Standpoint Position', in Maitrayee Chaudhuri, ed., *Feminism in India*, pp. 211–25. New Delhi.

———. 2006. *Writing Caste/Writing Gender: Narrating Dalit Women's Testimonies*. New Delhi.

Ribbentrop, Berthold. 1900. *Forestry in British India*. Calcutta.

Richards, John F. 1995. *The Mughal Empire*. Cambridge.

———. 2003. *The Unending Frontier: Environmental History of the Early Modern World*. Berkeley.

Richter, William L. 1971. 'Princes in Indian Politics', *Economic and Political Weekly*, Vol. 6, No. 9, pp. 535–42.

Risley, Herbert H. and William Crooke, eds. 1915. *The People of India*. Calcutta.

Rizvi, Saiyid Athar Abbas. 1972. *Fatehpur Sikri*. New Delhi.

———. 1978–83. *A History of Sufism in India*, Vols 1–2. Delhi.

———. 1986. *Socio-Intellectual History of the Isna 'Ashari Shi'isin India*, Vols 1–2. New Delhi.

Robb, Peter. ed. 1995. *The Concept of Race in South Asia*. New Delhi.

———. 1996. *Ancient Rights and Future Comfort*. Surrey.

———. 2011 [2002]. *A History of India*. London.

Robinson, Daniel. 2010. *Confronting Biopiracy: Challenges, Cases and International Debates*. London.

Robinson, Francis. 1974. *Separatism among Indian Muslims: The Politics of the United Provinces Muslims, 1860–1923*. Cambridge.

———. 1996.'Knowledge, Its Transmission and the Making of Muslim Societies', in Francis Robinson, ed., *The Cambridge Illustrated History of the Islamic World*, pp. 208–49. Cambridge.

———. 2004. 'Other-Worldly and This-Worldly Islam and the Islamic Revival', *Journal of the Royal Asiatic Society*, Third Series, Vol. 14, Part 1, pp. 49–58.

Rocher, Rosane. 1995. 'Weaving Knowledge: Sir William Jones and Indian Pandits', in Garland Cannon and Kevin Brine, eds, *Objects of Inquiry: The Life, Contributions, and Influences of Sir William Jones (1746–1794)*, pp. 51–79. New York.

———.2007. 'Henry Thomas Colebrooke and the Marginalization of Indian Pandits', in Birgit Kellner et al., eds, *Jnanashrimitra's Anupalabdhirahasya and Sarvashabdabhavacarca: A Critical Edition with a Survey of His Anupalabdhi-Theory, Wiener Studien zur Tibetologie und Buddhismuskunde*, Vol. 67, pp. 237–56. Vienna.

Rodrigues, Valerian, ed. 2002. *The Essential Writings of B.R. Ambedkar*. New Delhi/Oxford.

Roy, Arundhati. 2011. *Broken Republic*. New Delhi.

Roy, Manabendra N. 1926. *The Future of Indian Politics*. London.

Roy, Rammohan. 1804. *Tuhfut ul Muwahidin*. Murshidabad.

Roy, Srirupa. 2007. *Beyond Belief: India and the Politics of Postcolonial Nationalism*. Durham, NC: Duke University Press.

Roy, Tapti. 1994. *The Politics of a Popular Uprising: Bundelkhand in 1857*. New Delhi.

Roy, Tirthankar. 2006 [2000]. *The Economic History of India: 1857–1947*. New Delhi.

Rudolph, Susanne Hoeber and Lloyd Rudolph. 1968. *The Modernity of Tradition? Political Development in India*. Chicago.

Rushdie, Salman. 1991. '"Commonwealth Literature" Does Not Exist', in Salman Rushdie, *Imaginary Homelands: Essays and Criticism 1981–1991*, pp. 61–70. London.

———. 2005. *Shalimar the Clown*. London.

Rycroft, Daniel J. and Sangeeta Dasgupta, eds. 2011. *The Politics of Belonging in India: Becoming Adivasi*. London.

Saavala, Minna. 2010. *Middle-Class Moralities: Everyday Struggle over Belonging and Prestige in India*. Hyderabad.

Sahai, Nandita P. 2005. 'Crafts in Eighteenth-century Jodhpur: Questions of Class, Caste and Community', *Journal of the Economic and Social History of the Orient*, Vol. 48, No. 4, pp. 524–51.

Said, Edward. 1978. *Orientalism*. New York.

Sakarai, Lawrence J. 1980. 'Indian Merchants in East Africa, Part I: The Triangular Trade and the Slave Economy', *Slavery and Abolition: A Journal of Slave and Post-Slave Studies*, Vol. 1, No. 3, pp. 292–338.

Salvi, S., O. Porfiri, and S. Ceccarelli. 2013. 'Nazareno Strampelli, the 'Prophet' of the Green Revolution', *The Journal of Agricultural Science*, Vol. 151, No. 1, pp. 1–5.

Sangari, Kumkum and Sudesh Vaid, eds. 1989. *Recasting Women: Essays in Colonial History*. New Delhi.

Saradamoni, Kunjulekshmi. 1992. *Finding the Household: Conceptual and Methodological Issues*. Delhi.

Saraswati, Baidyanath. 1975. 'Study of Specialists in Traditional Learning: The Pandits of Kashi', *Journal of the Indian Anthropological Society*, Vol. 10, No. 2, pp. 103–16.

Sarkar, Sumit. 1973. *The Swadeshi Movement in Bengal 1903–1908*. New Delhi.

———. 1997. *Writing Social History*. Delhi.

Sarkar, Tanika. 2001. *Hindu Wife, Hindu Nation*. Delhi.

Sarkar, Tanika and Urvashi Butalia, eds. 1995. *Women and the Hindu Right: A Collection of Essays*. Delhi.

Sarma, Chandan Kumar. 2008. 'Introduction' in Chandan Kumar Sarma, ed., *Souvenir: North East India History Association (29th Annual Session)*, pp. 2–4. Dibrugarh.

Sastri, Sivanath. 1974. *History of the Brahmo Samaj*. Calcutta.

Sathe, Satyaranjan P. 2002. *Judicial Activism in India*. New Delhi.

Savarkar, Vinayak D. 1989 [1928]. *Hindutva: Who Is a Hindu?* New Delhi [Nagpur].

Schimmel, Annemarie. 2004. *The Empire of the Great Mughals: History, Art and Culture*. Chicago.

Schroeder, Doris and Thomas Pogge. 2009. 'Justice and the Convention on Biological Diversity', *Ethics and International Affairs*, Vol. 23, No. 3, pp. 267–80.

Scott, Paul. 1964. *Jewel in the Crown*. London.

Seers, Dudley. 1969. 'The Meaning of Development', *International Development Review*, Vol. 11, No. 4, pp. 3–4.

Sen, Amartya. 1983. 'Poor, Relatively Speaking', *Oxford Economic Papers*, Vol. 35, No. 2, pp. 153–69.

———. 1993. 'Positional Objectivity', *Philosophy and Public Affairs*, Vol. 22, pp. 126–45.

———. 1999. *Development as Freedom*. Oxford.

———. 2005. *The Argumentative Indian: Writings in Indian History, Culture and Identity*. London.

———, ed. 2003. *Social and Religious Reform: The Hindus of British India*. Delhi.

———. 2007. 'The Idea of Social Reform and Its Critique among Hindus of Nineteenth Century India', in Sabyasachi Bhattacharya, ed., *Development of Modern Indian Thought and the Social Sciences, History of Science, Philosophy and Culture in Indian Civilisation*, Vol. 10, Part 5, pp. 107–38. Delhi.

———. 2008. *Bankim Chandra Chattopadhyay: An Intellectual Biography*, pp. 5–15. Delhi.

———. 2012. *Raja Rammohun Roy:. A Critical Biography*. Delhi.

Sen, Indrani. 2001. 'Devoted Wife/Sensuous Bibi: Colonial Constructions of the Indian Woman, 1860–1900', *Indian Journal of Gender Studies*, Vol. 8, No. 1, pp. 1–22.

———. 2002. *Woman and Empire: Representations in the Writings of British India, 1858–1900*. New Delhi.

Sen, Samita. 1999. *Women and Labour in Late Colonial India: The Bengal Jute Industry*. Cambridge.

Sen, Siba P., ed. 1979. *Social and Religious Reform Movements in the Nineteenth and Twentieth Centuries*. Calcutta.

Sen, Sudipta. 1998. *Empire of Free Trade: The East India Company and the Making of the Colonial Marketplace*. Philadelphia.

Sethi, Manisha. 2000. 'Avenging Angels and Nurturing Mothers: Women in Hindu Nationalism', *Economic and Political Weekly*, Vol. 37, No. 16, pp. 1545–52.

Shackle, Christopher and Javed Majeed, trans. and ed. 1997 [1937]. *Hali's Musaddas: The Flow and Ebb of Islam*. Delhi.

Shah, Alpa. 2011. 'India Burning: the Maoist Movement', in Isabelle Clark-Decès, ed., *A Companion to the Anthropology of India*, pp. 332–53. Malden MA.

———. 2013. 'The Intimacy of Insurgency: Beyond Coercion, Greed or Grievance in Maoist India', *Economy and Society*, Vol. 4, No. 3.

Shah, Alpa and Judith Pettigrew, eds. 2011. *Windows into a Revolution: Ethnographies of Maoism in India and Nepal*. Delhi/Oxford [*Dialectical Anthropology*, Vol. 33, Nos 3–4, 2009].

Shah, Arvindbhai M. 1998. *The Family in India: Critical Essays*. Hyderabad.

Shaikh, Farzana. 1989. *Community and Consensus in Islam: Muslim Representation in Colonial India, 1860–1947*. Cambridge.

Shand, Hope. 1993. 'Control of Cotton: The Patenting of Transgenic Cotton'. *RAFI Communiqué*.

Shankara. 1948. *Brahmasutrabhashya*, Ram Narayan Acharya, ed. Bombay.

Sharafi, Mitra. 2009. 'The Semi-autonomous Judge in Colonial India: Chivalric Imperialism Meets Anglo-Islamic Dower and Divorce Law', *Indian Economic Social History Review*, Vol. 46, No. 1, pp. 57–81.

Sharma, Jayeeta. 2011. *Empire's Garden: Assam and the Making of India*. Durham NC.

Sharma, Kalpana. 2000. *Rediscovering Dharavi*. New Delhi/New York.

Sherman, Taylor C. 2007. 'The Integration of the Princely State of Hyderabad and the Making of the Post-colonial State in India, 1948–1956', *The Indian Economic and Social History Review*, Vol. 44, No. 4, pp. 489–516.

Saumarez Smith, Richard. 1996. *Rule by Records*. Delhi.

Sharar, Abdul Halim. 1975. *Lucknow: The Last Phase of an Oriental Culture*. London.

Sharp, Henry. 1920. *Selections from the Educational Records, Bureau of Education, India*, Vol. 1. Calcutta.

Shaw, Annapurna. 2007. *Indian Cities in Transition*. Chennai.

Sheth, Pravin. 1977. *Nav Nirman and Political Change in India: From Gujarat 1974 to New Delhi 1977*. New Delhi.

Shiva, Vandana, 1991. *The Violence of the Green Revolution: Third World Agriculture, Ecology, and Politics*. London/Penang.

———. 2001. *Protect or Plunder? Understanding Intellectual Property Rights*. London.

Shodhan, Amrita. 2001. *A Question of Community: Religious Groups and Colonial Law*. Calcutta.

Shome, M.G. 1948. *Report of the United Provinces, Zamindari Abolition Committee*, Vol. 1. Allahabad.

Shukla, Ramchandra. 1940. *Hindi Sahitya ka Itihas*. Banaras.

Siddiqi, Assiya. 1995. *Trade and Finance in Colonial India*. New Delhi.

Simpson, Edward. 2006. *Muslim Society and the Western Indian Ocean: The Seafarers of Kachchh*. London.

Singh, Girish P. 2003. *Ancient Indian Historiography: Sources and Interpretations*. New Delhi.

Singh, Khushwant. 2004 [1963]. *A History of the Sikhs*, Vols 1–2. Delhi.

Singh, Mahendra K. 2011. '12 Cities to Get Metro Rail Soon', *The Times of India*, 18 November, http://articles.timesofindia.indiatimes.com/2011–11–18/india/30414640_1_metro-projects-dmrc-model-project-report [last accessed on 30 January 2013].

Singha, Radhika. 2014. 'Punished by Surveillance: Policing "Dangerousness" in Colonial India, 1872–1918', *Modern Asian Studies*, http://dx.doi.org/10.1017/S0026749X13000462.

Sinha, Pradip. 1978. *Calcutta in Urban History*. Calcutta.

Sinha, Samita. 1993. *Pandits in a Changing Environment: Sanskrit Centres of Learning in Nineteenth Century Bengal*. Calcutta.

Sivaramakrishnan, Kavita. 2006. *Old Potions, New Bottles: Recasting Indigenous Medicine in Colonial Punjab*. Hyderabad.

Sivasundaram, Sujit. 2005. 'Trading Knowledge: The East India Company's Elephants in India and Britain', *Historical Journal*, Vol. 48, No. 1, pp. 27–63.

Sivathamby, Karthigesu. 1995. *Understanding the Dravidian Movement, Problems and Perspectives*. Madras.

Skaria, Ajay. 2009. '"No Politics without Religion": Of Secularism and Gandhi', in Vinay Lal, ed., *Political Hinduism: The Religious Imagination in Public Spheres*, pp. 173–210. Delhi.

———. [Forthcoming.] 'Daya Otherwise: The Notness of Ahimsa', *Journal of the History of Ideas*, Special Issue edited by Aishwary Kumar.

Smith, Brian K. 1993. 'How Not to Be a Hindu: The Case of the Ramakrishna Mission', in Robert D. Baird, ed., *Religion and Law in Independent India*, pp. 333–50. New Delhi.

———. 1994. *Classifying the Universe: The Ancient Indian Varna System and the Origins of Caste*. New York.

Smith, Donald E. 1963. *India: A Secular State*. Princeton.

Smith, Frederick M. and Dagmar Wujastyk. 2008. *Modern and Global Ayurveda: Pluralism and Paradigms*. Albany.

Smith, Jonathan Z. 1982. *Imagining Religion*. Chicago.

Smith, Wilfred C. 1946. *Modern Islam in India: A Social Analysis*. London.

Southworth, Franklin. 2005. *Linguistic Archaeology of South Asia*. London.

Spear, Percival. 1973. *Twilight of the Mughals: Studies in Late Mughal Delhi*. Karachi.

———. 1985. *History of India*, Vol. 2. Harmondsworth.

Speziale, Fabrizio. 2010. *Soufisme, Religion et Médecine en Islam Indien*. Paris.

Spivak, Gayatri C. 1988. 'Can the Subaltern Speak?' in Cary Nelson and Lawrence Grossberg, eds, *Marxism and the Interpretation of Culture*, pp. 271–316. Chicago.

———. 1999. *A Critique of Postcolonial Reason*. Cambridge.

Sridhar, Devi. 2008. *The Battle against Hunger: Choice, Circumstance, and the World Bank*. Oxford.

Srinivas, Mysore N. 1962. *Caste in Modern India and Other Essays*. Bombay.

———. 1989. *The Cohesive Role of Sanskritization and Other Essays*. Delhi.

Srinivasan, Thirukodikaval Nilakanta. 2007. 'Poverty Lines in India: Reflections after the Patna Conference', *Economic and Political Weekly*, Vol. 42, No. 41, pp. 4155–65.

Staal, Frits. 1965. 'Euclid and Panini', *Philosophy East and West*, Vol. 15, No. 2, pp. 99–116.

Stahlberg, Per. 2002. *Lucknow Daily*. Stockholm.

Steever, Sanford. 1981. *The Dravidian Languages*. London.

Stein, Burton, ed. 1992. *The Making of Agrarian Policy in British India, 1770–1900*. New Delhi.

———. 1998. *A History of India*. Oxford.

Steingass, Francis J. 1996 [1892]. *Comprehensive Persian-English Dictionary*. New Delhi [London].

Stepan, Alfred, Juan José Linz, and Yogendra Yadav, eds. 2011. *Crafting State-Nations: India and Other Multinational Democracies*. Baltimore.

Stewart, Tony K. 2000. 'Alternate Structures of Authority: Satya Pir on the Frontiers of Bengal', in David Gilmartin and Bruce B. Lawrence, eds, *Beyond Turk and Hindu: Rethinking Religious Identities in Islamicate South Asia*, pp. 21–54. Gainesville.

Stietencron, Heinrich von. 2005. 'Calculating Religious Decay: The Kaliyuga in India', in Heinrich von Stietencron, ed., *Hindu Myth, Hindu History: Religion, Art, and Politics*, pp. 31–49. Delhi.

Stokes, Eric. 1959. *The English Utilitarians and India*. Oxford.

———. 1986. *The Peasant Armed: The Indian Rebellion of 1857*, Christopher A. Bayly, ed. Oxford.

Subrahmanyam, Sanjay. 1990. *Merchants, Markets and the State in Early Modern India*. New Delhi.

Subramanian, Sreenivasan. 2012. *The Poverty Line*. Delhi.

Sunder, Madhavi. 2006. 'IP3', *Stanford Law Review*, Vol. 59, No. 2, pp. 257–332.

Sutherland, Gail H. 1997. *Nonviolence, Consumption, and Community among Ancient Indian Ascetics*. Shimla.

Swaminathan, Mankumbo S. 1993. *The Wheat Revolution—A Dialogue*. Madras.

Tagore, Rabindranath. 1921. *Greater India*. Madras.

———. 1951. *A Vision of India's History*. Calcutta.

Talbot, Ian and Gurharpal Singh. 2009. *The Partition of India*. Cambridge.

Talreja, Kajnayalal M.1996. *Pseudo-secularism in India*. Mumbai.

Tambiah, Stanley J. 1998. 'The Crisis of Secularism in India', in Rajeev Bhargava, ed., *Secularism and Its Critics*, pp. 418–53. New Delhi.

Tan, Tai Y. and Gyanesh Kudaisya. 2000. *The Aftermath of Partition in South Asia*. New York/London.

———. 2000. '"The Enigma of Arrival": 14–15 August 1947 and the Celebration of Independence', in Tai Y. Tan and Gyanesh Kudaisya, *The Aftermath of Partition in South Asia*, pp. 29–77. London/New York.

———, eds. 2008. *Partition and Post-Colonial South Asia: A Reader*, Vols 1–3. London.

Tandon, Bishan Narain. 2006. *PMO Diary: The Emergency*, Vol. 2. Delhi.

Tarlo, Emma. 1996. *Clothing Matters: Dress and Identity in India*. London/Chicago.

———. 2003. *Unsettling Memories: Narratives of India's Emergency*. New Delhi.

Tatla, Darshan S. 1999. *The Sikh Diaspora: The Search for Statehood*. London.

Tejani, Shabnum. 2007. *Indian Secularism: A Social and Intellectual History*. Ranikhet.

Teltumbde, Anand. 2010. 'One More Reservation', *Economic and Political Weekly*, Vol. 45, No. 14, pp.13–15.

Thakur, Pradeep. 2010. 'Tier II, III Cities Power Nation's Growth', *Times of India*, 24 September, http://timesofindia.indiatimes.com/business/india-business/Tier-II-III-cities-power-nations-growth/articleshow/6615628.cms [last accessed on 30 January 2013].

Thakurdas, Purushottamdas. 1944. *Plan for Economic Development for India* [Bombay Plan].

Thapar, Raj. 1991. *All These Years*. Delhi.

Thapar, Romila. 1980. *A History of India*, Vol. 1. Harmondsworth.

———. 1986. 'Society and Historical Consciousness: The Itihasa-Purana Tradition', in Sabyasachi Bhattacharya and Romila Thapar, eds, *Situating Indian History: For Sarvepalli Gopal*, pp. 353–83. Delhi.

———. 2002. *Early India: From the Origins to AD 1300*. Berkeley.

———. 2003. *The Penguin History of Modern India: From the Origins to AD 1300*. New Delhi.

———. 2011. *The Aryan: Recasting Constructs*. New Delhi.

Tharu, Susie and K. Lalita, eds. 1993 [1991]. *Women Writing in India, 600 BC to the Present*, Vols 1–2. New Delhi.

Thompson, Edward P. 1963. *The Making of the English Working Class*. London.

Thorat, Sukhdeo and Aryama Thorat, eds. 2007. *Ambedkar in Retrospect: Essays on Economics, Politics and Society*. New Delhi.

Thurston, Edgar. 1901. 'The Dravidian Head', *Bulletin of the Madras Government Museum*, Vol. 4, No. 2, pp. 79–86.

———. 1909. *Castes and Tribes of Southern India*, Vols 1–7. Madras.

Tod, James. 1832 [1829]. *Annals and Antiquities of Rajasthan or the Central and Western Rajpoot States of India*, Vols 1–2. London.

Tolstoy, Leo. 2008 [1885]. *What Men Live by and Other Tales*. Rockville MD.

Tomlinson, B.R. 1981. 'Colonial Firms and the Decline of Colonialism in Eastern India 1900–1914', *Modern Asian Studies*, Vol. 15, No. 3, pp. 455–86.

O'Toole, Marie-Therese and Antony Copley. 2003. 'Secularising the Sacred Cow: The Relationship between Religious Reform and Hindu Nationalism', in Antony Copley, ed., *Hinduism in Public and Private: Reform, Hindutva, Gender, and Sampraday*, pp. 84–109. Delhi.

Trautmann, Thomas R. 1997. *Aryans and British India*. Berkeley.

———. 2006. *Languages and Nations: The Dravidian Proof in Colonial Madras*. Berkeley/Delhi.

Trenckner, Vilhelm, ed. 1962. *Milindapanho*. London.

Tripathi, Dwijendra, ed. 1984. *Business Communities of India: A Historical Perspective*. New Delhi.

———. 1990. *Business Houses in Western India*. Ahmedabad.

———. 2004. *The Oxford History of Indian Business*. Oxford.

Tripathi, Dwijendra and Jyoti Jumani. 2007. *The Concise Oxford History of Indian Business*. New Delhi/New York.

Trivedi, Harish and Meenakshi Mukherjee, eds. 1996. *Interrogating Postcolonialism: Theory, Text and Context*. Shimla.

Trivedi, Lisa. 2003. 'Visually Mapping the "Nation": Swadeshi Politics in Nationalist India, 1920–1930', *The Journal of Asian Studies*, Vol. 62, No. 1, pp. 11–41.

Troll, Christian W. 1978. *Sayyid Ahmad Khan: A Reinterpretation of Muslim Theology*. New Delhi.

Tucker, Richard P. 1982. 'The Forests of the Western Himalayas: The Legacy of British Colonial Administration', *Journal of Forest History*, Vol. 26, pp. 112–23.

———. 1983. 'The British Colonial System and the Forests of the Western Himalayas, 1815–1914', in Richard P. Tucker and John F. Richards, eds, *Global Deforestation and the Nineteenth-Century World Economy*, pp. 146–66. Durham NC.

Tully, Mark and Satish Jacob. 1985. *Amritsar: Mrs. Gandhi's Last Battle*. Delhi.

Uberoi, Patricia. 1994. *Family, Kinship and Marriage in India*. Oxford.

Vajpeyi, Ananya. 2007. *Prolegomena to the Study of People and Places in Violent India*. New Delhi.

———. 2009. 'A History of Caste in South Asia: From Pre-colonial Polity to Bio-Political State', in Huri Islamoglu and Peter C. Perdue, eds, *Shared Histories of Modernity: India, China and the Ottoman Empire*, pp. 291–320. New Delhi.

———. 2012. *Righteous Republic: The Political Foundations of Modern India*. Cambridge MA/London.

Varma, Pavan. 1998. *The Great Indian Middle Class*. New Delhi.

Varshney, Ashutosh. 1998. 'India Defies the Odds: Why Democracy Survives', *Journal of Democracy*, Vol. 9, No. 3, pp. 36–50.

———. 2000. 'Is India Becoming More Democratic?' *Journal of Asian Studies*, Vol. 59, No. 1, pp. 3–25.

Vasubandhu. 1973. *Abhidharmakosa and Bhasya of Vasubandhu*, critically edited by Dwarkadas Shastri. Varanasi.

Vasudevan, Ravi. 2000. *Making Meaning in Indian Cinema*. New Delhi.

———. 2011. 'The Meanings of Bollywood', in Rachel Dwyer and Jerry Pinto, eds, *Beyond the Boundaries of Bollywood: The Many Forms of Hindi Cinema*, pp. 3–29. New Delhi.

Veer, Peter van der. 1994. *Religious Nationalism: Hindus and Muslims in India*. Berkeley.

———. 2001. *Imperial Encounters: Religion and Modernity in India and Britain*. Princeton/Oxford.

———. 2003. 'Religious Radicalism in South Asia', *South Asian Journal*, Vol. 6, pp. 16.

Venkatachalapathy, A.R. 2006. *In Those Days There Was No Coffee: Writings in Cultural History*. Delhi.

Verma, H. 1990. 'Secularism: Reflections on Meaning, Substance and Contemporary Practice', in Bidyut Chakrabarty, ed., *Secularism and Indian Polity*, pp. 32–9. New Delhi.

Visvanathan, Shiv. 1998. 'A Celebration of Difference: Science and Democracy in India', *Science*, Vol. 280, pp. 42–3.

———. 2005. 'Knowledge, Justice and Democracy', in Melissa Leach et al., eds, *Science and Citizens; Globalization and the Challenge of Engagement*, pp. 83–96. Hyderabad.

Viswanathan, Gauri. 1989. *Masks of Conquest: Literary Study and British Rule in India*. London.

———. 2000. 'The Ordinary Business of Occultism', *Critical Inquiry*, Vol. 27, No. 1, pp. 1–20.

Wagner, Kim A. 2010. *The Great Fear of 1857: Rumours, Conspiracies and the Making of the Indian Uprising*. Oxford.

Walsh, Judith E. 2004. *Domesticity in Colonial India: What Women Learned When Men Gave Them Advice*. Lanham MD.

Walton-Roberts, Margaret. 2004. 'Globalization, National Autonomy and Non-Resident Indians', *Contemporary South Asia*, Vol. 13, No. 1, pp. 53–69.

Washbrook, David A. 1982. 'Ethnicity and Racialism in Colonial Indian Society', in Robert Ross, ed., *Racism and Colonialism*, pp. 143–81. The Hague.

———. 1989. 'Caste, Class and Dominance in Modern Tamil Nadu: Non-Brahminism, Dravidianism and Tamil Nationalism', in Francine R. Frankel and M.S.A. Rao, eds, *Dominance and State Power in Modern India: Decline of a Social Order*, Vol. 1, pp. 204–64. Delhi.

Washbrook, David A. 1999. 'Orients and Occidents: Colonial Discourse Theory and the Historiography of the British Empire', in Robin W. Winks, ed., *The Oxford History of the British Empire: Historiography*, Vol. 5, pp. 596–611. Oxford.

Watkins, Calvert. 2000. *The American Heritage Dictionary of Indo-European Roots*. Boston.

Weber, Thomas. 1988. *Hugging the Trees: The Story of the Chipko Movement*. New Delhi.

———. 1996. *Gandhi's Peace Army: The Shanti Sena and Unarmed Peacekeeping*. Syracuse NY.

———. 2006. *Gandhi, Gandhism and the Gandhians*. New Delhi.

———. 2009. *The Shanti Sena: Philosophy, History and Action*. Hyderabad.

Wehr, Hans. 1980. *A Dictionary of Modern Written Arabic, Considerably Enlarged and Amended by the Author*, J. Milton Cowan, ed. Ithaca, NY. [Fourth Edition.]

Weir, David. 1987. *The Bhopal Syndrome: Pesticides, Environment and Health*. San Francisco.

Wensinck, Arent J. 1932. *The Muslim Creed: Its Genesis and Historical Development*. New York.

Werbner, Pnina. 1990. *The Migration Process: Capital, Gifts and Offerings among Manchester Pakistanis*. Oxford.

———. 2002. *Imagined Diasporas among Manchester Muslims: The Public Performance of Pakistani Transnational Identity Politics*. Oxford.

Wersch, Hubert W.M. 1992. *The Great Bombay Textile Strike*. Bombay.

Werth, Lukas. 2001. 'Castes among South Asian Muslims, Caste in South Asian Islam, Caste in Pakistan', in Dirk Lönne, ed., *Tohfa-e-Dil: Festschrift für Helmut Nespital*. Reinbek.

West, Martin L. 2007. *Indo-European Poetry and Myth*. New York/Oxford.

Whitcombe, Elizabeth. 1972. *Agrarian Conditions in Northern India: The United Provinces under British Rule, 1860–1900*, Vol. 1. Berkeley.

Wilberforce, William. 1813. 'Speech to the House of Commons', 22 June, *Parliamentary Debates*, Vol. 26, pp. 63–112.

Wiser, William H. 1936. *The Hindu Jajmani System: A Socio-Economic System Interrelating Members of a Hindu Village*. New York.

Wujastyk, Dagmar. 2003. *The Roots of Ayurveda*. London.

Wyatt, Robin and Nazia Masood. 2011. *Broken Mirrors: The 'Dowry Problem' in India*. New Delhi.

Yadav, Yogendra. 1999. 'Electoral Politics in the Time of Change: India's Third Electoral System, 1989–99', *Economic and Political Weekly*, Vol. 34, Nos 34–5, pp. 2393–99.

Yadav, Yogendra and Suhas Palshikar. 2009. 'Revisiting "Third Electoral System": Mapping Electoral Trends in India, 2004–2009', in Sandeep Shastri, K.C. Suri, and Yogendra Yadav, eds, *Electoral Politics in Indian States: Lok Sabha Elections in 2004 and Beyond*, pp. 393–429. Delhi.

Yang, Anand A. 1989. *Limited Raj: Agrarian Relations in Colonial India, Saran District, 1793–1920*. Berkeley.

Yasuda, Yoshinori and Vasant Shinde. 2004. *Monsoon and Civilization*. Delhi.

Young, Robert J.C. 2001. *Postcolonialism: An Historical Introduction*. Oxford.

Yule, Henry and A.C. Burnell. 1996, 1989 [1868]. *Hobson-Jobson, The Anglo-Indian Dictionary*. London.

Zachariah, Benjamin. 2005. *Developing India: An Intellectual and Social History, c. 1930–1950*. Delhi.

———. 2009. 'The Indian State, Nehruvian (Anti-)Nationalism and the Question of Belonging', *Contemporary Perspectives*, Vol. 3, No. 2, pp. 181–204.

———. 2011. *Playing the Nation Game: The Ambiguities of Nationalism in India*. Delhi.

Zachariah, K.C. and S. Irudaya Rajan. 2008. *Migration and Development: The Kerala Experience*. New Delhi.

Zamindar, Vazira Fazila-Yacoobali. 2007. *The Long Partition and the Making of Modern South Asia*. New York.

Zastoupil, Lynn and Martin Moir, eds. 1999. *The Great Indian Education Debate: Documents relating to the Orientalist-Anglicist Controversy of 1780–1840*. Richmond.

Zelliot, Eleanor. 1992. *From Untouchable to Dalit, Essays on the Ambedkarite Movement*. New Delhi.

Zillurrahman, Syed. 1994. 'Unani Medicine in India during 1900–1947', *Studies in History of Medicine and Science*, Vol. 13, No. 1, pp. 97–112.

Zimmermann, Francis. 1987. *The Jungle and the Aroma of Meats: An Ecological Theme in Hindu Medicine*. Berkeley.

Zutshi, Chitralekha. 2004. *Languages of Belonging: Islam, Regional Identity, and the Making of Kashmir*. New York/Oxford.

Zvelebil, Kamil. 1973. *The Smile of Murugan: On the Tamil Literature of South India*. Leiden.

Acts/Resolutions

'The Constitution (Seventy-Third Amendment) Act, 1992', 1993. New Delhi, http://indiacode.nic.in/coiweb/amend/amend73.htm [last accessed on 15 August 2013].

Government of India, 'The Hindu Succession (Amendment) Act, 2005', 5 September 2005, http://www.hrln.org/admin/issue/subpdf/HSA_Amendment_2005.pdf [last accessed on 25 May 2013].

Government of India, 'The Dowry Prohibition Act, 1961', 20 May 1961, http://wcd.nic.in/dowryprohibitionact.htm [last accessed on 25 May 2013].

Independent Citizen's Initiative [ICI]. 2006. *War in the Heart of India: An Enquiry into the Ground Situation in Dantewada District, Chhattisgarh*. New Delhi.

Industries (Development and Regulation) Act. 1951. http://dipp.nic.in/English/Policies/Industries_act1951.pdf [last accessed on 15 August 2013].

International Conference on Population and Development. 1995. Platform for Action. Cairo.

Ministry of Science and Technology, Department of Science and Technology, 'Scientific Policy Resolution 1958', 4 March 1958, New Delhi, http://www.dst.gov.in/stsysindia/spr1958.htm [last accessed on 15 August 2013].

Reserve Bank of India Publications, 'Foreign Exchange Regulation Act, 1973', http://www.rbi.org.in/scripts/ECMUserView.aspx?Id=21&CatID=12 [last accessed on 3 July 2009].

'The Bengal Goondas Act, 1923', also: 'The Bengal Act I, 1923', 28 February 1923, http://www.lawsofindia.org/pdf/west_bengal/1923/1923WB1.pdf [last accessed on 27 May 2013].

'The United Provinces Goondas Act, 1932', also: 'The United Provinces Goondas Act (Act I of 1932)' [India Office Records, The National Archives].

Tamil Nadu Amending Act 32, 2004.

UNHCR, The UN Refugee Agency, 2004. 'The Citizenship Act, 1955/2004', http://www.unhcr.org/refworld/pdfid/410520784.pdf [last accessed on 15 August 2013].

Debates

House of Commons Debate, March 1876, Vol. 228. pp. 75–164.

Indian Parliament [IP]. 1946–50. *India Constituent Assembly Debates* (Proceedings), Vol. 7, parliamentofindia.nic.in/ls/debates/debates.htm [[last accessed on 1 October 2012].

Judgment

Bhagwati, P.N., 'M.C. Mehta v. Union of India, WP 12739/1985 (1986.02.17) (Oleum Gas Leak Case), Judgment by Chief Justice Bhagwati.' http://www.elaw.org/node/2719, 1986 [last accessed on 15 August 2013].

Reports

Government of India [GOI]. 1880. *Report of the Indian Famine Commission.* Chairman: Richard Strachey, George Edward Eyre and William Spotteswoode. London.

Government of India [GOI]. 1911. *Census of India 1911, Central Provinces and Berar*, Vol. 10. Calcutta.

Government of India [GOI]. 1933. *Census of India 1931*, Vol. 1. Calcutta.

Government of India [GOI]. 1946. *Report of the Health Survey and Development Committee*, Vol. 2. New Delhi [Bhore Committee].

Government of India [GOI]. 1980. *Report of the Backward Classes Commission*, 1–7 Vols. Delhi.

Government of India [GOI]. 1993. *Report of the Expert Group on Estimation of Proportion and Number of Poor*. Planning Commission. New Delhi.

Government of India [GOI]. 2001. *Census of India 2001*, Online Version, 'List of Scheduled Tribes', Ministry of Home Affairs, http://censusindia.gov.in/Tables_Published/SCST/ST%20Lists.pdf [last accessed on 15 August 2013].

Government of India [GOI]. 2001. *Census of India 2001*, Online Version, 'Scheduled Castes and Scheduled Tribes Population', Ministry of Home Affairs, http://www.censusindia.gov.in/Census_Data_2001/India_at_glance/scst.aspx [last accessed on 15 August 2013].

Government of India [GOI]. 2004. Ministry of Home Affairs, 'Overseas Citizenship of India', http://mha.nic.in/uniquepage.asp?Id_Pk=553 [last accessed on 28 April 2013].

Government of India [GOI]. 2007. *Poverty Estimates for 2004–05*. Planning Commission. New Delhi.

Government of India [GOI]. 2008. *Development Challenges in Extremist Affected Areas, Report of an Expert Group to the Planning Commission*. New Delhi.

National Planning Committee. 1948a. *Report of the Sub-Committee on Population*. Bombay [Mukherjee Committee].

National Planning Committee. 1948b. *Report of the Sub-Committee on Women's Role in Planned Economy*. Bombay.

National Planning Committee. 1948c. *Report of the Sub-Committee on Health*. Bombay [Sokhey Committee].

Report of the High Level Committee [RHCL]. 19 December 2001. http:// indiandiaspora.nic.in/contents.htm [last accessed on 3 July 2009].

Series

The Clay Sanskrit Library, New York, 2005–9.

India Office Records, Finance Department, 5/191, 8 December 1930, London